Policy Issues in Insurance

Terrorism Risk Insurance in OECD Countries

No. 9

OECD

ORGANISATION FOR ECONOMIC CO-OPERATION AND DEVELOPMENT

ORGANISATION FOR ECONOMIC CO-OPERATION AND DEVELOPMENT

The OECD is a unique forum where the governments of 30 democracies work together to address the economic, social and environmental challenges of globalisation. The OECD is also at the forefront of efforts to understand and to help governments respond to new developments and concerns, such as corporate governance, the information economy and the challenges of an ageing population. The Organisation provides a setting where governments can compare policy experiences, seek answers to common problems, identify good practice and work to co-ordinate domestic and international policies.

The OECD member countries are: Australia, Austria, Belgium, Canada, the Czech Republic, Denmark, Finland, France, Germany, Greece, Hungary, Iceland, Ireland, Italy, Japan, Korea, Luxembourg, Mexico, the Netherlands, New Zealand, Norway, Poland, Portugal, the Slovak Republic, Spain, Sweden, Switzerland, Turkey, the United Kingdom and the United States. The Commission of the European Communities takes part in the work of the OECD.

OECD Publishing disseminates widely the results of the Organisation's statistics gathering and research on economic, social and environmental issues, as well as the conventions, guidelines and standards agreed by its members.

This work is published on the responsibility of the Secretary-General of the OECD. The opinions expressed and arguments employed herein do not necessarily reflect the official views of the Organisation or of the governments of its member countries.

Publié en français sous le titre :
Assurance du risque terroriste dans les pays de l'OCDE
N° 9

Foreword

The terrorist attacks of 11 September 2001 took a terrible toll of human life and have changed the course of history. Among other impacts, they were also the most costly disaster ever for the insurance industry. Insurers and reinsurers reacted responsibly to the attacks by assuming their part of the losses, demonstrating the crucial role that a well capitalised insurance sector can play both to compensate losses after a major disaster and more generally to help economies run smoothly. However, the 9/11 events fundamentally changed the perspective on future expected losses from terrorist acts. Driven by the fear of further (and possibly imminent) large-scale terrorist attacks, most insurers and reinsurers drastically reduced their exposure to terrorism risk, revised the terms of their policies, and increased their premiums.

A few years have now passed without another terrorist act of a comparable magnitude, and the terrorist insurance market has gradually relaxed. The tsunami which ravaged the coasts of southern Asia on 26 December 2004, at the end of a record year for the cost of natural disasters, came as a reminder of the diversity both of the catastrophic risks threatening our societies and the priorities for action.

Nevertheless, the attacks on three railway stations in the Madrid suburbs on 11 March 2004 as well as other terrorist acts and many foiled attempts, and the recurrent warnings of terrorism experts all bear witness to the persistence of the terrorist threat, and the need to improve preparedness and the response to terrorism.

In 2002, OECD Ministers asked the Organisation to help them to prepare for the financial consequences of possible further large-scale attacks and to provide compensation for such unforeseeable events. They requested "policy analysis and recommendations on how to define and cover terrorism risks and to assess the respective roles of the insurance industry, financial markets and governments, including for the coverage of "mega-terrorism" risks"[1]. In response to this request, the Insurance and Private Pensions Committee set up a Task Force of government and industry experts.

This volume compiles OECD policy conclusions[2], and leading academic analysis on the financial management of terrorism risk[3], nearly four years after the World Trade Centre attacks. It seeks to enhance understanding of the issues at stake and the options available to markets and governments facing the challenge of compensation for modern terrorism.

The publication consists of three main parts, allowing different levels of reading:

- Part I : Summary of conclusions and policy options ;

- Part II: Analyses of the major policy issues raised by the mandate, i.e. the respective role of the insurance industry, financial markets and governments in the coverage of terrorism risks, and the case of mega-terrorism risk.

- Part III: Reports by the consultants to the OECD Task Force on Terrorism Insurance.

The first two Parts are published under the responsibility of the OECD Insurance and Private Pensions Committee. The conclusions and policy options are not binding, and do not condition, compromise or prejudge measures adopted in several countries to compensate for losses resulting from terrorism. The reports in Part III (and the annex on terrorism compensation schemes in selected non-member countries) are written under the responsibility of their authors and the opinions expressed therein are not necessarily those of the Insurance and Private Pensions Committee, the Task Force on Terrorism Insurance, or the OECD member countries.

I would like to thank all those involved in this project. It was carried out under the aegis of the Insurance and Private Pensions Committee and is built on the work and close cooperation of the members of the Task Force on Terrorism Insurance. The project also benefited from the high quality of the work and the expert input of the consultants to the Task Force. This publication was produced under the direction of Cécile Vignial, Principal Administrator, Directorate for Financial and Enterprise Affairs, with the cooperation of Alberto Monti, Professor at Bocconi University (Italy) and technical support from Claire Dehouck and Edward Smiley.

Donald J. Johnston
Secretary-General

Notes

1   "We recognise the adverse effects of the shrinkage of affordable insurance cover for terrorism risks. We would welcome OECD policy analysis and recommendations on how to define and cover terrorism risks and to assess the respective roles of the insurance industry, financial markets and governments, including for the coverage of "mega-terrorism" risks." See OECD Council at Ministerial Level, 15-16 May 2002: Final Communiqué.

2   Various other documents with a more focused approach have been discussed within the OECD Insurance and Private Pensions Committee and its Task Force on terrorism insurance. The task of drawing up a list of criteria to define terrorism for purposes of compensation is the subject of a separate Recommendation (see *http://www.oecd.org/daf/insurance*).

3   The reader's attention is drawn to the fact that this publication deals almost exclusively with property insurance.

Table of Contents

PART I

SUMMARY OF CONCLUSIONS AND POLICY OPTIONS

PART II

POLICY ISSUES

PART III

REPORTS BY THE EXPERTS TO THE OECD TASK FORCE ON TERRORISM INSURANCE

Part I

Summary of Conclusions and Policy Options

Summary of Conclusions and Policy Options[*]

1. The new terrorism threat: a major challenge to the insurance world

1.1. The changing nature of international terrorism risk, as demonstrated in particular by the September 2001 attacks in the United States, translates into a tremendous and potentially lasting threat against which no country can claim to be protected. It calls for greater co-operation on an international scale. If loss prevention and mitigation perform a crucial function in terrorism risk management strategies, ensuring sustainable financial coverage of the terrorism risk[1], if prevention were to fail, is a no less important policy issue to mitigate the potentially devastating impacts of future attacks and to facilitate recovery.

Looking back at the historical record of small and large national and international terrorism acts committed over the last 30 years, terrorism was certainly not an unknown exposure before 2001. The increasing severity of terrorism acts, especially during the 1990s, was a rising source of concern. The damaging potential of terrorists and the urgency of a radical change in terrorism risk management remained, however, largely underestimated prior to the September 11 attacks in the United States.

On 11 September 2001, two aircraft hit the NYC World Trade Centre Twin Towers, while almost simultaneously another one hit the Pentagon and a fourth aircraft crashed in Pennsylvania. These attacks marked the advent of a new form of terrorism characterised by an unprecedented loss dimension, a transnational nature and much broader geographical scope. The attacks caused insured losses currently estimated at more than USD 30 billion, making them the single most costly event ever recorded in the history of the insurance and reinsurance industry, and changed the general perspective on the future expected losses and impact of terrorist attacks. Terrorism has become a worldwide issue, against which no country can claim to be protected. It has also become far more difficult to predict, detect and effectively prevent.

This new threat calls for co-ordinated action on an international scale. Gaining a proper understanding of what constitutes terrorism in the 21st century, and enforcing a strong and comprehensive multinational counter-terrorism policy are certainly important steps to be taken at this stage. Educating society, increasing public awareness of potential attacks, and preparing emergency and rescue plans are other fundamental policy goals to be pursued. If loss prevention and mitigation are crucial in terrorism risk management strategies, it is no less essential to provide compensation so as to permit rapid recovery if prevention were to fail. Given the potentially devastating impact of future attacks, this has become an important policy issue in OECD countries.

1.2. Before 2001, terrorism risk was widely considered by insurers to be a manageable exposure, and private non-life insurance routinely covered most terrorism risks related to property loss.

Private insurance used to cover most terrorism risks related to property and casualty loss, generally under fire policies which would provide compensation for fire and explosion damage of

---

*   References to the sources to which this summary is indebted are to be found in the detailed notes in Part II Chapters 1, 2, 3 and 4, infra.

any cause (except war). Not only was terrorism viewed as a manageable exposure, but it was usually considered so marginal that the additional risk was not subject to separate underwriting and pricing.

Spain (since 1954, through a mechanism which covers all extreme events) and the United Kingdom (since 1993) were the only OECD countries where the market was overwhelmed by the frequency and severity of attacks and where it was acknowledged that full protection against terrorism risks could not be made available through private (re)insurance alone[2].

1.3. The 2001 attacks have revealed the considerable increase in the potential size of losses in comparison with a finite market capacity. Attacks of comparable or even greater magnitude may be expected, and the threat of chemical, biological, radiological and nuclear (CBRN) weapons of mass destruction[3] is real. The possible multiplication of medium-size terrorist attacks within a limited time frame is another major challenge. Terrorism risks are also all the more complex to manage in that they can be highly correlated.

Comparing the September 11 losses with those caused by earlier events reveals a break in the historical series. In addition to the nearly 3000 victims[4] and the tragic human dimension of the attacks, the USD 31.7 billion insured losses are almost 1.5 times more than the insured losses from Hurricane Andrew, the second most costly event in the insurance industry[5], and more than thirty times as much as the worst terrorist attack in terms of insured property losses before 2001. The 9/11 attacks have thus evidenced that terrorism is potentially a catastrophic risk, sharing certain insurability features with other low probability and high consequences events, such as natural disasters.

The 2001 events called for a complete reassessment of loss scenarios for potential future attacks. Models of alternative terrorist attacks now include maximum loss scenarios considered unthinkable in the past, and a single attack resulting, for instance, in insured losses exceeding USD 90 billion for worker compensation losses alone are now considered plausible. Various features of modern terrorism can help to explain the rise in potential loss estimates. Terrorists' motives have shifted from often regional to global goals and to maximising the number of casualties and victims[6]. Their modus operandi, taking advantage of new technologies, the development of global networks and interdependencies between countries, allows for simultaneous attacks or the quasi-instantaneous propagation of damages at a low cost to the terrorists, entailing potentially exponential losses. The most worrying trend may be the ability to exploit the diffusion capacity of large critical networks (aviation, maritime and intermodal transport, water supply, electricity, public utilities, telecommunications, etc.), turning them against the target in order to maximize the destructive potential of attacks[7]. Lastly, today's terrorists may have access to far more lethal weapons. The possible use by terrorists of non-conventional chemical, biological, radiological and nuclear weapons (CBRN) represents a new and immense threat.

While massive attacks are to be feared, the possible accumulation of medium-size terrorist attacks in a limited timeframe may be equally challenging and end up having the same detrimental effects as a single very large attack. More generally, it should be stressed that new forms of terrorism might have more significant spill-over effects on the economy and society as a whole than other types of disasters. Large terrorist attacks may, for instance, entail a certain distrust in governments that have failed to prevent them and that terrorists have managed to defy. The threat of possible other attacks might affect economic outlook and investors behaviour, while increased security measures will also have a cost. Direct property losses may therefore turn out to be small compared to the global economic, social and political damage.

The considerable magnitude of potential future attacks is to be assessed against the available capacity of private insurance and reinsurance markets to withstand losses. Catastrophe insurance lines require a larger amount of capital (or easy access to alternative financing sources) to enable (re)insurers to pay the extremely high claim amounts that could result from extreme events, without facing the risk of bankruptcy. The September 11 terrorist attacks prompted many market players to point out that, while the capacity of insurers, backed by international reinsurance markets, was very large[8], it was also finite. Moreover, existing capacity had been hard hit by the joint impact of technical and financial losses. After 2001, the heavy losses suffered by the insurance and reinsurance industries, together with the capital markets' downturn, resulted in an estimated capital loss of USD 200 billion for the global property and casualty (P&C) industry.

Another common feature of terrorism attacks and natural hazards is that they usually involve temporally and spatially correlated risks. Risk correlation does not allow insurers to take advantage of the law of large numbers, thereby hindering risk diversification. Under these conditions, insurance is less effective as a mechanism for transferring risk. Moreover, one of the lessons of the September 2001 events was that modern terrorist attacks could also entail new types of correlation: a high degree of correlation between many different lines of insurance coverage, and between the liability and the asset side of insurers' balance sheets, which are further impediments to insurers' operation.

1.4.   Over and above its potential to generate extreme losses, modern terrorism risk is generally characterised by a set of specific features which translates into a general lack of predictability of the target(s), the severity, and, most of all, the frequency of future attacks. The conjunction of increased potential magnitude of highly correlated risks and growing risk unpredictability may fundamentally challenge the insurability of terrorism risk.

The debate about the ability of private insurance/reinsurance markets to cover terrorism risk has often focused on the issue of the magnitude of potential losses, the consequent capacity problems and the well-known insurability problems associated with low probability and high-consequence events, such as many natural disasters. Such conclusions fail, however, to take into account a number of additional challenges raised by (new forms of) terrorism that were brought to light by the analysis of recent terrorist attacks[9], in particular:

- *"Generalised"* and *"dynamic uncertainty"*, which refers to the acknowledgement that little information is publicly available on terrorism risk, and that existing information may not be reliable due to the constant evolution of the risk:

    - Past historical data are of limited relevance (no former attack can compare with that of 2001; more generally, analysis of terrorists' past intentions does not necessarily make their future agenda more predictable);

    - Both the insurer and the insured are affected by a "symmetry of non information" since the best informed party, *i.e.* governments, does not disclose information for national security reasons;

    - Above all, terrorists may change targets and methods of attack up to the last minute, to adapt to public and private prevention measures and to increase their chances of success and potential damages.

- *"Interdependent security"*, which refers to the fact that interconnections between firms will greatly increase their vulnerability to terrorism risk. Whatever their own level of protection against terrorism, firms may still be affected by the failure of a weak link in the system in which they operate. This will hinder efforts to predict and mitigate terrorism risk. Moreover, insurance will normally not cover resulting indirect losses.

- Lastly, *government influence on the risk* is an important difference between terrorism risk and other catastrophic risks: through its domestic and foreign policies, as well as counter-terrorism measures, the government can influence the level of risk and choice of targets, while adequate crisis management planning may mitigate the impact of an attack.

These challenges translate into high risk ambiguity and make terrorism more difficult to cover than natural or other man-made perils.

Under these conditions, can terrorism risks be shared and transferred via insurance mechanisms? Private insurance operations are based on a number of conditions which may be summarised under four criteria: the probability and severity of losses should be quantifiable (assessability); the time at which the insured event occurs should be unpredictable when the policy is underwritten, and the occurrence itself must be independent of the will of the insured (randomness); numerous persons exposed to a given hazard should be able to join together to form a risk community within which the risk is shared and diversified (mutuality); it should be possible to calculate a premium commensurate with the risk – the "actuarially justified premium"- (economic insurability). For the risk to be actually insured (if insurance is not mandatory), the premium will also need to be appropriate both for the insurer, who will assess it against the need for insurance supply to be profitable under given capital constraints, and for the insured, who should find it affordable and commensurate with his own perception of the risk. Clearly, new forms of terrorism risk as described above do not readily meet all of the insurability criteria. Not only the magnitude, but the combination of catastrophe-sized losses and modeling uncertainty constitute a critical challenge for the insurance industry, and may explain the disruptions in insurance markets that resulted from the 2001 terrorist attacks.

1.5. International insurance and reinsurance markets have assumed their share of the liabilities arising from the 11 September events. However, market reactions after the September 2001 attacks indicated that the industry would not be able in the future to manage new forms of terrorism risk under previous underwriting conditions. The drastic shrinkage of affordable insurance cover for terrorism risk which followed the WTC attacks, and the resulting adverse economic effects, raised the concern of OECD Ministers. In mid-2002, they mandated the OECD to develop policy analysis and recommendations on the financial management of terrorism risk.

Following the September 2001 attacks, initial uncertainty as to whether these risks were legally covered by insurance contracts and whether insurers with "acts of war" exclusions would rely upon them to deny coverage were rapidly lifted, and insurers and reinsurers demonstrated that they would assume their share of the loss. However, their attitude towards terrorism risk has radically changed and market reactions have followed a pattern typically observed in the wake of large-scale disasters. When the 9/11 events made the threat of potential future, and possibly imminent, large-scale terrorism acts explicit, reinsurers decided to exclude such risks as uninsurable through widespread terrorism exclusion clauses, or to drastically review their underwriting conditions so as to preserve their solvency. Unable to find sufficient reinsurance cover at affordable prices, insurers reacted likewise and the global capacity of the terrorism insurance market was subject to sudden shrinkage. Underwriting became far more selective and coverage was sharply reduced, so that terrorism insurance became almost unavailable in certain lines of business like commercial/industrial property and business interruption. The severely curtailed supply of cover and soaring premium rates often deterred entities at risk from taking out insurance, unless obliged to do so.

The social cost of the shrinkage of affordable insurance cover for terrorism risks, although difficult to quantify precisely, is probably high, thus threatening a negative spill-over across sectors and, possibly, the contraction of economic activity. The lack of insurance against terrorist attacks was especially disruptive in those economic activities most dependent on terrorism insurance *(e.g.,* aviation, tourism, construction, commercial lending, etc.) affected by a slow down or risk of complete freezing of activities as for commercial aviation and by increased business costs. Known and threatened adverse economic effects raised the concern of OECD Ministers, who requested the Organisation to "develop policy analysis and recommendations on how to define and cover terrorism risks and to assess the respective roles of the insurance industry, financial markets and governments, including for the coverage of "mega-terrorism" risks".

Restoring the financial coverage of terrorism risk, to accelerate recovery and prevent potential future attacks from having a debilitating impact on social and economic activity at national and international level, was recognised as a compelling need in many OECD countries. Yet, the sudden obsolescence of former terrorism risk compensation arrangements in most of them was raising many crucial questions: how should terrorism be defined for compensation purposes? What is the most effective and cost-efficient way to financially manage and cover terrorism risks? To what extent and under what conditions can insurers and reinsurers continue to cover losses arising from terrorism? Could capital markets provide additional capacity? Should governments be called upon to participate in the financial coverage of this unprecedented threat? Answers to these questions have gradually emerged in OECD countries and are continuing to take shape, according to the developments in risk perception and understanding, and also to the reactions of the various parties at stake.

2. Towards sustainable policy options to cover unpredictable terrorism risks

2.1. The financial coverage against modern terrorism called for the development of new insurability conditions and risk management tools. When reshaping their underwriting strategy in respect of terrorism risks, the first task of insurers and reinsurers was to (re)define terrorism acts unambiguously. This exercise, usually neglected before 2001, now appears as a crucial prerequisite for coverage or exclusion purposes.

The events of September 11 made the various actors in the insurance sector aware of the need to redefine and assess their commitments with respect to terrorism risks, before any new major terrorism attack occurred. Whether it is done to justify exclusion or to define the extent of the coverage by the market and/or any other compensation mechanism, terrorism risk, which was usually not even explicitly mentioned in contracts, now needs to be precisely defined in order to minimize ambiguities and the potential for lawsuits.

It is important to differentiate between terrorist acts and other manifestations of violence such as riots and vandalism, which may not trigger the same compensation mechanisms. Particularly crucial is the distinction between terrorism attacks and acts of war, the latter being systematically excluded from insurance cover.

Defining the nature of terrorism acts is a difficult task: past work on a general definition of terrorism has often been controversial, and no consensual definition has emerged at the international level. In response to the 2002 Ministerial mandate, the OECD Insurance Committee endeavoured to develop a flexible approach to the definition of terrorism risks for compensation purposes.

2.2. The following checklist of elements of a definition of terrorism acts, contained in the 2004 OECD Recommendation[10] and drawn from a comparison of the definitions commonly used for compensation purposes in a majority of member countries, may be useful to private sector entities as well as governments involved in terrorism risk coverage[11].

- *Means and effects*

  A terrorist act is:

  - an act including, but not limited to, the use of force or violence, causing serious[12] harm to human life, tangible or intangible property,

  - or a threat thereof entailing serious[12] harm;

- *Intention:*

  A terrorist act is committed or threatened:

  - with the intent to influence or destabilise any government or public entity and/or to provoke fear and insecurity in all or part of the population;

  - in support of a political, religious, ethnic, ideological or similar goal[13].

The OECD Recommendation also dealt with the criteria to be considered in determining whether a risk can be covered through insurance or other available mechanism.

2.3. The progress of terrorism risk modeling allows potential losses resulting from various attack scenarios to be quantified, but falls short of increasing the predictability of future attacks, and particularly their likelihood and frequency; terrorism risk-modeling also remains intrinsically more subjective than that of natural disasters in particular.

A substantial amount of investment has recently been devoted to the development of modeling techniques adapted to the specificities of terrorism risk. Models are intended for entities at risk which are willing to measure their vulnerability and need for coverage, for insurers and reinsurers having to increase risk predictability so as to improve pricing and set adequate policy conditions, and for governments anxious to assess the need and design the modalities of possible public involvement in terrorism compensation. Terrorism risk models are designed firstly to *assess the terrorism threat* and reduce uncertainty regarding three parameters of future attacks: possible targets, frequency and severity. Models also allow the development of extensive and informative data bases on *exposure inventories* (for property, but also life, liability, worker compensation etc. lines). Lastly, they measure the *vulnerability of targets* to different attacks, which, in the case of terrorism, can have an influence on the hazard.

Although terrorism modeling allows for the development of extensive data bases on exposure inventories and loss scenarios which are, for instance, a critical input for insurers when setting premium levels, it does have major shortcomings. The operations described above call for large, complex, and expensive information collection and analysis, limiting the geographical coverage of terrorism modeling. So far, it has mainly been developed in the United States. More fundamentally, while terrorism risk shares certain key features with natural disasters and other large-scale risks, the fact that it is man-made and intentional makes risk modeling not only more complex, but also less reliable. Events dictated by terrorists' malicious intentions are generally not predictable. Terrorism therefore requires a strategic approach to risk modeling: any probabilistic framework for evaluating and quantifying the risks associated with terrorist actions will ultimately need to involve a substantial measure of expert judgment. In particular, assessing the likelihood of attacks will remain intrinsically more subjective. The guidance that terrorism risk modeling may provide does not remove the need to assess the risk thoroughly and analyse exposure specificities that the model would not be able to take into account.

2.4. Insurers and reinsurers have adopted a rationalised strategy of careful underwriting, exposure control and premium setting, while building up further capacity in terrorism insurance.

Since the drastic market contraction that took place between end-2001 and mid/end-2002, insurers and reinsurers willing to cover terrorism risk have gradually revised their insurability conditions and adopted increased underwriting discipline, careful exposure control and premium setting.

At the same time, the sudden awareness of the threat hanging over insurers' solvency, the need to adapt their reserves to the new risk landscape, as well as the desire to take advantage of a potentially profitable market niche, have translated into capacity building in terrorism insurance. This was done via recapitalisation for those insurers who could afford it and the creation of new – usually offshore – ventures. Although far smaller than the global P&C insurance market, the so-called stand alone market has also benefited from this trend, while becoming more sophisticated as a result of increased competition.

Beyond the endeavours of individual (re)insurers to build further capacity, various initiatives aimed at the creation of private pooling mechanisms. Voluntary private pools would not of themselves create net additional industry capital. However, they could make for better risk spread and diversification, thereby reducing the likelihood of individual participants suffering heavy financial losses or becoming insolvent as a result of terrorism attacks (creation of additional capacity *for pool members*). Pooling initiatives have, however, known diverse fates. While private terrorism insurance pools have been set up at the national level in Austria and Finland for instance, various risk mutualisation initiatives for specific insurance lines or industries have been less successful. An interesting example of such an endeavour was recently provided by the US, where a feasibility study was conducted in 2004 for the setting up of a terrorism reinsurance pool to cover workers' compensation claims (one of the insurance lines most exposed to terrorism). It concluded that such a pool would be inadequate to compensate worker compensation claims in case of a major event. One should note that several risk retention groups initiated by the aviation industry have never been implemented either.

2.5. The financial markets may in the future provide some additional sources of capacity to cover terrorism risks: alternative risk transfer (ART) tools, such as risk-linked securities, may in theory be capable of complementing conventional insurance and reinsurance arrangements. However, a sustained market for such financial instruments to cover terrorism risks has not yet emerged, and these financial instruments are not expected to increase substantially market capacity for terrorism coverage in the short term, or to cover CBRN exposures in particular.

The shrinkage of capacity following September 11 was seen as an opportunity for new financial market instruments (comparable to those designed to cover natural catastrophe risks in the mid-1990s) to be developed as alternatives to the limited and expensive conventional insurance/reinsurance products. Considering their size, these markets have remarkable risk-spreading potential and might be willing to take on new risks if they considered them imperfectly correlated with those they routinely accept. In theory, by diversifying their investment portfolios, institutional investors may manage to absorb high-risk exposures, thereby optimizing their risk-return ratio.

Capital markets offer different types of alternative risk management solutions, which can be grouped in two main categories: alternative risk financing and alternative risk transfer instruments. Alternative risk transfer options currently appear far more promising than alternative risk financing as ways to cover catastrophic risks. Recent experience with the securitisation of natural disaster risks sets a particularly interesting precedent for the securitization of other catastrophic risks, such as man-made disasters: even though it has not matched expectations so far, with about USD 7.5 billion of capital at risk issued since 1996, and an accelerating increase in yearly new issues, the market for catastrophe bonds can be viewed as a stable, yet limited, source of alternative financing for catastrophic risks.

The idea of extending the securitisation of catastrophic risks to terrorism therefore emerged after the 2001 attacks. In 2003, a breakthrough was made with the Golden Globe Financing Ltd transaction[14]: not only was it the first time that a transaction *explicitly* covered terrorism risks, it was also oversubscribed, demonstrating that investors were ready to cover such exposure under certain conditions. Since then, a second transaction was initiated by Swiss Re in late 2003 to cover catastrophic mortality risk[15].

These transactions may pave the way for further terrorism risk securitisation. It is however clear that the issuance of terrorism catastrophe bonds requires many conditions to be met and careful monitoring of the different risks. Firstly, insurance companies, rating agencies, underwriters and investors need to evaluate the underlying risk exposure in order to make informed decisions. Yet, risk uncertainty and the perception that terrorism risk modeling is too subjective to be relied upon are limiting investors' appetite for terrorism bonds. It is therefore not surprising that, as of today, there have been no transactions purely securitizing terrorism risks despite the current strains on conventional reinsurance capacity. From this point of view the coverage of terrorism risk by means of multi-event bonds appears to be an important condition of success. Because of the uncertainty associated with the underlying risk and the fact that such transactions are new, they are both complex and take time to put in place, as well as being expensive. Also, the issuance of terrorism bonds may suffer from both moral hazard risk (if terrorist groups were to be connected to financial institutions and have a financial interest in the occurrence of an attack) and basis risk (*i.e.* the risk of imperfect correlation with the underlying exposure). For all these reasons, these alternative risk transfer solutions are not expected to substantially increase market capacity for terrorism coverage in the foreseeable future.

2.6. OECD member countries should rely, as far as possible, on the private sector to find solutions to the coverage of terrorism-related risks. However, where there is evidence of private markets' lacking capacity, indirect and direct government intervention may be considered as a means of increasing terrorism insurance availability and affordability and to support private market operations and enhance market efficiency. Any such government participation should be carefully tailored to avoid crowding out private initiatives.

While no country can claim to be immune from terrorism risks, the degree of exposure of OECD countries to terrorism risk nevertheless varies. The extent to which each country's insurance market has been affected by the 9/11 events differs, as do OECD countries' views of the appropriate level of government intervention in the sector.

Governments taking the decision to intervene in terrorism insurance markets will generally do so in the aftermath of an attack. The threat of major economic disruptions stemming from the market's incapacity, in the wake of a disaster, to provide sufficient cover at rates considered affordable by potential policyholders, may provide grounds for government action. Various other arguments may also support government involvement, in particular: governments may address capacity problems by achieving a far greater diversification of risk both among the wider population of tax payers as well as over time to future generations of taxpayers (while insurers are working under far shorter time constraints); as mentioned above, governments have a decisive influence on terrorism through counter-terrorism policy and foreign policy, and are the most informed party on terrorism risk, which makes this risk difficult to manage by the private sector alone; also, various externalities associated to terrorism risk hamper private market operations. On the political side, the involvement of governments in the financial compensation of terrorism related losses is likely to give credibility to its counter-terrorism policy.

Any government action however needs to be carefully designed to effectively extend terrorism risk insurance coverage while avoiding serious potential drawbacks, *e.g.*: the crowding out of private sector initiatives in the medium and long term[16], the offsetting of mitigation incentives, possible underwriting, pricing and claim management rigidities in the operation of national compensation schemes, and bureaucratic excesses which could result in high operating expenses.

Above all, any government intervention should be designed as a *condition* of private market operations and revitalisation, as well as a *complement* to private operators through the coverage of extreme risks that markets would in any case not be able to match, and not as a market substitute unless expressly required by specific political circumstances.

To this end, governments may consider a wide array of policy tools which may be broadly divided into two main categories: regulatory action and direct participation in mechanisms set up to cover terrorism risks.

2.7. Changes to the tax and accounting environment may be considered to reduce the cost to the insurer of building up reserves to cover expected future catastrophe losses and to promote the development of alternative risk transfer mechanisms to cover terrorism risk.

Regulatory action would be specifically needed to adapt tax and accounting rules to the needs of catastrophic risk management. However beneficial, such action may prove insufficient to restore private insurance market operations. Similarly, accounting and tax reforms may possibly be carried out to promote the catastrophe bond market, although this is not expected to greatly increase its potential to cover terrorism risks in view of the structure hindrances caused by risk ambiguity and the lack of specialised expertise among most potential investors. It should be noted, in any event, that regulatory action can be combined with direct forms of government intervention within an integrated strategy.

2.8. Direct government participation in terrorism risk compensation mechanisms, including some form of public-private partnership, may be considered as an option.

Solutions to cover terrorism risk are shaped according to a complex balance between possible policy aims, economic requirements, the historical context, national values, market conditions and regulation. If government participation in terrorism risk compensation is considered, some of the modalities of such intervention[17] should deserve special attention.

Regarding the *scope of government intervention,* governments may wish to rely on insurers and their broad networks and expertise to market and sell products, collect premia and manage claim reporting and payments after a disaster. In the resulting public-private risk and task-sharing mechanisms, the *form of government intervention* may vary from intervention as the primary insurer to reinsurer of last resort – an option that could possibly remain the centrepiece of government intervention in the foreseeable future. *Periodical reassessments of government intervention* should be explicitly organised. If envisaged, the scaling down of government commitments should be progressive and geared to market evolutions.

A key issue to be considered is that of *mandatory versus voluntary insurance*. This may refer to the mandatory participation of insurers and possibly reinsurers in government schemes (as in Spain or, as for insurers only, in the United States), the mandatory offer of terrorism insurance (as in Spain, in Australia, in the United States for commercial property and casualty insurance, or in France for firms offering commercial property insurance), and the mandatory purchase of terrorism insurance (as in Australia, France, Spain and the United States for workers compensation). In this context, the need to reduce or even eliminate risks of adverse selection, to broaden coverage and to extend compensation capacity shall be balanced against potential crowding out effects, as well as possible inefficiencies related to the fact that risk exposure varies among regions, industries, entities, etc.

No less important is the issue of *premium setting*. For public terrorism reinsurance (or insurance) premia, governments will need to choose between *ex ante* premia (as in France, United Kingdom, Germany and Spain) or allow for some *ex post* compensation for very high losses, as in the United States. Setting private terrorism insurance premia is generally at the discretion of the insurer. The issue also arises as to whether, for public reinsurance of terrorism[18] (as it is the case in the United Kingdom) as well as for primary insurance, premia should be risk-based to create incentives for mitigation, which would be logical if insurers were free to price the risk, or whether they should only be proportional to the insured value (as in Spain, France and Germany).

Governments involved in some form of public-private partnership will also have to define the extent of risk coverage, as well as their maximum involvement if the scheme is not open ended as in France or Australia.

Clearly, the choices made regarding the features described above in a public-private partnership will be critical to the success of the scheme.

2.9. Under current circumstances, for those countries where government participation is considered desirable, a layered approach to terrorism risk coverage[19] may be advisable. This could involve: the insured, through a deductible encouraging risk-mitigation measures, insurers and reinsurers, possibly through a private risk-sharing agreement such as a co-reinsurance pool, financial markets, reinsurance, and the government acting as reinsurer (and/or possibly lender) of last resort.

As observed in most existing government plans, the coverage should require a significant deductible requirement (at the lower-risk tier) and coinsurance component (at the middle-risk tier). This format provides good economic incentives for risk prevention and mitigation.

In the context of a customized risk coverage strategy, multiple layers of terrorism risk can be defined and allocated among the various parties involved: policyholders, private insurance and reinsurance companies, co-reinsurance pools, potential investors in risk-linked securities and other financial market instruments, international reinsurance, governments. Government intervention, in this respect, could be confined to the highest levels of risk exposures, for which private sector capacity does not at present appear to be available.

A balanced approach between the role assigned respectively to the insurance industry, financial markets and the government is recommended in order to avoid discouraging the private sector from developing effective responses to the new challenges that the terrorism risk will pose in the future.

There is no ready-made solution that governments can adopt to solve the problem of terrorism risk coverage; on the contrary, solutions need to be tailored to the specific needs of each country, taking into account their social, economic, historical and cultural backgrounds.

2.10. The institutional responses given by OECD member countries to the issue of terrorism risk coverage differ in various respects but, in many cases, involve some degree of permanent or temporary government participation, in the form of a layered public-private partnership.

Before 2001, Israel, South Africa, Spain, the United Kingdom in general, and Northern Ireland in particular, which have historically been highly exposed to terrorism risk, were the only places where the government had been asked to back up private markets, although to various degrees.

After the WTC attacks, insurers and reinsurers had initiated reflection and work on the establishment of private-public mechanisms for the compensation of terrorism-related losses. Several governments, faced with the incapacity of insurers to satisfy demand, have acknowledged the need to address problems in the availability and affordability of cover for terrorism risk via direct intervention. As of today, private-public mechanisms providing insurance coverage for terrorism risk have been implemented in seven OECD member countries[20]: Australia, France, Germany, The Netherlands, Spain, the United Kingdom and the United States. The Austrian pool does not involve the government at this stage.

2.11. Since terrorism risk may affect multiple insurance lines, it is crucial to understand which lines of insurance business and perils may need to be covered as a matter of priority under national arrangements. This exercise reflects a complex mix of technical, economic, legal and policy criteria, and may therefore vary between national compensation systems, as well as evolve over time.

Most of the schemes set up in OECD member countries focus on large commercial property and business interruption losses. While this is the common denominator of all institutional arrangements, it should be noted that: in Australia, the coverage offered by the national scheme extends to liability arising from ownership or occupation of eligible properties; in Austria, the pool covers all property lines other than transport insurance; in the Netherlands the scheme covers all lines (life and non-life) with the exception of aviation hull and aircraft liability; in Spain, in addition to damages to property (qualitative, as opposed to quantitative approach) and business interruption, the national scheme also covers personal injuries; and in the United States, coverage under the national terrorism compensation mechanism also extends to workers compensation.

Because terrorism is a fast-evolving phenomenon and future forms of terrorist action can hardly be anticipated, any definition of terrorist acts based on past experience may rapidly become obsolete. The list of risks covered also depends on the various stakeholders evolving ability to manage them. Any definition of terrorism risks eligible for compensation therefore needs to be periodically reassessed.

2.12. As a result of the private and public initiatives described above, terrorism insurance markets have stabilised to some degree and market conditions are expected to further improve in the absence of a new large-scale attack.

Terrorism insurance market conditions have improved substantially since 2001 in a number of markets. Capacity and prices have become more predictable and the very high prices observed in the months following the 9/11 attacks have come down. An illustration of this is provided by developments on the US market, where terrorism insurance represented roughly 4% of the property programme cost as a percentage of premia at end-2004, against 10% in early 2003. On the stand-alone market, prices have also benefited from more informed risk management and increased competition, falling by about 15 % since early 2002, and in some cases by as much as 25%. At the same time, insurance take-up rates have significantly increased in the United States, even though this general trend masks regional and sectoral disparities. When available, government participation in compensation mechanisms in OECD countries has turned out to be a condition for insurers to come back onto the terrorism risk market and was therefore a decisive factor behind the expansion of capacity and softening of insurance premia. In the absence of a new attack, and in the current regulatory frameworks, terrorism insurance market conditions may continue to stabilise over time.

2.13. The recent trend towards market stabilization leaves some major issues unanswered. Firstly, terrorism insurance take-up rates remain low in various countries where the purchase of this insurance is not compulsory. Under these circumstances, the economic and social impact of a new large-scale attack could be greater than in 2001. OECD member countries should endeavour to develop risk awareness and may consider incentives to extend coverage and increase the financial capacity of terrorism risk compensation mechanisms.

In various OECD markets where the purchase of coverage is not mandatory, terrorism insurance take-up rates remain low, leaving large parts of the economy financially exposed to possible future attacks if entities at risk have not opted for alternative coverage solutions. It has for instance been estimated that about half of all commercial entities remain uncovered in the United States, according to recent studies, while less than 3% of eligible firms had contracted with the government-backed Extremus mechanism in Germany, prompting a reduction in its reinsurance capacity. This situation raises serious concerns: in countries with low terrorism insurance take-up rates, a large-scale terrorist attack could be more damaging today than before 2001, since a far smaller portion of the risk would be spread across the national and international insurance and reinsurance community. Claimants in need of compensation would either have to draw on their own reserves (if any) and be exposed to the risk of ruin if these turned out to be insufficient, or hope for ex-post government action, which could put a serious strain on national budgets.

While a further fall in prices may increase insurance penetration, the decision not to purchase (or to purchase very low level of) terrorism insurance also depends on a complex set of factors, apart from the price of cover: behaviour bias, which may lead to an underestimation of the threat of future terrorist attack as the memory of recent attacks fades away, or to the feeling that "it can only happen to others", and the implicit hope that governments would intervene in case of large attacks, may deter from purchasing terrorism insurance ; the assessment of the cost of insurance against its potential benefits and the appraisal of insurance solutions against alternative types of coverage (such as self-insurance) may lead to similar risk management choices. Since little information is available on the motivations of entities at risks opting for no or a very low level of terrorism insurance cover, and on the amount of cover provided by alternative compensation mechanisms, the promotion of further risk awareness and understanding remains relevant. Under these conditions, the option of mandating the purchase of terrorism insurance may also be worth considering in countries with a low degree of market penetration for terrorism insurance, to ensure a broad premium base and steady capacity building under the national compensation scheme.

2.14. Because of the potential magnitude, spread and persistence of damages caused by chemical, biological, radiological and nuclear terrorism risks (CBRN), these exposures are for the time being generally considered as uninsurable by the insurance industry and are excluded from most insurance coverage.

CBRN risks represent a growing source of concern, since they may be an increasingly plausible scenario of attack. Although limited coverage can be found in some cases, they are generally considered as uninsurable and are therefore subject to exclusions because of the potential magnitude, spread and persistence of the damages potentially arising from such risks. Moreover, these risks are not always (fully) covered through existing government-backed insurance schemes. The coverage of CBRN risks for certain insurance lines is currently being debated in several countries, as well as at industry level. In the aviation sector in particular, some aviation insurers are proposing that all CBRN risks, and not just nuclear detonation and the associated radioactive contamination, be excluded through AVN48. Governments should consider the issue of CBRN risk and work, in cooperation with the industry, towards developing sustainable solutions to provide for their coverage[21].

2.15. Despite improvements in market conditions, the losses associated with very large-scale terrorist attacks may, under current conditions, remain beyond the capability of the private insurance and reinsurance industry to price and to absorb alone. The future evolution of the terrorism threat, and the ensuing capacity and willingness of the private market to cover resulting losses, is uncertain. The search for sustainable solutions to terrorism risk coverage should therefore be pursued to enable further private market recovery and avoid new insurability crises.

It is difficult to quantify aggregate efforts at capacity building since 2001, and more generally to assess the available capacity of the private insurance industry to cover the losses that a large-scale terrorist attack could involve. In the current context, in the United States for instance, the P&C insurers' surplus supporting all commercial property, general liability and workers' compensation insurance may be about USD 114 billion. Meanwhile, the terrorism risk landscape has changed considerably, based on the analysis of the September 11th and other recent attacks. Modeling firms are developing "plausible scenarios" in which estimated insured losses from a single event could amount to USD 50, USD 100 and up to USD 250 billion according to different studies. Such an illustration brings the insurability issue into perspective.

Over and above the capacity issue, while insurers have improved their capability to model "routine" terrorism, very large-scale events may remain beyond the industry's ability to price, due to high risk ambiguity.

Lastly, given the uncertainty surrounding the evolution of terrorism, any projection of market developments remains difficult. It is even harder to foresee the private sector reaction in the event of a major change in the conditions of operation, such as the withdrawal of government backing in countries where it is currently available, or in case of recrudescence of major terrorism event(s).

2.16. Flexibility and periodical assessments are recommended as key components of any institutional mechanism to be implemented by OECD member countries, in order to allow them to adapt to risk and market dynamics and to ensure the sustainability of compensation arrangements. Close monitoring of risks, markets and regulatory trends at international level will help countries to cope with terrorism risk compensation in the future.

The changing nature of terrorism risk and the potential ability of the private sector to develop new insurance techniques and build additional financial capacity over time call for a dynamic institutional approach. Policy measures to be implemented by OECD member countries should, therefore, allow for a high degree of flexibility. In particular, when a national mechanism for the compensation of terrorism risk is enforced, the possibility of progressively raising the level of retention to foster competition should be considered when appropriate and periodical assessment of the scheme could be foreseen. Private and public actors will benefit from further information and experience sharing at international level, which has already proven helpful in the development of the most recent national schemes for instance.

2.17. "Mega-terrorism" attacks may result in losses exceeding the joint capacity of private markets and governments in some countries to compensate for them without threatening national economic stability. International/regional ex ante cooperation between interested countries may be considered. Further examination as to whether mega-terrorism risk coverage may effectively be dealt with at international level may be worth pursuing by interested countries.

If the risk awareness of the public remains low, many experts agree that the threat of mega-terrorism[22] should be taken seriously and that it concerns, to varying degrees, all countries. Apart from the human distress created by such events, building the financial capacity to honour claims is desirable, not only as a way of compensating claimants, but also to avoid systemic impacts which may destabilise economies and societies. Given the potential magnitude of the losses involved, financial compensation for mega-terrorism related losses remains however highly problematic.

In a number of countries, the combined capacity of the private markets and the government may not be sufficient to compensate for mega-terrorism without threatening national economic stability. International/regional cooperation organised on a voluntary basis may be a solution to the indemnification of mega-terrorist events, and providing for such cooperation *ex ante* might minimise economic uncertainty. However, at this stage, the technical and political impediments to the implementation of an international terrorism risk-sharing agreement need to be highlighted. Also, an international/regional safety net may not be equally useful or desirable to all OECD member countries: such a mechanism may find most interest at the regional level. Further examination as to whether mega-terrorism risk coverage could effectively be dealt with at an international level by interested parties could therefore be worth pursuing *by those parties*.

2.18. Compensation of personal injuries deserves to be given the appropriate degree of priority. OECD member countries should carefully coordinate any backing of private insurance coverage with any financial protection already provided to victims of terrorist attacks through other publicly managed compensation mechanisms.

The shrinkage of insurance coverage for terrorism risks after the September 11 events mostly concerned commercial lines, while insurance companies in a number of OECD member countries continued to offer coverage in personal lines, without amending the existing conditions to exclude terrorism risks.

Several OECD countries, moreover, have set up special Compensation funds for victims of terrorism or other violent crimes, covering some of the consequences of terrorist acts. At the international level, the European Convention on the Compensation of Victims of Violent Crimes was signed on 24 November 1983. More recently, the Council of the European Union adopted a Directive on compensation to crime victims on 29 April 2004[23], on the basis of a proposal from the Commission, whose enactment had been called for by the European Council in the "Declaration on Combating Terrorism" of 25 March 2004.

In light of the above, proper coordination could be encouraged between all the existing mechanisms for the compensation of terror-related losses, so to avoid duplication of efforts and inefficient allocation of resources.

2.19. Terrorism is a universal exposure and a potential threat to every country. Both OECD and non OECD members may benefit from an increased exchange of information and experience at international level on the coverage of terrorism risks. The development of efficient solutions for compensating related damages may be an even more compelling need for the emerging economies which have limited access to financial resources. Policy dialogue and work in co-operation with emerging economies on appropriate ways to cover terrorist risks in these countries should be considered.

2.20. These conclusions and options are non-binding and do not condition, compromise or prejudge solutions and measures adopted in several countries to compensate for losses related to terrorism.

Notes

1   Except for paragraph 2.18, this summary, as the entire volume, will focus on the compensation of property losses (and not of personal injuries).

2   Outside of the OECD area, Israel (since 1961) and South Africa (since 1979) had also established State-backed terrorism compensation mechanisms. For more details on the compensation of terrorism in non-member countries, see infra, Annex.

3   See infra, Part II Chapter 1 on *Insurability of Terrorism Risk* for a definition of weapons of mass destruction.

4   2976 people perished in the 9/11 attacks. This number excludes the 19 hijackers. ISO, http://www.iii.org/media/facts/statsbyissue/catastrophes.

5   Hurricanes Ivan, Charley, Frances and Jeanne in August and September 2004 in the United States involved property and business interruption losses of USD 11, 8, 5 and 3.034 billion respectively. The aggregated amount of losses of the four hurricanes for these lines (*excluding liability and life insurance*), *i.e.* USD 27.034 billion, exceeds the hurricane Andrew and 9/11 *property and business interruption* losses.

6   The deliberate choice made by modern terrorists to magnify the impact of their attacks sets an important difference between terrorism and other types of disasters. Terrorist attacks may, for instance, target areas with the highest concentrations of people and values, and therefore result in greater damage.

7   See infra, Part III Chapter 6 on *Insurability of (mega-)terrorism risk: challenges and perspectives*, by H. Kunreuther and E. Michel-Kerjan.

8   Global Property and Casualty (P&C) industry capital at the end of 2004 is estimated at about USD 550 billion.

9   See infra, Part III Chapter 6 on *Insurability of (mega-)terrorism risk: challenges and perspectives*, by H. Kunreuther and E. Michel-Kerjan.

10   See Recommendation of the OECD Council on a checklist of criteria to define terrorism for the purpose of compensation, available at: http://www.oecd.org/daf/insurance.

11   This list is illustrative, non-binding, and can be adapted by the various parties concerned to meet the needs of their specific market and regulatory frameworks as well as their policy objectives. The criteria proposed do not, therefore, necessarily reflect the elements of definition currently used in all OECD member countries.

12   It is left to each country/entity to define the criteria more precisely, possibly quantitatively or qualitatively when relevant, according to their specific policies and technical considerations.

13   Such goals may be instrumental in the identification of terrorist acts. However, they may never be used to legitimate any terrorist act.

14   USD 260 million equivalent transaction securitizing the risk of cancellation of the Summer 2006 FIFA World Cup. Through this transaction, FIFA was able to cover its sponsoring earnings from that event.

15   In December 2003 Swiss Re concluded a financial arrangement with Vita Capital Ltd. to provide up to USD 400 million of payments to Swiss Re in certain extreme mortality risk scenarios. To fund potential payments under this arrangement, Vita Capital – a specially created insurance-linked security intermediary – issued USD 400 million of principal at-risk variable rate notes. The principal of the Vita Capital notes will be at risk if, during any single calendar year in the risk coverage period (the bond matures on 1 January 2007), the combined mortality index exceeds 130% of its baseline 2002 level (approximately 750 000 extra deaths). The catastrophe-indexed are linked to a rise in mortality from any source. According to certain estimations, the trigger threshold could be attained before the maturity date only if pessimistic lethality estimates are made for both a pandemic and a major terrorist attack involving the use of weapons of mass destruction.

16   It should however be emphasised that crowding out may in given circumstances have some positive welfare implications, for instance when private insurers are unable to price a risk and set prices that are too high for policies to be actually bought.

17   For more details, see infra, Part III Chapter 8 on *The role of government in the coverage of terrorism risks*, by D. Jaffee.

18   This may however be interpreted as disclosure of government information on likely targets. Also, it may be viewed as inequitable to charge higher premia for the higher risks.

19   Other forms of public participation which may have proven satisfactory for private markets, as is the case in Spain where State participation is based on the subsidiarity principle, should not be excluded.

20   For an analysis of the various national schemes, see infra, Part III Chapter 9 on *The coverage of terrorism risks at national level*, by J. Cooke. See also the tables on terrorism risk insurance schemes in OECD countries in Part II Chapter 5, infra.

21   While the CBRN threat may remain the most serious, it should be stressed that other risks, such as the cyber terrorism risk, are also raising great concern. This risk remains excluded from the Pool Re or Extremus AG cover for instance.

22   There is no ready-to-use definition of mega-terrorism. Nevertheless, orders of magnitude may be helpful in evaluating what governments would have to deal with. As a working hypothesis, a terrorist act resulting in losses of USD 100 billion for instance (not to mention the human cost), could be qualified as a mega-terrorist act, as would potentially be a nuclear, chemical, or biological attack, such as the explosion of a dirty bomb, the spreading of poisonous gas, or large-scale water contamination. The appreciation of what constitutes a mega-terrorist attack may nevertheless vary, depending for instance on the region/country targeted, and possibly on the level of protection that is available in the private insurance and reinsurance markets, or on whether the attack may have lasting repercussions, such as in the case of nuclear and radiological attacks, which long-tail consequences are highly difficult to measure, etc. Far smaller attacks may therefore well be considered as "mega-terrorism". Moreover, apart from the magnitude of individual events, the potential increase in the frequency of terrorism events may also have a debilitating effect on the economy and society.

23   Council Directive 2004/80/EC of 29 April 2004 relating to compensation to crime victims, in Official Journal of the European Union, L261 (2004), p. 0015-0018.

Part II

Policy Issues

Chapter 1

INSURABILITY OF TERRORISM RISK

Introduction[1]

With a considerable number of acts of national and international terrorism recorded in the last thirty years[2], terrorism was certainly not an unknown exposure for insurers before 2001. Private insurance covered most terrorism risks, which were viewed as a manageable exposure. Terrorism risk insurability was only an issue in a few countries historically highly exposed to terrorism, and mainly Israel, South Africa, the United Kingdom and Spain[3] – where governments had decided to step into the terrorism compensation process, although to various degrees.

The evolution of terrorism over the last decade, culminating in the September 11 attacks, confirmed the advent of a new form of terrorism characterised by a **broader geographical scope** and a **transnational character**, as well as a **completely new loss dimension**. On the one hand, terrorism has now become a global issue from which no country can claim to be protected. On the other hand, the 9/11 attacks caused insured losses currently estimated at around USD 31.7 billion[4], making it the single most costly event ever recorded in the history of the insurance and reinsurance industry worldwide, and changing the general perspective on future expected losses from terrorist actions.

As stated by the 9/11 Commission Report[5] "the 9/11 attacks were a shock, but they should not have come as a surprise". Despite recurrent warnings, no one was prepared for the events of September 2001, and insurers and reinsurers were no exception[6]. They became suddenly aware of the considerable and drastically underestimated exposure of their risk portfolio to terrorism. As a consequence, the insurability of terrorism risk was immediately put into question. Any answer to this question obviously has heavy financial implications for entities at risk, insurers, reinsurers and governments. Faced with the new features of terrorism risk which entail unprecedented challenges for the insurance industry, underwriters initially responded by withdrawing from the terrorism insurance market, which resulted in severe economic disruptions. More than three years later, market conditions have improved. However, many crucial questions regarding the ability of the conventional insurance and reinsurance markets to cover potential future attacks are still unanswered, and the debate on the issue of the insurability of risks related to terrorist acts therefore remains largely unsettled.

There is no simple answer to the question of terrorism risk insurability. The chapter which follows explores several elements in order to try to capture the full scope of this issue, and to guide the reflection and possible actions of the many actors involved.

1. New terrorism threat, new challenges for the insurance industry[7]

Due to a conjunction of increased potential magnitude of highly correlated risks and growing unpredictability, modern terrorism is one of the most challenging risks for insurers and reinsurers in the 21st century

Insurability is a dynamic concept. Many risks considered as "uninsurable" for decades are now covered by the insurance industry, which has been constantly extending the boundaries of insurance coverage in response to the emergence of new risks and market demand. Over time, the list of insurable risks has extended to cover new causes; "some have been economic in nature, such as credit insurance, and some political in nature, such as government expropriation of assets, civil disorder and terrorism"[8]. Nevertheless, developments in technological and legal frameworks (and of the liability regimes in particular), demographic changes and urbanisation, possible climate change, the evolution of the geopolitical context and now new forms of terrorism, confront insurers with risks of unprecedented magnitude and complexity which severely test the limits of the market.

1.1 Insurability criteria

Private insurance operations are based on a number of conditions[9], which could be summarised as follows:

- **accessibility**: the probability and severity of losses must be quantifiable;

- **randomness**: the time at which the insured event occurs must be unpredictable and the occurrence itself must be independent of the will of the insured;

- **mutuality**: numerous persons exposed to a given hazard must join together to form a risk community within which the risk is shared and diversified;

- **economic feasibility:** for a risk to be insurable, private insurers must be able to charge a premium commensurate with the risk it covers (the "actuarially justified premium"). For the policyholder to be able to acquire the cover he needs (if insurance is not mandatory), premia must be adequate both for the insurer, who will assess whether it permits the insurance supplied to be profitable under given capital constraints, and for the insured, who should find it affordable and commensurate with his own perception of the risk.

Risks that do not satisfy these criteria may be considered by professional risk carriers as uninsurable and, therefore, coverage may become unavailable on the private market. It should nevertheless be borne in mind that regulatory and legal constraints are other key factors determining the scope of insurability, although the first part of this chapter will put more emphasis on the technical criteria of insurability.

Clearly, new forms of terrorism risk do not readily meet all of the criteria enumerated above. Given its potential magnitude, it is generally recognised that new forms of international terrorism share certain insurability problems with other extreme hazards (natural perils and large-scale technological risks). However, the evaluation of new forms of terrorism risk for insurance purposes presents additional difficulties which stem from a combination of extreme loss potential and radical risk unpredictability or *ambiguity*.

1.2. New loss dimension, high risks correlation, and insurability problems of catastrophe risks

In light of the events of September 11, it is now recognised that new forms of terrorism may entail consequences of catastrophic proportions[10]. There is also a high correlation among the risks insured – another feature that is shared with other types of large-scale disasters. These features present well-known impediments to insurability.

Increase in loss magnitude

Terrorism risk was not perceived as a potentially catastrophic risk before 2001. Isolated threats posed by pockets of national or regional terrorists as well as international terrorism acts remained of *relatively* small scale[11] and therefore, except in very few countries most exposed to terrorism, coverage was not problematic.

The September 11, 2001 attacks have however revealed the **radical change in the scale of potential losses.** To take the full measure of these events, it should be highlighted that the

USD 31.7 billion[12] insured losses entailed are almost 1.5 times as much as the insured losses from Hurricane Andrew, the second most costly event in the insurance industry. The comparison of September 11 losses with those entailed by former terrorist attacks underlines the break in historical series on terrorism losses: the worst terrorist attack in terms of insured property losses before 2001 was the explosion of a bomb near the Nat West Tower in the City of London, which resulted in USD 907 million[13]. The 2001 events have therefore called for a complete reassessment of loss scenarios for potential future attacks. Models of alternative terrorist attacks now include Probable Maximum Loss (PML) considered as unthinkable in the past; scenarios in which total insured losses could exceed USD 250 billion are considered plausible by terrorism experts[14].

This change in magnitude is rooted in a **shift in the motivations of terrorists**[15]. Some terrorist organisations have declared their enemy to be, no longer just national or social orders, but the community of Western industrialised nations and their values. Terrorist groups now seek not only to draw attention to their cause, but also to maximise casualties, the number of victims and collateral damage, and do not hesitate to sacrifice their own lives to maximise the impact of attacks. **Modus operandi** of today's terrorists also allows for exponential damage, at low cost for the terrorists: they tend to form loose, trans-national organisations and affiliations based on religious, ideological and political affinity, often claiming that their destructive acts are part of a broader global plan or war against a common enemy. In this way, they enjoy a force-multiplier effect by establishing connections with other organisations around the world.

Furthermore, new technologies, the development of global networks and interdependencies between nations have considerably **increased terrorists' potential** to organise and to wreak damage, including through simultaneous attacks or quasi instantaneous propagation of damages. A major evolution lies in the **exploitation of critical networks** (transportation, water supply, energy, telecommunications, etc.) by terrorists in recent attacks[16]. The growing dependence of social and economic activities on the operation of networks, combined with increasing interdependencies among theses networks at national and international level, translates into a set of vulnerabilities associated with their potential failure to operate, leading to major disruptions. Networks can be targeted by terrorists: by their nature, networks interface with public life at many junctures and therefore offer almost unlimited possible points of attack. For example, it is difficult to protect rail lines or all rail cars. Moreover, elements of the network may not only be identified as a target but also used as a weapon. The use of aircraft to destroy iconic buildings in the 9/11 attacks is an explicit illustration of this strategy. The 2004 Madrid bombing followed the same pattern. Lastly, terrorists may exploit the diffusion capacity of large critical networks[17]. In October 2001, terrorists used the US postal network to widely diffuse anthrax poison. Such small but carefully targeted attacks can cause immediate large scale economic damages. Whatever the strategy chosen, the damage is all the greater that every element of network – every aircraft, train, or piece of mail – becomes a potential target or a potential weapon, putting the entire network at risk. This will call for large scale security measures, which may entail major economic disruptions: for instance, after the hijacking of several planes on 11th September 2001, the uncertainty over the total number of planes targeted motivated the shutting down of the entire US commercial airline system one hour after the first attack on the World Trade Center attacks, for the first time in history.

Also, the potential future use of **non-conventional chemical, biological, radiological and nuclear (CBRN) weapons** and weapons of mass destruction[18] should not be underestimated. Since the mid-1990s in particular, terrorism experts have been warning that terrorists may have gained greater access to far more effective and lethal weapons.

Consequences for insurability

For the reasons described above, the 9/11 attacks may turn out not to be an isolated event, and the possibility of other attacks of catastrophic proportions has to be contemplated[19]. In this respect, it may be affirmed that new forms of terrorism share the features of risks often referred to as **LPHC (low probability high consequences) events**. Policymakers and private sector players are well aware of the fundamental insurability problems that arise in the general context of catastrophe insurance[20] and that have been extensively analysed in relation to natural hazards in particular[21]. Firstly, both terrorist attacks and natural hazards result in losses that are potentially high and very uncertain. The procedure for estimating the probability that a certain level of loss will be exceeded during a given timeframe has evolved from a rather simplistic deterministic basis to a more sophisticated methodology based on loss exceedance probability (EP) curves, generated using dedicated catastrophe modeling software[22]. For LPHC events however, analysis of past events reveals wide variations in loss distribution; this hinders insurers ability to predict the severity and frequency of future events, and thus to set premia commensurate with such risks.

LPHC events also raise a serious financial challenge: to compensate for such events, the (re)insurance industry must be able to mobilise very large financial resources at short notice. The considerable magnitude of potential losses is to be assessed against the **available capacity of private insurance to withstand these losses.** The financial resources of the insurance market depend on three main sources: a) the capital and reserves held by insurers and the amount of new capital that they can raise quickly; b) the capital and reserves held by the global reinsurance network and its capacity to raise new capital; and c) part of the short-term cash flow from new business, since after a very large loss, insurance prices tend to rise sharply for a period of time[23]. Having to cover relatively infrequent, but extremely large losses that can have severe long-term economic and social consequences, firms underwriting catastrophe risks must hold **very large amounts of capital and reserves or have easy access to alternative financing source**. If catastrophe insurance is offered without access to the necessary amount of capital, then the professional risk carrier faces a substantial bankruptcy risk (also known as the risk of ruin), thereby frustrating the very purpose of insurance operations. Insurance companies can – and often do – avoid this risk simply by withdrawing from the catastrophe insurance market.

The September 11 terrorist attacks were the occasion for market players to remind that, while the capacity of insurers, backed by international reinsurance markets, was very large, it was also finite. Estimating the industry capacity and its ability to withstand a certain amount of losses is a difficult exercise. A study was undertaken in 2002 on the capacity of the US industry to compensate for losses resulting from natural disasters. It concluded that a USD 40 billion loss would probably be manageable, while a USD 100 billion loss would result in a large number of insolvencies and severely disrupt insurance markets[24]. On the global scale, suffice it to say at this stage that after 2001, the heavy losses suffered by the insurance and reinsurance industry[25] (reinsurers ended up covering about 70% of insured losses), combined with the very substantial capital markets downturn, resulted in an estimated capital loss of USD 200 billion for the global property and casualty (P&C) insurance and reinsurance industry[26].

High risk correlation, new forms of correlation

Another common feature of terrorism attacks and natural hazards is that they usually involve **temporally and spatially correlated risks**. Risk correlation does not allow insurers to take advantage of the law of large numbers[27]. This hinders geographical and inter-temporal diversification, and makes it difficult to build a well-balanced book of business[28]. Because insurance is predicated on the pooling of a large number of significantly independent risks exposures, failing to meet this condition, while not necessarily translating into uninsurability, will require increased capacity/higher premia to face risk concentration. A related problem is that of **risk of accumulation:** the same catastrophic event can cause losses involving many different insured properties and infrastructures at the same time, giving rise to overwhelming claims burdens in a single policy period. The dramatic increase in the concentration of population and economic wealth around the globe has considerably aggravated the risk of correlation and accumulation in recent times. The insurance industry has recently warned against the disproportionate exposure and vulnerability of fast growing megapoles to natural, technological and environmental disasters, as well as to terrorist attacks[29]. It should also be highlighted that the **major differences in hazard exposure**, adding to risk correlation, makes mutuality even more difficult to achieve. For instance, costal areas and earthquake prone regions, or landmark or "trophy' risks such as, iconic buildings, and major metropolitan areas, will be far more exposed to natural disasters or terrorism attacks respectively than other areas, and will be more likely to be insured, generating further imbalance in risk portfolio.

Moreover, one of the lessons of September 11th was that large-scale events may also result in a **high degree of correlation between different lines of insurance coverage**. Not only commercial property, but also business interruption, aircraft liability, workers' compensation, life, health, disability and general liability insurance were simultaneously triggered. Worker compensation for instance represented 5.7% of aggregated 9/11 losses[30], while in past extreme events losses were almost entirely compared on the basis of property losses (against which other losses were marginal). This trend towards higher correlation between insurance lines will also seriously hamper risk portfolio diversification for insurers holding catastrophic risks.

Lastly, the 2001 attacks highlighted the emergence of a third type of correlation. The magnitude of direct and indirect economic damages of the World Trade Center attacks caused large losses **not only on the liability side, but also on the asset side of their balance sheet**. The sharp decline in financial markets *immediately following the attacks* also affected insurance companies which saw steep drops in their stock prices. This in turn lowered their capacity to raise new capital in good conditions. Insurers were also affected by the financial market downturn in their role as major institutional investors. After such a major disaster, and depending on the financial market conditions and reactions, it may therefore become increasingly difficult to offset part of the catastrophic losses through investment policy. Insurers and reinsurers that are willing to cover terrorism risk may now have to improve correlations analysis among underwriting, investment, and credit and operational risks.

1.3. Terrorism-specific features and rising unpredictability

The debate over the ability of private insurance/reinsurance markets to cover terrorism risk has often crystallised over the issue of the magnitude and correlation of potential risks and consequent capacity problems. However, risk associated with new forms of terrorism can not simply be assimilated to the well known insurability problems associated with low probability and high consequences events. Beyond its extreme damage potential and the high risk correlation it entails, new terrorism risk is characterised by a set of specific features which translate into even greater uncertainty as to risk quantification and likelihood of occurrence. Given insurers aversion to ambiguity, these severe conditions of generalised uncertainty affecting terrorism risk strongly hinder its insurability[31].

The analysis of the 9/11 events and of past terrorist attacks has allowed for the identification of several challenges that make terrorism fundamentally different from other types of extreme events[32]:

- Limited relevance of historical data: analysis of past intentions of terrorists does not make their future agenda more predictable; more generally, available data from past events therefore reveals little about the future patterns of terrorist actions. Moreover, the emergence of new forms of terrorism, as confirmed by the 11 September events in particular, further invalidates the use of statistics on past events since no former attack can compare with that of 2001. This crucial difference between terrorism before and after 11 September 2001, as well as between intentional man-made events and unintentional or natural events, considerably hampers insurers' work, for which projections based on statistical series are most often a central tool for the development of a market.

- "dynamic uncertainty", results from the constant change in the mapping and nature of risks as terrorists adapt to evolving prevention strategies adopted by private parties and governmental authorities; they may for instance shift attention to unprotected targets: as certain targets become "harder" (e.g., increased security at governmental buildings), rational terrorist groups may switch to softer targets (e.g. commercial premises), in order to maximise the chances of success of the planned attack. Terrorists may even switch at the very last minute to targets of opportunity. The literature on terrorism risks has recently pointed to these negative externalities potentially generated by self-protection measures[33]. The hardening of certain locations might transfer additional risk burden to other targets, thereby diluting or entirely offsetting the effects of self-protection measures from a societal point of view and defying efforts to predict, mitigate and cover terrorism risk[34].

- "interdependent security"[35] is another possible source of negative externality affecting decision making processes in terrorism prevention. Even if the insured invests in efficient security measures, it may nevertheless suffer losses due to an insufficient level of prevention taken by other economic actors whose activities are connected with that of the insured. This may deter firms from investing in prevention, making it difficult for insurers to provide incentives (such as premium reduction) for terrorism coverage, and raises significant problems for insurance companies to relevantly measure the exposure of their client to terrorism.

- "symmetry of non information" refers to the unavailability of information on risks incurred. It affects both the insurer and the insured, since most of the information available is classified, and the most informed party, the government, do not disclose it for national security reasons. Historical databases on losses from natural perils in most regions are now generally available. To the contrary, data on terrorist activities and future possible targets are usually kept secret for security reasons. While insurance operation may often be impeded by asymmetry of information between the insured and the insurer, terrorism insurance is hampered by what has been wittily qualified as "symmetry of non information"[36].

- Lastly, the critical influence of governments on the risk through foreign policy and counter-terrorism measures, is a very specific feature of terrorism risk, adding, among other consequences, to risk unpredictability.

In the past, insurers have covered risks of hardly predictable likelihood – risks related to new technologies for instance. Similarly, insurers cover various large scale (and highly correlated) risks, and managing very large exposures is one of the very *raison d'être* of the reinsurance business in particular. The specificity of new forms of terrorism risk however lies in the conjunction of both potentially catastrophe-sized losses and very high risk unpredictability. This combination of two major challenges to insurance providers may radically influence their view on insurability, and provide a plausible explanation of a global disruption in insurance markets[37] as witnessed after the World Trade Center attacks. Terrorism therefore appears more challenging to insure than in the past, and in various respects more difficult to predict, prevent, mitigate and eventually cover than many other extreme events.

2. Market reactions after the 9/11 attacks: from drastic shrinkage in affordable insurance cover to the development of new insurability conditions

Market reactions immediately after the 2001 terrorist attacks on the United States followed a typical post disaster pattern, resulting in a drastic shrinkage in terrorism insurance cover. Private and public initiatives that followed converged to stabilise insurance market conditions and further improvements may be expected in the absence of new large scale attack.

2.1. Terrorism risk insurance before 2001

With a few exceptions of some countries highly exposed to terrorism, terrorism risk insurability was not an issue before 2001.

Before September 2001, private insurance routinely covered most terrorism risks related to property losses under fire policies which would provide compensation for fire and explosion damage of any cause (except war). Not only was terrorism viewed as a manageable exposure, but it was usually considered so marginal that this unnamed peril was not subject to separate underwriting and pricing. Regular demand was addressed to specialised underwriters by a limited number of countries most exposed to terrorism, *i.e.* mainly Algeria, Colombia, Israel, Indonesia, South Africa, Sri Lanka and the UK after 1992. For more than twenty years, two main political risk underwriters – the Lloyd's and AIG – covered this market, with rather old-fashioned types of products focusing on property and trade and investment exposure, failing in particular to adequately define triggering events and to distinguish terrorism from other political violence perils[38]. Spain (since 1954, through the Consorcio which covers all extreme events), Israel (since 1961), South Africa (since 1969), and the United Kingdom (since 1993) were the only countries where the market was overwhelmed by the frequency and magnitude of attacks and where it was acknowledged that full protection against terrorism risks could not be made available through private (re)insurance only.

2.2. Short term market reaction after the 9/11 attacks: insurability into question

The insurance sector reacted responsibly to the 2001 attacks in assuming its part of the losses. In parallel, it drastically reviewed its exposure to terrorism risk to adapt to the new dimensions of modern terrorism threat, and market capacity shrank at a time when terrorism risk appeared hardly insurable.

Right after the attacks, there was some uncertainty as to whether these risks were legally covered by insurance contracts and whether insurers with "acts of war" exclusions would rely upon them to deny coverage. Insurers and reinsurance however quickly demonstrated that they would assume their part of the loss, and, by general acknowledgement, they reacted in a fair and responsible manner[39]. However, when the 9/11 events made the threat of potential future major terrorism acts explicit, and in a context of general fear of new and imminent attacks, reinsurers decided to exclude this risk as uninsurable through widespread terrorism exclusion clauses, or to drastically review their underwriting conditions to preserve their solvency[40]. Unable to find sufficient reinsurance cover at affordable prices, insurers echoed this reaction, so that the global capacity of the terrorism insurance market suddenly shrank. Underwriting became far more selective and coverage was sharply reduced, so that terrorism insurance became almost unavailable in certain lines of business like commercial/industrial property and business interruption. Meanwhile, many businesses that had also taken the full measure of the terrorism threat, were seeking this insurance coverage. However, the severely curtailed offers for coverage and soaring premium rates often deterred entities at risk to insure, unless obliged. The sudden tightening in the provision of terrorism insurance had immediate adverse economic effects that were especially disruptive in economic activities most dependent on terrorism insurance[41] (e.g., aviation, tourism, construction, commercial lending, etc.). The global social cost of such shrinkage in affordable insurance cover, although difficult to quantify precisely, is probably high, entailing the threat of negative spill-over across sectors, and eventually of contraction of economic activity. This shrinkage of affordable insurance cover for terrorism risk caused concern among OECD Ministers, and was the source of the request addressed to the Organisation to develop policy analysis and recommendations on terrorism insurance.

2.3. Towards increased availability and affordability of terrorism insurance

A large array of solutions can help restore insurability after a disaster. Many have been implemented since September 11th. Insurers' endeavours to rebuild capacity, progress in risk modeling and government intervention have increased the affordability and availability of terrorism insurance. Market conditions may be expected to further improve in the absence of new large-scale attack.

A wide range of initiatives were taken immediately after the events, in an attempt to mitigate economic disruptions. In particular, some of the short-term forbearance measures[42] aimed at protecting insurers solvency through an easing of solvency funding, accounting and investment requirements. From a longer-term perspective, the mobilisation of insurers, reinsurers and brokers as well as of several governments, progressively allowed for the broadening of terrorism insurance supply and the definition of new insurability conditions. A number of trends and initiatives – some more decisive than others – deserve specific mention.

Recent progress in **catastrophe risk modeling**[43] improved risk assessment and risk management strategies. Substantial investment has recently been made to develop modeling techniques adapted to the specificities of terrorism risk, for use by entities at risk willing to assess their vulnerability and necessary coverage, by insurers and reinsurers needing to increase the predictability of the risks to improve pricing and set adequate policy conditions, and by governments to assess the need, and design the modalities of possible public involvement in terrorism compensation. Specialised modeling firms[44] played a decisive role in the development of the first generation of terrorism risk models. The protocols developed since 2001 are highly complex and wide-ranging; they involve extensive data and information collection and analysis[45], in an attempt to assess the terrorism threat, develop inventories of values and people at risk and estimate the vulnerability of targets.

Assessing the terrorism threat or hazard requires studying three parameters of future attacks: possible targets, frequency and severity. To develop probabilities on the likelihood of the attack, experts' judgements are confronted, which can be done through the Delphi method or the convening of a conference of experts. Modelers also attempt to gather information on terrorists' intentions and capabilities. Lists of likely targets are established, taking into account that terrorists may weight the need to maximise economic, political and psychological effects of the attacks against chances of success. The severity of attacks will also depend on the weapons used, and especially whether terrorists use conventional weapons or manage to manufacture or obtain weapons of mass destruction that have a far less predictable impact[46]. Game theory can be used to calculate probabilities regarding targets and attack modes. According to recent developments in terrorism risk modeling, terrorist organisational structure should also be viewed as a critical factor influencing the frequency and severity of terrorist attacks[47].

Inventories of exposures are made to estimate potential losses involving property, but also life, liability, worker compensation, etc. Work already conducted to model natural catastrophes scenarios can be used in this respect. One of the lessons of the September 11th attacks was the high exposure of worker compensation lines to terrorism, and a lot of work has been developed in the past three years to clarify the magnitude of exposures in this respect.

Vulnerability of targets to different attack modes is also analysed *(e.g.,* structural stability of buildings). In the case of terrorism, vulnerability levels have an influence on the hazard. Hence different and more sophisticated approaches (compared for example to modeling of natural perils) are required. Game theory may well serve this purpose. It predicts that, as prime targets are hardened, rational terrorists will turn to softer targets. This appears to be fully consistent with the strategy: "avoid the strength, and attack weakness", a fundamental precept in asymmetric warfare games since terrorist group – however well financed and armed – can not match the economic and technological capability of most nation states.

As a result, extensive and highly informative data bases on exposure inventories and loss scenarios have been generated to model the business impact of a wide range of events. However, while risk modeling has contributed to the rationalisation of the terrorism insurance market and allowed for more credible loss estimates, its application to terrorism has important shortcomings. First, the development of relevant models requires very large, complex, and expensive information collection and analysis, limiting its geographical coverage; so far, it has been mainly been developed in the United States. More fundamentally, while terrorism risk shares certain key features with natural disasters and other large-scale risks, the fact that it is man-made and intentional makes risk modeling not only even more complex, but also far less reliable. While the analysis of certain meteorological parameters preceding natural catastrophes as well as past disasters may be very helpful to anticipate those to come, events dictated by terrorists' intentions are generally not predictable. Terrorism therefore requires a strategic approach to risk modeling: any probabilistic framework for evaluating and quantifying the risks associated with terrorist actions will ultimately need to involve a substantial measure of expert judgment, whatever the sophistication of models used. In particular, assessing the likelihood of attacks will therefore remain intrinsically more subjective[48]. The guidance that terrorism modeling may provide does not discharge the need to thoroughly assess the risk, and analyse exposure specificities that the model would not be able to take into account.

Another major trend following the September 2001 attacks was the development of new terrorism insurance capacity. **Capacity building in terrorism insurance** resulted from the new awareness of the threat to the solvency of insurers who would continue to underwrite and who needed to adapt their capital to the new risk landscape. In addition, insurers wished to take advantage of a potentially profitable market niche when the increase in premia pointed to new business opportunities in the market. (Re)insurers increased their risk retention capacity by raising new capital (through the issue of new equity or the placement of subordinated debt) for those who could afford it, decreasing their dependence on risk transfers to others, and via the creation of new – usually off-shore – ventures[49]. More than three years after 9/11, and in the absence of another attack of similar magnitude, market capacity has substantially increased and more underwriters have re-entered the market. Changes in the legislative framework may have encouraged the increase in terrorism insurance offer, as in Australia, or the United States where new terrorism insurance mechanisms include a requirement for insurers to "make available" this line of business under certain conditions. Although far smaller than the global P&C (property and casualty) insurance market, the so-called free or stand alone market has also benefited from this trend[50], while becoming more sophisticated as a result of increased competition.

The shrinkage of capacity following September 11 was also seen as an opportunity to develop **new financial market instruments** (comparable to those first designed in the mid-1990s' to cover natural catastrophe risks). Because of their size, financial markets have a remarkable risk spreading potential and might be willing to take on new risks if they considered them imperfectly correlated with those they routinely accept. Such transactions may provide corporate entities with an alternative to limited and expensive conventional insurance products. They may also be used by large (re)insurers to allow them to increase their underwriting capacity and in turn increase insurability. This was the case of the transaction initiated by Swiss Re at the end of 2003 to cover catastrophic mortality risk, which was the second (and so far last) multiple event disaster bond covering terrorism risk. If financial markets may in the future provide some additional capacity through comparable transactions, no sustainable market for terrorism securitisation has emerged so far. Furthermore, financial markets are not expected to substantially increase market capacity for terrorism coverage in the short term, not least because capital markets demand a higher degree of precision in risk pricing than conventional (re)insurance markets: being more transaction based, they place a premium on tradability.

The insurance sector also endeavoured to foster **product innovation**, in response to the evolution of the terrorism threat, policyholders demand, and regulatory changes. New terrorism insurance facilities have emerged and continue to take shape, in particular via public-private schemes designed to compensate for terrorism risk (in countries where they exist), and through the stand-alone market[51], or as a combination of both. Insurance solutions become increasingly flexible and customised. Meanwhile, national schemes have evolved to cover new risks and adapt to new threats[52].

In an attempt to minimise individual carriers' difficulties in mutualising risk exposures, several **voluntary private pools** have also emerged[53]. A purely private co-reinsurance pool was for instance set up in Austria by the VVO (insurance association), to cover all property lines (industrial, commercial and private) other than transport insurance. Similar pools have also been created in non-OECD countries. Such pools do not of themselves create net or "new" additional industry capital. However, they can allow a better spread and diversification of the risk, thereby reducing the likelihood that individual participants will suffer heavy financial losses or become insolvent as a result of terrorism attacks. Through a more efficient capital allocation, therefore, pooling mechanisms may create additional capacity *for their members*. Pooling initiatives have however known diverse fates, and several initiatives at industry level have been aborted. Various risk retention groups designed for the needs of the aviation industry never came to be implemented (see box 1.1). An interesting example of such an endeavour was also recently provided by the United States, where a feasibility study was conducted in 2004 for the setting up of a terrorism reinsurance pool to cover the commercial line presenting the greatest risk of ruin to insurers: workers' compensation (for which there are no policy limits and the exclusion of terrorism coverage is not allowed). It concluded that such a pool would be inadequate to compensate worker compensation claims in case of a major event[54].

Meanwhile, since the end of 2001, insurers and reinsurers had initiated reflection and work on the establishment of private-public mechanisms for the compensation of terrorism-related losses. Several governments, faced with the incapacity of insurers to satisfy demand, have acknowledged the need to address problems in the availability and affordability of insurance cover for terrorism risk, and to help restore insurability[55]. Since September 2001, governments in five OECD countries – Australia, France, Germany, the Netherlands and the United States – have agreed to participate in national terrorism compensation schemes, based on a layered approach of compensation. Together with the long established Spanish Consorcio and UK Pool Re, there are now seven OECD countries disposing of **public–private partnerships** to compensate for terrorism losses. Government's direct involvement is usually foreseen only as last resort, to allow the insurability of larger risks[56]. More generally, government back-up has been seen as a key element to restore market confidence and helps to make the market possible, motivating insurers to re-enter the market by capping their exposure and allowing enlarged supply, even at lower levels of coverage. National schemes have however very different features, mirroring a complex interplay between economic, political, and historical considerations. The impact of a scheme on insurability conditions will obviously depend on several features, and mainly whether the offer of terrorism insurance coverage is mandatory (for certain lines) as in Australia, France, Spain and the United States, the level of State intervention, the business lines covered, or the pricing mechanisms and the greater or lesser freedom left to private players in this respect. Overall, it is widely recognised that these schemes had a decisive stabilising effect on the terrorism insurance market.

Box 1.1. **Aviation insurance**

1. Specificities of the aviation insurance

Aviation insurers provide insurance cover against loss, damage and liability for airlines, aerospace manufacturers, aircraft operators, airports, and service providers (air traffic control, refuellers, caterers, security screeners and the like). With regard to terrorism risk, aviation insurers face the same difficulties as their colleagues in other sectors of the insurance industry, and this is why third party liability cover is limited. In addition, there are two interrelated aspects of the aviation insurance market that present unique challenges to insurers: the narrow customer base; and the problem of accumulation. These challenges have prompted the development of specific insurance solutions for aviation after 9/11. They have also led some insurers to seek additional policy exclusions (see Box 1.3).

Third party liability cover

Prior to 9/11, war risk cover (which included terrorism) had been provided for passenger and third party liability at nominal cost, given the historical absence of major loss. Policy limits were as high as USD 2 billion for each and every occurrence. 9/11 was an unprecedented event with losses on a scale never contemplated by governments or the insurance industry. Insurers were concerned to preserve their solvency and ensure the survival of the aviation insurance market in the event of further such attacks. Their reserves were already severely depleted due to soft market conditions in the years immediately prior to 2001, and they were under pressure from their capital providers and reinsurers, who in turn were under pressure from their capital providers, to control their exposure to risk. The fundamental problem was the unquantifiable nature of the new third party terrorism risk. After the 9/11, insurers therefore invoked a contractual cancellation of war risks covers. A seven days notice was given to airlines, while revised covers were made available. New policies offered coverage for war risk third party claims initially limited to USD50million in the aggregate per annum at very significantly increased rates. It is however important to note that passenger liability arising out of war risks, being essentially quantifiable, was still covered up to the full policy limits. Clearly, underwriters from then on would have to take into account this previously unforeseen exposure when pricing aviation policies, and it will continue to be an element of the overall risk profile.

The customer base

The underlying principle of traditional insurance markets is that the premia of the many pay for the losses of the few. The aviation insurance market has always differed from most other insurance markets in that the customer base is very narrow, with just a small number of insureds: this is highlighted by the fact that the International Air Transport Association has only some 270 airline members. At the same time, the potential exposure of each airline is considerable. Because of this very large exposure it is almost unknown for a single insurer to underwrite the entire amount of an airline's overall risk. Usually, a number of insurers will each underwrite a small percentage of that risk, keeping the exposure for any one insurer within acceptable limits. Thus the law of large numbers does not apply, and it is difficult to achieve a satisfactory spread of risk.

The problem of accumulation

Consider a major international airport. All the risk exposures for the airlines operating there, the airport authority, the air traffic control authority, and the various service providers will be insured in the aviation insurance market. It has been estimated that the insured value of aircraft on the ground mid-morning at London Heathrow is in excess of USD8.3billion, and this does not include non-scheduled charter and general aviation aircraft. To this must be added the value of buildings, plant, equipment and stock, and the liability exposure for the thousands of employees and passengers at the airport at any one time. Given the extent of the total exposure, a concentration of events, such as a coordinated bombing attack leading to mass casualties and large scale property destruction, would nullify the spread of risk between insurers because the losses would all fall on the aviation insurance and reinsurance market. This could present individual insurers, and also the market as a whole, with an overwhelming accumulation of losses.

Source: International Union of Aviation Insurers

2. Aviation insurance schemes

After the 9/11 events, the drastic and instant reduction of cover for third party war risk and the considerable increase in base rates, to which added the cost of increased security measures, worsened the already fragile financial situation of many airlines. Since the war/terrorism third party liability cover available from the market was, in most cases, far smaller than that contractually or statutorily required, it was feared that this lack of adequate insurance could ground airline fleets. In this context, insurers, reinsurers and brokers, the government in the United States and in many European countries and the aviation industry itself endeavoured to develop viable coverage solutions for third party liability war/terrorism risk. Some were intended to be time limited, to cope with a crisis situation, others aimed to introduce sustainable cover in the longer term[57].

Market facilities led by AIG and the Allianz Group emerged at the end of September 2001 and in mid-2002 respectively, which provided for coverage in excess of the USD50million initially granted. Some other underwriters have since re-entered the market, while Allianz ceased to provide this type of cover at the end of 2004.

Meanwhile, governments decided to come to the rescue of airline industries and offered a variety of indemnity schemes at discounted rates both in the United States (temporary Federal Aviation Administration war risk insurance programme[58]) and Europe. Such direct government intervention was however criticised, due the possible crowding out effects on private initiatives as well as the serious competition problems it entailed. It was therefore phased out end of 2002 in Europe, and is scheduled to expire in August 2005 in the United States. Moreover, end of March 2005, the leading European insurers have committed to reforms to promote competition and transparency[59].

Lastly, various multinational schemes were proposed, with a view to spreading the risk across the industry and developing sustainable insurance cover in the longer term. Two regional risk retention groups were developed by the aviation industry: Equitime, focusing on US airlines, and Eurotime designed for European airlines. These schemes were to be backed by governments in an initial phase. A third initiative, called Globaltime, was launched by the ICAO (International Civil Aviation Organisation) to mutualise the risk on a global scale and offer equal rights of access to airlines internationally (thereby solving competition issues that the two regional schemes would have raised). This arrangement also foresaw governmental reinsurance. However, alike the two regional schemes, Globaltime did not become operational, for lack of universal acceptance of the scheme principles by governments involved.

It should be underlined that the development of a **more stable and predictable regulatory and legal environment** has also been an important prerequisite for the development of the terrorism insurance. For example, extensive work on the wording of far more precise definitions of triggering events and underwriting conditions has been carried out by both private and public actors. Conditions of operation under government schemes have also been clarified[60].

Lastly, to the immediate and drastic shrinkage in insurance offer that followed the World Trade Center attacks progressively succeeded a **rationalised strategy of careful underwriting, exposure control and premium setting.** Abiding to this reinforced underwriting discipline allows insurers and reinsurers to cover part of the terrorism risks, without endangering their solvency situation. It is obviously a core condition for sustained insurability, in the new risk landscape.

As a result of these trends, **terrorism insurance market conditions have substantially improved** in a number of markets. Capacity and prices have become more predictable and the very high prices after the disaster have come down to more sustainable levels. The evolution of the US market illustrates this point[61]. According to a market survey issued at the end of 2004[62], the premium structure for terrorism coverage is at a significantly reduced level than before the introduction of TRIA[63]. Terrorism insurance premia represents roughly 4% of the basic property insurance rate against 10% in early 2003. Another study highlights that on the stand-alone market, prices declined by about 15 since 2002, and in some cases by as much as 25%[64], because more players are ready to underwrite and geographical risk spreading has been improved. On this market, prices may be as little as 0.02% of the values insured. It should be noted that overall pricing for commercial property insurance continues to soften, which allows firms to free up funds to increase their purchase of terrorism insurance[65]. The various studies also reveal an important elasticity of take-up rates to prices. Insurance take-up rates at the national level (percentage of corporation covered by insurance) has therefore significantly increased, from 23.5% for the first quarter of 2003 to 44% by the end of 2004. Of course, these average figures hide many nuances. Examples include the fact that insurance take up rates remains at only about one third of the TIV (total insured value) when TIV is less than USD 100 million; some industries have been better able to secure their property limits than others: financial institutions for instance will tend insure far more than the energy, manufacturing or utility sectors; regional factors still play a key role, etc., and the same *caveats* apply to pricing. Nevertheless, there has undoubtedly been some stabilisation in the US market for terrorism insurance. Results from another survey in the United States[66] find an overall take-up rate of 57% for 2004, compared with about 25% in the first quarter of 2003. Beyond the softening of insurance premia, various incentives to insure certainly played a role in this evolution such as requirements imposed by corporate governance rules, Directors' and Officers' insurance, as well as, possibly, the pressure of secured lenders requiring terrorism insurance from borrowers as a protection of commercial real estate loans. More generally, in the United States[67], as on other markets where it is available, government backing has been an important factor in this respect.

In the absence of a new attack, and in the current business environment, terrorism insurance market conditions may continue to stabilise over time.

3. Outstanding questions, and the need for sustainable solutions commensurate to modern terrorism risks

The recent trend towards market stabilisation leaves important outstanding questions; the search of sustainable solutions to terrorism risk coverage should be pursued to further decrease exposure to terrorism risk where needed and avoid another insurability crisis in the event of a new attack

The progressive improvement of market conditions since 2001 would lead to a certain optimism concerning the ability of the market to manage this risk ever more smoothly in the future. However, many crucial questions regarding the ability of the conventional insurance and reinsurance markets to absorb terrorism risks – and large ones in particular – remain pending, and the debate on the issue of insurability of risks related to terrorist acts is therefore still largely unsettled.

3.1. Low insurance penetration in certain major OECD markets

Terrorism insurance take-up rates remain low in markets like Germany and the United States[68], leaving large parts of the national economy financially exposed to possible future attacks.

One of the main sources of concern related to terrorism insurance today, despite recent increases in terrorism risk coverage, is the continuing high financial exposure to terrorism risk in certain OECD markets, and in particular in two major ones: the United States and Germany. While many efforts have recently been devoted to increasing supply at affordable rates, demand does not always follow. Many companies in the United States and Germany skip terrorism coverage. If take-up rates have tended to increase in the United States as described above, probably more than half of commercial entities still remain uninsured. In Germany, out of the 40 000 German companies qualifying for terrorism coverage under Extremus[69], only 1100, *i.e.* about 2.75%, had actually contracted with the government backed specialised insurer by the end of 2004[70]. This in turn prompted a reduction of Extremus' aggregate capacity (as well as more difficulties to negotiate its reinsurance coverage). Under these conditions, the impact of a new large scale attack on the social and economic fabric of the United States and Germany would be greater than in 2001 if uninsured firms have not opted for alternative compensation solutions: corporations would end up supporting a large part of losses, which were mutualised among the insurance and reinsurance community at the time of the World Trade Center attacks[71]. Moreover, when assessing the potential damage of terrorism on the economy, it should be reminded that terrorism insurance will as a rule only compensate for losses if the insured is the direct target of the attack; indirect losses (as far as business interruption is concerned) – which may be considerable – remain in any case at the charge of the insured[72].

There may be different reasons leading to the decision not to purchase (or to purchase very low level) of terrorism insurance: an important reason is that entities at risk tend to underestimate the threat of future attacks, as the memory of recent terrorist events fades away. They may also be inclined to think that "it will never happen to them", especially in countries that have not been highly exposed to terrorism in the past[73]. The implicit hope that, after an attack, the government, faced with the so-called "Samaritan dilemma", will cover losses, may also have a significant influence on behaviour. In some cases, the insurance offer may not match expectations in terms of coverage or level of premium, and, premium rates, although decreasing, may still not be commensurate with the client perception of the risk. Since it has been suggested that individuals tend to underestimate or ignore LPHC risks[74], even a reasonably priced terrorism insurance coverage may be perceived as too costly by prospective policyholders – affordability being a highly subjective concept. In the absence of a claim, insurance might therefore be viewed as a poor investment. Lastly, low insurance rate may result from rational risk management choices and weighting of the cost of insurance against its potential benefits, based on available estimates of exposure to terrorism risk and on the assessment of insurance solutions against alternative types of coverage (such as self-insurance/risk diversification through a potentially large number of shareholders).

Since little information is available on the motivations of entities at risks opting for no or very limited terrorism insurance cover, and on the level of coverage provided by alternative risk management solutions, it is difficult to know to what extent and how the issue of low insurance coverage should be addressed[75]. Since low coverage could signal imperfect information and underestimation of the risk, as well as reliance on the assumption that government relief package will be granted after a disaster, options to promote an adequate level of insurance cover should still be considered, such as further promotion of risk awareness, and possibly the development of appropriate incentives on the demand side. Ultimately, the option of mandating the purchase of terrorism insurance may also be worth considering in countries with a low degree of market penetration for such insurance, to ensure a broad premium base and steady capacity building under the national compensation scheme.

3.2. Specificities of CBRN risks

CBRN technology consists of chemical (deadly chemicals and poisons), biological (biological viruses and bacteriological agents), radiological (dispersal of radioactive materials), and nuclear (detonation of nuclear fission weapons) devices. CBRN risks represent a rising source of concern, since they are increasingly reagarded as a plausible scenario of attack[76]. Intelligence experts have warned about the desire of some terrorism organisations to gain access to weapons of mass destruction. Meanwhile, information on how to develop or access such weapons, which previously was restricted to specialists, has now been widely disseminated, in particular through the internet[77].

Although limited coverage can be found in some cases, private carriers generally have no appetite to cover terrorism risks that are at the extreme end of the unpredictability spectrum. The greatest concern in this area regards CBRN terrorism risks. Because of the potential magnitude, spread and persistence of damages potentially caused by such risks, they are generally considered as uninsurable for the time being and are therefore subject to exclusions. Moreover, these risks are not always (fully) covered through existing government backed insurance schemes.

Box 1.2. Coverage of CBRN risks under existing national terrorism compensation scheme

Austria	No
Australia	Partial: all nuclear causes excluded.
France	Partial: exclusion of damage caused by conventional weapons or devices designed to explode by means of the structural modification of the atomic nucleus (with the exception of «dirty» bombs, whose effects are covered).
Germany	No
Netherlands	Yes
Spain	Yes
United Kingdom	Yes (since 2003)
United States	Partial (TRIA covers CBRN risks only to the extent that it is on the same terms and conditions of other coverages within the policy)

The coverage of CBRN risks for certain insurance lines is currently being debated in several countries. In France for instance, the government has refused to extend the protection against "dirty bombs' provided by GAREAT (minimum sum insured: EUR 6 million) to small enterprises and individuals, but remains open to further discussions. In the aviation sector, some aviation insurers are proposing that all CBRN risks, and not only nuclear detonation and the associated radioactive contamination, be excluded through AVN48.

Box 1.3. Aviation insurance: the exclusion issue

Existing exclusions

Claims arising from war, hostile detonation of nuclear weapons, civil commotion, terrorist acts, sabotage, political seizure, hijacking, and the like, are all excluded from aviation policies through clause AVN48. Although the majority of these can be written back into policies through the extended coverage clause AVN52, nuclear detonation and the associated radioactive contamination cannot, since the potential magnitude, spread, and persistence of damage is such that the insurance industry will not cover it. It is a weapon of mass destruction that could give rise to a major loss accumulation.

Proposed new exclusions

Intelligence analyses post-9/11 have repeatedly identified threats of terrorists using chemical, biological, radioactive ("dirty bombs"), and electromagnetic weapons in pursuit of their aims. These are perceived as weapons of mass destruction because they are similar to nuclear detonations in the magnitude, spread and persistence of their effects and their potential to generate major loss accumulations.

Some aviation insurers are proposing that these more recently identified weapons of mass destruction are also excluded through AVN48. It should be noted that all other major insurance markets, for example property, marine, and energy, already operate such exclusions. Thus the proposed aviation exclusions are neither novel nor extraordinary. These proposals are the subject of a lengthy and continuing consultation involving a wide cross section of interested parties including insurers, brokers, regulators and airlines.

Source : International Union of Aviation Insurers

Among CBRN risks, the **coverage of nuclear terrorism**[78] raises specific problems[79]. It has been judiciously argued that nuclear-weapon attacks would better be considered as a class of their own[80]. Since the mid-nineties, terrorism experts have highlighted that the risk of nuclear material proliferation was increasing and with it the threat of nuclear terrorism[81] (previously considered as unrealistic). This incited reinsurers in particular to screen the terms and conditions of the cover that they provide, in order to ensure that they could not be made liable for risks that have been long considered as uninsurable by conventional (re)insurance markets[82]. They concluded that inadequate nuclear risk exclusions could be one of the most threatening shortcomings in property insurance and reinsurance, and that new terrorism compensation schemes have generally not solved this problem. The risk of dirty bombs with conventional chemical explosives for instance would turn out to be covered under certain policies; and some national regulations requiring insurers to cover terrorism risk may invalidate nuclear terrorism exclusions. Policy and exclusions wordings should therefore be revised, and possible changes in related national legislation may need to be considered.

More generally, governments should consider the issue of CBRN risk, and work, in cooperation with the industry, towards developing stable solutions to guarantee their coverage[83].

3.3. Covering large-scale terrorist attacks in an ever changing risk landscape

Despite certain improvements in market conditions, the private insurance and reinsurance industries may not by themselves be able, under current conditions, to absorb alone the losses arising from large-scale terrorist attacks. Great uncertainty also remains as to the future evolution of the terrorism threat, and the consecutive capacity and willingness of the private market to (fully) cover resulting losses. The search for sustainable solutions to terrorism risk coverage should therefore be pursued to avoid new insurability crises, while enabling further private market recovery.

Assessing the available capacity of the private insurance industry to cover the losses that a large scale terrorist attack could involve is a difficult task. In the current context, in the United States for instance, P&C insurers' surplus supporting all commercial property, general liability and workers compensation insurance may be about USD 114 billion[84]. However, the terrorism risk landscape has considerably evolved, based on the analysis of the September 11th attacks. Modeling firms are developing "plausible scenarios" in which estimated insured losses for workers' compensation lines alone could amount to USD 90 billion[85] for a single event. Such an illustration brings into perspective the insurability issue. Together with the threat of a potential increase in frequency and of simultaneous attacks, this casts serious doubts on the financial capacity of the insurance and reinsurance sectors to fully absorb future large-scale terrorism risks on their own, under current conditions. Moreover, if insurers have improved their capacity to model "routine" terrorism, very large scale events may always remain beyond the industry's ability to price[86].

More generally, given the high uncertainty surrounding the evolution of terrorism, it is very hard to predict the appetite of the private market to cover this risk in the future and any projection about market evolution remains at best very hazardous. It is even harder to foresee the private sector reaction in case of a major change in conditions of operation, such as the withdrawal of government backing in countries where it is currently available or in case of recrudescence of major terrorism event(s)[87].

Conclusion

Conditions of insurability of terrorism risk have been fundamentally revised after the attacks on the Unites States on 11 September 2001, which first resulted in a drastic shrinkage in terrorism insurance cover. Private and public initiatives that followed converged to stabilise insurance market conditions and certain insurability criteria are easier to meet now that capacity has increased, risk management tools have become more sophisticated and, in several countries, governments have stepped into the compensation process. In the absence of a new attack, and in the current business environment, terrorism insurance market conditions may be expected to further improve over time.

Meanwhile, awareness and understanding of a number of issues remains concernedly low. Firstly, the fact that the modern terrorism threat is not a temporary condition, but is expected to be at least constant for the foreseeable future should be highlighted as a conclusion of most experts in the field. Also, the magnitude of losses involved may be expected to grow, while terrorism is and will continue to be far less predictable than other large-scale risks. This conjunction of factors is highly challenging for the insurance industry, and the assertion that "coverage for terrorist acts is not now amenable to normal insurance underwriting, risk management and actuarial techniques"[88] still holds true. It also explains why terrorism risk insurance is now, and should remain in the foreseeable future, subject to careful underwriting and close control over exposures and accumulation risk. Under these conditions, specific risks like CBRN terrorism exposures or large-scale terrorist attacks are generally considered as uninsurable by the private insurance industry alone, at least for the time being. Lastly, given the low terrorism insurance penetration in various markets where terrorism insurance is not compulsory, losses which were mutualised among the insurance and reinsurance community at the time of the World Trade Center attacks could be left to corporations to support, and the economic impact of a new large-scale attack on these markets may be greater than in 2001, would these firms not be able to diversify the risk through other tools.

In this context, the search for sustainable solutions to terrorism risk coverage should be pursued to further decrease exposure to terrorism risk where needed and avoid another insurability crisis in the event of a new attack. Future research in this respect should focus not only on compensation mechanism, but also on effective and innovative loss mitigation solutions – a particularly challenging task in the area of terrorism given the existence of various disincentives to investment in security measures as well as negative externalities that may result from prevention and mitigation. While risks tend to increase in magnitude and decrease in predictability, mitigation becomes ever more important in order to allow the private markets to operate efficiently and assume terrorism risk as far as possible, therefore reducing the financial exposure of corporations and governments. Beyond terrorism, the recent evolution of the global risk landscape in which insurers are now operating, marked by an increase in insured losses resulting from disasters that are also more frequent, is a strong incentive in this direction. It should indeed be reminded that "9/11 casts a very long and pervasive shadow, but it is far from being the only challenge. It is only the keystone of a global mutation in our emerging world, where crises must be anticipated, prepared for, prevented as far as possible and emergency situations tackled"[89].

Notes

1   This chapter is indebted to Kunreuther, H. and E. Michel-Kerjan (2005), *Insurability of (mega-)terrorism risk: challenges and perspectives* (see infra, Part III Chapter 6).

2   Some 20000 acts of international terrorism alone were recorded during the thirty years that preceded the World Trade Center attacks. Swiss Re (2003), *Terrorism risks in property insurance and their insurability after 11 September 2001*, p. 20.

3   In France, the government was not directly involved in the compensation of losses resulting from terrorism before 2001. However, in the aftermath of a series of terrorist attacks, terrorism cover for direct property losses and business interruption has become compulsory in 1986, within all policies covering property damage.

4   This includes liability claim costs. Property losses include USD1.1 billion due to a December 2004 federal jury decision that the World Trade Center losses resulted from two separate attacks; this is subject to appeal. See Insurance Information Institute (2005), *http://www.iii.org/media/facts/statsbyissue/catastrophes/*.

5   National Commission on Terrorist Attacks Upon the United States (July 22, 2004), *The 9/11 Commission Report*, p. 2.

6   While major reinsurers, echoing terrorism experts, had expressed their concerns since the 1980s about the evolution of modern terrorism threats and risks of large-scale attacks and accumulation, these warnings were not followed by changes in underwriting strategies.

7   Both insurers and reinsurers are referred to under this terminology. More generally, most of the issues presented in this paper concern not only insurance, but also reinsurance companies.

8   Dickinson, G. (2002), *Insurability Challenges for Large Terrorism and natural Catastrophe Risks*, unpublished manuscript, commissioned by the OECD (on file with the OECD).

9   Conditions of insurability have been extensively reviewed in the literature. See Swiss Re (2002), *Natural Catastrophes and man-made disasters in 2001*, Swiss Re Sigma series n.1/2002 ; Berliner, B. (1982), *Limits of Insurability of Risks*, Englewood Cliffs, NJ, Prentice-Hall, Inc.; Faure, M. G. (1995), *The Limits to Insurability from a Law and Economics Perspective*, Geneva Papers on Risk and Insurance, p. 454-462; Skogh, G. (1998), *Development risks, strict liability and the insurability of industrial hazards*, Geneva Papers on Risk and Insurance, p. 87 and 247.

10   While the September 11th attacks put forward the considerable threat of a possible similar large-scale event, it should not be forgotten that a single large-scale attack is not the only threat: the possible accumulation of medium-size terrorist attacks in a limited time frame represents a growing danger, which may end up having the same detrimental effects as a single very large attack.

11   It was however far from minor in some countries: in Spain for instance, terrorism caused, in 1982, the largest (in terms of material damages) single loss that the Consorcio, which covers all extreme risks, ever had to cover since it was created in 1954.

12   Another USD 7 billion payments, made by the 9/11 Victims compensation fund, should be added to measure the full scale of losses from the 2001 attacks for which financial compensation has been granted. See Congressional Budget Office (CBO) (January 2005), *Federal Terrorism Reinsurance: An Update* (available at: *http://www.cbo.gov*), p. 26.

13   Indexed to 2001 price levels. Swiss Re (2002), *Terrorism – Dealing with the New Spectre*, Focus Report.

14   Towers Perrin (April 2004), *Workers' Compensation Terrorism Reinsurance Pool Feasibility Study*, p.V.

15   See, for instance, Bremer, L. Paul (2002), in Guy Carpenter, *The terror risk: can it be managed?*, p. 5.

16   See Michel-Kerjan, E. (2003), *New Vulnerabilities in Critical Infrastructures: A US Perspective*, Journal of Contingencies and Crisis Management, Volume 11, Issue 3, p. 132-141.

17   See Lagadec, P. and E. Michel-Kerjan, *Meeting the Challenge of Interdependent Critical Networks under Threat: The Paris Initiative, "Anthrax and Beyond"*, Cahier du Laboratoire d'Econométrie n° 2004-014, Ecole Polytechnique.

18   Although the definition of weapons of mass destruction appears controversial, it often refers to chemical, biological, and nuclear weapons. However, weapons of mass destruction have also been recently defined as including radiological *and conventional weapons causing mass casualties*. This last and wider definition is referred to in this volume. In contrast, CBRN terrorist attacks may be of large or moderate scale, depending on several variables.

19   The nation has been told to expect more terrorist attacks, possibly including attacks more extreme than those of September 11. See National Commission on Terrorist Attacks Upon the United States (2004), p. 17.

20   Jaffee, D. and T. Russell (June 1997), *Catastrophe Insurance, Capital Markets, and Uninsurable Risks*, Journal of Risk and Insurance 64 No.2, p. 205-230; Jaffee, D. and T. Russell (2003), *Markets Under Stress: The Case of Extreme Event Insurance*, in Richard Arnott, Bruce Greenwald, Ravi Kanbur, and Barry Nalebuff editors, *Economics for an Imperfect World: Essays in Honor of Joseph E. Stiglitz*, MIT Press.

21   It has been highlighted that the recent multiplication of large-scale natural disasters may soon question the relevance of the low probability qualification to characterise these events. Some natural catastrophes such as hail or tornadoes may occur on a quite regular basis. 2004

provides an explicit illustration of this, with the succession of hurricanes and typhoons in the Caribbean, the United States and Asia in the summer and fall of 2004.

22   Woo, G. (2002), *Natural Catastrophe Probable Maximum Loss*, British Actuarial Journal, Volume 8, Part V.

23   Dickinson, G. (2002).

24   With reference to natural catastrophes risk, see: Cummins, J. David, N. Doherty and A. Lo (2002), *Can Insurers Pay for the 'Big One'? Measuring the Capacity of the Insurance Market to Respond to Catastrophic Losses*, Journal of Banking and Finance, Volume 26, Issues 2-3, p. 557-583.

25   "US insurers' total underwriting losses – the difference between their premium income and expenses – reached USD 52.6 billion in 2001 (ISO, *The Financial Services Fact Book*, p 62). With insufficient investment income in 2001 to offset those underwriting losses, the industry's net worth fell by USD 27.8 billion that year". ISO and NAII, in Congressional Budget Office (2005), p. 3.

26   Swiss Re economic research and consulting. See Mumenthaler, C. (November 2004), *The use of risk-linked securities to manage catastrophic risks*, presentation at the occasion of the OECD Conference on 'Insurance and catastrophic risks', available under the conference link at *http://www.oecd.org/daf/insurance*, p. 3.

27   The law of large numbers, formulated by Bernoulli, states that for a series of independent and identically distributed random variables, the variance around the mean of the random variables decreases as the number of variables increases.

28   As verifications of the insured risks may not be independent from one another, insurance companies operating in catastrophe lines cannot rely on cross-policy diversification to limit their exposure in any given year, or to limit the variation in total losses across different policy periods. Catastrophe risk carriers, therefore, face an extremely volatile loss ratio across years, with a significant mismatch between premia collected and claims paid in any given period. With reference to environment-related risks see also: Monti, A. (2003), *Environmental Risks and Insurance. A Comparative Analysis of the Role of Insurance in the Management of Environment-Related Risks,* Policy Issues in Insurance N°6, Chapters 1 and 3, OECD.

29   See Munich Re (2004), *Megacities-Megarisks, Trends and challenges for insurance and risk management.*

30   See Insurance Information Institute (2005), *http://www.iii.org/media/facts/statsbyissue/catastrophes.*

31   It will in particular weigh on premium rates: an aversion to ambiguity leads insurers to set premia at much higher rates than they otherwise would if they had more reliable information on the likelihood and consequences of future events (Kunreuther, Hogarth, and Meszaros, 1993). The premium charged to the insured comprises a series of loadings, some of which (e.g. safety and fluctuation loadings) are precisely aimed at covering the residual level of unpredictability that characterises every risk. If great uncertainty is associated to the risk, (re)insurers are typically lead to set such loading according to the most pessimistic model.

32 See, among other reports by these authors, Kunreuther, H.and E. Michel-Kerjan (2005), infra.

33 Lakdawalla, D. and G. Zanjani (September 2002), *Insurance, Self-protection, and the Economics of Terrorism*, US National Bureau of Economic Research, Working Paper 9215, Cambridge, MA: NBER. See also: Woo, G. (2003), *Insuring Against Al-Qaeda*, paper prepared for the US National Bureau of Economic Research meeting, p. 11. With target substitution, relocation of businesses for security purposes, for instance, which may depress local economic activity, is another form of negative externality of self-protection measures.

34 This is obviously an important difference with other types of hazards, for which prevention will mitigate the impact of a catastrophe in one place generally without increasing the risk that it may occur elsewhere.

35 On this concept, see Kunreuther, H. and G. Heal (2003), *Interdependent Security*, The Journal of Risk and Uncertainty, Volume 26, Numbers 2-3, p. 231-249.

36 See Michel-Kerjan, E., (2003) *Large-scale terrorism: risk sharing and public policy*, Revue d'Economie politique, n°5, p. 625-648.

37 Jaffee, D. (2005), *Report on the role of government in the coverage of terrorism risks* (see infra, Part III, Chapter 8).

38 Garston, B. (2005), *Terrorism insurance: an overview of the private market*, in *Catastrophic Risks and Insurance*, Policy Issues in Insurance N°8, OECD.

39 Dickinson, G. (2002).

40 Reinsurers could apply such exclusions as soon as the reinsurance treaties expired, i.e. in January or July 2002 for a most of them.

41 United States General Accounting Office (GAO) (February 2002), *Terrorism insurance – Rising Uninsured Exposure to Attacks Heightens Potential Economic Vulnerabilities*.

42 Liedtke, P. and C. Courbage (eds) (2002), The Geneva Association, *Insurance and September 11 one year after. Impact, Lessons and Unsolved Issues*, p. 245.

43 For more details, see Grossi P. and H. Kunreuther (Eds) (2005), *Catastrophe modeling – a new approach to managing risk*.

44 Lead by Applied Insurance Research (AIR), Eqecat and Risk management Solutions (RMS).

45 For instance, more than 300,000 US landmarks (corporate headquarters, energy installation, government buildings, etc.) have been incorporated in the AIR model.

46 The effects of a 'dirty' bomb for instance, using nuclear/radiological, biological or chemical components would depend, among other factors, on component, location, potency, amounts, weather, containment and device design. They are therefore highly difficult to predict. Nuclear attacks may be an exception in this respect, since work has been developed for a long time in an attempt to model the impact of nuclear attacks or accidents.

47   See Woo, G. (February 2002), *Quantifying Insurance Terrorism Risk*, paper presented at the US National Bureau of Economic Research Conference on Insurance, Cambridge, MA.

48   Modeling firms disagree for example on the most likely targets of terrorist attacks (few cities/properties with high visibility vs. low-profile targets demonstrating that no place is safe), see CBO (2005), p. 4.

49   It should however be noted that the increase in capacity, and the portion of new capacity actually devoted to terrorism coverage, are difficult to measure.

50   The limit available for a single risk would be of about USD1.210 billion. More actors have reentered the market, which is now characterised by active competition (as well as co-insurance) between the USA, Bermuda, and the London. See Aon (December 2004) *Terrorism Risk Management & Risk Transfer Market Overview.*

51   The stand-alone market is specifically instrumental in offering coverage for risks excluded from state-backed schemes or providing worldwide coverage for multinational firms (also, there is no uncertainty related to sun set provisions of the insurance schemes, as opposed to that provided through some national schemes). For instance, one month after the attacks, the Lloyd's released a new product known as T3, which met a strong demand. Terrorism public liability (not covered under Pool Re, Gareat or Extremus) or contingent banking risks, are among the most recent examples of product innovation capacity in this market.

52   Pool Re for instance was covering until 2002 only commercial property damage and business interruption costs arising from an act of terrorism which results in fire or explosion. Further to the 9/11 attacks, it was decided that policyholders should be granted wider cover; it now includes terrorist attacks causing commercial property damage and consequent business interruption by "all risks". The exclusion for damage caused by nuclear devices has also been suppressed. Since 1 January 2002, the Spanish Consorcio de Compensacion de Seguros provides business interruption cover.

53   Historically, additional capacity (in the absence of an increase in capital) was provided by commercial reinsurers. Given the reluctance of reinsurers to expand either the size or scope of their coverage of modern terrorism, alternative capacity-creating private mechanisms had to be sought, and the idea emerged of creating insurer pools – a solution already experienced with other types of insurance such as environmental insurance.

54   Current terrorism attacks scenarios include terrorism events that would generate worker compensation losses of USD 90 billion or more (see Towers Perrin, 2004) which is over three times the capital backing the private insurance industry's worker's compensation line of business.

55   Various economic arguments also support this choice, such as, among others, the fact that terrorism is partly a public good, given that governments influence on the risk through foreign policy and counter-terrorism strategy; the negative externalities associated with terrorism risk protection measures; more generally, governments can achieve a far greater diversification of risk, both among the wider population of tax payers and in time: "when catastrophic risks are difficult to insure, time diversification may provide a good substitute. (…) The State has the credit worthiness and the long time horizon that are necessary to implement time diversification"; they can spread the risk over future generations of tax payers when the insurance sector operates under far shorter time constraints. For this last argument, see Gollier, C. (2005), *Some aspects of the economics of catastrophe risk insurance,* in *Catastrophic Risks and Insurance*, Policy Issues in Insurance N°8, OECD.

56   Governments may also intervene according to the subsidiarity principle, as for the Spanish Consorcio de Seguros.

57   See Partner Re (2004), *Terrorism Insurance*, p. 41-46. For a more detailed analysis of developments in aviation insurance, see: Straus, Andrew (June 2005), *Terrorism Third Party Liability Insurance for Commercial Aviation, Federal Intervention in the Wake of September 11,* The Wharton School, Center for Risk Management.

58   See *http://insurance.faa.gov* for more details on this programme.

59   "Following an investigation by the European Commission, leading European aviation insurers have undertaken to reform their practices as regards the operation of aviation insurance in order to promote more competition and transparency. The reforms foresee inter alia greater transparency in key industry committees based in London, including one that establishes standard wordings for aviation insurance policies and clauses [in which customers will have a say in the development of published standard clauses]. In addition, the undertakings provide that if an unforeseeable crisis resulting from war or terrorism arises, insurers will limit any co-ordinated action to that which is indispensable to ensure that capacity continues to be available and customers can continue to buy insurance". See European Commission, Press Communiqué IP/05/361, 23 March 2005.

60   The issuance of a series of TRIA final regulation and interpretative letters illustrates this point.   Another example is the Pool Re 2002 reform which allowed insurers to have certainty about their maximum exposure – and therefore "to know in advance the maximum amount they could be called to pay out in any one year". See *Changes to the Pool Re scheme* (2002) at http://www.hm-treasury.gov.uk./media/648/AF/ACF1D0D.PDF.

61   The United States being by far the most significant market for terrorism risk, its evolution is of key relevance. Also, given the size of the market and the importance taken after the 2001 attacks by the issue of terrorism coverage, as part of a wider national security programme, much of the literature on terrorism insurance concerns the US.

62   Marsh Inc (2004), *Marketwatch Property Terrorism insurance Update-Third Quarter 2004*, Study based on a sample of 754 companies renewing their property insurance policies between July 1, 2004 and September 30, 2004.

63   Boris, Andrew S. (May 2004), Insurance Journal, *Question of coverage for Terrorism*.

64   Aon (2004).

65   According to Marsh (2004).

66   Aon (2004).

67   CBO (2005), p. 6.

68   In these countries (Germany and the United States), the purchase of terrorism insurance is not compulsory (even though, in the US, insurers must make it available in commercial lines of insurance).

69   Such coverage requests minimum sum insured of 25 million Euros, limiting it to larger entities or real estate.

70   Michel-Kerjan, E. and B. Pedell (February 2005), *Terrorism Risk Coverage in the Post-9/11 Era: A Comparison of New Public-Private Partnerships in France, Germany and the U.S*, The Geneva Papers and Risk and Insurance, Vol. 30, N° 1, p. 144-170.

71   Michel-Kerjan, E. and B. Pedell (2005). According to Macdonald, J. (Summer 2004), *Terrorism, Insurance and TRIA: Are We Asking the Right Questions?* The John Liner Review, Vol.18 N°2, almost 200 insurers and reinsurers shared the loss on September 11.

72   Kunreuther, H. and E. Michel-Kerjan (2004), *Dealing with Extreme Events: new Challenges for Terrorism Risk Insurance in the U.S.* Working paper, Center for Risk Management and Decision Processes, The Wharton School, Philadelphia.

73   See for instance Kunreuther, H., E. Michel-Kerjan and B. Porter (December 2003), *Assessing, Managing and Financing Extreme Events: Dealing with Terrorism*, US National Bureau of Economic Research, Working Paper 10179, Cambridge, MA, p. 13.

74   Camerer, C. and H. Kunreuther (1989), *Decision Processes for Low Probability Events: Policy Implications*, 8 Journal of Policy Analysis and Management, p. 565-592.

75   On the issue, see CBO (2005), p. 12.

76   E.g., according to a recent report published by RMS: "*Al Qaeda has conducted research into all four of these. Evidence of research into chemical agents includes videotapes of nerve gas tests on dogs and formula for sarin gas was recovered in Afghanistan. Unverified reports have circulated about Al Qaeda and Chechnyan agents enquiring about obtaining ex-Soviet nuclear weapons. In 1998, an unsuccessful attempt by Al Qaeda to purchase uranium from blackmarket sources suggested the development of at least a research interest in radiological weapons. A chapter in an Al Qaeda training manual "Encyclopedia of Jihad", gives schematic instructions on building a radiological dispersal bomb, or dirty bomb. (...) In Afghanistan, notes and documentation on anthrax production were found in the Al Qaeda sites. (...) Evidence suggests that detailed components on the process of mass producing anthrax have been mastered by Al Qaeda.*" RMS, *Catastrophe, Injury, and Insurance: The Impact of Catastrophes on Workers Compensation, Life, and Health Insurance* (2004), p. 46.

77   Bremer, P. (2002), p. 7. Until recently, one could also find on the internet key information on critical infrastructures - and potential vulnerabilities - such as the detailed location of nuclear power plants and nuclear waste facilities in the US for example.

78   Three basic scenarios of nuclear terrorism are conceivable: Radiological Dispersal Devices (RDD) or nuclear material dispersed through spraying devices or conventional chemical explosives, i.e. the so-called dirty bombs (which can not cause a nuclear explosion); attacks on nuclear installations; improvised Nuclear Devices (IND) as "home made" nuclear bombs or bomb from a military source. Swiss Re (2003), *Nuclear risks in property insurance and limitation of insurability*, p. 5.

79   This paragraphs draws on Swiss Re (2003).

80   Although CBRN risks are most often dealt with as a group, the following argumentation deserves serious consideration: *"It may make more sense to structure public policy based on the magnitude of the loss rather than the type of attack. Further work is needed to better understand what distinguishes CBRN attacks from other attacks and whether they deserve special treatment independent of their magnitude. Most discussions of CBRN attacks tend to lump together all four types of attacks: chemical, biological, radiological, and nuclear. However, the range of potential consequences of the four different types of attacks is considerable. While radiological or biological attacks can have devastating consequences, it is highly unlikely that they will be of the same scale or scope as a nuclear attack. Nuclear-weapon attacks are in a class of their own. The debate over CBRN attacks should consider the distinctions among these various types of unconventional attacks and their implications for insurance markets."* Dixon, L. *et al.* (2004), p. 20.

81   See for instance most recently: Allison, Graham (2004), *Nuclear Terrorism, The Ultimate Preventable Catastrophe.*

82   The existing nuclear insurance pools cover the peaceful utilisation of nuclear energy and are not intended to cover risks related to the use of nuclear weapons. However, reference should be made to the work developed since 2000 by the Nuclear Energy Agency to examine the potential impact of terrorist acts on the market for nuclear damage insurance and, in particular, the ability of nuclear operators to obtain insurance coverage for civil liability and material damage to nuclear facilities (used for peaceful purposes) resulting from a nuclear accident caused by a terrorist act. Information has been collected on the obligations imposed by national legislation on nuclear operators with regard to such liability, as well as the means by which nuclear operators usually guarantee their liability (through insurance or other). It is clear that, in the great majority of countries, these obligations have always been binding on nuclear operators, in that terrorist acts, unlike acts of war, are not events which relieve the liability of operators. It is also clear that in several countries nuclear operators still guarantee this liability through private insurance, although such coverage is not always "comprehensive" or has become more expensive since the events of 11 September 2001. In other countries, in contrast, private insurers no longer cover this risk, or only partially. Private nuclear insurers have never provided coverage for nuclear facilities used for non-peaceful purposes.

83   While the CBRN threat may remain the most serious, it should be highlighted that cyber terrorism is also raising concern. This risk remains excluded from the Pool Re or the Extremus cover for instance.

84   Hartwig, R. (Insurance Information Institute) (October 2004), *The Cost of Terrorism, How Much Can We Afford?* It should also be reminded that "only those companies whose policies are affected, not the industry as a whole, would pay claims resulting from a particular event" (see United states General Accounting Office (2005), *Catastrophe Risk, U.S. and European Approaches to Insure Natural Catastrophe and Terrorism Risks,* p. 5).

85   See Towers Perrin (2004), p. 25.

86   Liedtke, P. and C. Courbage (2002), p. 226.

87   Several recent studies put forward that the absence of governmental support on the terrorism insurance market in the United States could play as an incentive for increased investment by corporations in counter-terrorism measures, and, maybe, the development of alternatives to insurance solutions in particular. It would also probably entail substantive rise in premium rates; should a new attack occur, markets may be disrupted again, many carriers would

probably partially or completely withdraw from the market (if allowed to do so), while the stand alone market in particular, which is already a sellers'market, may be overwhelmed by demands for coverage and need to become far more selective.

88   United states General Accounting Office (GAO) (October 24, 2001), *Terrorism Insurance: Alternative Programs for Protecting Insurance Consumers,* p. 15.

89   Lagadec, P. (February 2005), *Crisis Management in the 21st Century, "Unthinkable" Events in "Inconceivable" Contexts,* Cahier du Laboratoire d'Econométrie, n° 2005-003, Ecole Polytechnique.

Chapter 2

FINANCIAL MARKET SOLUTIONS FOR TERRORISM RISK

Introduction[1]

The insurance and reinsurance markets are cyclical. Following large losses, premia tend to rise due to several factors, including the need of the (re)insurance industry to gradually rebuild financial capacity after the loss reserves have been drained[2], the increased level of generalised uncertainty that translates into higher safety and fluctuation loadings, and the growth in the demand for coverage.

The appalling terrorist actions perpetrated in the recent past caused a major shock in the international insurance and reinsurance markets: not only did prices soar, but terrorism coverage became almost unavailable in certain lines of business, notably commercial/industrial property and business interruption. Furthermore, the unprecedented nature of the attacks and the unexpected magnitude of the insured losses were such as to raise concerns about the capacity of the conventional insurance and reinsurance sectors to fully absorb terrorism risks in the future, without endangering the financial stability of the system[3].

After the 11 September 2001 attacks in particular, governments in various OECD countries decided to enter the compensation process and make financial commitments in order to ensure the availability of sufficient insurance coverage for losses caused by terrorist events[4]. At that time, the drastic shrinkage in (re)insurance cover also gave rise to a search for purely private alternative risk transfer mechanisms[5]. Solutions designed to cover natural catastrophe risks in the mid-1990s, after the hardening of (re)insurance markets that followed Hurricane Andrew, set a particularly interesting precedent for the securitisation of other catastrophic risks such as terrorism risk. Available capital market solutions to cover terrorism risks will be analysed in the first part of this chapter, while the second part will highlight the main challenges related to terrorism risk securitisation.

1. Available capital market solutions to cover terrorism risks

In order to overcome the limits of conventional insurance and reinsurance markets, suggestions have been made to turn to the international capital markets, with a view to developing new and innovative risk-transfer and risk-financing solutions. In consideration of their size, which exceeds USD 50 trillion[6], these markets have a remarkable risk spreading potential and might be willing to take on new risks if they consider them imperfectly correlated with those they routinely accept[7]. In theory, through the diversification of institutional investors' investment portfolios, they may manage to absorb high risk exposures, thereby optimising their risk-return ratio.

Capital markets offer different types of alternative risk management solutions[8], which can be grouped into two main categories: alternative risk financing and alternative risk transfer instruments. The market for alternative risk financing solutions comprises various types of committed credit facilities in the banking sector, as well as certain contingent capital instruments, while alternative risk transfer instruments include risk-linked securities, risk swaps and different kinds of exchange-traded and over-the-counter catastrophe derivatives. The main difference between the two categories is that while risk financing tools are aimed at securing the availability of funding for recovery on predetermined conditions in case of a disaster loss, alternative risk transfer solutions entail the shift of all or part of the financial burden associated with the risk from one party to another: in this perspective, only the latter is considered a functional alternative to conventional insurance and reinsurance contracts[9]. It shall be noted, however, that risk transfer and risk financing tools can be jointly used within the framework of an integrated risk management strategy[10].

Even if there is at present a substantial lack of experience with special reference to the case of terror-related losses, as well as several technical problems associated with high risk ambiguity issues, the global capital market might eventually be able to develop innovative solutions and additional capacity to finance and cover at least part of the costs associated with terrorism risks in the future. It is, therefore, worth exploring the field.

1.1. Alternative risk financing

As anticipated, the purpose of catastrophe risk financing instruments is not to transfer a risk of loss, but to secure access to future financing opportunities under prearranged conditions. Different forms of risk financing solutions have been explored within international financial markets, the most important of which are committed funding arrangements with commercial banking sector participants, such as committed revolving term facilities, and contingent capital instruments offered by investment banks and securities firms. These latter instruments may take the form of put option contracts or contingent surplus notes, the aim of which is to guarantee the issuance of medium-term securities on fixed terms if a certain event occurs. In any case, the proceeds of alternative risk financing solutions must be repaid according to the terms and conditions agreed upon in advance, adding to the debt burden of the borrower. It is worth noting, that, reportedly, to date no contingent capital instrument has been issued using natural disasters or terrorist attacks as triggering events[11].

Although captive insurance companies are usually risk transfer vehicles, they may also be used by large corporations for alternative risk financing where the conventional insurance market is unable to provide sufficiently flexible, stable and attractive conditions of coverage. It should however be underlined that, with regard to terror-related losses, captives do not seem to have the capacity to offer solutions adapted to the current constraints affecting the availability of reinsurance coverage for the highest layers of terrorism risk exposure.

1.2. Alternative risk transfer

In order to understand the potential role of alternative risk transfer tools in the management of terrorism risk, it is useful to look at the recent experience with natural catastrophe risk securitisation[12]. Since the mid-1990s – after the occurrence of major catastrophes such as Hurricane Andrew (1992) and the Northridge earthquake (1994) – insurance companies, reinsurance companies and capital markets actors have been developing alternative risk-transfer mechanisms in order to shift to the financial markets the burden of catastrophic losses associated with certain natural disasters, mainly hurricanes, windstorms and earthquakes. The first issuance of a capital market instrument linked to catastrophe risk dates back to 1994 and concerned a catastrophe bond (cat bond) linked to worldwide property catastrophe losses, with the exclusion of the United States and Japan. Since then, several insurers and reinsurers have turned to the capital markets and begun to securitise a portion of their catastrophe risk exposures in order to expand capacity and spread the cost of disaster losses among a large number of investors. Distributed across more than 50 issues and covering a variety of catastrophe risks, including hurricanes, typhoons, windstorms and earthquakes, the securitisation of natural disaster risks represents about USD 7.5 billion of capital at risk since 1996. The recent past registered a sharp increase in cat-bond issues, with 50% growth reported from year-end 2002 to year-end 2004, and a total of USD 4.3 billion in bonds outstanding[13]. This evolution is driven by several factors, and mainly: bond issuing costs are following a downward trend, investors have become more familiar with such transactions and the bonds so far have maintained their creditworthiness. Despite this positive trend, however, the total volume of these transactions remains very low compared to financial market or global property and casualty reinsurance market capacity; at present, moreover, the use of capital markets has been for relatively small-scale transactions and for only certain types of risk.

From a legal and financial point of view, cat bonds are the result of a modification of the asset securitisation technique applied to the reinsurance market. Risk-linked securities, including cat bonds, are offered via structured finance transactions through an entity called a special purpose reinsurance vehicle (SPRV) established offshore for tax and regulatory purposes. The SPRV is usually sponsored by an insurance or reinsurance company that enters into a reinsurance contract and pays reinsurance premia to the special purpose vehicle, in exchange for the coverage of specific risks. The reinsurance contract typically provides the sponsor with coverage of the upper layers of the risks, between specified attachment and exhaustion points, *i.e.,* excess of loss coverage. It is worth noting that this corresponds to practice also in the conventional catastrophe reinsurance market. The SPRV, in turn, issues the risk-linked securities for purchase by institutional investors. The proceeds from the bond issue are placed by the SPRV in a trust fund and then invested in liquid securities with high credit quality ratings, as collateral for the debt service payments due on the cat bonds[14].

The investors receive a relatively high interest rate, compared to standard corporate bonds of equal rating, but they face the risk of losing all or part of the invested principal in case of occurrence of the triggering catastrophic event before the maturity date[15]. The definition of the triggering event and the formula for determining the exact amount of compensation due from the investors to the SPRV may vary and are set by the issuer at the time of the securities offering. The trigger could be based on actual insurance losses incurred by the sponsoring party, *i.e.,* the insurance or reinsurance company, on a defined loss index, or it may be based on other indicators, such as wind speed during a hurricane, earthquake intensity, etc.[16]; the most sophisticated offerings involve a parametric trigger formula, linked to the loss exposure of the cedant (sponsor company), but objectively measurable, so that investors do not have to fully analyze the cedant's underwriting practices and moral hazard concerns are reduced[17]. Cat bonds are typically rated by major rating agencies on the basis of the underlying catastrophe risk evaluation performed by specialised risk modeling firms. The investor base for cat bonds has continued to increase during the past years and dedicated cat-bond funds have recently emerged.

From the point of view of the sponsoring company, cat bonds entail extremely low credit risk, since the assets needed to compensate insured losses in case of occurrence of the triggering event are placed in trust by the SPRV and invested in liquid securities. While conventional reinsurance contracts always entail a counterparty risk of default (credit risk), especially with respect to low probability and high consequences events, cat-bond issues provide a secure source of funds in case of a disaster. However, non-indemnity based risk-linked securities, *i.e.,* risk-linked securities whose triggering event is not directly based on the cedant's incurred losses but, for instance, on an index, a physical indicator or a parametric formula may not be a perfect hedge of the underlying exposure, being only imperfectly correlated to the actual insured losses caused by the occurrence of the triggering event. This uncertainty is known as basis risk[18].

One notable advantage of catastrophe risk securitisation is that it provides multiyear coverage at fixed price, while the cost and availability of (re)insurance – in current market conditions – fluctuate on an annual basis. However, the total costs associated with cat-bonds issues are sometimes perceived as high, compared with traditional reinsurance arrangements; this reflects several factors, including the high interest rate of return paid to the investors, the underwriting fees, and the legal fees involved in the complex structured finance transaction. Furthermore, cat bonds have so far been targeted to cover only the lowest frequency and highest severity losses.

In addition to cat bonds, other alternative risk transfer mechanisms have been explored during the 1990s to cope with catastrophic risks: these are over-the-counter and exchange-traded financial derivatives, including options contracts, futures contracts, catastrophe risk swap agreements, as well as other standardised contracts to hedge catastrophic exposures that have been offered to investors. With the limited exception of certain weather derivatives, however, such instruments have proved to be largely unsuccessful, since they require special expertise, deep insights into the reinsurance market and knowledge of specific catastrophe risk exposures, all of which most investors do not possess[19].

2. The challenge of terrorism risk securitisation

The idea of extending the securitisation of catastrophic risks to terrorism emerged after the 2001 attacks. The shrinkage of capacity following September 11 was seen as an opportunity to develop new financial market instruments that may be used by (re)insurers to enable them to increase their underwriting capacity. These instruments may also provide other corporate entities with an alternative to limited and possibly expensive conventional terrorism (re)insurance products.

In 2003, a breakthrough was made with the **Golden Globe Financing LTD transaction**. This transaction involving, *inter alia*, terror-related losses, was sponsored by the FIFA (Fédération Internationale de Football Association) to cover revenue losses that would arise in the event of the cancellation of the 18th FIFA World Cup scheduled to be held in the summer of 2006 in Germany.

Box 2.1. **The FIFA transaction (Golden Goal Finance Ltd.)**

Under the guidance of investment bank Credit Suisse First Boston (CSFB), the Fédération Internationale de Football Association (FIFA) transferred the financial risk of cancellation by issuing bonds in an amount equivalent to USD 260 million to international investors during September 2003. The securities issued in this structured finance transaction are linked to the risks of natural disasters as well as terrorist events precluding the completion of the final tournament. As a consequence, FIFA will no longer hold a traditional insurance policy to cover the mentioned risks. The world football's governing body opted for this capital market arrangement having carefully evaluated the traditional insurance alternative, which reportedly no longer met FIFA's objectives. Among the main concerns was the fact that, after September 11, the insurance market shifted from multi-year to annual renewable cover. Bondholders rather than insurance companies, therefore, have now taken on the risk of the 2006 tournament being postponed or cancelled.

Risk Management Solutions (RMS) performed analysis which examined the threat and impact of terrorism events and natural disasters on the 64-match FIFA World Cup final competition. The structure of the bond, devised to ensure that the same economic effect as an insurance contract was achieved, took about six months to evolve and it had to strike a delicate balance between FIFA's requirements and investor appeal.

According to the terms of the offering, in the event of cancellation, investors will lose 75% of their money invested in the bonds. In principle, all risks are covered, with two main exceptions: the outbreak of a world war and a boycott by players or participating associations, in which case the investors would be repaid. The bond came in four tranches, A1, A2, A3 and B, denominated in three currencies (USD, EUR and CHF) via a special purpose vehicle incorporated in Jersey, Channel Islands, and called Golden Goal Finance Limited. Class A bonds were rated A3, or mid-investment grade by ratings agency Moody's Investors Service, while class B bonds have not been rated[20].

This transaction is said to be the first to transfer event risk, *i.e.*, the risk of a sporting event being cancelled and the first to transfer the risk of terrorism and man-made catastrophe, as well as natural catastrophe to the capital markets[21]. However, given the unique characteristics of the FIFA bond issuance, it may not have broad applications to the overall securitisation of terrorism risk in the near future.

First, terrorism risk (defined as the risk of "any act or acts of one or more persons, whether or not agents of a sovereign power, for political, religious, ideological or similar purposes including the intention to influence any government and/or the public, or any section of the public and whether the loss or damage resulting there from is accidental or intentional.") has been pooled together with several other risks that may lead to the cancellation of the sporting event. The extent to which the rating agency relied on the predictions made by the modeling firm with regard to terrorism risk remains unclear, but in any case it concluded that terrorism is unlikely to affect the tournament.

Second, the trigger has been defined in an objective and highly verifiable manner, since Class A bondholders will lose 75% of their invested principal if no official result has been determined or declared in respect of the final match of the 2006 FIFA World Cup and no final match will be held on or before 31st August 2007.

Third, the sponsor is not an insurance or a reinsurance company, but the world football's governing body, acting in its capacity as event organiser. In this case, the structured finance transaction replaces primary insurance coverage, not excess of loss reinsurance.

Fourth, the transaction is not aimed at covering property damage or business interruption losses caused by terrorist attacks, but revenue losses from cancellation of the event. Coverage was reportedly requested by FIFA's marketing partners, in order to secure reimbursement of prepaid sums. In such an arrangement, the impact of basis risk is greatly reduced.

Fifth, moral hazard concerns appear to be extremely low in this case, since FIFA has a strong financial incentive to ensure that the event is not curtailed and reaches completion.

Sixth, it would require extraordinary circumstances for the final tournament to be cancelled, abandoned or truncated, since the world football's governing body has the possibility to reschedule matches and also to choose different locations.

Not only was the Golden Glove Financing Ltd transaction the first transaction covering *explicitly* terrorism risks, it was also oversubscribed, demonstrating that investors were ready to cover such terrorism exposure under certain conditions. However, the special features and circumstances of this transaction, as discussed in Box 2.1, contribute to rendering it somehow special: while it could certainly be used as a model for the management of the various risks – including terrorism – affecting similar events in the future, it does not provide clear indications as to the potential for risk-linked securities to become a viable complement to, or substitute for, conventional insurance and reinsurance in the coverage of terrorism risk exposures.

After the FIFA transaction, another securitisation transaction involving certain aspects of terrorism risk was sponsored in late 2003 by Swiss Re to obtain from **Vita Capital Ltd**. financial coverage up to USD 400 million in the event pre-determined extreme mortality risk scenarios materialise before the end of 2006. The catastrophe-indexed notes issued by Vita Capital are linked to a rise in mortality from any source, including epidemics, natural disasters, war, or terrorist attacks.

Box 2.2. **The Swiss Re – Vita Capital transaction (mortality risk)**

In December 2003 Swiss Re entered into a financial arrangement with Vita Capital Ltd. to provide up to USD 400 million of payments to Swiss Re in certain extreme mortality risk scenarios. To fund potential payments under this arrangement, Vita Capital – a specially created insurance-linked security intermediary – issued USD 400 million of principal at-risk variable rate notes[22].

The structure of the Vita Capital risk coverage is based on a combined mortality index similar to other index-based insurance-linked securities. The mortality index measures annual general population mortality in five selected countries (U.S., U.K., France, Switzerland, and Italy) by applying predetermined weights to publicly-reported mortality data from each country (70% US; 15% UK; 7.5% France; 5% Switzerland; 2.5% Italy); the risk has also been segmented according to age and gender. The principal of the Vita Capital notes will be at risk if, during any single calendar year in the risk coverage period (the bond matures on 1 January 2007), the combined mortality index exceeds 130% of its baseline 2002 level. In terms of an absolute number of extra deaths, this may be in the range of approximately 750,000. The catastrophe-indexed notes are linked to a rise in mortality from any source, including epidemics, natural disasters, war, or terrorist attacks. According to certain estimations, the trigger threshold could be attained before the maturity date only if pessimistic lethality estimates are made for *both* a pandemic *and* a major terrorist attack involving the use of weapons of mass destruction.

Swiss Re Capital Markets Corporation structured the Vita Capital securities and acted as the sole bookrunner in the distribution to institutional investors. The Vita Capital securities were rated "A+" by Standard & Poor's and "A3" by Moody's Investor Service. Under the terms of the agreement, investors are paid a quarterly coupon rate of USD three-month Libor plus a spread of 135 basis points for the principal at risk. Through this securitisation, Swiss Re has transferred mortality risk to the capital markets as an alternative to traditional retrocession.

A **few observations may be drawn in light of these two, and so far only publicly reported, terrorism securitisations**. While these transactions may pave the way for further terrorism risk securitisation, it is clear, however, that the issuance of terrorism cat bonds requires many conditions to be met and careful monitoring of the different risks.

Firstly, the ability to analyze, predict and estimate risk is a prerequisite not only for insurance, but also for securitisation. Capital markets may demand an even higher degree of precision in risk pricing than conventional (re)insurance markets: being more transaction based, they place a premium on tradability. Rating agencies, underwriters and investors, therefore, may benefit from specialised knowledge and skills to evaluate the underlying risk exposure in order to make informed decisions. Yet, risk uncertainty and the perception that terrorism risk modeling is too new and subjective to be fully relied upon may in particular be limiting investors' appetite for terrorism bonds[23]. At present, the challenges in predicting with some degree of reliability the frequency and severity of terrorist acts appear to be among the main obstacles to the securitisation of terrorism risks, just as they are obstacles to (re)insuring those risks. Specialised firms have been developing new risk evaluation models, but estimating the probabilities associated with future terrorist acts remains intrinsically far more subjective than assessing the risk of natural disasters[24]. As a consequence of the uncertainty associated with the underlying risk and the fact that such transactions are new, cat bonds transactions tend to be complex, long to put in place, and expensive as compared with traditional reinsurance, if it is available.

Furthermore, it should be emphasised that the issuance of terrorism bonds, like insurance, may suffer not only from basis risk (*i.e.* the risk of imperfect correlation with the underlying exposure, for the reasons mentioned above) but also from moral hazard risk.

Lastly, in the case of catastrophic terrorist events, due the magnitude of their potential macroeconomic impact, there may be consequences of the terrorist act to the general commercial risks that the institutional investors already have in their portfolio, so that the diversification potential could be at least partly frustrated.

It is therefore not surprising that, as of today, the OECD Insurance and Private Pensions Committee has not found more transactions securitising terrorism risks despite the current strains on conventional (re)insurance capacity. From this point of view, the coverage of terrorism risk by means of multi-event bonds appears to be an important condition of success[25]: future securitisation might try to mix-and-match different risks in order to dilute the terrorism component[26], or to make the loss of principal contingent on the occurrence of two or more trigger events[27].

A **proposal** was recently put forward to develop new derivatives instruments in the form of **catastrophe-linked swaption contracts** with specific reference to terrorism risk[28]. These instruments should cater the needs of issuers of financing for public spaces and construction projects, as well as municipals. While the idea of transferring a portion of terrorism risks to capital markets via new derivative contracts is appealing, it seems that the above mentioned proposal is still in its formative stages, and several crucial aspects of the proposal remain unclear[29] though swap contracts could provide substitutes for more traditional reinsurance coverage if a market developed.

Conclusion

The experience with natural catastrophe risks securitisation transactions during the past eight years[30] may offer some guidance in the possible use of risk linked securities to cover terrorism risks, and financial markets may in the future provide some additional capacity to cover terrorism exposures. However, the market for securitising natural catastrophe risk, despite certain shortcomings, currently appears to be far more feasible than the securitisation of terrorism risk. Financial market tools suitable to cover catastrophic terrorism risks have not yet been developed, and no sustainable risk-linked securities market covering losses associated with terrorism acts has emerged so far, owing mainly to the extremely high level of uncertainty and ambiguity that affects modern-day terrorism risk. Also, whereas governments in several OECD member countries have decided to step in and make permanent or temporary commitments in order to secure the availability of sufficient insurance coverage for losses caused by terrorist events, it is argued that the demand for such private risk sharing alternatives or other innovations might well be impeded by direct government involvement (and/or the expectation that the government will provide post-event disaster aid). For the specific case of terrorism risk securitisation, it is however unclear at this stage whether the absence of direct government intervention in the countries considered would have considerably changed the market prospects, risk ambiguity remaining by far the major obstacle to terrorism risk securitisation.

Up to now, only two known transactions have covered, explicitly or implicitly, terrorism risk, and there have been no transactions purely securitising terrorism risk, despite the current strains on conventional (re)insurance capacity. While these instruments are still being developed and may be capable of providing a complement to conventional (re)insurance arrangements in the future, especially in those cases where terrorism risk can be packaged together with other catastrophic risks, the role of risk-linked securities in the future management of terrorism risk remains currently uncertain.

Standardised financial derivatives on terrorism risk exposures may need further examination as to whether they present viable market-based alternatives to conventional insurance and reinsurance contracts; interesting proposals have been recently made to develop new derivative instruments in the form of terrorism risk swaption contracts, but they too seem to be in need of further elaboration at this stage.

It is worth noting that a friendlier fiscal and accounting environment could make the securitisation of terrorism risk more appealing and cost efficient. However useful, tax and accounting measures alone may yet prove insufficient to allow a substantial development of such transactions[31].

Alternative risk transfer solutions are therefore generally not expected to bring about a meaningful increase in the private capacity for terrorism coverage in the foreseeable future and, in the absence of substantial improvements in terrorism risk modeling, developing derivatives or other securities instruments to cover terrorism risks alone is probably not yet realistic[32]. As long as reinsurers themselves, with their long experience and great expertise in the coverage of a wide range of catastrophic risks, prove reluctant to cover large terrorism exposures due to the difficulty of quantifying and pricing such risks, the motivation of financial market players to develop securitisation solutions to terrorism risk is likely to remain rather low.

Notes

1   This chapter is indebted to Andersen, T. (2005), *International financing solutions to terrorism risk exposures* (see infra, Part III Chapter 7).

2   Jaffee, Dwight and T. Russell (June 1997), *Catastrophe Insurance, Capital Markets, and Uninsurable Risks*, Journal of Risk and Insurance 64, No. 2, p. 205-230.

3   See infra, Part II Chapter 1, *Insurability of terrorism risk*.

4   See infra, Part II Chapter 3, *Possible role of government in the coverage of terrorism risk*.

5   The need for a thoroughly interdisciplinary perspective on the issue of catastrophic risks, including terrorism risk, has been highlighted most recently by: Posner, Richard A. (2004), *Catastrophe: Risk and Response*, Oxford University Press.

6   As of end of March 2005, the total domestic stock market capitalisation of all members of the World Federation of Exchanges as well as international debt securities outstanding by all countries as reported by the BIS was about USD 51 trillion. Sources: Bank for International Settlements (BIS) (June 2005), *BIS Quarterly Review*; and World Federation of Exchanges (May 2005), *Focus* N. 147.

7   See: Froot, Kenneth A. (August 1999), *The Evolving Market for Catastrophic Event Risk*. NBER Working Paper No. W7287.

8   See Insurance Services Office – ISO (1999), *Financing Catastrophe Risk: Capital Market Solutions*, Insurance Issue Series.

9   See Culp, C. L. (2002), *The ART of Risk Management: Alternative Risk Transfer, Capital Structure, and the Convergence between Insurance and Capital Markets*. Wiley, New York, NY; Bock, K. J. and M. W. Seitz (2002), *Reinsurance vs Other Risk-transfer Instruments – The Reinsurer's Perspective*, in Lane, M. (Ed.) Alternative Risk Strategies. Risk Books, London, UK; Cummins, J. D., D. Lalonde and R. D. Phillips (2002), *Managing Risk Using*

Risk-linked Catastrophic Loss Securities, in Lane, M. (Ed.) Alternative Risk Strategies, cit.; Canter, M. S., J. B. Cole and R. L. Sandor (1996), *Insurance derivatives: A new asset class for the capital markets and a new hedging tool for the insurance industry*, The Journal of Derivatives, Winter, p. 89-104.

10   See Andersen, T. (2005), infra; Pollner, John (February 2001), *Catastrophe Risk Management: Using Alternative Risk Financing and Insurance Pooling Mechanisms,* World Bank Policy Research Working Paper No. 2560.

11   See Andersen, T. (2005), infra.

12   See for instance Mocklow, D., J. DeCaro and M. McKenna (2002), *Catastrophe Bonds*, in Lane, M. (Ed.), Alternative Risk Strategies. Risk Books, London, UK.

13   See: U.S. General Accounting Office (GAO) (February 28, 2005), *Catastrophe risk: US and European approaches to insure natural catastrophe and terrorism risks* and *Market Update: the Catastrophe Bond Market at Year-End 2003,* Guy Carpenter & Company, Inc. (2004).

14   See Andersen T. (2005), infra.

15   On the complex issue of pricing of these instruments, see: Froot, Kenneth A. and S. E. Posner (February 2001), *The Pricing of Event Risks with Parameter Uncertainty*, NBER Working Paper No. W8106; Lee, Jin-Ping and M. Yu (2002), *Pricing Default-Risky CAT Bonds With Moral Hazard and Basis Risk*. Journal of Risk & Insurance, Vol. 69, No. 2, p. 25-44; Young, Virginia R. (July 2004), *Pricing in an Incomplete Market With an Affine Term Structure*. Mathematical Finance, Vol. 14, No. 3, p. 359-381.

16   See *e.g.* Nell, Martin and A. Richter (April 2004), *Improving Risk Allocation through Indexed Cat Bonds*. Geneva Papers on Risk and Insurance, Vol. 29, p. 183-201.

17   According to Araya, R. (2005), *Catastrophic Risk Securitization: Moody's Perspective*, in *Catastrophic Risks and Insurance*, Policy Issues in Insurance N°8, OECD, *"there are four types of triggers used to determine losses to the holder of cat bonds: parametric, loss index, modeled-losses and indemnity triggers. Over time there has been a shift in the types of transactions brought to market. The early stages of the cat bond market were dominated by indemnity transactions whereas parametric transactions tend to be more prevalent nowadays"*.

18   See Cummins, John David, D. Lalonde and R. D. Phillips (May 2000), *The Basis Risk of Catastrophic-Loss Index Securities*. http://ssrn.com/abstract=230044.

19   See Andersen, T. (2005), infra.

20   See Moody's (September 2003), *Golden Goal Finance Ltd. – Fédération Internationale de Football Association ABS Risk Transfer Switzerland/Germany*, Moody's Pre-Sale Report.

21   See Woo, Gordon (2005), *Current Challenges in the Securitization of Terrorism Risk*, in *Catastrophic Risks and Insurance*, Policy Issues in Insurance N°8, OECD; Woo, Gordon (February 6-7, 2004), *A Catastrophe Bond Niche: Multiple Event Risk*, paper delivered at NBER Insurance Workshop, Cambridge Mass.

22   See: Official news release entitled *Swiss Re obtains US$ 400 million of extreme mortality risk coverage - its first life securitisation* (December 8, 2003), available at *www.swissre.com*; See also: *Vita Capital Ltd. – a Catastrophe Bond Linked to Catastrophic Mortality*, Moody's New Issue Report (January 2004); Beelders, O., D. Colarossi (July-August 2004), *Modelling Mortality Risk with Extreme Value Theory: the Case of Swiss Re's Mortality-Indexed Bonds*, in Global Association of Risk Professionals - GARP Risk Review, Issue 19; Woo, G. (2004).

23   According to Mumenthaler, C. (November 2004), *The use of risk linked securities to manage catastrophic risks*, presentation at the occasion of the OECD November 2004 Conference on 'Insurance and catastrophic risks', available under the conference link at *http://www.oecd.org/daf/insurance*, p. 15-16: there is "*some potential [for terrorism risk securitisation] (...) where models might not be essentials: 1. very low risk areas (FIFA deal) where investors basically think it is not possible or very remote; 2. high risk area where investors would basically 'bet' and get a high return*".

24   On this issue, see infra, paragraphs on modeling in Part II Chapter 1 on terrorism risk insurability.

25   For a discussion on the advantages and drawbacks of packaging terrorism risk as a multi-event transaction see: Woo, G. (2004).

26   See: Woo, G. (2005).

27   See Woo, G. (2004).

28   US Securities Industry Association (SIA) - *Research Reports*, Vol. 5, N.1: Brandon, K and A. Fernandez (January 31, 2004), *Terrorist risk: insurance market failures and capital market solutions*.

29   In particular: who would actually be willing to act as counterparty in such terrorism risk swap transactions; what would be the proposed duration of these contracts (swap contracts generally have an extremely short maturity), as one of the reasons for seeking capital market solutions is to secure multiyear coverage at fixed price though shorter term contracts could provide substitutes for more traditional reinsurance coverage if a market developed; how could the underlying terrorist exposure be effectively fragmented and distributed across a large number of credit worthy counterparties; and, finally, whether these instruments would be able to provide the necessary financial capacity to cover mega-terrorism risks.

30   See Guy Carpenter & Company, Inc. (2004), *Market Update: the Catastrophe Bond Market at Year-End 2003*.

31   For more details on this issue, see infra, Part II Chapter 3.

32   See GAO (2005), p. 6-7: "catastrophe bonds have not been issued to address terrorism risk in the United States, and according to industry participants such bonds are not considered feasible at this time given the uncertainties associated with forecasting the timing and severity of terrorist attacks". See also David, M. (2005), *The Potential for New Derivatives Instruments to Cover Terrorism Risk*, in *Catastrophic Risks and Insurance*, Policy Issues in Insurance N°8, OECD: "While the development of new derivatives instruments and markets to cover terrorism risk is possible, the use of derivatives to transfer terrorism risk is probably not feasible until we have a way to accurately measure and price terrorism risk. Market

participants would like to find a new form of capacity, but without a way to price the risks involved the premiums for these types of derivatives would likely be cost prohibitive. The mismatch in the perceived level of risk needs to be resolved through the use of reliable and widely accepted models before derivatives can provide a viable source of capacity for terrorism risk".

Chapter 3

POSSIBLE ROLE OF GOVERNMENT IN THE COVERAGE OF TERRORISM RISK

Introduction[1]

Even if material damages and economic losses are primarily suffered by targeted businesses and individuals, terrorist acts are ultimately directed against governments, often with a view to influencing their domestic and/or foreign policies. Terrorism risk, therefore, is a political issue that necessarily calls for informed governmental decision making at a national and international level[2]. Governments play a crucial role in the prevention and management of terrorism risks. The enforcement of a strong and comprehensive counter terrorism policy, aimed at limiting the occurrence of terrorist attacks and the incidence of potential future terror-related losses, has been recognised as an important step to be taken at this stage[3]. Educating society, increasing public awareness of potential attacks, enforcing prevention measures and preparing emergency and rescue plans are other fundamental policy goals to be pursued.

If loss prevention and mitigation perform a crucial function in terrorism risk management strategies, it is no less important to foresee compensation in case prevention fails. Since modern-day terrorism may have a potentially debilitating impact on the social and economic activities of a country, it is critical to assure business and social continuity should the terrorists be successful.

Beyond the need to solve a possible crisis situation on private markets after an attack, a number of underlying goals might be considered in the design of terrorism risk compensation mechanisms, and mainly economic efficiency, equity, and national security[4]. The extent to which they would interplay and may also need to be prioritised in certain contexts, would have to be clarified, according to each country's circumstances.

For a wide spectrum of economic, social and political risks, private insurance has emerged in developed countries as a highly efficient tool to manage risks through its pooling and diversification capabilities. Obviously, private insurance is not the only possible component of compensation; it should be viewed as an element of a more comprehensive strategy in which additional ways to compensate for losses may be provided by government programmes, dedicated compensation funds, tort liability[5], charitable contributions, etc. Private insurance nevertheless remains a corner stone in compensation management[6]. One of the key issues that governments and policymakers face in the institutional design of an effective terrorism risk management and compensation system therefore concerns the role that private insurance can and should play in such system[7].

The 11 September 2001 attacks in particular have radically changed the perspective in this respect. They have brought to light the new features of the modern terrorism threat, and cast doubts on the ability of the private insurance and reinsurance market to price and absorb alone large-scale terrorism risks in the future[8]. Following the attacks, the global capacity of the terrorism insurance market was subject to sudden shrinkage and, in a number of OECD countries, government where called to provide some form of guarantee to the private terrorism insurance market. Questions suddenly emerged that had only been addressed in the past in the countries most exposed to terrorism: Should the insurance market disruptions following a large scale attack be considered as a short-term problem only? To what extent are private insurance mechanisms suited to cover terrorism risks? Should they be complemented by government intervention?

Would the benefits of such intervention exceed its potential costs, and if so, under which conditions? Above all, who can/should pay for terrorism losses, and how should the risk be shared between entities at risks, insurers, reinsurers, possible institutional investors on the capital markets and eventually the larger community of tax payers?

Several years after the 9/11 events, the proper role of governments in the financial compensation for terror-related losses remains a highly controversial issue in various OECD countries, where different types of direct and indirect government intervention are still being discussed. In some countries, the insurance industry has been calling for government support without success, while in others the renewal of the government backed mechanism is being questioned. At international level, the comparison of terrorism risk compensation mechanisms in the various countries reveals diverging views on the appropriate level of government involvement.

The main forms and rationale of government intervention, as well as potential drawbacks, are addressed in Section 1 from a theoretical viewpoint. Where there was evidence of private markets lacking capacity, and taking into account the economic advantages that the *ex ante* insurance approach may bring about, a number of OECD countries have established mechanisms devoted to the compensation of losses from terrorism with a view to restoring the availability and affordability of insurance cover[9]. As of today, eight schemes providing insurance coverage for terrorism risk have been implemented in OECD member countries, among which seven involve government participation. The main features of such institutional arrangements are discussed in Section 2, while Section 3 touches upon some initiatives that have been contemplated at international level.

1. Possible forms of government intervention in the terrorism insurance market, their advantages and drawbacks

1.1. Rationale of government intervention

While no country can claim to be immune from terrorism risks, the degree of exposure of OECD countries to terrorism risk nevertheless varies. The extent to which each country's insurance market has been affected by the 9/11 events also differs, as do OECD countries' views of the appropriate level of government intervention in the sector.

Government involvement in the compensation of terrorism related losses may be supported on political grounds. Terrorism risk is a specific exposure in that the choice of the compensation system and the degree in which it promotes mitigation in particular, may impact not only on the extent of losses incurred, but also on the likelihood of the hazard itself. As they may reduce chances of success and/or minimise the impact of an attack, prevention measures may deter terrorist action. To that extent in particular, the organisation of the compensation of losses caused by terrorist attacks may have an impact on national security[10].

Starting from the assumption that foreign policy choices have a decisive impact on transnational terrorism[11] and that terrorism compensation is a matter of national security as previously mentioned, it has been argued that the government should participate in a national insurance programme covering economic losses due to terrorist attacks as part of its national security policy[12]. Recent trends in terrorist activities may further increase the potential influence on national security of the government support of insurance or direct compensation of victims[13]. Governments, therefore, may want to explore options to "bridge the gaps between business motivation and national security interest"[14]. Such intervention may also give credit to national counter-terrorism policy.

From an economic viewpoint, the discussion about the proper role that governments may be called upon to play in the field of terrorism risk insurance stems from the recognition of certain failures that may negatively affect the functioning of private insurance markets. Consequent market incapacity to provide sufficient cover at affordable rates may have negative spill-over effects on the broader economy, result in a contraction of economic activity, and threaten both recovery and growth in the aftermath of an attack[15]. Analyses however diverge on the proper extent and modality of government intervention in private markets in order to address these issues[16].

1.2. Modalities of government intervention

According to insurance industry representatives in particular, among the most important problems currently affecting terrorism risk insurance markets are *(a)* the **limited availability of financial capacity**, *(b)* the **generalised uncertainty and risk ambiguity.**

As concerns the first issue, it became clear after the September 11 events that terrorist acts may entail previously unforeseen catastrophic consequences. Insurance companies, however, have finite capital and reserves, and access to additional resources is typically limited and costly after a disaster. The shrinkage of reinsurance capacity, after the World Trade Center events for instance, provoked the sudden disruption of terrorism risk insurance markets worldwide[17]. The capacity issue remains acute today: while the terrorism insurance market conditions have improved since 2001, and supply has broadened as prices were decreasing, the private insurance and reinsurance markets could be overwhelmed by a large-scale terrorism attack[18].

In order to address the capacity problem, a first **"indirect" or "implicit" form of government intervention** can be characterised by the adoption of policy measures aimed at providing specific incentives to restart private (insurance and non-insurance) markets. In this perspective, governmental action would not set up a substitute for or a complement to purely private solutions, but it would rather attempt to revitalise private markets[19]. Examples of this type of intervention could be *fiscal*[20], *accounting and regulatory measures aimed at facilitating the raising and reserving of capital by insurance firms* involved in catastrophe insurance lines[21]. *Fiscal and regulatory incentives to the purchase of terrorism coverage* could also be considered.

Another example would be targeted regulatory measures aimed at fostering the *development of alternative risk transfer tools* that would serve the purpose of spreading the risk on capital markets[22]. Changes in related accounting rules are being considered in countries like the United States[23]. Fiscal measures could also play a significant role in the development of cat bonds: in particular, granting the SPVs for cat bonds a tax-free conduit status would allow them to locate outside of off-shore tax-havens (where they are currently typically located), and therefore reduce transaction costs. However, while cat bonds may be a more attractive and competitive option in a friendlier tax and accounting environment, it is unlikely that such measures alone will be sufficient to allow for a significant development of financial market solutions for terrorism risk coverage in particular.

Lastly, discussing the possible indirect role of governments, it is also relevant to note that the legal framework might facilitate private capacity building and larger mutuality in several ways, for instance, by providing incentives and favourable regulatory environments, *e.g.,* granting of tax-free conduit status to *private sector risk-mutualisation schemes*.

Unfortunately, indirect public sector initiatives to rebuild private markets for terrorism risk insurance appear to have had limited success to date in OECD countries. Moreover, while such initiatives may provide at least partial solutions to the current shortage of available financial capacity, they do not address the crucial issue of risk ambiguity and generalised uncertainty.

As concerns this second issue, a high level of generalised uncertainty negatively affects risk insurability. In particular, the malicious nature of the terrorist threat, the potential impact of governmental policies on future terrorist acts, and the fact that most relevant information on the hazard (the current terrorist threat) are not available to insurers since they are classified for obvious national security reasons, all contribute to rendering terrorism risk insurance extremely challenging, and may be used to plead in favour of some government action. Indirect forms of government intervention do not address these issues, and may therefore not be sufficient to avoid the rise in insurance premia and consequent low levels of terrorism insurance penetration[24], while coverage for certain risks (such as the risks of very large scale events and CBRN attacks, which private insurers appear very reluctant to underwrite, at present) may remain unavailable in the short/medium run. Under current circumstances, indirect forms of governmental intervention may be considered as a complement to direct forms of intervention, as part of an integrated terrorism risk management strategy. In consideration of the above, **"direct" or "explicit" types of government intervention** have been contemplated as a means of increasing terrorism insurance availability and affordability. Such types of intervention may take a wide range of different forms, addressing both the capacity and the uncertainty issues outlined above.

It may be useful to distinguish the "market micro structures", through which the sale of policies and the adjustment of claims take place, from the "insurance functions", through which risk bearing occurs[25]. As will be seen below, most existing government interventions in OECD countries are mixed private/public enterprises with the private markets being responsible for most, if not all, of the market micro structure functions, while the government may assume certain insurance functions. This sharing of responsibilities will allow taking advantage of insurers experience and expertise in writing policies, collecting premia and adjusting and settling claims, as well as to benefit from their extensive networks.

The most far-reaching form of "explicit" intervention[26] has the government acting as the **primary insurer**, taking on all insurance functions, including defining the coverage, setting the prices, and bearing the risk. An example of such government involvement is offered by the solution adopted in Israel, where very comprehensive terrorism coverage is provided without direct costs to the beneficiaries. The government of Israel bears the entire risk, which is funded from property tax revenues[27]. Another example of an institutional arrangement in which the government may play, *inter alia*, the role of direct insurer is provided by the Spanish Consorcio de Compensación de Seguros, covering all extraordinary risks, including terrorism[28].

Other possible forms of intervention have the government serving as the **reinsurer of last resort**, within a layered approach to terrorism risk coverage. This integrated risk management strategy involves both the private and the public sector[29], the government stepping in to provide reinsurance at the highest risk levels, while private insurers and possibly reinsurers retain some or all of the lower tiers of risk. The sharing of risk with the private industry is achieved through a deductible limit at the lowest risk level and possibly through co-reinsurance at intermediate risk levels. This solution allows accessing the exclusive capacity of the government to provide coverage for the larger risks, as it enjoys much wider diversification capabilities: it may spread the loss over the entire population, as well as across time to future generations of taxpayers, while insurers operate under far shorter time constraints[30].

Finally, the government may act as **lender of last resort**. A government agency may stand ready to make loans to insurance firms who are in need of liquidity after a terrorist event. Private insurance firms may refuse to offer terrorism coverage due to the costs of financial distress that arise if the firm does not have access to the resources to pay future claims. Thus, a lender of last resort may serve to activate the private market for terrorism insurance at low cost to the government.

One should note that these solutions are not exclusive. Direct and indirect intervention may be combined. Regarding direct intervention, governments may act both as primary insurer and guarantee fund, as under the Spanish Consorcio designed according the subsidiarity principle. More commonly, governments may combine the function of reinsurer and lender of last resort.

1.3. Potential limits and drawbacks

Having illustrated the rationale and possible forms of government participation in terrorism compensation schemes, it is essential to evaluate the potential limits and drawbacks to government intervention[31]. Among the potential drawbacks of government action, possible underwriting, pricing and claim management rigidities in the operation of national compensation schemes, as well as bureaucratic excesses[32] which could result in high operating expenses, have, for instance, been highlighted. Another particularly important question, from both economic and political perspectives, is whether the government intervention **crowds out or otherwise displaces private markets**[33] – be it the operation of conventional (re)insurance markets, or the emergence of possible innovative solutions such as terrorism insurer pools or terrorism risk securitisation.

Potential operational rigidities and more fundamental threats of crowding out of the private sector may be significantly reduced by carefully structuring and periodically reassessing institutional arrangements chosen, so that market mechanisms are used wherever possible. Generally speaking, when governments act as primary insurers, little room for manoeuvre may be left for the industry[34]. Where governments act as reinsurers of last resort instead, the crowding out of private sector players could occur only at the highest risk tier. Private firms are, in any case, unlikely to have a major market presence in any risk layer at which the government continues to intervene actively[35]. Various more detailed options are discussed in part 2 of this chapter.

The possibility that government interventions may **displace private actions to mitigate damages** that may be created by terrorist actions is another possible drawback to government activity in terrorist insurance markets. Reduced incentives to mitigation and delay in private sector's adjustments to a continuing threat of terrorism can be understood as an application of the principle of moral hazard, in which insurance coverage provides individuals and firms incentive to take on greater risk.

Terrorism risk mitigation[36] is however a complex issue: while mitigation is highly desirable with regard to other disaster, precautionary measures against terrorism risks might under certain conditions be of limited use for entities at risk and even detrimental on a global scale. Firstly, private markets may not be able to provide adequate incentives for companies to invest in security measures because interconnections between firms increase their vulnerability to terrorism risk to an extent that is difficult to quantify: firms that have invested in counter-terrorism protection measures may still be affected by the failure of a weak link in the system in which they operate. Insurers, therefore, may not be willing or able to offer premium incentives for investment in protective measures[37]. As a consequence, public-sector intervention through the enforcement of security standards and regulations in particular may be desirable in order to limit risk exposure and cope with externality problems.

Secondly, while mitigation generally remains desirable, adopting protective measures against terrorism risk may also generate negative externalities. Security measures taken by one entity may shift the risk to other targets while entities at risk may not consider such negative effects (*i.e.,* negative externalities) when making their decisions[38]. The social benefit of mitigation may thus be limited to the extent that it only serves to change the location at which an attack will occur. The widespread availability of insurance at affordable rates would encourage individuals and firms to rely more heavily on such a risk transfer mechanism to cover their losses than on investment in overly costly preventive measures or adoption of socially undesirable avoidance measures.

The interplay of these forces is important in the evaluation of the impact that government intervention may have on terrorism risk mitigation. Given the partially public nature of terrorism risks, some mitigation efforts may be influenced by factors other than the narrowly defined economic incentives, and some of the effects of terrorism may exceed the reach of mitigation by private sector firms and individuals. In this respect, terrorism risk may pose some of the economic problems that are typical of so-called "public goods"[39].

Lastly, one should bear in mind that individuals generally anticipate the provision by governments of emergency aid and relief following a terrorist attack, independent of any formal government insurance program and *ex ante* commitment. *Ad hoc* compensation mechanisms are often criticised for raising problems of uncertainty and inequality in the treatment of those who suffer losses from different types of events. *ex post* aid is also likely to create a harmful form of crowding out, since the aid can be seen as the equivalent of a zero-cost government insurance program. Lastly, *ex post* aid is likely to create disincentives to mitigate, to the extent that there is the expectation that the government will indemnify losses, whatever the size. While these crowding out and mitigation effects of *ex post* aid programs are undesirable, realism suggests that governments may continue to provide such aid in the face of unexpected events, and that citizens will expect their government to do so. A practical solution, therefore, would be to control the details of the *ex post* aid in a way that minimises the undesirable effects of crowding out private initiatives. For example, it is important to clarify that purchasing insurance will not reduce the payout that otherwise would be expected from *ex post* aid. It is also useful to tie aid payments in a positive way to the amount of *ex ante* mitigation that was carried out. Another problem however arises at this point: *ex post* aid is normally provided on the basis of *emergency need*, and it may not be credible for the government to announce on an *ex ante* basis that it will not reduce award payments due to insurance or mitigation effort[40].

Box 3.1. **Different Types of Government Intervention**

Governmental intervention in the management of terrorism risk may take very different forms:

a) ex post **aid v.** *ex ante* **solutions:** the initial and fundamental policy choice is between *ex post* aid and *ex ante* financial coverage of terrorism risk. *ex ante pre funded* mechanisms will aim at providing foreseeable, efficient and possibly rapid allocation of the resources destined to the compensation of terror-related losses, although the risk of crowding out private market initiatives will need to be addressed. *ex post* solutions will often be motivated by the wish to enforce a certain degree of redistributive justice[41], while governments would retain flexibility on the modalities of the aid it provides. It will however need to take into consideration various potential drawbacks, and mainly crowding out effects on insurance and induced disincentives on mitigation.

b) **Direct (explicit) vs. Indirect (implicit) modalities of intervention:**

Indirect modalities ⇨ to facilitate the re-emergence of private markets; governments may adopt certain policy actions, such as fiscal, accounting and regulatory measures aimed at facilitating the raising and reserving of capital by insurers involved in catastrophe insurance lines.

Government as the **primary insurer** ⇨ to offer insurance coverage directly to policyholders; this is the most comprehensive, but also invasive (in terms of crowding out effects), form of direct government intervention. Such public intervention would most probably be motivated by specific political context with regard to terrorism.

Government as the **reinsurer of last resort** ⇨ to provide a backstop to private sector exposures; governmental backing may take the form of excess of loss (XL) or stop-loss reinsurance coverage. The backstop facility may be offered free of charge by the government but subject to some degree of recoupment (as under the US TRIA) or may be paid for (as in other OECD schemes).

Government as the **lender of last resort** ⇨ to provide easy access for the insurance and reinsurance industries to the necessary liquidity after the occurrence of a major insured loss.

---

2. The OECD countries' terrorism compensation schemes: some lessons to be drawn[42]

In order to proceed with a comparative analysis of the different solutions experienced by OECD member countries, the following specific features shall be taken into account: basic structure of the scheme; limitation of exposure of private sector; duration of government participation; cost of government coverage; voluntary or mandatory nature of the scheme; minimum sum insured; coverage of CBRN terrorist attacks; lines covered and pricing mechanism. The institutional responses they have given, before and after the September 11 events, to the issue of terrorism risk coverage diverge in many respects, even if it shall be recognised that most of them involve a partnership between the public and the private sectors, with some degree of *ex ante* government participation in the financial management of terrorism risk exposures.

2.1. Basic structure of the national schemes

In Australia, the Australian Reinsurance Pool Corporation (ARPC) – a hybrid pool/post funded scheme – was established in 2003 by the Terrorism Insurance Act; the relevant legislation overrides terrorism exclusion clauses in eligible insurance contracts and eligible terrorism risks can be reinsured with ARPC.

In Austria, the Österreichischer Versicherungspool zur Deckung von Terrorrisiken was created on October 1, 2002 by the Verband der Versicherungsunternehmen Österreichs (VVO, the Austrian insurance association) as a purely private co-reinsurance pool.

The French GAREAT is a reinsurance pool offering reinsurance protection to direct insurers provided that they cede the terrorism risk forming part of all qualifying policies within their portfolio. The French State acts as reinsurer of last resort, offering unlimited protection through the *Caisse Centrale de Réassurance (*CCR).

EXTREMUS Versicherungs-AG, a specialist insurance company with a share capital of €50 million writing only large property risk against terrorism, was established in Germany in September 2002. EXTREMUS benefits from a limited participation offered by the German State.

The Nederlandse Herverzekeringsmaatschappij voor Terrorismeschaden (NHT), established in 2002, is a dedicated reinsurance company writing terrorism risks in the Netherlands. A "Terrorism Cover Clause" was added to all new and/or amendable policies providing for overall terrorism exposures to be limited to €1 billion per year. Pursuant to an agreement with the Government, if needed, emergency legislation will restrict terrorism exposures in non-amendable life insurance policies to conform to the overall NHT exposure limit of €1 billion.

In Spain, terrorism is traditionally part of a series of risks known as "extraordinary risks", which have special insurance treatment within a system that includes other political risks and natural catastrophes. Coverage for extraordinary risks in certain classes of insurance (see below) is mandatory and it is available from the Consorcio de Compensación de Seguros (CCS). All extraordinary risks can legally be covered by private insurance companies. Otherwise, CCS will automatically take charge of the extended cover. In practice, the private market does not directly cover those risks, thus CCS is the direct insurer[43]. CCS also acts as a warranty fund when a private insurer can no longer fulfil its obligations, following bankruptcy, for example. CCS is supported by an unlimited State warranty if the losses are above its own capacity for payment, though as yet this has never been necessary.

Pool Re is a mutual reinsurance company authorised to transact reinsurance business in the United Kingdom. The scheme covers losses resulting from an Act of Terrorism, as defined in the enabling Act of Parliament, the Reinsurance (Acts of Terrorism) Act 1993. Pool Re's Retrocession Agreement with HM Treasury provides funding in the event that it exhausts all its financial resources following claim payments. The government, therefore, is acting as lender of last resort.

In the United States, pursuant to the Terrorism Risk Insurance Act of 2002 (TRIA), while insurers are required to make available, in certain lines of commercial property and casualty insurance policies, coverage for losses arising from an act of terrorism – as defined under Section

102 of the Act -, a special risk-sharing arrangement has been set up by the federal government to limit market exposure. In particular, the federal government offers a backstop facility aimed at limiting private sector exposure that is not pre-funded, but subject to recoupment.

It is worth noting that the French and UK plans create an explicit reinsurance pool, into which reinsurance premia are pre-paid, and from which compensation for losses is received (including the additional support provided by the government as insurer of last resort). This creates an automatic mutualisation of the risk, which moderates the risks retained by the insurance firms. In contrast, the United States TRIA plan creates no *ex ante* pool, thus requiring the primary insurers to generate their own mechanisms for risk sharing. This can be seen as a positive feature if it allows the private markets to develop efficient mechanisms for risk sharing, or as a negative feature if turns out that the private markets are unable to develop such risk-sharing structures for terrorism risks.

2.2. Limitation of exposure of private sector

While participation in government backed plans reduces firms' exposure, it still leaves varying amounts of the risk to be held in an industry pool or by the firm directly. In Germany for instance, there are limits to the government's retention at the highest risk tier. In contrast, in the revised Pool Re plan in the United Kingdom, the risk of individual insurers is now capped per event and per annum, with the cap levels depending on the firm's market share. In France, insurance firms face losses proportional to the total losses to be paid by pool members, but the French government retains all the risk at the highest tier. The US legislation provides for an industry-wide maximum retention amount, while the insurance industry and federal government's share of losses is also capped to a combined annual amount, beyond which neither the government nor the insurers are responsible for paying claims.

Overall, the greater the amount of risk transferred from the private sector by the government plan, the greater that plan's contribution to the revival of the terrorism insurance market may be, but also the greater the extent to which it might crowd out future private market activity[44]. In this context, it is worth noting that in most plans the private sector exposure increases over time[45]. More generally, a balanced approach between the role assigned respectively to the insurance industry, financial markets and the government will avoid discouraging the private sector from developing effective responses to the new challenges posed by terrorism risk.

2.3. Duration of government participation

Government participation is permanent only in Spain, while in all other countries it is designed as temporary. Some countries have set a terminal date, such as France (currently until end-2006), Germany (currently end of 2005), The Netherlands and the United States (currently until end-2005). In Australia and in the United Kingdom no terminal date has been set, but government programs are subject to periodic assessment and revision.

It may prove difficult to terminate such schemes, in particular if terminating the government plan means switching from a high level of government support to none at all on a particular date. The most operational option may be that of gradual reduction of the government role when appropriate, through an increase in industry retention, and periodic assessment of the scheme. This allows as much flexibility as possible in the decision to extend, or not, its duration, which appears relevant given that the evolution of terrorism risk and of the market financial capacity and technical ability to manage it in the future are currently not predictable. Decision about the future of the national scheme should be made early enough to allow insurers and reinsurers to take this key parameter into account when defining the conditions of policy renewals.

2.4. *Voluntary or mandatory nature of the scheme*

The voluntary or mandatory nature of the sheme is a multifaceted problem (see Box 3.2, below). In one country (the United States), insurance companies have to make terrorism insurance available on certain lines of commercial property and casualty insurance, but policyholders, with limited exceptions, are free to turn the offer down. In the United Kingdom, Pool Re members are required to provide terrorism coverage to policyholders if requested.

Box 3.2. **Mandatory Nature of the Schemes**

National terrorism schemes vary with respect to their mandatory nature.

One should distinguish between:

- *Mandatory offer* of terrorism risk insurance coverage in certain lines ⇨ the United States.

- *Mandatory purchase* of terrorism risk insurance coverage in certain lines ⇨ Australia, France, Spain (in the United States only with respect to workers' compensation).

- *Mandatory participation* in terrorism risk insurance schemes ⇨ Spain and the United States.

In some countries *(e.g.,* Australia, France and Spain), terrorism insurance cover is compulsory for certain insurance classes. In a substantial number of countries (Austria, Germany, the Netherlands, United Kingdom) terrorism risk insurance coverage is marketed on a voluntary basis.

Another aspect concerns the voluntary or mandatory nature of the participation by insurers in the national scheme. Participation is voluntary in Australia, Austria, France[46], the Netherlands and the United Kingdom, while it is mandatory in Spain and in the United States (for insurers selling certain lines of commercial property and casualty insurance).

Mandating the purchase of terrorism insurance will allow to spread risks and collect premia over a larger base, thereby ensuring steady capacity building. It will also allow for eliminating risks of adverse selection, and ultimately limiting the dependency on government support after a disaster. These advantages will however need to be balanced with possible drawbacks such as moral hazard problems (*i.e.* the lack of incentive to prevent attacks or mitigate losses due to insurance protection[47]), a possible increase in premium regulation and standardisation and rigidity that would disconnect premia from the actual risk and generate cross subsidisation. It may as well constrain insurers to cover risks they may otherwise not have insured, entail crowding out effects for alternative types of cover such as self-insurance and, more generally, restrict the ability of buyers to choose the mode and extent of coverage according to their own circumstances[48] and given that risk exposures may vary among regions, industries, entities, etc. The relevance of an insurance coverage requirement will therefore need to be assessed according to the specific features and possible shortcomings of each national terrorism insurance market. It may, for instance, be considered in priority in countries where terrorism insurance penetration is low. Lastly, the decision to require insurance cover and its political acceptability will ultimately depend on the social and historical context, and, in particular, on past exposure of the population to terrorism.

2.5. Minimum sum insured

Of all the countries that have implemented a special plan to cover terrorism risks, only France and Germany have introduced a minimum sum insured, in the amount of € 6 million and € 25 million respectively.

2.6. Coverage of CBRN terrorist attacks

CBRN risks are generally considered as uninsurable, and purely private insurance solutions to cover them appear to be very limited in OECD countries at present. While they are covered under the schemes implemented in The Netherlands, Spain, United Kingdom (since 2003) and the United States[49] under strict conditions, CBRN attacks are excluded from coverage in Austria and Germany, and only partial coverage is offered in Australia and France.

Box 3.3. Coverage of CBRN risks under existing national terrorism compensation scheme

Austria	No
Australia	Partial: all nuclear causes excluded.
France	Partial: exclusion of damage caused by conventional weapons or devices designed to explode by means of the structural modification of the atomic nucleus (with the exception of «dirty» bombs, whose effects are covered).
Germany	No
Netherlands	Yes
Spain	Yes
United Kingdom	Yes (since 2003)
United States	Yes (to the extent that the underlying insurance policy covers such losses)

The coverage of CBRN risks for certain insurance lines is currently being debated in several countries. In France, for instance, the government has just refused to extend the protection against "dirty bombs' provided by GAREAT (minimum sum insured: 6 million Euros) to small enterprises and individuals, but remains open to further discussions.

Governments may wish to consider the issue of CBRN risk, address the issue of gaps in insurance coverage when they exist, and work in cooperation with the industry towards developing stable solutions to guarantee their coverage[50].

2.7. Lines covered

The September 11 events and the Madrid bombing showed that terrorist acts may entail claims in many different lines of insurance. It is therefore crucial to understand which segments of the insurance market need to be complemented. Most of the schemes set up in OECD member countries focus on large commercial property and business interruption risks. While this is the common denominator of all institutional arrangements, different priorities as regards other lines have emerged in OECD countries. In the United States, coverage under TRIA is also extended to workers compensation; in Australia the coverage offered by ARPC extends to liability arising from ownership or occupation of eligible properties; the Spanish system includes coverage for personal injury (independently from the compensation funds for the victims of terrorism); lastly, in the Netherlands, the scheme covers all lines (life and non-life) with the exception of aviation hull and aircraft liability.

One should note that the shrinkage of insurance coverage for terrorism risks after the events of September 11 mostly concerned commercial lines, while insurance companies in several

OECD member countries continued to offer coverage in personal lines, without amending the existing conditions to exclude terrorism risks. Moreover, several OECD countries have set up special compensation funds for victims of terrorism or other violent crimes, covering certain consequences of terrorist acts, *e.g.*: the Austrian *Verbrechensopfergesetz* (Act on granting aid to crime victims, VOG), the French FGTI (Compensation Fund for Victims of Terrorist Actions and other Offences), the German *Opferentschadigungsgesetz* (Victim Compensation Act, OEG), the compensation mechanism set up in Italy by laws n. 446/1980, n. 302/1990 and n. 407/1998, the Spanish compensation system governed by Regulation on Benefits and Compensation to Victims of Terrorist Crimes (RATV) and by the Act n. 32/1999, and the US September 11 Victims Compensation Fund of 2001[51].

At an international level, the European Convention on the Compensation of Victims of Violent Crimes was signed in Strasbourg on 24 November, 1983. More recently, the Council of the European Union adopted a Directive on compensation to crime victims on 29 April, 2004[52], on the basis of a proposal from the Commission, whose enactment had been called for by the European Council in the "Declaration on Combating Terrorism" of 25 March, 2004. The Directive will ensure that by 1 July 2005, each Member State has a national scheme in place which guarantees fair and appropriate compensation to victims of crime. Secondly, the Directive ensures that, in practice, compensation is easily accessible regardless of where in the EU a person becomes the victim of a crime by creating a system for cooperation between national authorities, which should be operational by 1 January 2006.

In light of the above, proper coordination should be ensured among the existing mechanisms for the compensation of victims of terrorist attacks, so as to avoid duplication of efforts.

2.8. Pricing mechanism

Generally speaking, primary insurers in the countries reviewed have wide discretion to set the premia they charge their customers for terrorism coverage. As regards reinsurance premia charged by national schemes to their members, they may be linked to different parameters. Under the UK Pool Re scheme, damage rates charged by the pool are related to geographic zones (the United Kingdom being divided into three types of areas according to the level of risk, except for business interruption for which there is a single rate). In France, the reinsurance premium charged by the government plan is proportional to the total property coverage premium charged to the policyholder by the primary insurer; but this still leaves the primary insurer in control of the premia it charges its clients.

Failure to apply risk-based premia in most government reinsurance programs may create disincentives to mitigation[53] as well as inefficient distortions (since the private sector is in a better position than governments to set rates[54]). Flat pricing is however motivated by some other factors. For example, the government may fear that risk-based pricing, by revealing the government's information with respect to the locations and structures it knows to be at the greatest risk, would be used by the terrorists themselves. The government might also consider it inequitable to charge higher premia for the higher risks, given that international terrorism targeting the nation as a whole will often be the source of the risks.

3. National vs. international solutions

To date, risk sharing arrangements to cover property and casualty losses resulting from terrorism have been entered into at a national level. Meanwhile, some sort of international cooperation has been viewed by some as a desirable target, taking into account that larger mutualisation and diversification could have a positive effect on prices, efficient allocation of capacity and availability of coverage. Moreover, a coherent international approach to terrorism risk insurance coverage across jurisdictions might be welcomed by those insureds who conduct their business at a multinational level (none of the pools currently in operation provide international coverage[55]).

Against this background, in November 2001, the Comité Européen des Assurances (CEA) made a proposal for a European terrorism risk insurance solution based on a layered system combining cover by the private (direct insurance and reinsurance) and by the public (supplementary guarantee by governments) sectors. The novelty of the proposal laid in the replacement of the government layer provided in various national schemes by an international public layer of compensation. Each government intervention would not be limited to the coverage of its local risks, but public resources would be combined at European Community (EU) or European Economic Area (EEA) level. This proposal has, however, not been implemented, for lack of sufficient political will. At the OECD level, discussions within the OECD Task Force on Terrorism Insurance and the Insurance Committee on an international cooperation scheme to compensate for mega-terrorism losses revealed marked differences in countries' views on such initiative. An international scheme may not be equally useful or desirable to all OECD Member countries, and it may find most interest at the regional level. Discussions thus concluded that international/regional *ex ante* cooperation may be called for *between interested countries*, and that further examination of the feasibility of such a mechanism may be worth pursuing *by these countries*[56].

Conclusion

Several years after the WTC attacks, the proper role of government in the financial compensation for terror-related losses remains a highly controversial issue. OECD countries have different and sometimes diverging views on the appropriate level of government intervention in the terrorism insurance markets, while the relevance of various types of direct and indirect government intervention are still being discussed at national level.

Prior to or after 2001, seven OECD countries have set up permanent or temporary private-public partnerships for the compensation of terrorism related losses. Such flexible public-private schemes, which involve in all but one case a layered approach to terrorism risk coverage, appear as a promising institutional arrangement under current circumstances to address the potential magnitude of losses involved but also the generalised uncertainty characterising modern terrorism. Under this broad framework, many different compensation systems can emerge and have emerged.

Depending on how terrorism risks evolve over time, the level of the call for government intervention may decrease, in consideration of the development of private sector solutions. Among other things, time will allow the industry to further recover and expand its capital base, and maybe to develop better capabilities to model terrorism risks, as far as this is possible. At present, some OECD countries have already renewed the government backed programme or will be considering doing so in the near future. To our knowledge, governments of other OECD members not mentioned in this chapter have not taken any major initiative in the field of terrorism compensation.

The first assessments of the terrorism compensation schemes implemented after September 11 in particular highlight that in most countries, government participation, possibly as reinsurer or lender of last resort, may act as a *stimulation* for the private sector to come back into the terrorism insurance market after having suffered heavy losses. Government participation may also be a *complement* to private market capacity, through the coverage of extreme risks that markets would not be capable to meet. It may therefore encourage the restoration of terrorism insurance availability and affordability, increase terrorism insurance penetration, as well as provide some stabilisation of market conditions. However, arguments have been made that government backed schemes might slow down the emergence of purely private sector alternatives, such as the development of mutual reinsurance pools for instance[57]. The extent of crowding out of private markets depends on a number of specific features of the national compensation mechanism, most of which are highlighted above.

There is certainly no ready-made solution that governments should adopt to solve the problem of terrorism risk coverage, and each arrangement will have to be tailored to the specific needs of each market. The success, since the mid-fifties, of the Spanish Consorcio, that stands out as an original solution among all other OECD country systems based on a layered approach to compensation, is an illustration of the singularity of each nation in its approach of the new challenges raised by modern terrorism risk.

What part of this risk will be assumed by individual and commercial policy holders, the (re)insurance sector, potential investors on the capital markets, and the general population of taxpayers, will eventually depend on national choices and trade-offs based on historical factors such as the past exposure to terrorism, economic structures, social and political organisation, values and acceptability, as well as projections on welfare optimisation in various institutional scenarios. The reliability of such projections however varies; in particular, the reactions of all actors at stake are hardly predictable in case of major institutional changes[58], while even information and data on the *current* national terrorism insurance markets – and on the scope of alternative coverage – remains scarce. The merely partial assessments that could be made available more than three years after the 9/11 attacks may call for more data and information collection, further analysis and planning and more systematic exchange of information on relevant market and regulatory developments at international level, as a basis for informed policy decision. More specifically, the possibility for fine-tuning the various features of existing compensation mechanisms as well as implementing some possible degree of indirect government intervention in order to spur private initiatives, while avoiding a possible sudden shrinkage in insurance availability, deserve further consideration.

Notes

1   This chapter is indebted to Jaffee, D. (2005), *The role of government in the coverage of terrorism risks* (see infra, Part III Chapter 8) and Cooke, J. (2005), *The coverage of terrorism risks at national level* (see infra, Part III Chapter 9).

2   *"Terrorism attacks the values that lie at the heart of the Charter of the United Nations: respect for human rights; the rule of law; rules of war that protect civilians; tolerance among peoples and nations; and the peaceful resolution of conflict."* *A More Secure World: Our Shared Responsibility* Report of the High-level Panel on Threats, Challenges and Change, United Nations (December 2004), p. 47.

3   On the complex issues raised by the enforcement of counter-terrorism measures and its impact on civil liberties see e.g. Viscusi, W. Kip and R. J. Zeckhauser (January 2003), *Sacrificing Civil Liberties to Reduce Terrorism Risks*. Harvard Law and Economics

Discussion Paper No. 401; and KSG Working Papers Series No. RWP03-017. *http://ssrn.com/abstract=380620.*

4 See Dixon, L., J. Arlington, S. Carroll, D. Lakdawalla, R. Reville, D. Adamson (2004), *Issues and Options for Government Intervention in the Market for Terrorism Insurance*, *Occasional Paper*, RAND Center for Terrorism Risk Management Policy, p. 3-4; this report can also be referred to for a definition of economic efficiency and equity.

5 See the discussion in: Koch, B. A. (ed.) (2004), *Terrorism, Tort Law and Insurance. A Comparative Survey*, Springer.

6 Note that private insurance and reinsurers covered more than half of the total payout of the compensation system after 9/11.

7 See: Dixon, L. *et al.* (2004), p. xi; Kunreuther, Howard and E. Michel-Kerjan (Fall 2004), *PolicyWatch: Challenges for Terrorism Risk Insurance in the United States*, Journal of Economic Perspectives, Vol. 18, Number 4, p. 202.

8 See e.g.: Jaffee, Dwight and T. Russell (2003), *Markets under Stress: The Case of Extreme Event Insurance*, in Arnott, Greenwald, Kanbur and Nalebuff (eds.) Economics for an Imperfect World: Essays in Honor of Joseph Stiglitz, MIT Press.

9 Some OECD countries most expose to terrorism had already paved the way for such initiatives years before 2001.

10 "*Compensation systems in other settings typically do not have implications for national security. However, the type of compensation system chosen for losses from terrorism may feed back into the frequency and effectiveness of terrorist attacks. Incentives to take precautions may (or (...) may not) reduce vulnerability to attacks. Policies that reduce panic, social fragmentation, economic uncertainty, or economic ripple effects will reduce the impact of terrorist attacks. Reduced vulnerability to an attack and reduced impact from an attack may discourage terrorists from carrying out the attack in the first place.*" Dixon, L. *et al.* (2004), *cit.*, p. 4.

11 See *e.g.* Pillar, P. (2001), *Terrorism and U.S. Foreign Policy*. Washington, D.C.: Brookings Institution Press; see also: National Commission on Terrorist Attacks Upon the United States (July 2004), *The 9/11 Commission Report*, Washington, D.C., *e.g.* p. 375-377.

12 According to Levmore, S., K. Logue (2003), *Insuring Against Terrorism – and Crime*, 102 Michigan Law Review 268, governments should cover losses from terrorism because doing so would lead them to carefully consider the costs and benefits of their foreign policies.

13 See : Dixon, L. and R. Reville (2005), RAND Center for Terrorism Risk Management Policy, *National Security and Compensation Policy for Terrorism Losses*, in *Catastrophic Risks and Insurance*, Policy Issues in Insurance N°8, OECD: "We suggest (...) that terrorism insurance (as well as direct government compensation as in the 9/11 Victims' Compensation Fund) ought to be considered part of the portfolio of policy measures available to policymakers to counter the threat of terrorism. Particularly in light of evidence that recent trends in terrorism suggest increased risk of economically-motivated attacks against private sector targets, government support of the compensation system may be a means of protecting financial assets in a manner that is complementary to the physical protection of targets and the direct disruption of terrorist activities".

14   Tritak, John S. (2002) in Guy Carpenter, *The terrorism risk, can it be managed?*, p. 18.

15   After September 2001, concerns related to international competition also raised the issue of the opportunity of government intervention: in countries where there was a shortage of affordable terrorism insurance, it was feared that national businesses were at competitive disadvantage, as compared to their competitors in other countries where government backing was allowing access to more affordable and more widely available terrorism insurance coverage. See U.S. General Accounting Office (GAO) (February 2005), *Catastrophe risk: US and European approaches to insure natural catastrophe and terrorism risk*, p. 42.

16   For a summary of policy options, their advantages and drawbacks, see Dixon, L. *et al.* (2004), p. 4; for arguments in favour of government implication in terrorism compensation mechanisms, see for instance Michel-Kerjan, E., B. Pedell (2005), *Terrorism Risk Coverage in the Post-9/11 Era: A Comparison of New Public-Private Partnerships in France, Germany and the U.S.*, The Geneva Papers on Risk and Insurance, 30, (p. 144-170); See also on the US case: Kunreuther, H. and E. Michel-Kerjan (2004), p. 201-214. For arguments in favour of government intervention with regard to critical infrastructure protection, see Orszag, Peter (September 4, 2003), *Critical Infrastructure Protection and the Private Sector: The Crucial Role of Incentives*; Testimony before the Subcommittee on Cybersecurity, Science and Research & Development and the Subcommittee on Infrastructure and Border Security, House Select Committee on Homeland Security.

17   See Jaffee, Dwight and T. Russell (2003); See also *e.g.* Brown, Jeffrey R., B. H. Jenn and R. S. Kroszner (October 2002), *Federal Terrorism Risk Insurance*. NBER Working Paper No. W9271.

18   For more information on the industry capacity issue, see infra, Part II Chapter 1 on insurability.

19   In a recent article entitled *Insuring Against Terrorism: The Policy Challenge* (NBER Working Paper No. w11038, January 2005), Ken Smetters argued that mostly unfettered insurance and capital markets are capable of insuring large terrorism losses. According to this author, if there is any 'failure', it rests with government tax, accounting and regulatory policies that have made it costly for insurers to hold surplus capital. Smetters maintains that government policy has also hindered the implementation of instruments that could securitise the underlying risks and that correcting these policies would likely enable private insurers to cover both terrorism and war risks. In other words, the 'market failures' that appear to justify government intervention into the terrorism insurance market are viewed by the author as 'government failures'. See also: Gron, A., A. O. Sykes (2003), *Terrorism and Insurance Markets: A Role for the Government as Insurer?*, 36 Indiana Law Review 447.

20   In Germany for instance, the building of reserves for terrorism risk coverage has been exempted from corporate income taxes in May 2003 (although exemption is capped). See Michel-Kerjan, E and B. Pedell (2005), p. 12.

21   Surplus impairment risk has been identified as an important obstacle to the insurability of terrorism risks in countries like the United States for instance: "Insurers are *not allowed to post reserves for losses that have not occurred.* Therefore, insurers are not allowed to post reserves to cover catastrophe losses from natural perils or terrorism until they actually occur. As a result, a terrorism loss would deplete an insurer's capital and surplus base intended for the security of all policyholders". Macdonald, James W. (Summer 2004), *Terrorism, Insurance, and TRIA: Are We Asking the Right Questions?* The John Liner Review, Vol. 18

No. 2, p. 7. A proposal has been made to change US tax laws and accounting standards to allow insurers to set aside funds on a tax-deductible basis to establish reserves for potential future natural catastrophes or terrorist attacks. Such measure is however controversial. See GAO (2005), p. 7 and 25. As of 2004, accounting standards and tax laws in various countries covered by the GAO report (France, Germany as mentioned above, Italy, Spain, Switzerland, United Kingdom) allowed insurance companies to establish tax-deductible "catastrophe" or "equalisation" reserves. However, the IRFS 4 issued in March 2004 by the IASB includes guidance that prohibits the use of catastrophe and equalisation reserves. The implementation of this guidance is contrasted for the time being.

22   On the role of alternative risk transfer and alternative risk financing tools in the management of terrorism risks see also infra, Part II Chapter 2, *Financial market solutions for terrorism risk*.

23   For more details, see U.S. General Accounting Office (GAO) (September 24, 2003), *Catastrophe Insurance Risks. Status of Efforts to Securitize Natural Catastrophe and Terrorism Risk*, GAO-03-1033; and Jaffee, D. (2005), infra, in which two main accounting issues are highlighted. First, "accounting standards (….) do *not* allow insurance firms to reflect the risk transfer achieved by *non-indemnity* catastrophe bonds on their financial reports". See also GAO (2005). Second, "new Accounting Standards Board proposal (….) clarifies accounting rules for *special purpose vehicles* (SPVs), including those that hold the government bond collateral for catastrophe bonds. The proposal enlarges the conditions under which the assets and liabilities within the SPV must be consolidated on the books of the issuing firm (…).The change will be detrimental to the use of catastrophe bonds by insurance companies if it is determined to apply in these cases".

24   Thus, in case of an attack, most risks would be uninsured and the government would be called upon to intervene *ex post* to provide compensation on an *ad hoc* basis. "*Even though these options [of indirect government involvement] attempt to place most of the risk for terrorism losses on the private sector, they may end up shifting most of the risk to the public sector because the purchase of insurance may not be widespread even with these fixes. [In the US] the precedent set by the 9/11 attacks will make it difficult for the political process to let those who do not buy insurance go uncompensated. Expectations of government compensation may in turn reduce incentives to buy insurance and would undermine this approach.*" Dixon, L. *et al.* (2004), p. 24.

25   See Jaffee, D. (2005), infra.

26   This chapter focuses on medium and long term government intervention. It should nevertheless be emphasised that governments in Europe and in the United States have granted direct financial support (indemnity schemes at discounted rates in particular) to airlines companies in order to avoid a crisis in the international airline industry after 9/11. Although it was meant to be limited in time, government backing lasted for several months in Europe, and is scheduled to expire in August 2005 in the United States. Such direct intervention arose many critics, on the grounds that it may have crowded out potential private risk mutualisation initiatives, as well as generate serious competition issues.

27   See: Sommer, H. (2003), *Providing Compensation for Harm Caused by Terrorism: Lessons Learned in the Israeli Experience*, 36 Indiana Law Review 335.

28   The Consorcio nevertheless strongly relies on private market mechanisms. The extraordinary risks coverage is offered via policies underwritten by private insurance companies, and funding is based on premia paid by policyholders.

29   *"Policymakers, thus, do not have to view the choice between private insurance and public compensation programs as an either/or but can design hybrid systems that combine the attractive features of both."* Dixon, L. *et al.* (2004), p. 17.

30   Gollier, C. (February 1, 2001), *Insurability*. Paper presented at the NBER Insurance Group Workshop. Cambridge, MA.

31   Limits and drawbacks of government intervention in insurance markets are emphasised by: Smetters, K. (January 2005)*., Insuring Against Terrorism: The Policy Challenge*, NBER Working Paper No. w11038; Gron, A., A. O. Sykes (2003); Priest, G. (1996), *The Government, the Market, and the Problem of Catastrophic Loss*, Journal of Risk and Uncertainty, Volume 12, Numbers 2-3, p. 219-237. See also: Levmore, Saul and K. D. Logue (May 2003), *Insuring Against Terrorism - and Crime*. Michigan Law and Economics Research Paper No. 03-005; University of Chicago, Public Law Working Paper No. 47; U Chicago Law & Econ, Olin Working Paper No. 189. *http://ssrn.com/abstract=414144.*

32   The experience of OECD countries in this respect seems to be quite contrasted. For instance, the possible ultimate operating cost entailed by the management of TRIA could be rather high (estimated at USD14 million for 2003-2005, in the absence of claims filed under the scheme - see Congressional Budget Office (CBO) (January 2005), *Federal Terrorism Reinsurance: An Update*, available online at: http://www.cbo.gov), as compared to the low operation costs of Pool Re in the United Kingdom, or of the Spanish Consorcio for instance.

33   See the discussion in Brown, Jeffrey R., J. D. Cummins, C. M. Lewis and R. Wei (March 2, 2004), *An Empirical Analysis of the Economic Impact of Federal Terrorism Reinsurance, http://ssrn.com/abstract=516483.* On crowding out effects and the cost of TRIA in the United States see CBO (2005).

34   In this respect, the Spanish compensation mechanism, based on the subsidiary principle, is nevertheless radically different from the Israeli solution for instance.

35   See Jaffee, D. (2005), infra.

36   Mitigation measures may comprise: moving operation to a less exposed location, improving security systems, protecting computerised information, etc. see CBO (2005), p. 13.

37   See: Kunreuther, H., G. Heal (2003), *Interdependent Security*, *Journal of Risk and Uncertainty*, Vol. 26, Nos. 2 and 3.

38   Lakdawalla, D., G. Zanjani (July 2004), *Insurance, Self-Protection, and the Economics of Terrorism*, RAND Center for Terrorism Risk Management and Policy, Working Paper WR-171-ICJ.

39   See e.g.: Coase, R. H. (October 1974), *The Lighthouse in Economics*, Journal of Law & Economics, University of Chicago Press, vol. 17(2), p. 357-376.

40   Buchanan, J. M. (1975), *The Samaritan's Dilemma,* In *Altruism, Morality and Economic Theory*, edited by E.S. Phelps, p. 71-85. New York: Russell Sage Foundation.

41   See Dixon, L. *et al.* (2004), p. 4.

42   For more detailed analysis on OECD terrorism compensation schemes, see Cooke, J. (2005), infra, as well as, for instance, Partner Re (May 2004), *Terrorism Insurance. Pools & Market Solutions in Europe.*

43   See footnote 28.

44   For instance, on possible crowding out effects of TRIA in the United States, see CBO (2005).

45   One should note that in most countries, government participation, although vital when triggered, is not triggered in a great majority of scenarios. Government participation has, for instance, never been required in the long history of Pool Re in the United Kingdom. In the United States, the TRIA scheme may not be triggered in 98% of scenarios (because of high retention levels). Even if triggered, the cost for government under this scheme may be limited by the post loss recoupment funding mechanism. See Hartwig, R. (Insurance Information Institute) (October 2004), *The Cost of Terrorism, How Much Can We Afford?*

46   Although not mandatory, participation into the GAREAT scheme is nevertheless quasi automatic in France.

47   This classic insurance shortcoming can however be reduced through the enforcement of deductibles and the promotion of risk-reducing activities that insurers themselves have an interest to develop in order to alleviate the costs of attacks. See Orszag, P. (2003).

48   See for instance the summary provided by the RAND Center for Terrorism Risk management Policy (2004), *Issues and Options for Government Intervention in the Market for Terrorism Insurance*, p. 16. For arguments in favour of a requirement to purchase terrorism insurance, see for instance Kunreuther, H. and E. Michel-Kerjan (2004).

49   It shall be noted, however, that TRIA covers CBRN losses to the extent that the underlying insurance policy covers such losses. In some states, regulators have prohibited exclusions of CBRN losses, but according to the available data, nearly all insurers exclude coverage for CBRN attacks whenever they can, regardless of the magnitude of loss. As a result, CBRN coverage in the United States varies considerably across States. See: Marsh, Inc. (April 2004), *Marketwatch: Property Terrorism Insurance 2004*, Marsh & McLennan Companies.

50   While the CBRN threat may remain the most serious, it should be highlighted that other risks, such as the cyber terrorism risk, is also raising much concern. This risk remains excluded from the Pool Re cover for instance.

51   See: Koch, B. A. (ed.) (2004), *Terrorism, Tort Law and Insurance. A Comparative Survey*, Springer.

52   Council Directive 2004/80/EC of 29 April 2004 relating to compensation to crime victims, in Official Journal of the European Union, L 261 (2004), p. 0015 – 0018.

53   This point, however, remains highly controversial in the literature.

54   See for instance Jerry, R.H. II (2002), *Insurance, Terrorism and 9/11: Reflections on Three Threshold Questions*, in 9 Connecticut Insurance Law Journal, p. 118.

55   See GAO (2005), p. 54.

56   See also infra, Part II Chapter 4 on *Compensation of mega-terrorism risk*.

57   See CBO (2005), p. 15, 17. Yet, it will prove difficult to assess the possible disincentives entailed by government-backed schemes while they remain in operation.

58   See for the United States, for instance: CBO (2005); Kunreuther, H., E. Michel-Kerjan, E. (2005), infra.

Chapter 4

COMPENSATION OF MEGA-TERRORISM RISK

Introduction

"According to security specialists, terrorists could at some stage attempt to explode a nuclear device or release contagious viruses in a populous metropolitan area (…). An attack against, for instance, New York City using a nuclear weapon could leave most of the metropolitan area uninhabitable for years. The direct impact would reduce the country's production potential by about 3%, that is, the equivalent of a small OECD country's GDP. (…) In view of this, preparedness should be seen as essential, even if the possibility of such an attack is considered as remote"[1]. Similar warnings against the potential for large-scale or "mega" terrorist attacks, possibly using non conventional weapons, are periodically issued by intelligence agencies and other sources of expertise on terrorism. The fact that nations should be prepared for attacks of comparable or greater magnitude was also a key lesson from the analysis of the September 2001 events[2]. These attacks have called for a complete reassessment of loss scenarios for potential future attacks, to include Probable Maximum Loss (PML) considered as unthinkable in the past. The compensation of losses that could result from a mega-terrorist attack raises policy and financial issues that may reach beyond national boundaries.

The success of a mega-terrorist attack would require a number of challenging conditions to be met, from the acquisition or fabrication of the required devices/substances to their activation or dissemination in the case of CBRN attacks for instance. Preparing to respond to smaller and more likely terrorism events remains a priority. Nevertheless, the potential social, economic and political impact of a mega-terrorist attack would be too broad for this threat to be ignored.

While OECD countries agree on the importance of the issues at stake (as set out in part 1 and 2 of this chapter), their views on how mega-terrorism should be addressed diverge. Starting from the assumptions that some member countries may not be able to cope at national level with the financial consequences of a mega-terrorism attack, the OECD Task Force on Terrorism Insurance and Insurance and Private Pensions Committee discussed the relevance and feasibility of some form of international compensation mechanism for mega-terrorism risks. Beyond the challenges and highly controversial issues that the establishment of an international safety net would raise, it clearly appeared that this option may find most interest at the regional level, while a number of countries would not be prepared to join such initiative (see part 3 of this chapter).

1. A mega-terrorist attack could have a devastating impact on economies and societies, thus programs organising adequate and rapid compensation may need to be considered to mitigate losses

There is no ready-to-use definition of mega-terrorism, and assessing the economic impact of large scale terrorist attacks is a highly complex exercise. Nevertheless, "orders of magnitude may be helpful to evaluate what governments would have to deal with"[3]. As a working hypothesis, a terrorist act resulting in USD 100 billion[4] of losses for instance (not mentioning the human cost), could certainly be qualified as a mega-terrorist act, as would potentially be a nuclear, radiological, chemical, or biological attack, such as the explosion of a dirty bomb, the spreading of poison gas, or large water contamination.

The figure of USD 100 billion is given by way of an example. The appreciation of what constitutes a mega-terrorist attack may nevertheless vary, depending for instance on the region/country targeted, and possibly on the level of protection that is available in the private insurance and reinsurance market, or on whether the attack may have lasting repercussions, such as in the case of nuclear and radiological attacks which long-tail consequences are highly difficult to measure, etc. Far smaller attacks may therefore well be considered as "mega-terrorism". It should also be emphasised that, beyond the magnitude of individual events, the potential increase in the frequency of terrorism events may as well have a debilitating effect on the economy and society.

Even if public risk awareness or concern remains low, the threat of mega-terrorism should be taken seriously[5] and concerns most, if not all, countries – to varying degrees. No terrorist act can be viewed as unthinkable anymore. Prevention of such risks – as of any terrorism risk – is of utmost priority. Several recent initiatives, including through co-operation of intelligence agencies, have strengthened prevention efforts and the fight against terrorism financing at national and international level. If loss prevention and mitigation are of crucial importance, it is no less important to help ensure some level of compensation if prevention were to fail. Beyond the human distress created by such events, the financial capacity to honour claims is a critical consideration to allow rapid recovery, and to mitigate potential systemic impact which may destabilise economies and societies.

2. In some OECD countries, the joint capacity of the private markets and of the government may not be sufficient to compensate for mega-terrorism without threatening national economic stability

Given the potential magnitude of losses involved, the financial compensation for mega-terrorism related losses may be problematic in some member countries. Compensation for mega-terrorism may go beyond the current technical and financial *capacity of the private (re)insurance sector.* In 2002, the OECD ministers were concerned by the shrinkage of affordable insurance cover for terrorism risks and its adverse effects on the economy, as well as by the issue of mega-terrorism coverage[6]. As of today, the insurance and reinsurance industry is still often reluctant to cover large terrorism risks[7] at prices that potential buyers may consider reasonably consistent with the risk incurred. Obviously, the greater the risk, the more problematic its coverage. The case of mega-terrorism therefore raises the most serious concerns.

Since end-2001, private (re)insurance capacity to cover terrorism risks has increased, terrorism risk modeling has become more sophisticated and government intervention has increased the affordability and availability of terrorism insurance. However, the *private insurance and reinsurance industries* may not by themselves be able, under current conditions, to absorb alone mega-terrorist attacks[8]. It should also be noted that, by virtue of coverage limitations/exclusions, the insurance industry may not be involved at all in the coverage of many of the most threatening types of mega-risks such as the risk of CBRN attacks, which is generally excluded from private insurance and reinsurance contracts. Above all, average terrorism insurance penetration remains low in several OECD countries. In these markets, only a small part of the risk would therefore be mutualised among insurers and the international reinsurance market in case of a major attack.

After the 2001 attacks, the idea emerged to transfer large-scale terrorism risks to *financial markets,* which were presented as a promising alternative to limited insurance capacity. However, capital markets instruments have not yet developed to the extent that they would be a substantial complement to insurance and reinsurance markets[9], and more work needs to be done in this area.

Lastly, even *governments* – at least some of them – might not be able to compensate for the financial cost of such an attack (or for the part of losses not covered by private mechanisms) without threatening national economic stability. Only the largest OECD member countries, up to a certain level of damages, would be able to cope with the losses entailed by a mega-terrorist attack.

Many other OECD countries may well face grave financial consequences should a mega-terrorist attack occur.

3. International/regional cooperation may be a solution for the compensation of mega-terrorist events in many countries; foreseeing such cooperation ex ante could minimise economic uncertainty and facilitate recovery efforts after an attack. Such a scheme may find most interest at the regional level, while some countries may not have the same incentives to join it

If a mega-terrorist attack were to strike a country which could not manage the necessary recovery efforts alone without endangering its general economic stability, other governments might offer financial assistance to the targeted country[10]. However, such an approach might translate into a non optimal allocation of resources and possible delays in recovery, due to the general lack of coordination that might follow a disaster and to the potential difficulty of organising coherent *ad hoc* international/regional support under emergency conditions. Moreover, any such *ex post* assistance would be entirely dependant on other countries' willingness to offer their cooperation after the attack.

A second option would be to design *ex ante* a *private* international/regional scheme. It could take the form of private reinsurance/coinsurance pools, covering terrorism exposures from all lines of insurance business[11] (aviation, worker compensation, etc.), or of a specialised reinsurance entity or "super mutual". Purely private risk sharing agreements could bring wider diversification and mutualisation, reduce the risk of insolvency and enhance information sharing, though they may not significantly expand the available aggregate market capacity for mega-terrorist events.

A third option would be to agree ex ante, on a voluntary basis, on a flexible system of international/regional co-operation based on a *public-private partnership*. The establishment of an international compensation scheme for mega-terrorism would add an international layer to current private-public multi-layer risk sharing agreements already established in some OECD countries to cover terrorism risks.

Multilayered private/public schemes already exist to cover the nuclear reactor risk, which may be comparable in magnitude[12] to that of a mega-terrorism attack. In the nuclear field, the Paris Convention and the Brussels Supplementary Convention for the compensation of losses resulting from the peaceful use of nuclear energy established a multi-layer risk sharing scheme, with a top layer organising an *ex post* funding by all parties to the Convention. Early in 2004, the OECD Council noted the revision of the nuclear Conventions which aimed at adapting the compensation scheme to current economic environment.

If such multi-layered risk-sharing scheme were to be considered to cover mega-terrorism risk, some key design aspects could include it being called into play only as a last resort safety net[13], in case of a very large-scale attack, with no pre-funding required from participating governments and the amount of contributions by the parties to the agreement after an attack being capped. Also, such agreement could remain temporary and its relevance could be reassessed periodically, in order to take into consideration the development of private markets capacity. However, preventing any international/regional governmental layer from "crowding out" the private sector should also be considered, as well as providing incentives for the private stakeholders to participate as far as possible in the terrorism insurance market[14].

The implementation of such a risk-sharing scheme, if considered, would encounter a number of complex technical and political obstacles. One of them would be how to ensure an effective bridge between the various reinsurance coverage or national schemes and the framework for international intervention: so far, eight OECD countries have set up either a permanent or temporary terrorism-specific compensation scheme, and each of them has different features, in particular regarding the maximum amount of compensation involved. Among other concerns might be the range of events to be covered and how non-signatory countries should be treated.

Moreover, the establishment of an international/regional scheme may not be equally useful or desirable to all OECD Member countries. Such a mechanism may find most interest at the regional level, while some countries may not have the same incentives to join such an agreement. Further examination as to whether mega-terrorism risk coverage might be effectively dealt with at an international level by interested parties may therefore be worth pursuing *by these parties*.

It is worth mentioning that a proposal for the setting up of such a multi-layered scheme was made in November 2001 by the *Comité Européen des Assurances* (CEA). The CEA proposed the creation of a European terrorism risk insurance solution based on a layered system combining cover by the private (direct insurance and reinsurance) and by the public (supplementary guarantee by governments) sectors. The scheme foresaw the addition of an international layer of compensation to those already existing in several EU countries[15]. This proposed scheme has, however, not been formalised or implemented, for lack of sufficient political will. A government-led initiative would by nature not suffer from the political handicap of the CEA proposal; nevertheless, the failure of such endeavour may be an element questioning the likelihood of an international solution to the compensation of mega-terrorism in the close future.

Conclusion

Future terror-related loss scenarios are extremely difficult to predict. Nevertheless, the demonstrated ability of terrorists to exploit the diffusion capacity of large critical networks and the potential use of non-conventional chemical, biological, radiological and nuclear weapons of mass destruction in particular, bring about the need to evaluate circumstances in which one or more terrorist acts cause catastrophic losses that exceed the capacity of usual sources of compensation. Because of the potential magnitude and unpredictability of damages that a mega-terrorist attack could cause, insurance and reinsurance companies are reluctant to carry the financial burden of large terrorism risk coverage while they keep the risk of accumulation of smaller but potentially correlated exposures under close control. Moreover, in some OECD countries, even the government may find itself overwhelmed by losses in case of a mega-terrorist attack, and the joint capacity of the private markets and of the government may not be sufficient to compensate for losses without threatening national economic stability. In these countries, international/regional cooperation designed *ex ante* could appear as an appealing solution under current circumstances. It could for instance take the form of a flexible scheme based on a public-private partnership.

However, also in the post September 2001 era, the issue of mega-terrorism risk compensation remains technically and politically difficult to address, and highly controversial. The discussions within the OECD Task Force on Terrorism Insurance and the Insurance and Private Pensions Committee on the feasibility and relevance of such an international cooperation mechanism to compensate for mega-terrorism losses emphasised that many technical obstacles and political hindrances would need to be overcome in order to implement such a scheme; above all, they brought to light marked differences in countries' interest in such initiative, since an international safety net may not be equally useful or desirable to all OECD Member countries. Discussions thus concluded that international/regional *ex ante* cooperation may be called for *between interested countries*, and that further investigations on the feasibility of such a scheme may be worth pursuing *by these countries*. However, to date there has been no evidence of the governments of any group of countries banding together to further investigate the feasibility of an international scheme.

Notes

1   OECD (June 2002*), OECD Economic Outlook n°71*.

2   See National Commission on Terrorist Attacks Upon the United States (July 22, 2004), *The 9/11 Commission Report*, p 364: "Americans have also been told to expect the worst: An attack is probably coming; it may be terrible". See also infra, Part II Chapter 1 on *Insurability of terrorism risk.*

3   OECD (2002).

4   As a background, it is, for instance, interesting to note that in 2003, four OECD countries had a GDP below USD100 billion, and seven OECD countries had a GDP below USD150 billion. See *OECD Fact Book 2005, Economic, environmental and Social Statistic*, OECD (2005).

5   See infra, Part II Chapter 1 on *Insurability of terrorism risk.*

6   See OECD Council at Ministerial Level, 15-16 May 2002: Final Communiqué.

7   When the provision of terrorism coverage is not compulsory.

8   See infra, Part II Chapter 1 on *Insurability of terrorism risk.*

9   See infra, Part II Chapter 2 on *Financial market solutions for terrorism risk.*

10   Public solidarity after the December 2004 tsunami that devastated South East Asia provides an example of such international cooperation.

11   Taking into consideration certain restrictions, such as the common exclusion of CBRN risks from private institutions/mechanisms coverage for instance; this again limits the relevance of such mechanisms for large-scale risks in particular.

12   It should however be emphasised that the nuclear reactor risk and the mega-terrorism risk have different features. In particular, risks related to nuclear reactor accidents are easier to model (the number of power plants is known and the potential losses that an accident could cause are broadly foreseeable), while the estimates of potential damages entailed by a mega-terrorism attack remain most often highly uncertain.

13   Unless potential coverage discrepancies with underlying layers, especially concerning CBRN risks, indicate the need for more direct participation.

14   Whereas governments in some OECD member countries have decided to step in and make commitments in order to secure the availability of sufficient insurance coverage for losses

caused by terrorist events, the demand for private risk-sharing alternatives or other innovations might be impeded by direct government involvement or the expectation that the government will provide post-event disaster aid. The same argument could be raised regarding the involvement of governments in the compensation process at international level. However, there is in practice little chance that the private markets would be willing to compete at such risk level and cover alone extreme terrorism risks in the foreseeable future.

15   According to the CEA, the scheme could be indicatively structured in four layers: (1) retention by the insured; (2) intervention by the direct insurer; (3) intervention by a private trans-European reinsurance pooling system combining insurers' and reinsurers' retentions up to the maximum of the combined capacity; (4) Governments intervention (by way of excess or stop loss) to take over after the pooling system's resources are exhausted, in a harmonised way between EU (European Union) or EEA (European Economic Area) Member States and through the production of a "certificate of cover" issued by the public authorities involved. The scheme would provide coverage for all the categories of risks resulting from terrorist acts, except aviation, marine and nuclear risks, which, according to the CEA, should be addressed separately.

Chapter 5

TERRORISM INSURANCE SCHEMES
IN OECD COUNTRIES (2005) : COMPARATIVE TABLES

Terrorism Insurance Schemes in OECD Countries (2005) – Comparative Table

(data current as of 1 May 2005)

Countries[1]	Australia	Austria	France	Germany	Netherlands	Spain	United Kingdom	United States
Name of scheme	ARPC (Australian Reinsurance Pool Corporation)	Österreichischer Versicherungspool zur Deckung von Terrorrisiken	GAREAT (Gestion de l'Assurance et de la Réassurance des Risques Attentats et Actes de Terrorisme)	EXTREMUS Versicherungs-AG	NHT (Nederlandse Herverzekeringsmaatschappij voor Terrorismeschaden)	CCS (Consorcio de Compensacion de Seguros)	Pool Re	TRIA (Terrorism Risk Insurance Act of 2002)
Date of establishment	July 2003	October 2002 (covering risks from January 2003)	December 2001 (covering risks from January 2002)	September 2002 (covering risks from November 2002)	July 2003	1954	1993	November 2002
Basic structure	Hybrid pool/post funded model established by the Terrorism Insurance Act of 2003. The legislation overrides terrorism exclusion clauses in eligible insurance contracts. Eligible terrorism risks can be reinsured with ARPC.	Purely private co-reinsurance pool set up by the Verband der Versicherungsunternehmen Österreichs (VVO, the Austrian insurance association). The pool is open to insurers and reinsurers writing business in Austria. 99% of VVO members belong to the Pool.	GAREAT is a co-reinsurance pool offering reinsurance protection to direct insurers provided that they cede the the terrorism risk forming part of all qualifying policies within their portfolio. The French State acts as reinsurer of last resort, offering unlimited protection through the CCR.	EXTREMUS is a specialist insurance company with a share capital of €50 million writing only terrorism business. The German State offers limited guarantee. The annual maximum indemnity for each client is limited to € 1.5 billion.	NHT is a dedicated reinsurance company writing terrorism risks. A "Terrorism Cover Clause", was added to all new and/or amendable policies providing for overall terrorism exposures to be limited to €1 billion per year. Pursuant to an agreement with the Government, if needed, emergency legislation will restrict terrorism exposures in non-amendable life insurance policies to conform to the overall NHT exposure limit of €1 billion.	In Spain, terrorism is part of a series of risks known as "extraordinary risks", which have special insurance treatment within a system that includes other political risks and natural catastrophes. Coverage for extraordinary risks in certain classes of insurance (see below) is mandatory. A specific extraordinary risks coverage clause is compulsorily attached to the ordinary policies issued by private insurers[2] in said classes of insurance. The Consorcio does not issue policies[2]. All extraordinary risks can legally be covered by private insurance companies. Otherwise, the Consorcio will automatically take charge of the guarantee, following the said coverage included in the policy underwritten with the private insurer. In practice, the private market does not directly cover those risks, thus the CCS is the direct insurer. The CCS also acts as a warranty fund when a private	Pool Re is a mutual reinsurance company authorized to transact reinsurance business. The scheme covers losses resulting from an Act of Terrorism, as defined in the enabling Act of Parliament, the Reinsurance (Acts of Terrorism) Act 1993. Pool Re's Retrocession Agreement with HM Treasury provides funding in the event that it exhausts all its financial resources following claim payments.	Pursuant to the Terrorism Risk Insurance Act of 2002 (TRIA), while insurers are required to make available, in all property and casualty insurance policies, coverage for losses arising from an act of terrorism – as defined under Section 102 of the Act -, a special risk-sharing arrangement has been set up by the federal government to limit market exposure.

Countries[1]	Australia	Austria	France	Germany	Netherlands	Spain	United Kingdom	United States
Layers of coverage	**First** – accumulation of a cash pool of $300 million funded by premia **Second** – $1 billion commercial line of credit, in excess of $300 million. **Third** – $9 billion Government indemnity, in excess of $1.3 billion, to give a total of $10.3billion available to meet claims. If this amount will be insufficient to meet losses from a series of events then the Treasurer must declare a pro rata reduction in claim payments in order to contain the Commonwealth's liability within the $10.3 billion limit.	**First** – up to an annual aggregate of €50 million, co-insured by direct insurers, in proportion to their market share; **Second** – up to an annual aggregate of €150 million, in excess of €50 million, underwritten by the international reinsurance market.	**First** – €400 million in annual aggregate: co-reinsurance provided by pool members (*i.e.* direct insurers, in proportion to their market share) **Second** (for 2005) – €1,2 billion in annual aggregate, excess of €400 million: coverage provided by international insurance market **Third** (for 2005) – € 400 million in annual aggregate, excess of €1.6 billion: coverage provided by international reinsurance market **Fourth/Overspill** – above € 2 billion: unlimited protection provided by CCR, backed by state guarantee.	**First** – €2.0 billion in annual aggregate: provided by primary insurers and reinsurers domiciled in Germany and international reinsurers. **Second** – €8 billion in annual aggregate, excess of €2 billion: State guarantee.	**First** – €7.5 million: provided by participating "franchise" primary insurers **Second** – €400 million in the aggregate: pooled cover provided by participating primary insurers **Third** – €400 million in annual aggregate, excess of €400 million: provided by international reinsurers **Fourth** – € 200 million in annual aggregate, excess of €800 million: provided by international reinsurers and Dutch government (50% each)3. Should the aggregate limit of €1 billion ever be exceeded, there would be pro-rated reductions in amounts to be paid against claims, in accordance with a detailed protocol.	insurer, **having assumed the coverage of a extraordinary risk (like terrorism)**, can no longer fulfil its obligations, such as following bankruptcy. The CCS is supported by an unlimited State warranty if the losses are above its own ability of payments, though as yet this has never been necessary.	**First** – industry retention amounts (see below) **Second** – Pool Re coverage up to the full amount of its fund. **Third** – UK government indemnity up to 100% of claims above fund's value. A £500 million loan facility is available to Pool Re should the government indemnity obligation be triggered, as the Treasury only disburses funds on certain dates.	**First** – each insurer is responsible for an annual deductible based on a percentage of its prior year direct earned premium. The percentage varies over the three-year period of operation: 7% in 2003, 10% in 2004, and 15% in 2005. **Second** – once an insurer has met its backstop deductible, the Federal Government is responsible for paying 90% of the insurer's losses above that amount, subject to annual marketplace aggregate retention amounts (see below) and related mandatory recoupment provisions.

Countries[1]	Australia	Austria	France	Germany	Netherlands	Spain	United Kingdom	United States
Limitation of exposure of private sector	Retention set at the lesser of $1 million or 4% of gross Fire and Industrial Special Risks (ISR) premium revenue per insurer per annum, and $10 million across the industry per event.	Not applicable.	€1.5 billion (2002) €1.75 billion (2003) €2 billion (2004, 2005)	€3 billion (2002, 2003) €2 billion (since March 2004). The State Guarantee, however, is *not* unlimited (currently €8 billion in the annual aggregate in excess of the €2 billion provided by private sector).	€800 million	Not applicable	Industry-wide retentions: Year 2003 – £30 million (per event) / £60 million (per year) / Year 2004 – £50 million (per event) / £100 million (per year) / Year 2005 – £75 million (per event) / £150 million (per year) / Year 2006 – £100 million (per event) / £200 million (per year) Individual insurers' retentions are based on market share.	Industry-wide maximum retention amounts: $10 billion in 2003; $12.5 billion in 2004 $15 billion in 2005 The insurance industry and federal government's share of losses is capped to a combined annual amount of $100 billion.
Temporary /permanent government participation	Temporary. No terminal date, but subject to periodic revision.	Not applicable.	Temporary. Currently until end-of 2006.	Temporary. Currently until end-of 2005.	Temporary. Has been renewed for 2005.	Permanent	No terminal date, but subject to periodic assessment.	Temporary. Currently until end-of 2005
Gratuity of government coverage	No. Insurers must pay reinsurance premia to ARPC.	Not applicable.	No. Government receives premium for unlimited guarantee.	No. Government receives premium for guarantee.	No. Government receives premium for guarantee.	No. Because the extraordinary risks coverage system (terrorism included) is financed with the surcharges paid by policyholders.	No. Government receives premium for coverage under the scheme.	No initial premium, but amounts paid to insurers subject to mandatory and discretionary recoupment via shurcharge on policyholders as set by the Secretary of the Treasury, but not to exceed 3% of policy premium charged.

Countries[1]	Australia	Austria	France	Germany	Netherlands	Spain	United Kingdom	United States
Voluntary/mandatory	Reinsurance with ARPC is voluntary. Coverage of terrorism risks in eligible insurance contracts is mandatory.	Insurance of terrorism risks covered by the scheme is voluntary. Participation in the pool is voluntary.	Coverage of terrorism risk is a compulsory element of insurance policies covering property damage, including motor policies, since 1986. Pool membership is not compulsory. However, it is currently automatic for insurance company members of the Fédération Française des Sociétés d'Assurances (FFSA) and mutual insurers in the Groupement des Entreprises Mutuelles de l'Assurance (GEMA).	Coverage of terrorism risk is optional. As EXTREMUS is an incorporated primary insurance company membership requirements are not applicable. EXTREMUS provides its services to all clients, brokers, agents etc.	Coverage of terrorism risk is optional. Membership of NHT is optional. Participating insurers, however, are required to cede all their terrorism exposure to the pool.	Coverage of extraordinary risks, including terrorism, is mandatory for all of the classes listed below since 1954 (business interruption since 2004).	Membership of Pool Re is not obligatory. Direct insurers that are members are deemed to provide terrorism cover, in the terms of the scheme, to those policyholders that request it. Even if coverage is not mandatory, insureds are not permitted to select which properties to insure against terrorism risk. Their choice is to select to have terrorism cover either for all of their properties or none at all. An insured purchasing terrorism cover for material damage may elect not to do so for business interruption.	Insurers are required to make terrorism risk coverage available in all commercial property and casualty insurance policies. Clients can turn down the offer. Coverage is however compulsory for Workers Compensation.
Minimum sum insured	No	No	€6 million	> €25 million	No	No	No	Aggregate losses must exceed $5 million before any government sharing of losses from a certified act of terrorism.

Countries[1]	Australia	Austria	France	Germany	Netherlands	Spain	United Kingdom	United States
Coverage of CBRN terrorist attacks	Partial: all nuclear causes excluded.	No	Partial: exclusion of damage caused by conventional weapons or devices designed to explode by means of the structural modification of the atomic nucleus (with the exception of «dirty» bombs, whose effects are covered).	No	Yes	Yes	Yes (since 2003)	Yes, but only if covered under same terms and conditions of other risks covered under the policy.
Lines covered	Commercial property and business interruption (arising from loss of or damage to or inability to use eligible property). Liability arising from ownership or occupation of eligible property (Definition of eligible property in Section 3 of the Act)	All property lines (industrial, commercial and private) other than transport insurance.	Commercial and industrial risks for direct property losses and business interruption. The scheme includes a waiver of subrogation rights against motor insurers in the event of a terrorist attack involving a vehicle.	Commercial and industrial property damage and business interruption (provided that the business interruption is linked to an insured property damage loss) arising from fire, explosion, collision or falling objects from airplanes or flying objects as well as vehicles of all types, parts thereof or their cargo or other malicious damage	All lines are covered (life and non-life), with the exception of aviation hull and aircraft liability.	Indemnification by CCS is linked to insurance policies from any company in the market for the following classes: fire and natural events, land vehicles (vehicle damages, not civil liability), railways vehicles, other damages produced to goods (robbery, plate glass, machinery breakdown, electronic equipments and computers), business interruption and accident insurance.	Commercial property damage and consequent business interruption Coverage was originally limited to fire and explosion as named peril. Since 2003 it is offered on an all risks basis. Still excluded: war and related perils, computer hacking, virus and denial of service.	Commercial property and casualty lines (including excess insurance, workers' compensation and surety), with certain exclusions.
Pricing mechanism	Reinsurance premium levels between 2 and 12 per cent (depending on risk and location) of underlying commercial	Rating structure for reinsurance premia: from 0.75% to 4.0% of the sum insured (for participants in the Pool); from 2.25% to 12.0% of the sum	Direct insurers set the rates to be applied on original business. Pool members cede the following rates (expressed as % of property insurance	Ratings are between 0.25‰ and 0.6‰ of the sum insured. Pricing does not vary with the location of the risk. The premium rate	Not publicly available.	The premium for the cover of extraordinary risks is taken by the original policy insurer. A 5% administration charge is deducted before the insurer transfers the appropriate amount to CCS. For Property damage, the rates	Reinsurance is provided to members at rates stipulated in the Underwriting Manual. The material damage rates are related to geographic zones by	Direct policy premia subject to state law, with exception for premia charged prior to 12/31/03. No initial premium for government reinsurance backstop,

Countries[1]	Australia	Austria	France	Germany	Netherlands	Spain	United Kingdom	United States
	property insurance premia have been mandated from October 1, 2003. Reinsurance rates may be increased up to three times after an event. Direct insurers are free to set premia to be paid by insureds.	insured (for non-participants in the Pool). Direct insurers are free to set premia to be paid by insureds.	premia) to GAREAT: - Insured value between € 6 million and € 20 million: 6% - Insured value between € 20 million and € 50 million: 12% - Insured value above € 50 million: 18%	depends only on the original sum insured for the conventional cover and the yearly aggregate limit purchased by the insured. If the latter is lower than the original sum insured, a discount will be given and the ratings may even remain under 0.25 ‰.		applied on sums insured differ accordingly with the risks covered: homeowners 0.009%, buildings 0.014%, commercial 0.018%, industry 0.025%, motor fixed premium based on the vehicle, civil works 0.034% to 0.195%For personal insurance (accidents): 0.00096%". For business interruption: real property, rate of 0.0005% to be applied on the amount insured for material damages; and other risks, rate of 0.025% on the amount insured for business interruption.	postcode within the United Kingdom; in broad terms these are grouped in Central and Inner London, other city centres, and the rest of England together with Scotland and Wales. There is a single rate for business interruption, which is not allocated to particular zones. Rates are applied to the full value at risk. Members are free to set the premia for their underlying policies.	but amounts paid to insurers are subject to mandatory and discretionary recoupment via surcharge on policyholders as set by the Secretary of the Treasury, but not to exceed 3% of policy premium charged.
Other public sector victims compensation schemes	No scheme is administered at the national level. Some states established criminal injuries compensation funds.	Compensation of victims of intentional crimes is offered, under certain conditions, by the Verbrechensopferg esetz (Act on granting aid to crime victims, VOG).	FGTI – Fonds de Garantie des Victimes des Actes de Terrorisme et d'autres Infractions (Compensation Fund for Victims of Terrorist Actions and other Offences).	Opferentschadigung sgesetz (Victim Compensation Act, OEG).	Criminal Injuries Compensation Fund Act	Article 93 of Act 13/1996 and the Regulation on Benefits and Compensation to Victims of Terrorist Crimes (RATV) passed by RD 288 of 7 March 2003. Act n.32/1999 on solidarity with the victims of terrorism (LSVT)	Criminal Injuries Compensation Scheme administered by the Criminal Injuries Compensation Authority (CICA) Criminal Damage (Compensation) (Northern Ireland) Order 197 (SI n.1247 - N.I. 14).	U.S. September 11 Victims Compensation Fund of 2001. Other State Compensation Funds.

Notes

1. It should be noted that initiatives at national level for the compensation of terrorism risk have been taken in 2 other OECD countries:

    – *Switzerland* has established the "Swiss Market Solution' on 1 September 2003; **Basic structure**: the Swiss market solution foresees a terrorism exclusion for commercial/industral property policies with a total sum insured > CHF 10 million each for contents and business interruption and for all buildings with a total sum insured > CHF 10 million. Clients may "buy back" the exclusion, and insurers have bought a facility to cover such risks up to maximum total sum insured of CHF 100 million each (contents/buildings/BI) with a 10% deductible (min. CHF 50 000, max. CHF 500 000 each). Some highly exposed occupancies are excluded; **Layers of coverage**: None, facility is quota share with an event limit of CHF 300 million and sublimit of CHF 150 million (3x50million)/insured, (accumulation tool limits cessions within 250 metre radius); **Limitation of private sector exposure**: Not applicable – no government participation, private sector exposure limited per coverage described above; **Voluntary/mandatory**: voluntary; **Minimum sum insured**: CHF 10 million each for contents, business interruption, buildings,...; **Types of events covered (definition/government declaration)**: no government declaration required (private market solution); **Coverage of CBRN terrorist attacks**: none – excluded; **Lines covered**: Commercial/industrial property and private buildings; **Pricing mechanism**: based on a matrix with minimum risk rates according to relationship between Total Sum Insured/limit; **Other public sector victims compensation schemes**: Opferhilfegesetz (Victim Compensation Fund Act).

    – *Finland*: at the start of 2002, six Finnish non-life insurers (not comprising the two largest insurers in Finland, however) set up a terrorism pool of their own. The original intention was to build a more comprehensive, Scandinavia-wide pool but the plan failed. The terrorism pool operates under the roof of the Finnish Motor Insurers' Centre. Instead of paying annual contributions, the pool members have undertaken to cover any damage arising from terror acts initially in excess of a deductible of €0.5 million up to €10 million jointly and severally.

2. CCS is a State company attached to the Ministry of Economy and Finance through the General Department of Insurance and Pension Funds. Although public, it is managed as a private company with a board half of whose members are from the private insurance market and half from the Public Administration. It has its own status and assets separate from the State's, and operates under commercial law as a private company.

3. Before 2005, the Dutch government was covering alone this third layer.

Definitions of terrorism acts for the purpose of compensation in OECD countries

Country	Status of definition of terrorism	Intention of terrorist act	Identification of authors/people behind the act	Means used	Targets/effects
Australia	Contained in s.5 Terrorism Insurance Act 2003 *Act of terrorism has to be certified by the Commonwealth Treasurer, after consultation with the Commonwealth Attorney-General.*	Action done, or threat made, with the intention of advancing a political, religious or ideological cause, with the intention of coercing or influencing by intimidation the government of Australia or the Australian States or Territories, or a foreign country, or intimidating the public..	Not specified	An act (or threat of an act), that is not advocacy, protest, dissent or industrial action, that causes specified damage.	An action that causes serious harm to a person, serious damage to property, causes death or endangers life or creates a serious health or safety risk, or seriously interferes with, or disrupts or destroys an electronic system.
Austria	Industry definition	To influence the government or put the public or any section of the public in fear.	Terrorist organisations or individuals NB: Standard policy conditions for property and loss insurance excludes *inter alia* damages incurred as a consequence of acts of violence committed by (political or) terrorist *organisation* (not defined). Such damage can only be covered through a special agreement.	Act or threat of violence	Human life, tangible or intangible property or infrastructure
France	Article L421-1 of the Criminal Code (no distinction between the notions of "attack" and "terrorist act")	Seriously and intentionally disrupt law and order	Individual or joint undertaking	Intimidation or terror List of offences: 1. Deliberate attempts on people's lives, deliberate attacks on people's wellbeing, abduction and false imprisonment, as well as the hijacking of aircraft, ships and any other means of transport; 2. Theft, extortion, destruction and damage, as well as computer-related crime; 3. Offences relating to combat groups and movements that have been disbanded; 4. The manufacture or possession of arms, lethal weapons and explosives, as defined in Article 3 of the Act of 19 June 1871 repealing the Act of 4 September 1870 on the manufacture of weapons of war;	

Country	Status of definition of terrorism	Intention of terrorist act	Identification of authors/people behind the act	Means used	Targets/effects
France *(continued)*					– the production, sale, import or export of explosive substances, as defined in Article 6 of Act No. 70-575 of 3 July 1970, amending the regulations applying to explosive powders and substances.
Germany	Definition of EXTREMUS AG	Acts committed for political, religious, ethnic or ideological purposes suitable to create fear in the population or any section of the population and thus to influence a government or public body.	Persons or groups of persons	The insurer shall indemnify, if this has been specially agreed, in respect of insured property which is destroyed, damaged or lost due to: a) fire, explosion, b) impact or crash of aircraft or aerial bodies and vehicles, also craft, of all kinds, their parts or their cargo, c) other malicious damage, insofar as the mentioned perils are caused by an act of terrorism committed in the Federal Republic of Germany.	
Netherlands	Definition used for the operation of the Terrorism Risk Reinsurance Company (start of activities: 1 July 2003)	Attacks or series of attacks likely to have been planned or carried out with a view to serve certain political and/or religious and/or ideological purposes.	Whether or not in any organisational context	Any violent act and/or conduct – committed outside the scope of one of the six forms of acts of war as referred to in Article 64(2) of the Insurance Business Supervision Act [1993 wet toericht verzekeringsbedrijf] – in the form of an attack or a series of attacks connected together in time and intention, as a result whereof injury and/or impairment of health, whether resulting in death or not, and/or loss of or damage to property arises or any economic interest is otherwise impaired	Acts against persons and property of any nature.

Country	Status of definition of terrorism	Intention of terrorist act	Identification of authors/people behind the act	Means used	Targets/effects
Spain	Definition of the risks covered by the Consortium (no prior government statement is needed in order to compensate for damage under this heading)	Every act committed with the object of destabilising the established political order or generating fear and insecurity in the social environment in which they are perpetrated	Not specified	Act of violence	People and goods
	Specific case of state terrorism Criminal Code definition of terrorism (Section 2, Art. 571)	Disrupt the Constitution or seriously undermine law and order	Members of armed factions or people working for or in co-operation with armed factions, organisations or groups whose aim is to disrupt the Constitution or seriously undermine law and order	Acts of destruction or fires started deliberately	Not specified
Switzerland	Definition of the insurance association	In pursuit of political, religious, ethnic, ideological or similar purpose which may result in putting the public or any section of the public in fear or influencing any government or governmental organisation.		Act or threat of violence. The definition shall not include civil unrest (act of violence against persons or property committed in the course of unlawful assembly, riot or civil commotion or associated looting)	

Country	Status of definition of terrorism	Intention of terrorist act	Identification of authors/people behind the act	Means used	Targets/effects
United Kingdom	Reinsurance (Acts of Terrorism) Act 1993 (for Pool Re arrangements in Great Britain – other arrangements apply in Northern Ireland). *The issue of a certificate by the UK Treasury (or, if refused, by a decision of a Tribunal) is required for an act to be recognised as a "terrorist act" for the purpose of the scheme, under the Reinsurance (Acts of Terrorism) Act 1993.*	Acts of persons acting on behalf of, or in connection with, any organisation which carries out activities directed towards the overthrowing or influencing, by force or violence, of her Majesty's government in the United Kingdom or any other government *de jure* or de facto.		Not specified	Targets are not specified in the definition of terrorism itself. However, the Pool Re scheme is limited to damages to commercial property and consequent business interruption costs arising from an act of terrorism.
United States	Terrorism Risk Insurance Act of 2002 – Public Law 107-297 *An act of terrorism is an act certified by the Secretary of the Treasury in concurrence with the Secretary of State and the Attorney General of the United States; Any certification or decision not to certify an act or event as an act of terrorism shall be final and may not be subject to judicial review;* Acts or events committed in the course of a war declared by Congress, or losses resulting from acts or events which, in aggregate, do not exceed $5 000 000, shall not be certified as terrorist acts	Part of an effort to coerce the civilian population of the United States, or to influence policy or affect the conduct of the US by coercion	Committed by one or more individuals acting on behalf of any foreign person or foreign interest	Violent act or dangerous act	Endanger human life, property or infrastructure Result in damages within the United States, or outside the US in the case of an attack of an air carrier or vessel, or premises of a US mission.

Part III

Reports by the Experts to the OECD Task Force on Terrorism Insurance

Chapter 6

INSURABILITY OF (MEGA-) TERRORISM RISK : CHALLENGES AND PERSPECTIVES[*]

Catastrophic events present special challenges for economics and risk management since they have an immediate impact on a wide range of stakeholders, can have severe long-term economic and social consequences, and are difficult to assess quantitatively. As these events normally have a low probability of occurrence, there are limited historical data on which to base estimates of the risks, and there is considerable uncertainty associated with experts' risk assessments.

The terrorist attacks of September 11, 2001 are the most costly disaster in the history of insurance and have led both insurers and reinsurers to reevaluate under what conditions they can provide coverage against this risk. We examine the conditions for insurability of risks and conclude that terrorism presents special problems due to the dynamic uncertainty of the risk, information-related issues as well as correlated catastrophic losses between different lines of coverage and government influencing the risk through foreign policy and national security. These factors may explain the unwillingness of private insurers in the United States to offer coverage alone following 9/11 and why the US Congress passed legislation that provides government protection against catastrophic terrorist losses.

We argue that the special characteristics of terrorism call for government participation in any terrorism insurance program to be based on public-private partnerships. This need has been recognized by most countries through the creation of national temporary programs based on public-private partnerships for covering (mega)-terrorism. Since the creation of these programs, the level of demand for non-compulsory commercial terrorism coverage has remained low in countries such as the U.S. and Germany. The paper discusses some factors that explain this behavior. If the low level of demand continues, a large-scale terrorist attack will likely have a more devastating effect on business and social continuity today than after 9/11 because losses will not be diversified in the national and international insurance and reinsurance industry. This raises the question as to whether terrorism insurance should be mandatory and, if so, how would such a program be administered?

The report also discusses the most recent developments in quantitative risk modeling. A wide range of stakeholders are likely to find these models useful for evaluating their exposure through alternative scenarios but they currently are not able to predict the likelihood of specific terrorist actions. We conclude that better data are needed to evaluate alternative public-private partnerships for encouraging risk reduction measures and providing sustainable programs of insurance against terrorism should new large-scale attacks occur.

[*]   This report was written by Pr. Howard Kunreuther, Cecilia Yen Koo Professor of Decision Sciences and Public Policy, Operations and Information Management Department, Wharton School, University of Pennsylvania, Philadelphia, USA, and Dr. Erwann Michel-Kerjan, Center for Risk Management and Decision Processes, OPIM Department - The Wharton School, Philadelphia, USA.
The data in this report is current as of end-November 2004.

1. Introduction

Catastrophic events present special challenges for economics and risk management since they have an immediate impact on a wide range of stakeholders, can have severe long-term economic and social consequences, and are difficult to assess quantitatively. As these events normally have a low probability of occurrence, there are limited historical data on which to base estimates of the risks, and there is considerable uncertainty associated with experts' risk assessment estimates.

An aversion to ambiguity leads insurers to set premiums much higher than they otherwise would if there were agreement among experts as to the likelihood and consequences of future events (Kunreuther, Hogarth, and Meszaros, 1993). On the demand side, it is well known that potential purchasers may underestimate the risks and consider the insurance premiums as being too expensive, thus refusing to purchase coverage if they have the choice (Kunreuther, 1996).

Because these events are capable of having a debilitating impact on the country, providing adequate financial protection to victims of catastrophes often becomes a national issue. Facing unprecedented large-scale potential damage, the private sector may severely restrict the insurance supply or even refuse to provide coverage. In such cases, the government is likely to intervene by offering insurance at prices that property owners can afford (Moss, 2002). This report discusses some of the challenges associated with the insurability of (mega)-terrorism today in the post-9/11 era. It is structured around the following four main themes:

Section 2 discusses new frontiers for dealing with terrorism as an extreme event: September 11, 2001 (9/11) highlighted the radical change in the nature of international terrorism and its consequences that have occurred over the past 20 years.

Section 3 focuses on the insurability of catastrophic events and on the characteristics of terrorism risk that make it more challenging to deal with than major natural hazards.

Section 4 analyzes the need for developing public-private partnership to deal with (mega)-terrorism as indicated by the challenges faced by private insurers and reinsurers after 9/11. The paper describes the risk-sharing mechanisms operating in the United Kingdom, France, Germany, and the United States.

Section 5 provides features of the new models developed after 9/11 to help quantify terrorism risks and discusses some of their strengths, limitations, and possible applications.

Section 6 summarizes the arguments for public-private partnership for dealing with catastrophic losses from terrorism and raises some questions for future research.

2. New Frontiers

2.1. Insuring 9/11: A New Loss Dimension

Prior to September 11, 2001 terrorism exclusions in commercial property and casualty policies in the U.S. insurance market were extremely rare (outside of ocean marine). The private insurance market had functioned effectively in the U.S. because losses from terrorism had historically been small and, to a large degree, uncorrelated. Attacks of a domestic origin were isolated, carried out by groups or individuals with disparate agendas and did not create major economic disruption nor many casualties.

In fact, insurance losses from terrorism were viewed as so improbable that the risk was not explicitly mentioned in any standard policy and hence the rate for providing such coverage to firms was never calculated. Even the first attack on the World Trade Center (WTC) in 1993 was not seen as being threatening enough for insurers to consider revising their view of terrorism as a peril to be explicitly considered when pricing a commercial insurance policy (Kunreuther and Pauly, 2004).

The 1993 bombing of the WTC killed 6 people and caused USD725 million in insured damages (Swiss Re, 2002-a). Prior to Sept. 11th the Oklahoma City bombing of 1995, which killed 168 people, had been the most damaging terrorist attack on domestic soil, but the largest losses were to federal property and employees and were covered by the government. So insurers and reinsurers felt that they did not have to pay close attention to their potential losses from terrorism in the United States.

Table 6.1. **The 10 Most costly terrorist attacks in terms of insured property losses - 1970-2001**

Insured property USD million, indexed to 2001 (excluding liability and life)	Event	Injured	Fatalities	Date	Location
19,000	Terror attacks against WTC, Pentagon and Pennsylvania by hijacked airliners	2250	3,000	11 Sept. 01	USA (NYC, Wash. DC, PA)
907	Bomb explodes near NatWest tower (City)	54	1	24 Apr. 93	UK (London)
744	Explosion of IRA car bomb near shopping mall	228	0	15 Jun. 96	UK (Manchester)
725	Bomb explodes in garage of World Trade Center	1,000	6	26 Feb. 93	USA (New York)
671	Bomb explodes in financial district	91	3	10 Apr. 92	UK (London)
398	Rebels destroy 3 airliners, 8 military aircraft and heavily damage 3 civilian aircraft	15	20	24 Jul. 01	Sri Lanka / Colombo Airport
259	IRA bomb attack in South Key Docklands	100	2	09 Feb. 96	UK (London)
145	Truck bomb attack on government building in Oklahoma City	467	166	19 Apr. 95	USA (Oklahoma City)
138	PanAm Boeing 747 crashes due to bomb	0	270	21 Dec. 88	UK (Lockerbie)
127	Hijacked Swissair DC-8, TWA Boeing 707 and BOAC VC-10 dynamited	0	0	06 Sep.70	Jordan (Zerqa)

Sources: Swiss Re (2002-a)

The terrorist attacks of September 11, 2001 killed over 3,000 people[1] from over 90 countries and injured more than inflicted damage currently estimated at nearly $80 billion, about $32.5 billion of which was covered by insurance. (Hartwig, 2004). Of the total insured losses[2], those associated with property damage and business interruption are estimated at $21 billion. Prior to 9/11, most terrorist attacks did not have a major impact on liability coverage[3]; most published comparisons were based only on insured property losses. Table 6.1 details the 10 most costly terrorist attacks between 1970 and 2001 in terms of insured property losses (including also business interruption and aviation hull losses, but excluding liability and life).

The insured losses from 9/11 illustrate the high degree of risk correlation between different lines of insurance coverage. Indeed, these attacks not only affected commercial property, caused business interruption and aircraft hull damage, but also led to significant claims from other lines of coverage: workers' compensation, life, health, disability, and general liability insurance. Figure 6.1 depicts the composition of the $32.5 billion total insured loss estimates due to these terrorist attacks (as of July 2004).

Figure 6.1. **Composition of 9/11 Insured Loss Estimates (total: $32.5 billion), by Line ($ billion)**

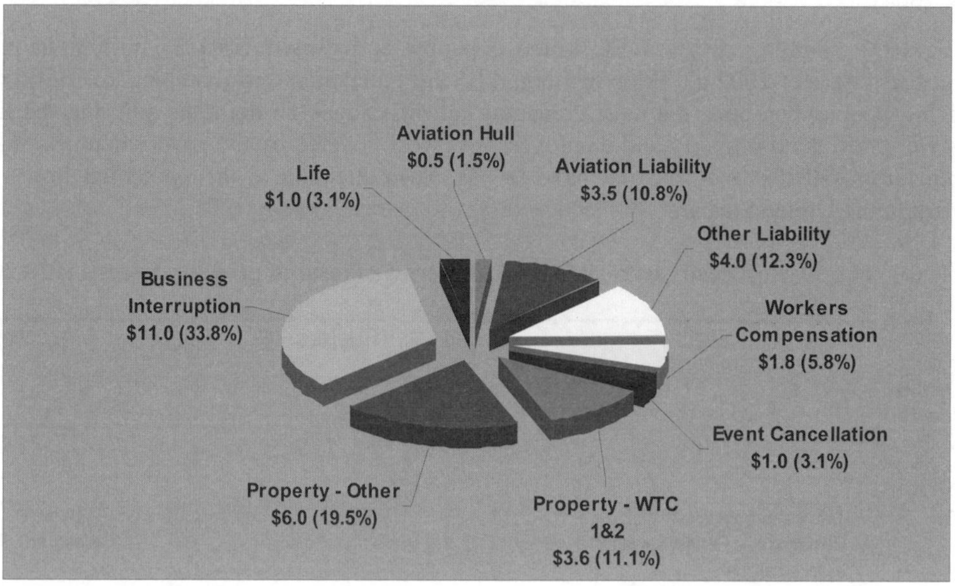

Sources: Insurance Information Institute (Hartwig, July 2004).

To more fully understand the losses from 9/11 from an insurability perspective, it is important to compare this event with other types of catastrophic events, such as natural disasters, that have affected the (re)insurance industry. Table 6.2 presents the 10 largest worldwide insurance losses due to natural catastrophes and man-made disasters from 1970 to 2003. Prior to 9/11 losses, the most-insured event was Hurricane Andrew, which devastated the coasts of Florida in August 1992 and inflicted $20.9 billion insured losses (indexed to 2003). Adding claims to insurers and reinsurers ($32.5 billion) to payments by the US federal Victim Compensation Fund to victims of 9/11 and their family (nearly $5 billion), the claims from the 9/11 terrorist attacks are almost 1.5 times as much as those from Hurricane Andrew.

Taking an even broader perspective, Figure 6.2 depicts the trend in worldwide insurance losses due to natural catastrophes and man-made disasters from 1970 to 2003 showing how insured losses have increased in recent years. Of the 40 most costly events over this period of time, 75% of them occurred between 1990 and 2003 (in constant prices).

Table 6.2. **The 10 most costly insurance losses 1970-2003.**

US$ Billion (indexed to 2002)	Event	Victims (Dead and missing)	Year	Country
32.5[4]	9/11 Attacks	3,025	2001	USA
20.90	Hurricane Andrew	43	1992	USA, Bahamas
17.31	Northridge Earthquake	60	1994	USA
7.60	Typhoon Mireille	51	1991	Japan
6.44	Winterstorm Daria	95	1990	France, UK et al
6.38	Winterstorm Lothar	110	1999	France, Switzerland et al
6.20	Hurricane Hugo	71	1989	Puerto Rico, USA et al
4.84	Storms and floods	22	1987	France, UK et al
4.48	Winterstorm Vivian	64	1990	Western Europe
4.45	Typhoon Bart	26	1999	Japan

Sources: Swiss Re, sigma No. 1/2004 and Hartwig (2004).

In particular, the insured losses from Hurricane Andrew and the Northridge Earthquake led insurers and reinsurers to pay much more attention to the catastrophic potential of natural disasters. Some of the smaller insurers were forced to declare insolvency due to these events. Those that survived began to rethink what is meant by an insurable risk and the roles of catastrophic models to estimate the likelihood and consequences from specific hazards that might cause damage in specific locations (Grossi and Kunreuther, in press).

Figure 6.2. **Worldwide Evolution of Insured Losses, 1970-2003**

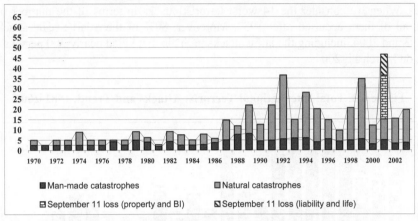

- ■ Man-made catastrophes
- ▨ Natural catastrophes
- ⊞ September 11 loss (property and BI)
- ▨ September 11 loss (liability and life)

(Property and business interruption (BI); in US$ billon indexed to 2003)
Source: Swiss Re, Sigma no.1/2004 (2004) and Hartwig (2004)

The events of September 11th confronted the insurance and reinsurance industries with an entirely new loss dimension. Reinsurers (most of them European) will be responsible for a large portion of the $40 billion claims. The 9/11 terrorist attacks came on top of a series of catastrophic natural disasters over the past decade and portfolio losses due to stock market declines. Having their capital base severely hit, most of them decided to drastically reduce their exposure to terrorism, or even stopped covering this risk. The few who marketed policies charged extremely high rates for very limited protection. This directly affected insurance supply and most insurers stopped covering terrorism.

While the prices of commercial property-liability insurance were beginning to rise prior to September 11, 2001[5], the terrorist attacks appeared to have hardened the general liability market even further. Take the case of insuring Chicago's O'Hare airport. Prior to 9/11, the airport had $750 million of terrorist insurance coverage at an annual premium of $125,000. After the terrorist attacks insurers only offered the airport $150 million of coverage at an annual premium of $6.9 million. The airport purchased this coverage and could not obtain any more (Jaffee and Russell, 2003). Golden Gate Park was unable to obtain terrorism coverage and its non-terrorism coverage was reduced from $125 million to $25 million. Yet the premiums for this reduced amount of protection increased from $500,000 in 2001 to $1.1 million in 2002.

By early 2002, 45 states in the U.S. permitted insurance companies to exclude terrorism from their policies[6], leading to a call for some type of federal intervention (U.S. Congress Joint Economic Committee, 2002). In other countries, similar reactions were observed. Deprived of reinsurance at an affordable price, most insurers decided to stop covering terrorism risk and turned to the government to fill the gap.

2.2. Empirical Evidence on Change in the Nature of Terrorism Risk

There is evidence collected by Enders and Sandler (2000) that terrorism risk has changed radically over the past two decades. On the one hand, the total number of international terrorist attacks worldwide has been decreasing on average in the 1990s compared with the 1980s, as shown in Figure 6.3 (U.S. Department of State, 2003)[7]. This decrease is mostly due to the end of the East/West conflict that led to the reduction in activities of several political terrorist groups. (Pillar, 2001).

On the other hand, there has been a significant change towards attacks that create more injuries and fatalities. When we consider the 14 worst terrorist attacks in terms of the number of casualties (Table 6.3), all of them occurred after 1982. Moreover, 80% of these large-scale attacks occurred between 1993 and 2004, including the latest attacks in Spain that killed nearly 200 persons and injured 1500 others on March 11, 2004.

Figure 6.3. **Total International Terrorist Attacks and Trend, 1981-2002**

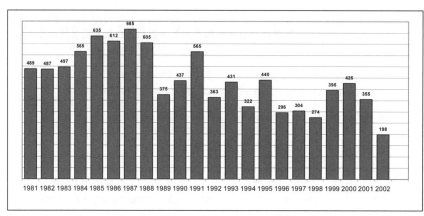

Sources: U.S. Department of State (2003)

In this context, as pointed out by Sandler and Enders (2004), "the events of 11 September with their massive casualties of innocent people of all ages came as no surprise to those of us who study terrorism and warned of an ominous changing nature of transnational terrorism." The question today is not really whether other terrorist attacks will be perpetrated but rather who, where, and with what type of weapons.

Dealing with this new spectrum of terrorism risk, the use of non-conventional chemical, biological, radiological, and nuclear weapons (CBRN) also has to be considered. Although the use of such weapons requires higher level of technical skill and the WMD capability of active terrorist organizations is low, the intent of several of them to acquire such a capability is beyond doubt. (Woo, 2004). For example, Al Qaeda clearly expressed interest in acquiring and deploying these weapons of mass destruction. (Central Intelligence Agency, 2003).

Table 6.3. **The 14 worst terrorist acts in terms of fatalities**[8]

Date	Location	Event	Fatalities	Injured
11 Sep 01	USA	Terror attack	3,000	2,250
23 Oct 83	Lebanon/Beirut	Bomb attack on US Marine barracks and French paratrooper base	300	100
12 March 93	India/Bombay	Series of 13 bomb attacks	300	1,100
21 Dec 88	UK/Lockerbie	PanAm B-747 explodes mid-air	270	0
07 Aug 98	Kenya/Nairobi	Bomb attacks on US embassy complex	253	5,075
11 March 04	Madrid, Spain	Bomb attacks on trains	192	1,500
12 Oct 02	Indonesia/Bali	Bomb attack in a night club	190	300
19 Apr 95	USA/Oklahoma City	Truck bomb attack on government building	166	467
23 Nov 96	Comoros/Indian Ocean	Hijacked Ethiopian Airliner B-767 ditched at sea	127	0
13 Sep 99	Russia/Moscow	Bomb destroys apartment building	118	0
31 Jan 96	Sri Lanka/Colombo	Bomb attack on Ceylinco House	100	1,500
04 Jun 91	Ethiopia/Addis Ababa	Arson in arms warehouse	100	0
18 Jul 94	Argentina/Buenos Aires	Bomb attack	95	147
26 Feb 93	USA New York	Bomb explodes in garage of world Trade Center	6	1,000

In this regard, the 9/11 events and the anthrax attacks during the fall of 2001 demonstrated a new kind of large-scale vulnerability. Attackers can use the diffusion capacity of our large critical networks and turn them against the target population so that each element of the network (*e.g.* every aircraft, every piece of mail) now becomes a potential weapon and the entire network becomes at risk (Michel-Kerjan, 2003-a).

During the anthrax episode, for example, the attacks were not turned against a specific postal office. Rather the attackers used the whole United States Postal Service network to spread threats throughout the country and abroad. Any envelope could have been considered as contaminated by anthrax so that the whole postal service was potentially at risk (Boin, Lagadec, Michel-Kerjan, and Overdijk, 2003). Less than one hour after the first aircraft crashed against the North WTC Tower, the U.S. Federal Aviation Administration (FAA) ordered all private and commercial flights grounded and suspended. It was on September 12th, 2001 that they were authorized to resume their flights, as the number of hijacked planes on 9/11 was not known and each flying aircraft was a potential danger. It was the first time and only time that the FAA has ever shut down the airline system.

These examples demonstrate that a small but carefully targeted attack can cause large-scale economic consequences because they have an impact on interdependent and large-scale operating networks. In 1998, U.S. Presidential Decision Directive 63 classified those sectors, among others (*e.g.* aviation, transportation, water supply, electricity[9], telecommunications, banking, finance, and energy), as "critical infrastructure sectors" for the social and economic continuity of the country. (White House, 2003). Since then, new programs have been launched in other countries to understand this source of mega-terrorism and undertake actions to manage this new type of vulnerability. (OECD, 2003; Lagadec and Michel-Kerjan, 2004).

The growing globalization of economic activities, combined with increasing interdependencies and terrorist threats, makes the question of protection (physical and financial) even more crucial as the malevolent/terrorist use of these networks can inflict mega-terrorism. A single event can be sufficient to destabilize the insurance industry and perhaps the economy.

Two related features need to be considered also. First, the antecedents to catastrophes can be quite distinct and distant from the actual disaster, as in the case of the 9/11/01 attacks when security failures at Boston's Logan airport led to crashes at the WTC and Pentagon. The same was true in the case of recent power failures in the northeastern US and Canada, where the initiating event occurred in Ohio but the worst consequences were felt hundreds of miles away.

Second, as illustrated by the FAA's decision on 9/11, when there is a high degree of uncertainty on which are the risky elements the response to a terrorist attack can be highly disruptive by imposing negative effects on elements of the infrastructure that are not actually at risk. There may be also negative impacts on every other network that depends on it. As a whole, these reactions can create economic losses that are greater than the direct impacts of the attack itself. Terrorism insurance today will not provide coverage for many of these indirect losses resulting from the response to an attack[10] (Kunreuther and Michel-Kerjan, 2004).

3. Insurability Of Extreme Events: Why Is Terrorism Different?

We first consider the conditions for a risk to be insurable by focusing on natural hazards and then turn to terrorism. There are some crucial differences between these two types of events which make terrorism a more challenging risk for the private sector to insure alone.

3.1. Insurability of Catastrophe Risks

In most developed countries, insurance is one of the principal mechanisms used by individuals and organizations for managing risk. Insurance allows the payment of a relatively small premium for protection against a potentially large loss in the future. In the United States, some property insurance coverage is required by law or by a lending institution. For example, homeowners normally have to purchase fire coverage as a condition for a mortgage. Automobile liability insurance is also required in most states as a condition for licensing a car. However, earthquake insurance is usually not required by lenders on property even in seismically active regions of the country such as California.

Insurance pricing can be a signal as to how risky certain activities are for a particular individual. To illustrate, consider automobile insurance. For cars that are the same price, younger, inexperienced drivers of sporty vehicles pay more in premiums than older drivers of more conservative cars. For life and health insurance, smokers pay more for coverage than non-smokers. This allocation of risk seems appropriate since it is tied to the likelihood of outcomes resulting from the nature of an individual's lifestyle. If one individual is more susceptible to a specific risk, then the cost for coverage against a loss from that risk is greater. Of course, since insurance rates are subject to regulation, the price of the policy may not fully reflect the underlying risk.

The key challenge is how to allocate catastrophe risk among stakeholders in a manner similar to what is done for the more frequent events where there is a large historical database to estimate insurance premiums for individuals with different risk characteristics. For example, for automobile coverage the large number of data points and the absence of correlation between accidents allow the use of actuarial-based models to estimate risk.

Conditions for Insurability of a Risk

Consider a standard insurance policy whereby premiums are paid at the start of a given time period to cover losses during this interval. Two conditions must be met before insurance providers are willing to offer coverage against an uncertain event. The first is the ability to identify and quantify, or estimate at least partially, the chances of the event occurring and the extent of losses likely to be incurred. The second condition is the ability to set premiums for each potential customer or class of customers.

If both conditions are satisfied, a risk is considered to be insurable. But it still may not be profitable. In other words, it may be impossible to specify a rate for which there is sufficient demand and incoming revenue to cover the development, marketing, operating, and claims processing costs of the insurance and yield a net positive profit over a prespecified time horizon. In such cases, the insurer will opt not to offer coverage against this risk.

To satisfy the first condition, estimates must be made of the frequency of specific events and the likely extent of losses. Such estimates can be based on past data coupled with data on what experts know about a particular risk. The insurer can then construct an exceedance probability (EP) curve that depicts the probability that a certain level of loss will be exceeded on an annual basis[11].

To illustrate with a specific example, suppose one was interested in constructing an EP curve for dollar losses to homes in Los Angeles from an earthquake. Using probabilistic risk assessment, one combines the set of events that could produce a given dollar loss and then determines the resulting probabilities of exceeding losses of different magnitudes. Based on these estimates, one can construct the mean EP depicted in Figure 6.4. By its nature, the EP curve incorporates uncertainty associated with the probability of an event occurring and the magnitude of dollar losses. This uncertainty is reflected in the 5% and 95% confidence interval curves in the figure.

Figure 6.4. **Example of Exceedance Probability (EP) Curves**

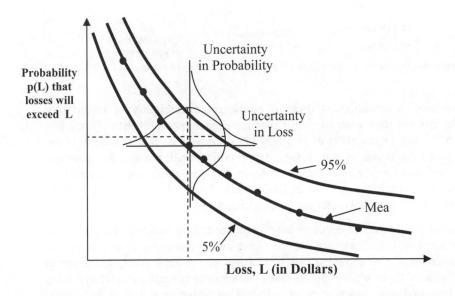

A key question that needs to be addressed in constructing an EP curve is the degree of uncertainty regarding both probability and outcomes. It is a lot easier to construct such a curve for natural disasters and chemical accidents than it is for terrorist activities. But even for these more predictable accidents or disasters, there may be considerable uncertainty regarding both the likelihood of the occurrence of certain risks and the resulting damage. For low probability-high consequence risks, the spread between the three curves depicted in Figure 6.4 shows the degree of indeterminacy of these events. Providing information on the degree of uncertainty associated with risk assessments should increase the credibility of the experts producing these figures.

Extreme events, such as natural disasters or large-scale terrorism, pose a set of challenging problems for insurers because they involve potentially high losses that are extremely uncertain. In the case of natural disasters, Figure 6.5 illustrates the total number of loss events from 1950 to 2000 in the United States for three prevalent hazards: earthquakes, floods, and hurricanes. Events were selected that had at least $1 billion of economic damage and/or over 50 deaths (American Re, 2002). Looking across all the disasters of a particular type (earthquake, hurricane, or flood), for this 50-year period, the median loss is low while the maximum loss is very high. Given this wide variation in loss distribution, it is not surprising that insurers are concerned about the uncertainty of the loss in estimating premiums. With respect to terrorism, the events of 9/11 were totally unexpected by insurers based on past experience. As shown in Table 6.1 (Section 2) there was considerable variation in the losses from the top 10 terrorist events over these past 31 years.

Figure 6.5. **Historical economic losses in $ millions versus type of significant U.S. natural disaster**

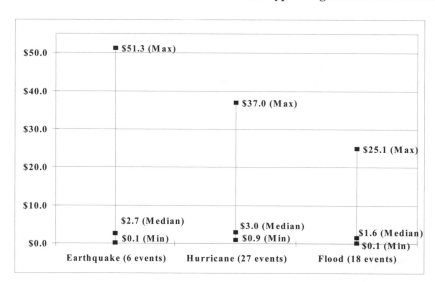

With respect to the second condition, if there is considerable ambiguity or uncertainty associated with the risk, insurers may wish to charge a much higher premium than if they had more precise estimates of the risk (Kunreuther *et al.* 1993, 1995). Moreover, if the capacity of the insurance industry is reduced due to recent large losses, then premiums will rise due to a shortage in supply. The situation will be exacerbated if the recent losses trigger an increase in demand for coverage, as was the case after Hurricane Andrew in 1992 and the Northridge earthquake in 1994 (Kunreuther and Roth, Sr., 1998) as well as after the terrorist attacks of 9/11.

Once the risk is estimated, the insurer needs to determine a premium that yields a profit and avoids an unacceptable level of loss. State regulations often limit insurers in their rate-setting process, and competition can play a role in what may be charged in a given marketplace. Even in the absence of these influences, there are two other issues that an insurer must consider in setting premiums: problems associated with asymmetry of information (adverse selection and moral hazard) and the risk of highly correlated losses.

Adverse Selection

If the insurer sets a premium based on the average probability of a loss, using the entire population as a basis for this estimate, those at the highest risk for a certain hazard will be the most likely to purchase coverage for that hazard. In an extreme case, the poor risks will be the only purchasers of coverage, and the insurer will lose money on each policy sold. This situation, referred to as *adverse selection*, occurs when the insurer cannot distinguish between the probabilities of a loss for good- and poor-risk categories[12].

The assumption underlying adverse selection is that purchasers of insurance have an informational advantage by knowing their *risk type*. Insurers, on the other hand, must invest considerable expense to collect information to distinguish between risks. For example, suppose some homes have a low probability of suffering damage (the good risks), and others have a higher probability (the poor risks). The good risks stand a 1 in 1000 probability of loss and the poor risks, a 3 in 1000 probability. For simplicity, assume that the loss is $100,000 for both groups and that there are an equal number of potentially insurable individuals in each risk class.

Since there is an equal number in both risk classes, the expected loss for a random individual in the population is $200[13]. If the insurer charges an actuarially fair premium across the entire population, only those in the poor-risk class would normally purchase coverage, since their expected loss is $300 (*i.e.,* .003x$100,000), and they would be pleased to pay only $200 for the insurance. The good risks have an expected loss of $100 (*i.e.,* .001x$100,000), so they would have to be extremely risk-averse to be interested in paying $200 for coverage. If only the poor risks purchase coverage, the insurer will suffer an expected loss of $100 on every policy it sells.

It is important to remember that the problem of adverse selection only emerges if the persons considering the purchase of insurance have more accurate information on the probability of a loss than the firms selling coverage. If the policyholders have no better data than the insurers, both sides are on an equal footing. Coverage will be offered at a single premium based on the average risk, and both good and poor risks will want to purchase policies.

Moral Hazard

Providing insurance protection to an individual may lead that person to behave more carelessly than before he or she had coverage. If the insurer cannot predict this behavior and relies on past loss data from uninsured individuals to estimate rates, the resulting premium is likely to be too low to cover losses.

Moral hazard refers to an increase in the probability of loss caused by the behavior of the policyholder. Obviously, it is extremely difficult to monitor and control behavior once a person is insured. How do you monitor carelessness? Is it possible to determine if a person will decide to collect more on a policy than he or she deserves by making false claims (so called "ex post moral hazard")?

Highly Correlated Risks

Correlated risk refers to the simultaneous occurrence of many losses from a single event. In general, insurance markets flourish when companies can issue a large number of policies whose losses are spatially and otherwise independent. The statistics for this type of portfolio illustrate the theory of the *law of large numbers,* introduced by Bernoulli (1738). This law states that for a series of independent and identically distributed random variables, the variance around the mean of the random variables decreases as the number of variables increases.

Fire is an example of a risk that satisfies the law of large numbers since losses from this type of event are normally independent of one another. Of course, there are exceptions to this rule, such as the Oakland conflagration fire of October 20, 1991 where 3,000 structures were damaged for a total insured loss of $1.7 billion. More recently, the fires in Southern California between October 23 and November 6 of 2003, destroyed over 700,000 acres of land and approximately 3,600 residential properties.

To illustrate this law's application to spatially independent events, suppose that an insurer wants to determine the probability of losses from fire for 1,000 identical homes valued at $100,000, each of which has a 1/1000 chance of being completely destroyed by fire; otherwise the house will be unscathed. Since there are 1000 homes in the risk pool, the fire will destroy on average one structure per year. The average annual loss (AAL) for each home would be $100, or the product of the probability, p, and the value of the home, L, or 1/1000 x $100,000.

If the insurer issued only a single policy rather than 1000, then a variance of approximately $100 would be associated with its AAL[14]. As the number of policies issued increases, the variance of the AAL per policy will decrease in proportion to the number of policies, n. Thus, if n = 10, the variance of the mean will be approximately $10. When n = 100 the variance decreases to $1, and with n = 1,000 the variance is only $0.10. This clearly demonstrates that it is not necessary to issue a large number of policies to reduce the variability of expected annual losses to a relatively small value if the risks are independent.

However, losses from natural hazards or terrorism attacks do not follow the law of large numbers, as they are not independent. Catastrophic risks involve spatially correlated losses or the simultaneous occurrence of many losses from a single event. For example, due to their high concentration of homeowners' policies in the Miami/Dade County area of Florida, State Farm and Allstate Insurance paid $3.6 billion and $2.3 billion in claims respectively in the wake of Hurricane Andrew in 1992. Given this unexpectedly high loss, both companies began to reassess their strategies of providing coverage against wind damage in hurricane-prone areas (Lecomte and Gahagan, 1998).

The terrorism attacks of 9/11 caused significant losses from different lines of an insurers' portfolio, another form of correlated risk, as shown in Figure 6.1. Due to their high concentration of policies in the World Trade Center, Lloyd's, Munich Re, and Swiss Re would pay $2.9 billion, $2.4 billion, and $2.4 billion in claims respectively in the wake of 9/11. Among the important number of insurers that suffered losses, Allianz, AIG, and AXA paid $1,300 million, $820 million, and $550 million, respectively. (Hartwig, 2002).

3.2. Determining Whether to Provide Coverage

If an insurer's portfolio leaves them vulnerable to the possibility of extremely large losses from a given disaster, then the insurer will want to reduce the number of policies in force for these hazards, decide not to offer this type of coverage at all or increase the capital available to for dealing with future catastrophic events.

Capital Constraints

Cummins Doherty and Lo (2002) have undertaken a series of analyses in the context of natural catastrophes that indicate that U.S. property-liability insurance industry could withstand a loss of $40 billion with minimal disruption of insurance markets. According to their model, a $100 billion loss would create major problems for the insurance industry by causing 60 insolvencies and leading to significant premium increases and supply side shortage.

In the aftermath of the terrorism attacks of September 11th, there was a severe shortage of capital provided to insurers, as the reinsurers were reluctant to provide protection against this risk except at very high prices. Hence for insurers to provide their clients with the same coverage they were offered in the past, they had to find capital from other sources. Most insurers were unable to do this so they either excluded terrorism from the standard commercial property coverage or reduced the amount of protection they were willing to offer while at the same time raising premiums. The experience of O'Hare Airport in obtaining coverage after September 11th discussed in Section 2.1 illustrates the latter strategy by insurers.

Survival Constraints

In his study on insurers' decision rules as to when they would market coverage for a specific risk, Stone (1973) develops a model whereby firms maximize expected profits subject to satisfying a constraint related to the survival of the firm[15]. Following the series of natural disasters that occurred end of 1980's and in the 1990s, insurers focused on the survival constraint in determining the amount of catastrophe coverage they were willing to provide. In particular, insurers were caught off guard with respect to the magnitude of the losses from Hurricane Andrew in 1992 and the Northridge earthquake in 1994. Insurers only marketed coverage against wind damage in Florida because they were required to do so and state insurance pools were formed to limit their risk. In California insurers refused to renew homeowners' earthquake policies after the 1994 Northridge earthquake and the California Earthquake Authority was formed by the State of California in 1996 with funds from insurers and reinsurers. (Roth, Jr., 1998).

An insurer satisfies the survival constraint by choosing a portfolio of risks with an overall expected probability of insolvency less than some threshold, p_1. A simple example illustrates how an insurer would utilize the survival constraint to determine whether the earthquake risk is insurable. Assume that all homes in an earthquake-prone area are equally resistant to damage such that the insurance premium, z, is the same for each structure. Further assume that an insurer has $A dollars in current surplus and wants to determine the number of policies it can write and still satisfy its survival constraint. Then, the maximum number of policies, n, satisfying the survival constraint is:

$$Probability\ [Total\ Loss > (n \cdot z + A)] < p_1$$

Whether the company will view the earthquake risk as insurable depends on whether the fixed cost of marketing and issuing policies is sufficiently low to make a positive expected profit. This, in turn, depends on how large the value of n is for any given premium, z. Note that the company also has some freedom to change its premium. A larger z will increase the values of n but will lower the demand for coverage. The insurer will decide not to offer earthquake coverage if it believes it cannot attract enough demand at any premium structure to make a positive expected profit. The company will use the survival constraint to determine the maximum number of policies it is willing to offer, with possibly an adjustment of the amount of coverage and premiums and/or a transfer of some of the risk to others (larger insurers, reinsurers or capital markets).

3.3. Why is Terrorism Different?

Although terrorist activities and natural disasters can be both characterized as extreme events, there are crucial differences between them. These include: availability of historical data, dynamic uncertainty, shifting attention to unprotected targets, existence of negative externalities, and government influencing the risk. These characteristics are discussed now and summarized in Table 6.4.

Availability of Historical Data

There are large historical databases on losses from natural hazards that are in the public domain. These data have been utilized by modeling firms in conjunction with estimates by scientists and engineers on the likelihood and consequences of future disasters in specific locations. Data on terrorist groups' activities and current threats are normally kept secret for national security reasons. Moreover, while some time series data on terrorist acts over the past years are in the public domain, they may not reflect the changing expectations of planned activities of terrorist groups today. As discussed above, the nature of terrorist activities and targets has radically changed in the last 20 years and may do so again over the next 20 years.

Shifting Attention to Unprotected Targets

Terrorists may respond to security measures by shifting their attention to more vulnerable targets. Keohane and Zeckhauser (2003) analyze the relationships between the actions of potential victims and the behavior of terrorists. Establishing publicly observable protective measures against a given mode of attack on a specific building should reduce the probability of an attack against it because the marginal benefit of the attack (*i.e.*, the likelihood of success) as perceived by the terrorist group decreases. However, shielding that building makes an attack on an unprotected structure more likely[16].

Rather than investing in additional security measures, firms may prefer to move their locations from large cities to less populated areas to reduce the likelihood of an attack. Of course, terrorists may choose these less protected regions as targets if there is heightened security in the urban areas. They also may change the nature of their attack if protective measures in place make the likelihood of success of the original option much lower than another course of action (*e.g.* switching from hijacking to bombing a plane). This *substitution effect* has to be considered when evaluating the effectiveness of specific policies aimed at curbing terrorism (Sandler, Tschirhart, Cauley, 1983). CIA director, George Tenet, suggested this behavior in his prophetic unclassified testimony of February 7, 2001, (prior to 9/11) when he said: "As we have increased security around government and military facilities, terrorists are seeking out "softer" targets that provide opportunities for mass casualties" (CIA, 2001). Khalid Sheikh Mohammed, the Al Qaeda chief of military operations, arrested in March 2003 has since explicitly admitted such a soft target strategy (Woo, 2004).

Dynamic Uncertainty

Since terrorists are likely to design their strategy as a function of their own resources and their knowledge of the vulnerability of the entity they want to attack, the nature of the risk is continuously evolving. The likelihood and consequences of a terrorist attack is determined by a mix of strategies and counterstrategies developed by a range of stakeholders and changing over time. This leads to *dynamic uncertainty* (Michel-Kerjan, 2003-b).

More formally, the analyst is confronted with a dynamic game where the actions of the terrorist groups in period *t* are dependent on the actions taken by those threatened by the terrorists (*i.e.* the defenders) in period *t-1*. Hence terrorism risk will change depending on at least two complementary strategies by the defenders. The first entails protective measures adopted by those at risk. The second consists of actions taken by governments to enhance general security and reduce the probability that attacks will occur. In this sense, terrorism is a mixed public-private good. From the terrorists' point of view, they must determine what targets to attack and the commitment of resources to specific activities.

In contrast, actions can be taken to reduce damage from future natural disasters with the knowledge that the probability associated with the hazard will not be affected by the adoption of these protective measures. In other words, the likelihood of an earthquake of a given intensity in a specific location will not change if property owners design more quake-resistant structures. For example, damage due to a future large-scale earthquake in Los Angeles, Tokyo, or Monaco can be reduced through adoption of mitigation measures; however, it is currently not possible to influence the occurrence of the earthquake itself.

The firms that have modeled the risks from natural disasters have attempted to develop estimates of terrorist risk, but they are the first to acknowledge that there is considerable uncertainty in their projections. Moreover, the models do not provide distributions of expected loss from terrorism, in the statistical sense, but rather estimate potential losses associated with specific scenarios. (Kunreuther, Michel-Kerjan and Porter, 2004). Section 5 of this report discusses in more detail new developments in terrorism risk models and how they can be used to price the risk.

Interdependent Security

Another type of negative externality that affects the decision to invest in protective measures relates to problems of *interdependent security*. Kunreuther and Heal (2003) and Heal and Kunreuther (2003) have addressed this issue by asking the following question: What economic incentives do residents, firms or governments have for undertaking protection if they know that others are not taking these measures and that their failure to do so could cause damage to them?

Investing in airline security illustrates the nature of the interdependency problem. Suppose Airline A is considering whether to institute a sophisticated and costly passenger security system knowing that some passengers who transfer from other airlines to their planes may not have gone through a similar screening procedure. The more airlines that do not invest in these measures, the less incentive Airline A has to incur this cost. The interdependent risks across firms may lead all of them to decide not to invest in protection.

The crash of Pan America's flight 103 over Lockerbie, Scotland in December 1988 that killed 259 people on board and 11 others on the ground illustrates this point. The explosion was caused by a bomb loaded at Gozo, Malta on Malta Airlines where there were poor security systems, transferred at Frankfort Airport to a Pan Am feeder and then loaded onto Pan Am 103 at London's Heathrow Airport. The bomb was designed to explode only when the aircraft flew higher than 28,000 feet, which would normally not occur until the plane started crossing the Atlantic to its final destination, New York. There was not a thing that Pan Am could do to prevent this tragedy unless they inspected all transferred bags, which is both a costly and time-consuming process. The terrorists who placed the bomb knew exactly where to check the bag. They put it on Malta Airlines, which had minimum-security measures, and Pan Am was helpless. Hence the terrorists took advantage of the weakest link in a chain of interdependencies (Lockerbie, 2001). Similarly, the collapse of the World Trade Center on September 11, 2001 could be attributed in part to the failure of security at Logan airport in Boston where terrorists were able to board planes that flew into the twin towers.

Internalizing these externalities can be particularly challenging for insurers. Their pricing may adequately reflect the risk of an insured party being contaminated by others particularly if they are some distance away, as was the case in the airline example. We will return to this issue in discussing the need for public-private partnerships for terrorism insurance.

Information Sharing

The sharing of information on terrorism risk is clearly different than the sharing of information regarding natural hazard risk. In the latter case, new scientific studies normally are common knowledge so that insurers, individuals or businesses at risk, as well as public sector agencies, all have access to these findings. With respect to terrorism, information on terrorist groups' activities, possible attacks or current threats is kept secret by government agencies for national security reasons.

One justification for government intervention in insurance markets relates to the asymmetry of information between buyers and sellers and the problems this may cause, such as adverse selection. In the case of terrorism, there is a very peculiar case of *symmetry of non-information* on the risk between those insured and insurers, where government is the most informed party[17] (see Table 6.4). However, for obvious reasons, government agencies are often reluctant to share knowledge of terrorist plans and activities due to national security concerns. This constitutes a notable feature of terrorism as catastrophic risk[18]. Combined with a dynamic uncertainty, as introduced above, that presents special challenges for insurers who need information in order to establish predictability –and then pricing their coverage– for at least one year, but preferably over a period of years. Moreover, even perfect information on the likelihood of an attack during the coming month does little for an insurer that issues annual or even multi-year policies.

Government Influencing the Risk

Finally, there are also more fundamental differences between catastrophic natural hazards and mega-terrorism. International terrorism is a matter of national security as well as foreign policy. It is obvious that the government can influence the level of risk of future attacks through appropriate counter-terrorism policies and international cooperation as well as through adequate crisis management to limit consequences should an attack occur.

Table 6.4. **Natural Hazards versus Terrorism Risks**

	Natural Hazards Potential catastrophic losses	Terrorism Risks Potential catastrophic losses
Historical Data	Some historical data: Record of several extreme events already occurred.	Very limited historical data: 9/11 events were the first terrorist attacks worldwide with such a huge concentration of victims and insured damages.
Risk of Occurrence	Risk reasonably well-specified: Well-developed models for estimating risks based on historical data and experts' estimates.	Considerable ambiguity of risk: Terrorists can purposefully adapt their strategy (target, weapons, time) depending on their information on vulnerabilities; dynamic uncertainty.
Geographic Risk	Specific areas at risk: Some geographical areas are well known for being at risk (e.g., California for earthquakes or Florida for hurricanes).	All areas at risk: Some cities may be considered riskier than others (e.g., New York City, Washington), but terrorists may attack anywhere, any time.
Information	Information sharing: New scientific knowledge on natural hazards can be shared with all the stakeholders.	Asymmetry of information: Governments keep secret new information on terrorism for obvious national security reasons.
Event Type	Natural event: To date no one can influence the occurrence of an extreme natural event (e.g., an earthquake).	Resulting event: Governments can influence terrorism (e.g., foreign policy; international cooperation; national security measures).
Preparedness and Prevention	Insureds can invest in well-known mitigation measures.	Weapons and configurations are numerous. Negative externalities of self-protection effort; substitution effect in terrorist activity. Insureds may have difficulty in choosing measures to reduce consequences of an attack; Federal agencies may be in a better position to develop more efficient global mitigation programs.
Catastrophe Modeling	Developed in late 1980's and early 1990's.	The first models were developed in 2002.

Some decisions made by a government as part of their foreign policy can also affect the will of terrorist groups to attack this country or its interest abroad (Lapan and Sandler, 1988; Lee, 1988; Pillar, 2001). Governments can also devote part of their budget to the development of specific measures on national soil to protect the country. The creation of the new U.S. Department of Homeland Security in 2002 confirms the importance of this role in managing the terrorist risk. In that sense, terrorism risk is partly under the government's control and will change depending on at least two complementary strategies by the defenders. The first entails protective measures that could be adopted by those at risk. The second consists of actions taken by governments to enhance general security and reduce the probability that attacks will occur. Hence terrorism is a mixed private-public good. (Kunreuther and Michel-Kerjan, 2004).

Summary

Both terrorist activities and natural disasters have the potential to cause catastrophic losses, thereby posing limitations for the insurability of the risk. Terrorism has additional challenges due to the lack of current data on terrorist activities, the dynamic uncertainty due to the ability of these groups to purposefully adapt their strategy in reaction to new security measures and the existence of interdependencies that could reduce firms' incentives to adequately invest in security measures. Moreover, the risk of terrorist attacks is partly under the government's control. These features of terrorism make this risk very different than catastrophic risks associated with natural hazards, as summarized in Table 6.4. We argue that they call for the development of adequate and long-term partnerships between the public and private sectors to provide adequate protection to victims of terrorism, should new attacks occur.

4. Covering Mega-Terrorism: The Need For Public-Private Partnerships

These characteristics of terrorism, along with the difficulty insurers face in finding new capital for covering potential losses from future events, raise the question as to how the government and the insurance industry can work together in providing protection against terrorist risks. As this section discusses, the need for public-private partnerships was actually recognized in most countries in the aftermath of 9/11.

4.1. Private Market Responses to 9/11

Given the challenges in estimating the likelihood of specific terrorist attacks and their consequences, a question that is being posed today is whether the private insurance market can offer coverage without some public sector involvement. As discussed above, if there are limited data on which to estimate the risk and there is the potential for catastrophic losses, then insurers will want to charge premiums reflecting their aversion to ambiguity and restrict coverage to reduce the possibility of insolvency. If, in addition there are negative externalities associated with the risk, then the private insurer will not be able to encourage risk-reducing measures through premium reductions, as it would be able to do without these interdependencies. The insurer knows that even if a firm undertakes security measures to reduce its own risk, other firms that have not been as prudent can still affect it, thus increasing the risk from what it would otherwise be. (Kunreuther and Heal, 2003).

This section examines the demand and supply for terrorism insurance after the terrorist attacks of 9/11. For obvious reasons, most available data and publications relate to the U.S. insurance market[19]. We show that there was a very thin market for protection and explore why private sector solutions, such as a mutual pool and a sustained market for terrorist catastrophe bonds did not emerge.

We conclude that the failure of the insurance industry to satisfy the unsatisfied demand for coverage during the year following September 11th was the principal reason that the U.S. Federal government passed new legislation requiring insurers to provide terrorism coverage.

Market Reactions to 9/11

The response by the insurance industry to the terrorist attacks could have been predicted by the literature on insurance firm behavior following catastrophic events[20]. In the short run, large losses from a specific disaster reduce surplus and hence capacity to provide coverage. Given the high transaction costs of raising outside capital to replenish surplus and the relatively high interest rates associated with these funds, firms reduce the amount of coverage they offer and increase the price of insurance for the particular risk that caused the losses.

Consider the impact that 9/11 had on the supply of terrorism coverage. Insurers were unable to obtain reinsurance for these events except at very high prices and felt that losses from another terrorist attack of comparable magnitude could do irreparable damage to the industry[21]. As a result, many insurers refused to offer coverage to their clients. The few that did provide insurance charged very high prices so only organizations that were required to have this coverage actually purchased it.

Unlike reinsurers, primary insurers must obtain approval from state regulatory agencies when implementing new coverage restrictions. In October 2001, the Insurance Services Office (ISO), on behalf of insurance companies, filed a request in every state for permission to exclude terrorism from all commercial insurance coverage (except for workers' compensation coverage for which terrorism can not be excluded) (U.S. General Accounting Office, 2002). In the U.S., as of February 2002, 45 states, the District of Columbia and Puerto Rico had approved the insurance industry's applications for terrorism exclusion language. The states that had not approved the new exclusion were California, Florida, Georgia, New York, and Texas accounting for about 35 percent of the commercial insurance market (U.S. Congress, Joint Economic Committee, 2002)[22].

Potential Role for Mutual Insurance

One way the private market might have developed a larger market for terrorism insurance without governmental participation would have been to create mutual insurance, such as risk retention groups. A risk retention group (RRG) is an entity that provides liability insurance to its owner-members. Traditionally, it is created when insurance is not available or premiums are so high that few buyers feel they can afford coverage.

The airline industry considered forming such a mutual company when coverage for third party liability for terrorism and war risks was withdrawn within 10 days after 9/11. New policies offered by insurers limited their aggregate third party liability to $50 million, falling far short of the $3.5 billion of aviation liability losses from 9/11 (Hartwig, 2002). For airlines, the question of adequate third party liability coverage became vital for the continuity of their activities. As a temporary measure, the federal government provided this protection for U.S. airlines, as did other governments worldwide. When first warned that government coverage was going to cease, the U.S. airlines created their own RRG, *Equitime* in June 2002.

However, this group never became operational[23]. A principal reason for the failure of this RRG has been the continued subsidized financial protection of airlines by the federal government, crowding out the emergence of private solutions at a competitive price. Indeed, a temporary FAA (Federal Aviation Administration) terrorism insurance program, which covers approximately 75 U.S. air carriers, had been in effect since September 2001 for a six-month period. It was then extended to the end of 2004 and more recently to December 31, 2007 (U.S. House of Representatives, 2003).

Potential Role for Terrorism Catastrophe Bonds

Since another chapter of this publication will discuss the role of new financial instruments, we will not provide a detailed analysis of this new asset and the potential for using these instruments as a complement/subsitute for insurance and reinsurance in the coming months or years[24]. Rather, we provide some explanation as to why no sustained market for terrorist catastrophe bonds has emerged to date.

In the aftermath of Hurricane Andrew and the Northridge Earthquake in the early 1990s, property catastrophe reinsurance was in short supply and the price of reinsurance more than doubled in the U.S. compared with late 1980s, as illustrated by Figure 6.6. For insurers to provide their clients with the same amount of coverage they offered prior to these events they had to find capital from other sources. They collaborated with the investment banking community to develop new classes of financial instruments. Alternative risk transfers, such as options and catastrophe bonds, emerged to cover these losses by transferring part of the risks to the capital markets. Though the market for risk-linked securities is still in its early stages, insurers and reinsurers have over $4.3 billion in catastrophe bonds outstanding at the end of 2003, an increase of more than 50% over 2002. The total amount of risk-linked securities since its inception is over $9.5 billion (Swiss Re, 2004). However, this market is still considerably below the expectations of insurers, reinsurers, and investment bankers, accounting in 2002 for less than 3% of worldwide catastrophe reinsurance coverage. (U.S. General Accounting Office, 2003).

A market for catastrophe bonds to cover losses from terrorist attacks has **not** emerged since 9/11. To date, only two terrorism-related cat bonds have been issued. None of them is actually a pure terrorism cat bond issued for a specific type of attack only but multi-event cat bonds associated with the risk of natural disasters or pandemics[25].

Figure 6.6. **Catastrophe Reinsurance Price Index, 1989-2002 (1989 = 100)**

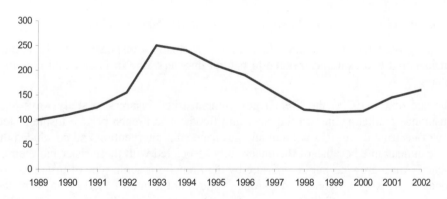

Sources: U.S. General Accounting Office (2003)

Bantwal and Kunreuther (2000) specified a set of factors that might account for the relatively thin market in catastrophe bonds for natural hazard risks that may partially explain the lack of interest in terrorist catastrophe bonds. In their paper the authors conjecture that the reluctance of institutional investors to enter this market is due to a combination of ambiguity aversion, myopic loss aversion, and fixed costs of education on a new type of asset.

Four additional elements may explain the lack of interest in new financial instruments for covering terrorism risk. Unlike investments in traditional high-yield debt, money invested in a natural or terrorist catastrophe bond can disappear instantly and with no warning. Those marketing these new financial instruments may be concerned that if they suffer a large loss on the catastrophe bond, they will receive a lower annual bonus from their firm and have a harder time generating business in the future.

More specifically, investment managers may fear the repercussions on their reputation from losing money by investing in an unusual and newly-developed asset or making money based on loss of human life. The short-term incentives facing investment managers differ from the long-term incentives facing their employers. If this is a major problem in marketing catastrophe bonds, then there is a need to develop strategies for bringing the principal (employer and its shareholders) and its agents (investment managers) into alignment.

Second, there may be a moral hazard problem associated with issuing such bonds if terrorist groups are connected with financial institutions having an interest in the U.S. For example, the recent aborted DARPA terrorism futures market experimented by the Pentagon, suffered from moral hazard: a terrorist group supported by specific investors might have an obvious financial interest to perpetrate and benefit from a terrorist attack against a public figure on whose life odds were placed (Woo, 2004).

A third reason why there has been no market for terrorist catastrophe bonds was the reluctance of reinsurers to provide protection against this risk following the World Trade Center attacks of September 11th. Financial investors perceive reinsurers as experts in this market. Upon learning that the reinsurance industry required high premiums to provide protection against terrorism, investors were only willing to provide funds to cover losses from terrorism if they received a sufficiently high interest rate.

Finally most investors and rating agencies consider terrorism models recently developed (see Section 5) as too new and untested to be used in conjunction with a catastrophe bond covering risks. The models are viewed as providing useful information on the potential severity of the attacks but not on their frequency. Without the acceptance of these models by major rating agencies, the development of a large market for terrorist catastrophe bonds is unlikely (U.S. General Accounting Office, 2003).

4.2. Terrorism Risk Coverage: Need for Government Participation

When the private insurance market fails there is normally a response from the public sector. Let's consider first two examples related to natural disasters, one in France and the other in the United States.

At the end of the 1970s, the French government asked insurers to study ways to create a private insurance market against earthquakes and floods. The French private insurers studied the possibility of insuring these risks without any governmental intervention and concluded that these events were uninsurable because of the uncertainty associated with these risks and their concerns of insolvency. Amid growing public pressure by the French for some type of insurance following major floods in the Rhône, Saône, and Garonne valleys at the end of 1981, France created a new and so far unique system the following year. The "Cat. Nat. System" is based on a public-private partnership, which covers all major natural hazards except storms, with unlimited state-guaranteed public reinsurance. The system has been operating for 22 years now. (Michel-Kerjan, 2001).

In the U.S., insurers were prepared to cancel windstorm coverage in hurricane-prone areas of Florida following Hurricane Andrew in 1992. The state legislature passed a law the next year that individual insurers could not cancel more than 10 percent of their homeowners' policies in any county in any one year and that they could not cancel more than 5 percent of their property owners' policies statewide. At the same time the Florida Hurricane Catastrophe Fund was created to relieve pressure on insurers should there be a catastrophic loss from a future disaster (Lecomte and Gahagan, 1998).

In the same spirit, government protection against catastrophic losses associated with mega-terrorism is particularly important as such events pose severe problems of liquidity and possible insolvency to insurers and reinsurers. Government has the capacity to provide this type of coverage, as it can diversify the risks over the entire population and spread past losses to future generations of taxpayers, a form of cross-time diversification that the private market cannot achieve because of the incompleteness of inter-generational private markets (Gollier, 2002).

Government participation in any insurance program to cover against terrorism is even more crucial than for natural disasters since the risk of terrorist attacks is partly in the government's control and that government can have more information on ongoing terrorist groups' activities though intelligence services, as discussed in Section 3.

Building on the capacity of insurers to levy and collect premiums as well as to estimate damage should attacks occur, the need for government participation was recognized in most countries as they develop national program to cover the risk associated with terrorism (Liedtke and Courbage, 2002). Below we provide some features of programs operating in three European countries (U.K., France, and Germany) and United States as chronologically launched.

United Kingdom

In the wake of the two terrorist bomb explosions in the City of London in April 1992 and an announcement seven months later by British insurers that they would exclude terrorism coverage from their commercial policies, the UK established a mutual insurance organization (Pool Re) to accommodate claims following terrorist activities. Pool Re charges a separate, optional premium for terrorism coverage that can be calculated as a percentage of the total sum insured under a fire and accident policy and mainly depends on the location of the property. The four different rates established by Pool Re are based on the risks, with the highest rate in Central London and the second highest in the rest of the city. The Treasury backs Pool Re as the reinsurer of last resort.

Until September 11, 2001 terrorism exclusions within insurance policies in the UK were limited to property policies. They were based on the Terrorism Act of 1993 and designed to deal with the IRA bombing campaign on mainland Britain. Fire and explosion were excluded by insurance companies, but were covered under Pool Re. The scale of the 9/11 attacks in the United States led to the need for extending protection under Pool Re to "all risks" (including damage caused by chemical and biological as well as nuclear contamination). As of January 1, 2003 the Pool Re policy cover all these risks which has resulted in doubling of the pre September 11th 2001 premiums. Moreover, insurers are now free to set the premiums for underlying terrorism policies, thereby introducing competition into the terrorist insurance market[26].

Michel-Kerjan and Pedell (forthcoming) provide a detailed comparative analysis, relative to each country's market, of the new terrorism insurance programs developed after 9/11 in France, Germany, and the U.S as well as analysis of the current market penetration. Below we briefly discuss key features associated with risk sharing between the public and private sectors in each of these three programs and whether terrorism coverage is compulsory or not[27]. The Appendix of this report provides a comparison of the main features of these three public-private partnerships.

France

France suffered several terrorist attacks during the 1980's. A law enacted in September 1986 requires the French insurers to provide terrorism coverage up to the overall limits of a standard commercial property insurance policy. After 9/11 French insurers were forced to renew terrorist coverage and retain most of the risk, as most reinsurers refused to cover acts of terrorism in their policies. Discussions between FFSA, GEMA[28] and the French government led to the creation of the first post 9/11 State-backed reinsurance pool for terrorism worldwide, the GAREAT (*Group of Insurance and Reinsurance against Terrorism*), on January 1, 2002[29]. A scale of premiums charged by the pool is established nationwide. Those premiums only depend on the insured value and not on the location at risk. All insurers must be members of the pool. In order to avoid adverse selection and low demand for insurance that may result in large uncovered losses as well as to bring the largest part of the risks to the pool, terrorism coverage is mandatory in France (Godard et al., 2002; Michel-Kerjan, 2003).

As of 2004, the current partnership between the government and the insurance industry is a four-layer scheme. Private insurers retain the first portion of losses up to 400 million euros; the next layer is placed in the international insurance and reinsurance market up to 1.65 billion euros (a 1.25 billion euros trench). A third layer is comprised of reinsurance covering losses between 1.65 and 2.0 billion euros. Losses greater than 2.0 billion euros are covered by the government (unlimited guarantee for which the pool pays an annual premium), and managed by the Caisse Centrale de Réassurance, a public-owned reinsurer.

Germany

Discussions between the German federal government and the insurance industry led to the creation of a special insurer for terrorism risks, Extremus AG. The company has been operating since November 2002. Extremus, a corporation whose shareholders are essentially private insurers and reinsurers operating in Germany, directly insures terrorism risk through the participating companies. As in France, a premium scale is established nationwide that depends on the sum insured and not on the location at risk. Coverage by Extremus is non-compulsory and is only offered if the total insured value per policy is at least 25 million euros.

From March 1, 2004 on, the annual reinsurance capacity has been limited to 10 billion euros and is provided in three layers. The shareholders of Extremus provide the first layer of 1.5 billion euros. International reinsurers, led by Berkshire Hathaway, provide the second layer of €0.5 billion. The Federal Government of Germany would provide an additional capacity of 8 billion euros if needed. It is worth noting that the low demand for terrorism insurance coverage in Germany during 2003 (see below) contributed to the decision to reduce this second layer from €1.5 billion in 2003 to €0.5 billion as of March 1, 2004 in order to decrease reinsurance premiums paid by Extremus and to enable Extremus to operate cost-covering. At the same time, the state coverage decreased from €10 billion to €8 billion (Frankfurter Allgemeine Zeitung, 2004).

United States

No state or federal insurance legislation was enacted during the year following 9/11 in the United States. As a result many firms remained largely uncovered at the time of the first anniversary of the 9/11 attacks (Hale, 2002). The lack of available terrorist coverage at an affordable price delayed or prevented certain projects from going forward due to concerns by lenders or investors in providing financing for these efforts. These concerns led to the passage of the Terrorism Risk Insurance Act of 2002 (TRIA) on November 26, 2002.

While TRIA may have been welcome news for commercial enterprises[30], it appears to have been a mixed blessing for insurers, as TRIA requires that insurers offer a policy covering against terrorism to all their clients who can decline the offer.

Under TRIA's three-year term –the act expires on December 31, 2005–, insured commercial property and casualty losses from terrorism are covered only if the U.S. Treasury Secretary certifies the event as an "act of terrorism" carried out by foreign persons or interests[31] and only for losses above $5 million.

There is a specific risk-sharing arrangement between the federal government and insurers that operates in the following manner. First, each insurer is responsible for an annual deductible based on a percentage of its prior year direct earned premium. The percentage varies over the three-year operation of TRIA: 7% in 2003, 10% in 2004, and 15% in 2005. Once an insurer has met its backstop deductible, the federal government is responsible for paying 90% of the insurer's losses above that amount. The insurance industry and federal government's share of losses is capped to a combined annual amount of $100 billion. Should this amount ever be reached, the Act contemplates that Congress will reconvene to determine a mechanism for further funding.

Second, the Act contemplates that Treasury may recoup the entire federal share of losses through a post-event policyholder surcharge administered by insurers. That surcharge is applied to all property and casualty insurance policies whether or not the insured has purchased terrorist coverage, with a maximum of 3% of the premium charged under that policy per year. Hence the federal government would pay only for insured losses above specific insurance marketplace retention amounts. That amount is specified as $10 billion in 2003, $12.5 billion for 2004 and $15 billion for 2005.

An important element of this program is that the federal government does not receive any premium for providing this coverage. Although the overall effect on the crowding-out of private solutions is not clear a priori, this limits the role of reinsurance companies to covering the deductible portion of the insurer's potential liability from a terrorist attack. With respect to catastrophic losses, there is no way reinsurers can compete with a zero cost federal terrorism reinsurance program.

Currently it is unclear what type of terrorism insurance program will emerge in the United States after 2005. One possibility is that TRIA will be renewed with the same or a new risk-sharing arrangement between the insurance industry and the federal government. However, if the program is terminated on December 31, 2005, alternative solutions will need to be found. The challenge is to develop an efficient program that will satisfy the different interested parties, each of whom has their own set of values and concerns. In addition to insurance coverage, there are ways of encourage investment in loss-reduction measures before an event so as to reduce the need for the public sector to provide financial aid following a disaster (Kunreuther and Michel-Kerjan, in press).

4.3. A Low Degree of Market Penetration

Empirical Evidence

As the U.S. TRIA and the German Extremus have been operating for less than 2 years at the time this report go to press, it is too early to get a robust analysis on the market penetration of terrorism insurance in these countries. However, in these two countries where coverage is non-compulsory, the limited available data present an interesting picture of the demand for terrorism coverage two years after the 9/11 attacks.

In the U.S., when Congress passed the Terrorist Risk Insurance Act of 2002 (TRIA) in November 2002, the expectation was that it would ease insurers' concerns about providing coverage and enable buyers at risk to purchase coverage at reasonable prices. Although insurance is now available nationwide, there have been few takers (Treaster, 2003).

The Council of Insurance Agents and Brokers (CIAB)[32] undertook the first national survey on the level of demand for terrorist coverage (CIAB, March 2003). At that time, 48% of its members that handle the largest accounts (customers who pay more than $100,000 annually in commission and fees to the broker) indicated that less than 1 in 5 of their customers had purchased terrorism insurance.

The low demand was even more pronounced for smaller companies (less than $25,000 in commission and fees to the broker): 65% of the brokers indicated that less than 1 in 5 customers were purchasing insurance against terrorism. According to another national survey by the CIAB a few months later, 72% of the brokers indicated that their commercial customers are still not purchasing terrorism insurance coverage (CIAB, July 2003).

Even in locations like New York City, the level of demand remains low. During the autumn of 2003, the New York-based insurance brokerage firm Kaye Insurance Associates surveyed 100 of its clients at middle market real estate, retail, and manufacturing in the New York area on a series of insurance-related issues, including terrorism insurance. Only 36% of the companies indicated that they had purchased terrorism insurance (Kaye, October 2003).

More recently, Marsh Inc. undertook another national survey of 2,400 of its client organizations in the United States for the second, third, and fourth quarters of 2003. Over that entire time period, the take-up rate for terrorism insurance averaged 27% (Marsh, 2004)[33].

The U.S. Treasury Department is required by Congress to assess the effectiveness of TRIA no later than June 30, 2005 as well as to analyze the supply and demand for terrorism coverage as inputs to the process of determining whether TRIA should be renewed after 2005. Some studies, launched by the U.S Treasury in December 2003, should contribute to a better understanding of the evolution of demand for terrorism insurance in the coming months.

In Germany, the demand for terrorism insurance is even lower than in the United States[34]. As of August 2004, according to data provided by Extremus, the number of contracts managed by Extremus amounts to nearly 1,000 over an estimated 40,000 firms eligible for such coverage in Germany; *i.e.* only 2.5 percent of eligible contracts are covered[35]. If one focuses on just the largest German companies, the level of demand is higher. According to a survey published in 2003, 40% of the DAX30 companies[36] (13 of the 30) had insurance contracts with Extremus (Frankfurter Allgemeine Zeitung, 2003).

Risk Perception and Other Factors

Since most businesses have little or no information on terrorism risk and no new attack has occurred on U.S. soil since 9/11, U.S. firms may perceive the chances of another event to be extremely low. A few years after 9/11, concern with damage from terrorism appears to have taken a back seat. In 2003, most firms believed that if a terrorist attack occurs, it would not affect them, whereas in the first few months after 9/11, they had the opposite belief. The aforementioned CIAB study indicated that more than 90% of the brokers said that their customers eschew terrorism insurance because they think they don't need it (CIAB, 2003b). The Kaye survey also asked those who had not yet purchased terrorism coverage why they had not done so. The top reason was that the company was not a target (66%), followed by high cost (17%) (Kaye, 2003).

This behavior has been well documented for natural hazards where many individuals buy insurance after a disaster occurs and cancel their policies several years later if they have not suffered a loss. It is difficult to convince these individuals that the best return on an insurance policy is no return at all. In other words, there is a tendency for most people to view insurance as an investment rather than as a form of protection (Kunreuther, 2002). These firms consider insurance, even at relatively low premiums, to be a bad investment.

The expectation that government may financially aid affected businesses whether or not they are covered by insurance, as illustrated by the airline industry following 9/11, may also contribute to limiting interest in spending money on coverage. Finally, the definition of terrorism coverage can also be problematic. More specifically, the distinction between an *act of terrorism* that would be covered and an *act of war* that would be excluded is not always very clear.

Should terrorism insurance be compulsory?

If the low level of demand continues, a mega-terrorist attack will likely have a more devastating effect on business continuity and social activity today than after 9/11 because losses will not be diversified in the national and international insurance and reinsurance industry, but mainly incurred by those at risk unless the government intervenes again. This may be partially alleviated by introducing some degree of mandatory coverage, as currently is done in France. As mentioned, such a compulsory component of national programs leads to a high degree of risk mutualization and hence lowers prices of terrorism insurance in large cities as well as reduces concern about adverse selection since everyone would be insured.

It is obviously much easier to defend a voluntary private market approach for providing terrorism insurance when no losses have been incurred. The lessons of September 11th indicate that there will be strong pressure for public sector involvement following any large-scale disaster. Considering some type of required insurance before such an event occurs should alleviate the political pressure for federal relief and facilitate the recovery process through insurance claims dispersed rapidly to those suffering losses. Whether terrorism coverage should be required in other countries by private institutions (*e.g.* banks as a condition of mortgage) or even by the government remains, however, an open question. As each country may have its own culture, habits, and its own characteristics of insurance markets, there is no easy answer and this question needs more open discussion.

Finally, it seems also difficult –if not impossible– to measure the real degree of efficiency of terrorism insurance programs implemented in different countries and to make a quantitative comparison between them. Indeed, most European programs have defined rates that depend on simple variables such as the level of total insured value or a few separate geographical areas, and do not result explicitly from quantification of risk exposure. Without the ability to estimate terrorist risks and potential damages associated with a wide range of scenarios of attacks, any economic evaluation of these programs, at least in relative terms, remains impossible.

5. Modeling Terrorism Risk[37]

This section presents some key features of the new models developed after 9/11 to quantify the risk associated with terrorism. The development of terrorism risk models could constitute helpful tools based on more understandable metrics for decisions by firms, (re)insurance industry and government to be made. Loss estimates generated by terrorism models are of interest to all parties. The insureds would like a better understanding of their exposure to potential terrorist attacks in order to determine whether to purchase coverage. Insurers and reinsurers can use model output to develop their pricing and reinsurance needs and fashion policy conditions such as deductibles, exclusions, and coverage limits. They can also use the output of these models to determine their implication in a particular national program of terrorism risk coverage based on a public-private partnership. Governments can establish their program with rates reflecting at least partially the exposure of the insureds.

Insurance markets function best when losses are relatively small, random, and uncorrelated, and when there is an abundance of historical loss data to which statistical techniques can be applied to predict future losses. As has been discussed throughout this report, when it comes to natural disasters or terrorism, losses can be of catastrophic proportion and are often highly correlated. Furthermore, because such natural disasters occur infrequently, loss data are relatively scarce, making reliance on traditional actuarial techniques dubious at best.

As limited as the data is for nature catastrophes, there is much less information available on terrorist attacks for risk estimation purposes. To the extent that data do exist and are available from government sources, they may not be representative of current threats. Even more important, unlike earthquakes and other natural disasters, whose occurrence has a physical basis that can be understood by scientists, terrorist attacks are a function of the malicious intent of groups of individuals of varying sizes and varying agendas. The groups themselves come and go and their ability to attract resources in terms of both financial and human capital waxes and wanes as the larger political and/or economic climate changes over time. As discussed in Section 3, it is clear that the uncertainty surrounding the frequency, location and severity of future terrorist activity is much higher than for natural hazards, making the task of modeling much more complex. In the absence of historical data to which probability distributions can be fit, the models are by necessity more subjective in nature.

To explore the alternative approaches that modelers have used to overcome the challenges of quantifying terrorism risk, it is useful to begin with a simple modeling framework as illustrated by Figure 6.7.

Figure 6.7. **Terrorism Catastrophe model components**

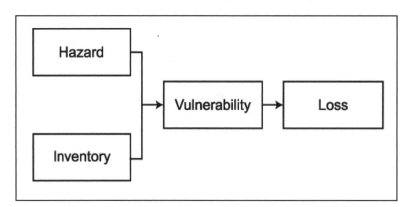

5.1. Terrorism Hazard

A terrorism model must first address three basic issues regarding the hazard itself: frequency of occurrence, the most likely locations of future terrorist attacks, and their severity in terms of insured loss. In undertaking this analysis, the different potential targets plus the interdependencies among networks and systems must be taken into account. For example, the loss of electric power or contamination of the water supply could create long-term business interruption risks and require residents in the affected areas to relocate.

The management of international terrorism risks has traditionally relied upon the experience and judgment of a specialist underwriter. For certain individual risks, recourse might be made on the advice of security professionals. For a portfolio, maximum loss would be carefully capped, but the overall risk assessment procedure would remain essentially qualitative and subjective. The most basic terrorism risk model is thus one encoded within the working experience of an underwriter and dependent on his personal expert judgment. To cover rare catastrophic acts of terrorism, beyond the experience of even the most seasoned underwriter, the judgment of external terrorism experts might be invoked.

Terrorism risk management would still be firmly judgment-based, but the underwriter would be supported by the greater knowledge and perception of terrorism experts. Recognizing that experts' risk estimates are based on their own set of assumptions and may reflect a set of biases, the challenge is to evaluate these figures carefully in modeling terrorism risk. Terrorism models incorporate the judgment of teams of experts familiar both with limited available historical data and current trends. These experts have operational experience in counter-terrorism at the highest national and international levels, with many specializing in terrorism threat assessment. Because each expert is privy to his own sources of intelligence and has his own security clearances, there is no common database of information upon which all experts can form their judgments. In fact, much of the crucial information is confidential.

Determining Likelihood of Attacks

To elicit expert opinion on the likelihood of attacks several different approaches have been utilized. Some modeling firms employ the Delphi method while others convene a conference of experts to capture and statistically combine various opinions into a useful and cohesive form that can be used to generate probabilities. For complex problems not governed by scientific laws, the judgment and intuition of experts in their field is not only an appropriate ingredient in any model, but a critical one.

The Delphi Method is a well-known and accepted approach developed by the RAND Corporation at the start of the Cold War. Among its first applications was the forecasting of inter-continental warfare and technological change. The Delphi method comprises a series of repeated interrogations, usually administered by questionnaire where the responses are anonymous. Direct interaction between the participants is precluded to eliminate the natural bias to follow the leader. After an initial round of interrogation, individuals are encouraged to reconsider and, when appropriate, to change their views in light of the replies of others in the group that are shared with everyone (Adler and Ziglio, 1996). While the methodology is highly structured, the final estimates by each participant still only represent opinions, informed by other members of the group.

Experts are asked to weigh in on several aspects of event frequency and intensity: the number of attacks per year, the type of target, the attack mode or weapon type, and finally the specific target of each potential attack. Each of these issues depends in part on the nature of the terrorist organization originating the attack. Critical to the results is the team's operational understanding of the likely terrorist actions in the context of the current state of security countermeasures. Targets and attack methods that were once undefended may now be more vigorously protected by federal homeland security, state and local policy, and private security resources.

An alternative to the Delphi method is using a conference of experts where participants can exchange views. The agenda can be topics, such as the kind of weapons a specific terrorist group is more likely to use or what areas/countries are more susceptible to attack. When some experts are unable to attend the conference, their judgment can be elicited separately and fed back to others using the Delphi method.

The lack of historical data makes the use of experts the only way for modelers to determine the likelihood of new attacks. However, experts have their own limitations in forecasting future behavior, as each of them has specialized knowledge. Some are much more focused on a given terrorist group and disregard dangers from others. Others are specialized on a given type of weapon or on a very specific kind of biological or chemical agent. In other words, each expert can be accurate within his or her small window of expertise, but the whole group of experts can be wrong about the reality of the global threats – a kind of illusory expertise (Linstone and Turoff, 1975).

Another pitfall is the possible optimism/pessimism bias of experts. For instance, if a terrorist attack recently occurred, a natural trend would be to overestimate the likelihood of new attacks in the short run. Conversely, if a governmental agency arrested leaders of a terrorist group, a natural bias could be to concentrate only on that group and overlook other terrorists, resulting in misconceptions of the likelihood of other attacks.

Identifying Likely Targets and Attack Modes

Target types vary depending on the nature and goals of the individual terrorist groups or organizations. For example, the targets that the Animal Liberation Front is likely to find attractive will differ from those chosen by Al Qaeda, not only because of differences in the resources at this group's disposal, but because of its different political agenda.

Once the target types are identified, databases of individual potential targets are developed. In the case of terrorism, targets within the U.S. might include high profile skyscrapers, government buildings, airports, chemical plants, nuclear power plants, dams, major tunnels and bridges, large sports stadiums, major corporate headquarters and marine terminals. Trophy targets normally represent a higher value to the terrorists due to the publicity associated with them, and they therefore have a higher probability of attack, other things being equal. Target databases can comprise tens of thousands or even hundreds of thousands of structures (White House, 2003).

In the simulations developed by modelers, the terrorist group receives value or utility from the damage inflicted on its adversaries. The expected loss is determined by the probability of success in carrying out the attack and the economic and psychological value of the target. In turn, the probability of success is determined not only by the amount of resources the terrorist group allocates to the attack but also by the resources its opponent allocates to detecting terrorist activity and defending the target. Both parties are constrained by the funds and person power at their disposal and the game becomes one of strategic decisions as to how to deploy those resources, *i.e.* which targets to attack and with what weapons, and which to defend. Therefore, game theory can be used to analyze likely targets and attack modes.

The severity of the attack is a function of the weapon type. Modeled weapon types include so-called conventional weapons, such as package, car and truck bombs, as well as aviation crash. In light of Al Qaeda's clearly expressed interest in acquiring and deploying weapons of mass destruction, models also account for the possibility of non-conventional weapon attacks including chemical, biological, radiological, and nuclear (CBRN) (Central Intelligence Agency, 2003).

5.2. Inventory

The 9/11 attacks revealed that not only are the terrorist targets themselves at risk, but so are the surrounding buildings. Nevertheless, the effects of terrorist attacks with conventional weapons are likely to be highly localized compared to natural disasters such as hurricanes and earthquakes. The resulting damage depends on such things as the kind explosive material used, the amount of material, and the density and verticality of the surrounding buildings. For non-conventional weapons, the spatial extent of damage depends on the delivery mechanism and on external factors such as wind speed and wind direction.

Terrorism models can estimate total losses as well as aggregate insured or insurable losses for individual buildings, insurance company portfolios and/or the entire insurance industry. While the large losses resulting from natural catastrophes have historically been to property, terrorist attacks can affect multiple insurance lines that include life, liability, workers' compensation, accident, and health. They can also result in severe stress on the psyche of a nation under siege.

The databases that are utilized in natural catastrophe models are also relevant for terrorism models. Modelers have developed industry databases of employees by building occupancy and construction type at the ZIP code level. These can be supplemented with state payroll and benefit information, generally available to insurance companies, to create an inventory at risk. Since 9/11, modelers are emphasizing to insurers the importance of gathering detailed data on the buildings they insure and the employees who work in them. (Insurance Accounting, 2003).

5.3. Vulnerability

Research on the impact of explosives on structures has been ongoing since the 1950s. The Department of Defense and the Department of State have examined blast loading in the course of developing anti-terrorism designs for U.S. embassies. In addition, research activity has surged since the bombing of the Alfred P. Murrah Federal Office Building in Oklahoma City (1995) and the U.S. military housing facilities in Dhahran, Saudi Arabia (1996) (Olatidoye et al., 1998).

Modelers have developed damage functions that incorporate historical data from actual events combined with the results of experimental and analytical studies of how different building types respond to such attacks. In the case of a terrorist attack using conventional and nuclear weapons, buildings sustain damage as a result of a variety of assaults on their structural integrity and their non-structural components. In the case of non-conventional weapons, the structure of the building is likely to be unaffected but the resulting contamination may render it unusable for long periods and result in extensive cleanup costs. In either case, the damage functions determine loss to building, contents and loss of use.

Conventional Weapons

In terrorism modeling, damage is a function of the attack type and building type. The type of attack, whether package, car or truck bomb, can be expressed as a TNT-equivalent. The size of this charge can be thought of as the intensity of the event. Damage to the target building results from the resulting shock wave, the subsequent pressure wave, and fire.

The target building may sustain total damage from the point of view of insured loss even if it remains standing. If the building collapses, however, it will increase the number of fatalities. Furthermore, different modes of collapse, such as an overturn versus a pancake collapse, will affect the degree of damage to surrounding buildings and thus the total area affected by the event. The buildings surrounding the target building are also likely to be damaged by the resulting shock and pressure waves and/or by falling or flying debris.

Non-conventional Weapons

The effects of nuclear weapons on both structures and populations have been subjects of extensive research for decades (Glasstone and Dolan, 1977). Chemical, biological, and radiological (CBR or "dirty bomb") attacks are more problematical. Accidental releases of chemical agents, such as the one that occurred at the Union Carbide chemical plant in Bhopal, India (1984) have been analyzed, as has the 1986 accident at the Chernobyl nuclear power plant. Other events include the 1995 sarin attack in the Tokyo subway and the more recent distribution of weaponized anthrax through the mail in autumn 2001 in the U.S. (U.S. Department of State, 2003). These examples provide data for empirical analysis and research. Fortunately, those attacks have been extremely rare so there is limited historical data.

Some modelers have developed relationships between the use of non-conventional weapons and potential damage; others employ models developed for various government agencies that follow what is known as a source/transport/effects approach. The *source* refers to how a hazard agent originates, including the type, yield, effectiveness, and other properties of the agent. Various attack types are simulated, including chemical agents such as sarin, VX, and tabun, and biological agents such as anthrax and smallpox. Nuclear and radiological agents such as cesium, cobalt, and plutonium are also simulated (Central Intelligence Agency, 2003).

Transport refers to the means by which the agent disperses or moves from the source to the people, or facilities presumed to be the targets. A full range of mechanisms is considered ranging from mail-borne dispersal to wide area dissemination via aerosol spraying and conventional bomb blast. *Effects* refer to the physical, performance, and psychological impacts of the attack on humans as well as on the environment. While even a small suitcase nuclear device can cause extensive physical damage to buildings over a relatively large geographical area, the primary effects of other non-conventional weapons is contamination, which may render the structures unusable for long periods of time. In fact, in some cases, the most cost-effective way of dealing with badly contaminated buildings may be demolition under very cautious and well-defined procedures.

5.4. Workers' Compensation Loss

In addition to property damage, terrorism models estimate fatalities under both workers' compensation and life insurance policies, as well as losses from injuries arising from workers' compensation, personal accident and other casualty lines. The number of injuries and fatalities, as well as the severity of injuries, is a function of the nature of damage sustained by the structural and non-structural components of buildings and their contents. Figure 6.8 illustrates the process for computing workers' compensation loss.

Figure 6.8. **Modeling workers' compensation loss**

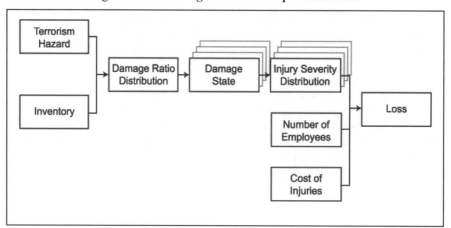

In estimating workers' compensation loss, models account for variability in damage to individual buildings so that one can estimate the extent of injuries and fatalities. For each level of severity, a mean damage ratio is calculated along with a probability distribution of damage. Because different structural types will experience different degrees of damage, the damage functions vary according to construction materials and occupancy. A distribution of damage for each structure type is mapped to different damage states. These may be, for example, slight, moderate, extensive, and complete, as shown in Figure 6.9 for a specific building.

Figure 6.9. **Building damage distribution mapped to different damage states**

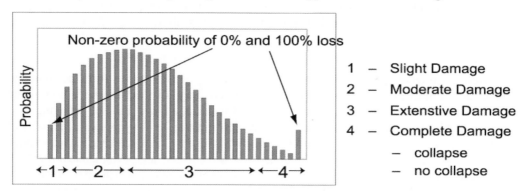

At the level of complete damage, the building may or may not have collapsed. Complete damage means that the building is not recoverable. Collapse will typically result in more severe injuries and larger numbers of fatalities than if the building is still standing. Estimates of workers' compensation (and other casualty lines) loss are based not only upon the number of people injured, but also on the severity of the injuries, such as minor, moderate, life threatening, and fatalities. Distributions of injury severity are then developed for each damage state for each building and occupancy type.

By combining information on the number of employees in each damaged building and the cost of injuries, the model generates the total loss distribution for a particular structure. Losses are calculated based on the number of employees in each injury severity level and on the cost of the injury as shown in Figure 6.10. To calculate losses arising from life insurance and personal accident claims, potential losses are calculated for both residential and commercial buildings using assumptions about the distribution of the population between these two types of structures at the time of the attack.

Figure 6.10. **Calculation of workers' compensation loss for an individual building**

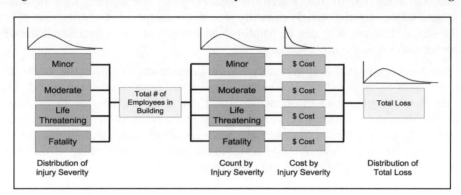

5.5. *National Programs of Risk Coverage: the Use of Terrorism Models*

Since these terrorism models have been applied to thousands of potential targets, they can provide a picture of the relative risk by state, city, ZIP code and even by individual location. The Insurance Services Office (ISO) used the estimates provided by one of its subsidiaries, AIR Worldwide, to file commercial property advisory average loss costs with the insurance commissioner for each state at the end of 2002[38]. ISO defined three tiers for the country, with certain areas within Washington, DC, New York, Chicago and San Francisco in the highest tier, with assigned loss costs of approximately $0.10 per $100 of property value. A second tier consisted of Boston, Houston, Los Angeles, Philadelphia and Seattle as well as other portions of the highest rated cities; the rest of the country fell into the third tier.

In pre-filing discussions with regulators, ISO's advisory loss costs were challenged by some regulators who felt that such premiums would lead businesses to relocate to other areas (Hsu, 2003). Negotiations ensued and compromises were made. ISO filed loss costs for first-tier cities based on zip code level model results, which differentiated between the higher risk of downtown city centers and the lower risk of properties on the outskirts. But nowhere did the filed loss costs exceed $0.03 per $100 of property value[39]. Thus, while the new official advisory average loss costs no longer adequately reflected the risk in the eyes of the modelers, they became more palatable to other stakeholders. The Departments of Insurance in all 50 states eventually approved these ISO advisory loss costs that covered the years 2003, 2004, and 2005.

A few months later, rates started decreasing. According to a national survey undertaken by Marsh Inc., of over 2,400 client firms during the second, third and fourth quarters of 2003, the median rate for terrorism insurance applied to the total insured value over that three-quarter period of 2003 was 0.056‰. That rate increased to 0.08‰ and 0.076‰ in the first and second quarters of 2004, respectively; virtually the same pricing as a year ago (Marsh, 2004).

6. Conclusion and Open Questions

This report focuses on the question as to how to provide adequate financial protection through insurance to firms who may be victims of terrorism. It discusses the question as to whether (mega)-terrorism can be covered by private insurance alone. We argue that the specific characteristics of terrorism make the risk difficult to quantify and hence not insurable by the private sector alone.

The development of terrorism models assists in the risk assessment process but it is difficult to estimate the likelihood of future terrorist attacks given our current state of knowledge. Although none of the terrorist models currently provides well-specified distributions of expected loss in the statistical sense, they can be helpful in enabling insurers to understand the degree of their exposure under specific attack scenarios.

Our report concludes that it is necessary for the government to participate in any terrorism insurance program to cover extreme losses that could result from large-scale attacks. This need has already been recognized in most industrialized countries and has led to the creation of temporary risk-sharing partnerships between the public and private sectors. However, in countries such as Germany and the United States where purchase is voluntary, the demand for terrorism coverage is currently quite low. A large-scale attack could be debilitating if the market for insurance protection in these countries continues to be thin.

There are no easy answers as to what type of public-private partnerships should evolve in the future but there are lots of questions that can be posed in this regard such as:

- Should terrorism coverage be mandatory and if so, to what extent?

- What role can the private sector institutions play in encouraging firms to purchase coverage? Will financial institutions require terrorism insurance as a condition for a mortgage as they have done with other types of coverage?

- What role should the government play with respect to requiring terrorism insurance?

- How well those programs would work should terrorists be successful in perpetrating a mega-attack? How would the terrorism coverage demand and supply react?

- How does one deal with issues of interdependency and the challenges of linking risk mitigation measures, as well as public and private responses to an attack, with insurance compensation?

The answer to these questions will vary across countries and will be partially determined by addressing the question as to who should pay for terrorism prevention and coverage of victims of attack.

We also need to recognize that insurance has to be incorporated as part of a risk management strategy that requires a wide range of policy tools ranging from information provision to regulations and standards. These policies need to be informed by risk assessments and an understanding of risk perception in order to implement a strategy for dealing with terrorism that is likely to be politically viable and cost-effective. Each country could have a different response that would depend on national characteristics of insurance markets, cultural and legal impediments, as well as loss history. In any case, the question of terrorism insurance will be with us for a long time as terrorism activities worldwide remain a real threat, as illustrated by other terrorist attacks since 9/11, including the large-scale one in Madrid on March 11, 2004.

Finally, as terrorist groups are much more likely today to try and inflict casualties on the population, there are sets of important related questions that need to be analyzed, although they go beyond this report. For example, what financial protection is currently provided to individuals who may be victims of attacks in OECD member countries? How do these programs work in practice? How could they be improved in the future?

Notes

1   This number represents victims of the attacks in New York, Washington, DC, and Pennsylvania as well as among teams of those providing emergency service.

2   Most published studies refer to this level of $40 billion of insured losses. It reflects actually the estimation by the U.S. Information Insurance Institute as of July 2002 (Hartwig, 2002). Three years after the attacks, it is worth noting that when taking into account both lowered liability loss expectations and greater utilization of the US federal Victim Compensation Fund than initially expected, which will have paid nearly $5 billion to 9/11 victims and their family (Smetters, 2004), insured losses could be eventually more likely to fall to a range between $30 and $35 billion (Lehman, 2004). We consider $32.5 billion, the latest available estimation (Hartwig, 2004).

3   An important exception is the terrorist attacks against the Pan American Flight 103, which exploded over Lockerbie, Scotland in December 1988 and inflicted $520 million insured losses under liability coverage (ICAO, 2002).

4   Including life and liability insurance losses; Sources: Hartwig (2004).

5   See the evolution of the catastrophe reinsurance price index, Figure 6.6.

6   Except for workers' compensation insurance policies that cover occupational injuries without regard to the peril that caused the injury.

7   That number has sharply increased during the year 2003. However, as of June 11, 2004, there was no consistent official estimation of the total number of international terrorist attacks worldwide in 2003 (Associated Press, 2004).

8   Multi-Sources: US Department of States (2003), Swiss Re (2002, updated March 2003), Press releases.

9   This is illustrated by the August 14, 2003 power failure in the U.S. and the September 27, 2003 one in Italy.

10   For example, the City of Chicago was denied for insurance compensation for business losses that resulted from FAA's decision to ban takeoffs of all civilian aircraft regardless of destination on September 11, 2001 (U.S. District Court, 2004).

11   It is not necessary to have a precise estimate of the probability for a risk to be covered by insurance (Eeckhoudt and Gollier, 1999). For example, the first U.S. satellite launch was covered (Explorer I in 1958) despite the lack of historical data and the difficulty of calculating the risk of failure. There are also some anecdotal cases: for example, Lloyd's covered the discovery of the Loch Ness monster in 1973. In 2001, potential attacks by the Yeti for travelers in the Himalaya Mountains have been covered too (Godard *et al.*, 2002).

12   For a survey on adverse selection issues, see Dionne and Doherty (1992).

13   This expected loss is calculated as follows: [50(.001x\$100,000) + 50(0.003x\$100,000)]/100 = \$200.

14   The variance for a single loss L with probability p is Lp $(1-p)$. If L = \$100,000 and p = 1/1,000, then $Lp(1-p)$ = \$100,000(1/1,000)(999/1,000) or \$99.90.

15   Stone also introduces a constraint regarding the stability of the insurer's operation. However, insurers have traditionally not focused on this constraint in dealing with catastrophic risks.

16   One exception would be if terrorist groups attack trophy buildings to prove that they can inflict damage to well- protected structures.

17   For this reason, any adverse selection phenomenon would result essentially from an asymmetry of risk perception between insureds and insurers rather than an asymmetry of information about the risk the insured faces *per se* (as this is the case from traditional adverse selection).

18   Of course, that may constitute a real limitation of the development of an insurance market if government determined the price of terrorism coverage without agreement with insurance industry joining the partnership, which is currently not the case in most countries, including the United States.

19   For a macroeconomic study of the economic consequences of the attacks of 9/11, see Lenain, Bonturi, and Koen (OECD) (2002).

20   See Winter (1988, 1991), Gron (1994); Doherty and Posey (1997), Cummins and Danzon (1997); Froot and O'Connell (1997, 1999).

21   Maurice Greenberg, CEO of AIG made this point by saying "The industry is going to pay its loss in the World Trade Center events. What we're saying is that if terrorist events continue, this is an industry with finite capital" (Hamburger and Oster, 2001).

22   There is no reliable information, however, on the share of the commercial property and casualty insurance market in the 5 states that did not approve the exclusion (U.S. General Accounting Office, 2002).

23   European airlines planned also to create their own RGG, *Eurotime,* which never became operational either.

24   The readers interested in these new developments as well as risk financing for catastrophic risks can turn to several other publications: Godard, Henry, Lagadec, and Michel-Kerjan (2002), Lane (2002), Grossi and Kunreuther (eds.) (in press).

25   The first bond was issued in Europe in August 2003. The world governing organization of association football (soccer), the FIFA, which organizes the 2006 World Cup in Germany, developed a \$262 million bond to protect its investment. The bond is actually not a terrorist bond per se, but a multi-event bond. Under very specific conditions, the catastrophe bond covers against *both* natural and terrorist extreme events that would result in the cancellation of the World Cup game without the possibility of it being re-scheduled to 2007 (U.S. General Accounting Office, 2003).
        The second terrorist-related bond is a securitization of catastrophe mortality risk that has been undertaken in 2003 by Swiss Re, the world largest life reinsurer. Mortality is measured with respect to a mortality risk index, weighted according to Swiss Re's exposure in several

countries. The trigger threshold for the mortality index is 30% higher than expected up to the end of 2006, based on 2002 mortality in these countries. This may represent 750,000 deaths. According to Woo (2004), the trigger threshold might be attainable before the end of 2006 only if pessimistic lethality estimates are made for both a pandemic and a terrorist attack using weapons of mass destruction killing several hundred thousand people.

26   There was also an intention to set the *maximum* insurance retention for the next four years, with individual insurers' retentions being based on market share. It is now set at £30 million (43 million euros) per event and £60 million (86 million euros) per annum for 2003; it will increase up to £100 million (144 million euros) per event and £200 million (288 million euros) per annum for 2006.

27   Annual studies by Partner Re provide a very comprehensive description of the terrorism insurance programs currently in place in European countries; see Partner Re (2004).

28   The French Federation of Insurance Companies and the French Group of Mutual Insurance Firms, respectively; the two major representative institutions from the French insurance market.

29   The reaction in this country has been swift for several reasons. First, France suffered several waves of deadly terrorist attacks during the 1980's and the 1990's. The explosion of the chemical factory AZF on September 21, 2001 –only 10 days after 9/11– in the densely populated French city of Toulouse killed 30 people and injured several thousands. This disaster constitutes one of the most important industrial catastrophes of the last 15 years in Europe. But at that time it was not clear whether this explosion was an accident or an attack and thus increased the perceived threat of terrorist attacks on French soil. Second, from a legal perspective, the situation in France was especially acute because the law does not allow commercial property insurers to dissociate terrorism coverage from commercial property. Indeed, the law of September 9, 1986 obligates insurers to provide terrorism coverage up to the overall limits of a property policy. Hence, in the aftermath of 9/11, French insurers who had decided to stop covering terrorism would have had also to stop covering commercial property at the 2002 renewals. As a result, many businesses would have been left not only without coverage against terrorism but also without commercial property damage and business interruption protection. (Michel-Kerjan and Pedell, forthcoming).

30   According to a study by the U.S. Council of Insurance Agents and Brokers (CIAB), 85% of insurance brokers who responded, estimated that terrorism was more available in the market in June 2003 than it was in January 2003 (CIAB, July 2003).

31   An event like the Oklahoma City bombings would not be covered under TRIA.

32   The council represents the top tier of the nation's insurance brokers who collectively write 80 percent of the commercial property/casualty premiums annually.

33   Although the take-up rate has increased for the first and second quarters of 2004 –mainly due to new alerts released by the US federal government and to a continuous decrease of the overall pricing for commercial property insurance, firms may hence have freed up funds to purchase terrorism insurance coverage– more than 50% of firms are still not purchasing terrorism insurance in the U.S.

34   The following data have been provided by members of Extremus, AG (personal communication).

35   This estimate has to be dealt with carefully as the size of the contracts is not accounted for, but according to expert opinion of members of Extremus, it gives a fairly realistic picture and underlines the prevailing very low dimension of market penetration. Unfortunately, it is impossible to get more precise information for the time being.

36   The DAX30 comprises the 30 largest listed companies in terms of market capitalization of the free float.

37   This section builds on Kunreuther, Michel-Kerjan and Porter (2003; 2004).

38   A *loss cost* is defined by ISO as that portion of a rate that does not include provision for expenses (other than loss adjustment expenses) or profit. It may be used by ISO companies as a starting point to set insurance rates, after reflection of company specific expenses and profit. Once an ISO advisory loss cost has been approved by a state, an ISO participating insurance company can usually adopt it without having to undertake its own often lengthy and expensive rate filing process.

39   The second tier (third tier) settled at $0.018 ($0.001) per $100 of property value.

References

Adler, Michael and Ziglio, Erio (eds). (1996). Gazing Into the Oracle: The Delphi Method and Its Application to Social Policy and Public Health, London, Kingsley Publishers.

American Re. (2002). Topics: Annual Review of North American Natural Catastrophes 2001.

Associated Press. (2004). "U.S. Wrongly Reported Drop in the World Terrorism in 2003", The New York Times, June 11.

Bantwal, Vivek and Kunreuther, Howard. (2000). "A Cat Bond Premium Puzzle?" Journal of Psychology and Financial Markets. 1, pp.76-91.

Boin, Arjen, Lagadec, Patrick, Michel-Kerjan, Erwann and Overdijk, Werner (2003). "Critical Infrastructures under Threat: Learning from the Anthrax Scare." Journal of Contingencies and Crisis Management. 11: 3, pp.99-105.

Central Intelligence Agency (2003). "Terrorist CBRN: Materials and Effects (U)", CIA: Directorate of Intelligence, May 2003, CTC 2003-40058.

Central Intelligence Agency (CIA). (2001). Statement by Director of Central Intelligence George J. Tenet before the Senate Select Committee on Intelligence on the "Worldwide Threat 2001: National Security in a Changing World". CIA: February 7, 2001.

Council of Insurance Agents and Brokers. (2003, b). "Commercial Market Index Survey." News Release, July 22.

Council of Insurance Agents and Brokers. (2003). "Many Commercial Interests Are Not Buying Terrorism Insurance, New CIAB Survey Show." News Release, March 24.

Cummins, J David, Neil Doherty and Lo, Anita. (2002). "Can Insurers Pay for the "Big One'? Measuring the Capacity of the Insurance Market to Respond to Catastrophic Losses" Journal of Banking and Finance, 26: 2-3, pp. 557-83.

Cummins, J. David and Danzon, Patricia. (1997). "Price, Financial Quality and Capital Flows in Insurance Markets." Journal of Financial Intermediation, 6, pp.3-38.

Dionne, Georges and Doherty, Neil (1992). "Adverse Selection in Insurance Markets: A Selective Survey" in Georges Dionne (ed) Contributions to Insurance Economics (Kluwer: Boston).

Doherty, Neil and Posey, Lisa. (1997). "Availability Crises in Insurance Markets: Optimal Contracts with Asymmetric Information and Capacity Constraints." Journal of Risk and Uncertainty. 15, pp. 55-80.

Eeckhoudt, Louis and Gollier, Christian. (1999). "The Insurance of Low Probability Events" Journal of Risk and Insurance, 66: 17-28.

Enders, Walter and Todd, Sandler. (2000). "Is Transnational Terrorism Becoming More Threatening?" Journal of Conflict Resolution. 44: 3, pp. 307-332.

Frankfurter Allgemeine Zeitung. (2004). March 25, 2004, p. 19.

Frankfurter Allgemeine Zeitung. (2003). April 1st 2003, p. 16.

Froot, Kenneth and O'Connell, Paul. (1999). "The Pricing of U.S. Catastrophe Reinsurance". In Froot, Kenneth. (ed.). *The Financing of Catastrophe Risks*. Chicago: University of Chicago Press.

Froot, Kenneth and O'Connell, Paul. (1997). "On the Pricing of Intermediated Risk: Theory and Application to Catastrophe Reinsurance". *Working Paper 6011*, National Bureau of Economic Research, Cambridge, MA.

Glasstone, Samuel, and Dolan, Philip J. (editors) (1977). *The Effects of Nuclear Weapons*, Third Edition, 1977, Prepared and published by the United States Department of Defense and the United States Department of Energy.

Godard, Olivier, Henry, Claude, Lagadec, Patrick and Michel-Kerjan, Erwann. (2002). *Treatise on New Risks. Precaution, Crisis Management and Insurance.* (in French). Paris: Editions Gallimard, Folio-Actuel, p.620.

Gollier, Christian. (2002). "Insurability". Paper presented at the NBER Insurance Group Workshop. Cambridge. MA, February 1.

Gron, Anne. (1994). " Capacity Constraints and Cycles in Property-casualty Insurance Markets." *Rand Journal of Economics.* 25:1, pp.110-127.

Grossi, Patricia and Kunreuther, Howard (eds.), with Chandu Patel (in press). *Catastrophe Modeling: A New Approach to Managing Risk.* Norwell, MA: Kluwer Academic Publishers.

Hale, David. (2002). "America Uncovered." *Financial Times*. September 12.

Hamburger, Tom and Oster, Christopher. (2001). "Insurance Industry Backs U.S. Terrorism Fund." *Wall Street Journal*. October 9, p. A3.

Hartwig, Robert. (2002). "September 11, 2001: The First Year. One Hundred Minutes of Terror that Changed the Global Insurance Industry Forever." Insurance Information Institute.

Heal, Geoffrey and Kunreuther, Howard. (2003). "You Only Die Once: Managing Discrete Interdependent Risks." *Working Paper 9885*, National Bureau of Economic Research, Cambridge, MA.

Hoffman, Bruce. (1998). *Inside Terrorism*. New York: Columbia University Press.

Hoffman, Bruce. (1997). "The Confluence of International and Domestic Trends in Terrorism." *Terrorism and Political Violence*. 9:2, pp. 1-15.

Hsu, Spencer. (2003). "D.C. Disputes Insurance Study Raising Rates For Terrorism" *Washington Post*, January 7, page A01.

International Civil Aviation Organization (ICAO). (2002). *Special Group on Aviation War Risk Insurance. Report of the Second Meeting.* 28-30 January 2002., Montreal: ICAO.

Insurance Accounting (2003). "Knowledge a Key for Terror Risk Pricing", January 27, 2003, Thomson Media.

Jaffee, Dwight and Russell, Thomas. (2003). "Market Under Stress: The Case of Extreme Event Insurance" in Richard Arnott, Bruce Greenwald, Ravi Kanbur and Barry Nalebuff (eds), *Economics for an Imperfect World: Essays in Honor of Joseph E. Stiglitz*. MIT Press.

Kahn, Jeremy. (2004). "Storm Chasing on Wall Street". *The New York Times*, September 19, 2004.

Kaye Insurance Associates. (2003). *Middle Market Survey*. October 2003, New York.

Keohane, Nathaniel and Zeckhauser, Richard. (2003). "The Ecology of Terror Defense." *Journal of Risk and Uncertainty*. 26: 2/3, pp. 201-229.

Kunreuther, Howard and Michel-Kerjan, Erwann.. (in press). "PolicyWatch: Challenges for Terrorism Risk Insurance in the United States", *Journal of Economic Perspectives*.

Kunreuther, Howard, Michel-Kerjan, Erwann and Porter, Beverly. (2004). "Extending Catastrophe Modeling to Terrorism and Other Extreme Events" in Grossi and Kunreuther (eds) with Patel. *Catastrophe Modeling: A New Approach to Managing Risk.* Kluwer Academic Publisher, Boston.

Kunreuther, Howard, Michel-Kerjan, Erwann. (2004). "Dealing with Extreme Events: New Challenges for Terrorism Risk Insurance in the U.S." Working paper, Center for Risk Management and Decision Processes, The Wharton School, Philadelphia.

Kunreuther, Howard and Pauly, Mark. (2004). "What You Don't Know Can Hurt You: Terrorism Losses and All Perils Insurance." Paper presented at the Annual Meeting of the American Economic Association, San Diego, January 2004.

Kunreuther, Howard, Michel-Kerjan, Erwann and Porter, Beverly. (2003). "Assessing, Managing and Financing Extreme Events: Dealing with Terrorism", *Working Paper 10179*, National Bureau of Economic Research, Cambridge, MA.

Kunreuther, Howard and Heal, Geoffrey. (2003). "Interdependent Security." *Journal of Risk and Uncertainty*. 26: 2/3, pp.231-249.

Kunreuther, Howard. (2002). "The Role of Insurance in Managing Extreme Events: Implications for Terrorism Coverage." *Risk Analysis*. August 2002, 22, pp. 427-437.

Kunreuther, Howard and Roth, Richard Sr. (1998). *Paying the Price: The Status and Role of Insurance Against Natural Disasters in the United States.* Washington, D.C: Joseph Henry Press.

Kunreuther, Howard. (1996). "Mitigating Disaster Losses through Insurance". *Journal of Risk and Uncertainty*. 12, pp.171-187.

Kunreuther, Howard, Robin Hogarth, Jacqueline Meszaros and Spranca, Mark. (1995). "Ambiguity and underwriter decision processes," *Journal of Economic Behavior and Organization*, 26, pp.337-352.

Kunreuther, Howard, Hogarth, Robin and Meszaros, Jacqueline. (1993). "Insurer Ambiguity and Market Failure." *Journal of Risk and Uncertainty*. 7: 1, pp.71-88.

Lagadec, Patrick and Michel-Kerjan, Erwann. (2004). "A Framework for Senior Executives to Meet the Challenge of Interdependent Critical Networks Under Threat: "The Paris Initiative, Anthrax and Beyond"". Working paper, Center for Risk Management and Decision Processes, WP#04-28, The Wharton School, Philadelphia.

Lane, Morton (ed.) (2002). *Alternative Risk Strategies.* London, Risk Books, Haymarket House, May 2002.

Lapan, Harvey and Sandler, Todd. (1988). "To Bargain or Not to Bargain: That is The Question". *American Economic Review*. 78: 2, pp. 16-20.

Lecomte, Eugene and Gahagan, Karen. (1998). "Hurricane Insurance Protection in Florida" in Kunreuther Howard and Roth, Richard, Sr. (eds.), *Paying the Price: The Status and Role of Insurance Against Natural Disasters in the United States.* Washington, D.C: J. Henry Press.

Lee, Dwight. (1988). "Free Riding and Paid Riding in the Fight Against Terrorism". *American Economic Review*. 78: 2, pp. 22-26.

Lehmann, Raymond. (2004). "Twin Towers Insured Loss Estimate Drops to Between $30 and $35 Billion", Bestwire, May 10.

Lelain, Patrick, Bonturi, Marcos and Koen, Vincent. (2002). "The Economic Consequences of Terrorism" *OECD Working paper 334*, Department of Economics, Paris: OECD.

Liedtke, Patrick and Courbage, Christophe. (eds.). (2002). *Insurance and September 11 One Year After. Impact, Lessons and Unsolved Issues.* The International Association for the Study of Insurance Economics.

Linstone, Harold and Turoff, Murray. (1975). *The Delphi Method. Techniques and Applications.* Addison-Wesly Publishing Company.

Lockerbie, Verdict. (2001). *Her Majesty's Advocate, v. Abdelbaset Ali Mohmed Al Megrahi and Al Amin Khalifa Fhimah*, Case No.: 1475/99 (High Court of Justiciary at Camp Zeist-January 31).

Marsh Inc. (2004). "Marketwatch: Property Terrorism Insurance. Update-2nd Quarter 2004", August 2004.

Michel-Kerjan, Erwann and Pedell, Burkhard. (forthcoming). "Terrorism Risk Coverage in the post-9/11 Era: A Comparison of New Public-Private Partnerships in France, Germany and the U.S." Working paper, Center for Risk Management and Decision Processes, The Wharton School, October 2004; forthcoming in the *Geneva Papers on Risk and Insurance*.

Michel-Kerjan, Erwann. (2003-b). "Large-scale Terrorism: Risk Sharing and Public Policy." *Revue d'Economie Politique.* 113: 5, pp. 625-648.

Michel-Kerjan, Erwann. (2003-a). "New Vulnerabilities in Critical Infrastructures: A U.S. Perspective." *Journal of Contingencies and Crisis Management.* 11: 3, pp.132-141.

Michel-Kerjan, Erwann. (2001). "*Insurance against Natural Disasters: Do the French Have the Answer? Strengths and Limitations*", Laboratoire d'économétrie, 2001-007, Paris: Ecole Polytechnique.

Moss, David. (2002). *When All Else Fails: Government as the Ultimate Risk Manager.* Cambridge, MA: Harvard University Press.

Olatidoye, O., Sarathy, S., Jones, G., McIntyre, C., Milligan, L. (1998). "A Representative Survey of Blast Loading Models and Damage Assessment Methods for Buildings Subject to Explosive Blasts", Clark Atlantic University, Department of Defense High Performance Computing Program, CEWES MSRC/PET TR 98-36.

Organisation for Economic Co-operation and Development. (2003). *Emerging Systemic Risks in the 21st Century: An Agenda for Action.* Paris: OECD.

Partner Re. (2004), "Terrorism Insurance". Available on www.partnerre.com, May 2004.

Pillar, Paul. (2001). *Terrorism and U.S. Foreign Policy.* Brookings Institution Press. Washington, DC.

Roth, Richard, Jr. (1998). "Earthquake Insurance Protection in California" in Kunreuther Howard and Roth, Richard, Sr. (eds.), *Paying the Price: The Status and Role of Insurance Against Natural Disasters in the United States.* Washington, D.C: Joseph Henry Press.

Sandler, Todd and Enders, Walter. (2004). "An Economic Perspective of Transnational Terrorism" *European Journal of Political Economy.* 20:2, pp.301-316.

Sandler, Todd, Tschirhart, John and Cauley, Jon. (1983). "A Theoretical Analysis of Transnational Terrorism." *American Political Science Review.* 77, pp.36-54.

Stone, James. (1973). "A theory of capacity and the insurance of catastrophe risks: Part I and Part II," *Journal of Risk and Insurance*, 40, pp. 231-243 (Part I) and 40, pp. 339-355 (Part II).

Swiss Re (2004). *Insurance-linked securities quarterly* (New York: Swiss Re Capital Markets Corporation) January.

Swiss Re, Sigma. (2004). "Natural catastrophes and man-made disasters 2003: many fatalities, comparatively moderate insured losses". *Sigma* no1/2004, Zurich: Swiss Re, Economic Research and Consulting.

Swiss Re. (2002-b). "Natural catastrophes and man-made disasters 2001: high flood loss burden". *Sigma* no2/2002, Zurich: Swiss Re, Economic Research and Consulting.

Swiss Re. (2002-a). *Focus Report: Terrorism–dealing with the new spectre.* Zurich: Swiss Re, February.

Treaster, Joseph. (2003). "Insurance for Terrorism Still a Rarity". *New York Times*. March 8.

U.S. Congress, Joint Economic Committee. (2002). *Economic Perspectives on Terrorism Insurance.* Washington, DC: May 2002.

U.S. Department of State. (2003). *Patterns of Global Terrorism-2003.* Washington, D.C.: April.

U.S. General Accounting Office (GAO). (2004). *Terrorism Insurance. Effects of the Terrorism Risk Insurance Act of 2002.* Testimony of Richard Hillman. GAO-04-720T. Washington, D.C.: April 28.

U.S. General Accounting Office (GAO). (2003). *Catastrophe Insurance Risks. Status of Efforts to Securitize Natural Catastrophe and Terrorism Risk.* GAO-03-1033. Washington, D.C.: September 24.

U.S. General Accounting Office (GAO). (2002). "Terrorism Insurance: Rising Uninsured Exposure to Attacks Heightens Potential Economic Vulnerabilities." Testimony of Richard J. Hillman before the Subcommittee on Oversight and Investigations, Committee on Financial Services, House of Representatives. February 27.

U.S. House of Representatives. (2003). "'H.R. 2115 – Flight 100–Century of Aviation Reauthorization Act'". *Section 105.* Washington, DC.: June, 2003.

White House. (2003). *National Strategy for Physical Protection of Critical Infrastructures and Key Assets.* Washington, DC, February 2003.

Wedgwood, Ruth. (2002). "Al Qaeda, Terrorism, and Military Commissions." *American Journal of International Law*. 96: 2, pp. 328-337.

Winter, Ralph. (1991). "The Liability Insurance Market". *Journal of Economic Perspectives*. 5:3, pp. 115-136.

Winter, Ralph. (1988). "The Liability Insurance Crisis and Dynamics of Competitive insurance Markets." *Yale Journal of Regulation*. 5, pp. 455-499.

Woo, Gordon. (2004). "Parameterizing the Evolving Threat" in Risk Management Solutions, *Managing Terrorism Risk in 2004.*

Appendix

TERRORISM RISK COVERAGE AFTER 9/11: COMPARISON OF THE PUBLIC-PRIVATE PARTNERSHIPS IN FRANCE, GERMANY AND THE UNITED STATES

	GAREAT (France)	Extremus (Germany)	TRIA (US)
Basic structure of the partnership for annual aggregate losses	Co-reinsurance pool with unlimited state guarantee for losses higher than €2.00 billion	Insurance company with federal reinsurance of last resort for losses higher than €2 (3) billion and less than €10 (13) billion in 2004 (respectively in 2002, 2003)	Risk-sharing arrangement between the federal government and insurers, up to $100 billion
Limited exposure of the private sector	€1.5 billion (2002) €1.75 billion (2003) €2 billion (2004)	€3 billion in 2003 €2 billion in 2004	Market retention as defined by TRIA $10 billion (2003) $12.5 billion (2004) $15 billion (2005)
Estimations of the total 2004 terrorism premiums	€260 million	€77 million	$3.6 billion
Temporary governmental involvement	Yes. Agreement with the government limited to the end of 2003 ; renewed to the end of 2006.	Yes. Agreement with the federal government limited to the end of 2005	Yes. Agreement with the federal government limited to the end of 2005
Gratuity of governmental coverage	No. Government receives premiums for its unlimited guarantee	No. Government receives premiums for its guarantee	Yes
Compulsory insurance	Yes	No	Insurers are required to offer terrorist coverage; Clients can turn down the coverage; compulsory for worker compensation
Minimum sum insured	€6 million	€25 million (refers to the basic sum insured in the conventional insurance policy; smaller limit for terrorism coverage might be chosen by insured)	No minimum sum insured, but a minimum of $5 million insured losses to be covered by TRIA
Risk pricing: National rate scale	Yes	Yes	No (only the 2002 ISO advisory loss cost scale)
Insurance price depends on risk location	No	No	Yes
Risk segmentation by sum insured	Yes	Yes	No

Sources: Michel-Kerjan and Pedell, forthcoming

Chapter 7

INTERNATIONAL FINANCING SOLUTIONS
TO TERRORISM RISK EXPOSURES[*]

Capacity and prices in the reinsurance market are sensitive to recent loss experiences and follow a highly cyclical pattern influenced by major catastrophe events. In the face of tighter conditions in the conventional reinsurance market, alternative risk financing solutions have received increasing attention, including catastrophe derivatives, risk-linked securities, contingent capital instruments, and committed credit facilities. The market for risk-linked securities has emerged as a stable source of risk-transfer solutions for different natural hazards and two recent transactions (Golden Goal Finance and Vita Capital) included cover for terrorism risk exposures. In contrast, exchange traded catastrophe derivatives have not been economically viable and contingent capital instruments are not currently focused on catastrophe risk financing. Different types of committed credit facilities constitute a well-developed area of the banking market that may serve as a complementary credit reservoir. Hence, some alternative risk-transfer and financing solutions have become steady elements of the financial markets and provide incremental capacity for catastrophe risk cover. The market for new risk-transfer solutions constitute a viable risk-transfer alternative but is not expected to dramatically expand the market for terrorism risk cover.

Given the extreme loss potential of large catastrophes these risks are often not insurable on commercial terms after mega-events. Therefore, some government inducement may be required to ensure availability of insurance cover for risk exposures inflicted by major terrorist acts until commercial insurance capacity is restored in the market. However, intervention should be structured so cover is provided on a professional arms-length basis without government subsidization and political influence on commercial operations that would reduce risk mitigation incentives and jeopardize economic efficiencies.

---

[*]   This report was written by Pr. T. J. Andersen, Associate Professor, Copenhagen Business School, Denmark.
The data in this report is current as of end-November 2004.

Summary:

Issuance of risk-linked securities has become a stable source of risk-transfer solutions and can provide cover for specific terrorism risk exposures.

The inherent uncertainties associated with terrorism exposures make it more difficult to securitize these types of risk.

Contingent capital instruments are not currently geared to cover catastrophe risks.

Traded catastrophe derivatives have not been economically viable.

The new risk-transfer solutions are not expected to expand market capacity dramatically.

Some government inducement is required to make cover available for mega-catastrophe exposures associated with terrorist acts.

Government intervention should be conducted prudently to avoid adverse economic effects associated with subsidization and operational interference.

1. Introduction

When we discuss catastrophe risk exposures we normally distinguish between natural catastrophes and man-made disasters. In turn, man-made disasters can be categorized as unintended events, caused by accidents, failures, crashes, explosions, fire, etc., and willful events, often referred to as civil unrest and terrorist acts. Until recently, willful events and specifically terrorist acts constituted a relatively modest share of the total catastrophe losses but suddenly turned into a sizeable loss potential with the terrorist attack on the World Trade Center in 2001. This incidence made substantial demands on the reserves of the global reinsurance industry. With total insured losses estimated around US$ 40 billion this incident counts among the most costly single catastrophe events[1].

The insurance and reinsurance markets showed remarkable resilience to the financial impact of this event, but the sensitivity of capacity and pricing in the reinsurance market to large current events had an adverse effect on the immediate availability of terrorism cover in property insurance and other lines. This situation was feared to have negative spillover effects on new construction projects and other business ventures. Generally speaking as higher uncertainty increased the cost of doing business, the general prospects for economic growth were lowered. Whereas governments in exposed countries have taken some initial steps to introduce coverage for excess losses from terrorist events there has also been a search for new market oriented risk-transfer solutions. The aim of this report is to present and evaluate alternative risk-transfer and financing approaches to accommodate this need for terrorism risk exposure management.

1.1 Background

Changing environmental conditions have increased the direct economic damages derived from catastrophes around the world. The seeming increase in catastrophe risk exposures has hit across the board in industrialized as well as developing countries, although the emerging economies by far have taken the heaviest toll in terms of human devastation inflicted by catastrophe events. The direct economic impact from catastrophes is increasing faster in the developing world, which may reflect that vulnerability is influenced by man, as economic infrastructure investments and human settlements increase in volume and concentration in exposed areas. Total insured losses, which apply mostly to economic assets in developed economies[2], have increased significantly over the past decade and have periodically strained capacity in the conventional insurance markets. This situation has in turn spurred the development of new innovative risk-transfer and financing products in the international financial markets.

Total insured catastrophe losses have increased to a considerably higher level over the past fifteen years compared to the previous period (Figure 7.1). The uncertainty associated with these loss exposures has increased at the same time as illustrated by a steady increase in the standard deviation of reported direct losses.

The direct economic losses associated with man-made disasters have evolved at a more moderate trend over the past decades displaying a relatively steady level of uncertainty. However, the general loss level took a dramatic jump in connection with the World Trade Center (WTC) terrorist incident in September 2001. However, the loss level has been back to previous levels over the subsequent two years.

Figure 7.1. **Direct Economic Losses Associated with Natural Catastrophes 1973-2003**
(insured property and business interruption losses)

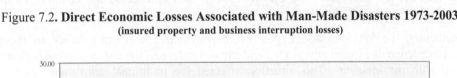

Source: Sigma No.1/2004, Natural catastrophes and man-made disasters in 2003, Swiss Re.

Figure 7.2. **Direct Economic Losses Associated with Man-Made Disasters 1973-2003**
(insured property and business interruption losses)

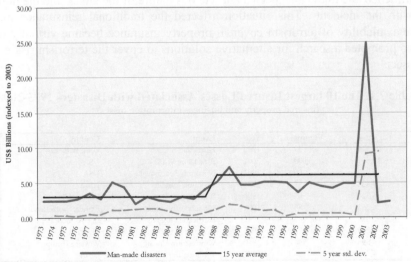

Source: Sigma No.1/2004, Natural catastrophes and man-made disasters in 2003, Swiss Re.

Figure 7.3. **Total Direct Economic Losses Associated with Disasters 1973-2003**
(insured property and business interruption losses)

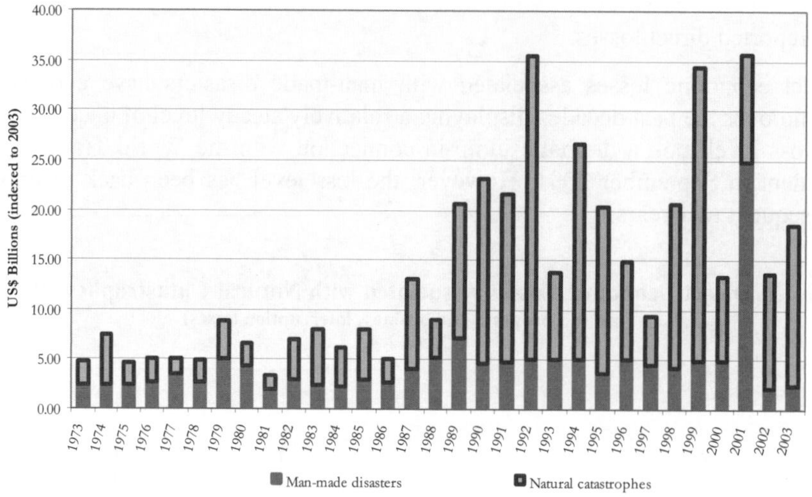

Man-made disasters   Natural catastrophes

Source: Sigma No.1/2004, Natural catastrophes and man-made disasters in 2003, Swiss Re.

Historically the losses associated with man-made disasters have been at levels somewhat comparable to the direct losses caused by natural hazards. This situation has changed over the past fifteen years, as direct losses from natural catastrophes have increased to a much higher level. However, with the WTC event, the level of losses from man-made disasters increased dramatically to become the dominant influence on the catastrophe reinsurance market during 2001. Fortunately, the level of natural disaster losses fell to a somewhat lower level during that same year, so the overall disaster related losses were not dramatically higher than previous high exposure years (Figure 7.3).

Both natural catastrophe and man-made disaster losses influence conditions in the markets for risk-transfer. In this context the economic exposure of the WTC incident was not more extreme than previous events. Hurricane Andrews in 1992 is still considered the costliest single event measured in fixed dollars (Table 7.1).

Nonetheless, the World Trade Center event provided a temporary shock to the general business confidence due to the unexpected and vicious nature of the attack and the high death toll associated with the incident[3]. This situation affected the traditional reinsurance market to an extent where availability of terrorism cover in property insurance became virtually unavailable. This situation prompted a search for alternative solutions to cover the terrorism risk exposures of economic assets.

Table 7.1. **The 10 largest Insured Losses Associated with Disasters 1973-2003**
(insured property and business interruption losses)

[US$ Million]	Victims	Year	Event	Country
20,511	38	1992	Hurricane Andrew	USA, Bahamas
19,301	3,000	2001	Attacks on WTC	USA
16,989	60	1994	Northridge earthquake	USA
7,456	51	1991	Typhoon Mireille	Japan
6,321	95	1990	Winterstorm Daria	France, UK
6,263	80	1999	Winterstorm Lothar	France, Switzerland
6,087	61	1989	Hurricane Hugo	Puerto Rico, USA
4,749	22	1987	Storms and floods	France, UK
4,393	64	1990	Winterstorm Vivian	Western Europe
4,362	26	1999	Typhoon Bart	Japan

Source: Sigma No.1/2004, Natural catastrophes and man-made disasters in 2003, Swiss Re.

1.2 Organization

This report first describes a series of alternative risk-transfer and financing instruments that have been introduced in the international financial markets in recent years. The analysis looks at ways in which risk transfer can take place in the form of conventional reinsurance treaties as well as newer derivative instruments and risk-linked securities. Then the report discusses possibilities for combining conventional insurance approaches and new alternative risk management instruments in insurance pools that may provide cover for terrorism risk exposures on a commercial basis. Finally, the report analyzes a recent transaction and discusses the potential for similar risk-transfer solutions.

The report is structured around three main sections under the following headings:

- Possible forms of market intervention

- Includes a discussion of reinsurance treaties, capital market instruments, and financial derivatives

- Other private risk-transfer mechanisms

- Includes a discussion of the uninsurable risk phenomenon and different catastrophe risk pooling programs

- Hypothetical risk management solutions

- Discusses the conditions of and potential for different instruments and alternative risk financing solutions.

2. Forms of Market Intervention

This report considers the two major types of risk management instruments, namely instruments for risk-transfer and instruments for risk financing. The markets for risk-transfer instruments comprise conventional insurance policies and different types of reinsurance treaties, newer capital market solutions including securitized instruments such as cat-bonds and risk-linked securities, bilateral agreements like catastrophe risk swaps, and exchange traded and over-the-counter catastrophe derivatives. The markets for risk financing instruments include different types of committed credit facilities in the banking industry and the money market, as well as various contingent capital instruments that converge between the insurance sector and the capital market.

2.1. Insurance and Reinsurance

The direct insurance and the reinsurance markets have been and remain the major reservoir for catastrophe risk-transfer. Until the mid-1990s, the reinsurance market was the only source to transfer risk exposures associated with catastrophes. The primary insurers provide cover to homeowners and commercial entities and act as financial intermediaries that aggregate the major economic exposures associated with underlying risk events across large portfolios of individual customers.

The primary insurance companies may insure homeowners' properties, industrial facilities, agricultural crops, automobiles, etc. Insurance policies can combine exposures to a variety of hazards within comprehensive policies although they may exclude specific event risks[4]. As long as hazardous events that expose the insurance portfolio happen independently of each other, the risks can be diversified and an insurance premium determined probabilistically. If primary insurers have accumulated large exposures within similar types of insurance they may trade part of the portfolio among each other to diversify the risk exposures further. This basic diversification principle is refined in the reinsurance market. Primary insurance companies cede part of their exposures to global reinsurance companies and the reinsurance companies may in turn retrocede part of their exposures to other reinsurance companies and thereby diversify the risk exposures among the international insurance community.

Catastrophe risk exposures are special in the sense that their occurrence is highly uncertain and they represent extreme loss potentials. Furthermore, catastrophe loss events are not independent of each other but are highly correlated within geographical areas, which make it impossible to diversify them through portfolio aggregation. Economic losses from natural disasters occur relatively infrequently within short time intervals that are depicted statistically as event spikes rather than evenly distributed loss events. Hence, for these types of events there is a need to cede excess exposures directly to the reinsurance market where agents with global coverage can obtain wider geographical diversification for the related loss exposures (Figure 7.4).

Figure 7.4. **Risk Diversification in Global Reinsurance Market**

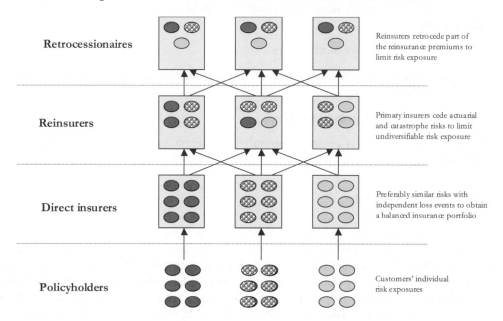

Balanced insurance portfolios are often covered through proportional reinsurance treaties where a share of all the written insurance policies is ceded to another primary insurer or a reinsurance company. Catastrophe risk exposures are typically ceded in the reinsurance market as facultative non-proportional treaties. Facultative insurance treaties cover for specified risk factors, such as windstorm, earthquake, etc. A non-proportional treaty does not have a pro-rata division of aggregate premiums and losses but typically defines a deductible or attachment point, up unto which the ceding party assumes all losses. The re-insurer is then obliged to cover losses in excess of the deductible up to a certain maximum amount, the exhaustion point.

Coverage provided within the loss range determined by the attachment point and the exhaustion point is typically referred to as a *layer* (Figure 7.5). A given insurance exposure can then be divided into different layers, each of which may be covered by different insurance treaties and risk transfer mechanisms. The ceded insurance exposure within a given layer may cover a certain percentage of total losses incurred between the deductible and the contractual maximum (Figure 7.5).

The cost of reinsurance coverage is normally indicated by the rate-on-line (ROL) derived as the premium divided by the limit of the insurance cover:

ROL = Premium/Cover limit

The expected loss-on-line (LOL) is determined by the actuarial probability that the event with corresponding loss characteristics will occur:

LOL = Actuarial probability of loss

Figure 7.5. **Reinsurance Layers and Retention Structures**

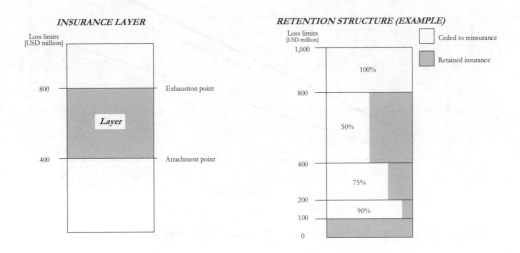

The relative price of the reinsurance cover is indicated in comparison to the actuarial probability that the loss will occur within the covered limit:

Relative price = ROL/LOL – 1
= ROL/Actuarial probability – 1
= Premium/(Actuarial probability x Cover limit) – 1

A positive price relationship indicates that the re-insurer receives a premium in excess of the actuarially expected loss and a negative price indicates that the re-insurer gets a premium below the expected loss of the contract. The price is typically positive because it includes the administrative cost and capital returns to the insurance company.

In principle, future catastrophe losses can be infinitely high, *i.e.,* there is really no upper loss limit on mega-catastrophes although these events are statistically extremely unlikely to happen[5]. The predictability of higher loss levels becomes increasingly uncertain and therefore the insurance premium for these exposures tends to increase[6]. With an indicative size of the property catastrophe reinsurance market around USD 75 billion[7] it is evident that covers for upper level risk exposures become excessively expensive.

Premium (P$_{cat}$) $= p \cdot \sigma_{cat} / \sigma_{non\text{-}cat} \cdot$ *Cover limit*

where; p *= probability of catastrophe event*
σ_{cat} *= standard deviation of catastrophe losses*
$\sigma_{non\text{-}cat}$ *= standard deviation of non-catastrophe losses*

The underlying market uncertainty has continued to decrease since the WTC incidence as illustrated by a falling ROL/LOL relationship across all risk layers (Figure 7.6).

Figure 7.6. **The Development in US Property Reinsurance Prices 2002-03**

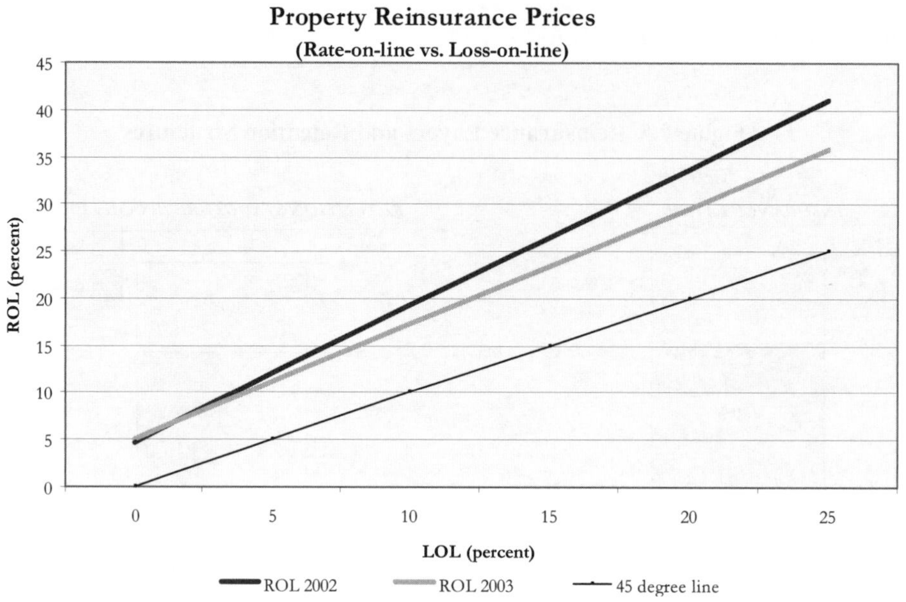

Property Reinsurance Prices
(Rate-on-line vs. Loss-on-line)

Source: Guy Carpenter, The World Catastrophe Reinsurance Market, Sept. 2003.

By experience capacity and pricing conditions in the reinsurance market is highly influenced by recent event losses. This is caused partially by an increase in uncertainty after major unexpected catastrophe events have occurred and partially because claims after major losses have occurred will drain total reserves of the insurance industry so premiums are increased to allow the reinsurance companies to gradually replenish their solvency ratio. Hence, the reinsurance premium can be further expressed as:

$$P_{cat,\,t} = p \cdot \sigma_{cat} / \sigma_{non\text{-}cat} \cdot loss_t / loss_{t\text{-}1} \cdot Cover\ limit$$

where; $loss_t$ = loss claims in current period t
            $loss_{t\text{-}1}$ = loss claims in previous period t-1

Accordingly, it appears that the rate-on-line has followed a cyclical path with upward trends following major loss events, *e.g.,* Hurricane Andrews in 1992, and after major storms in 1999 and the WTC incidence in 2001 (Figure 7.7). From the historical price development it also seems like the global reinsurance market has become more resilient to these kinds of mega-catastrophes. Hence, the market reaction has been more modest after 9/11 compared to the reaction experienced in conjunction with Andrews.

Figure 7.7. **The Development in Global Reinsurance Prices 1990-2003**

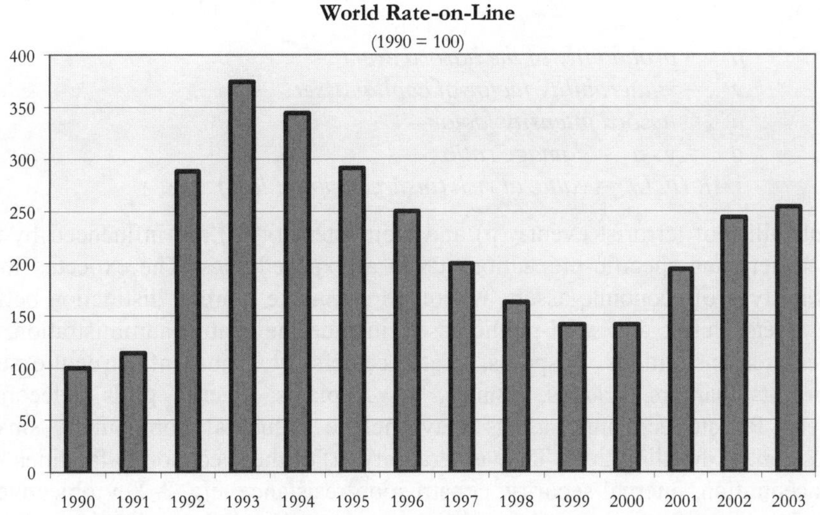

World Rate-on-Line
(1990 = 100)

Source: Guy Carpenter, The World Catastrophe Reinsurance Market, Sept. 2003.

The expected direct economic losses from catastrophe events are typically determined through sequential calculation modules. The hazard module outlines the potential intensity of different hazards at exposed sites. The exposure module identifies the exposed economic assets at the sites and quantifies the value at risk. The vulnerability module determines the damage ratio ascribed to asset classes of different quality. Finally, the loss analysis module calculates the total direct economic losses determined through computerized simulations of possible hazard events (Figure 7.8).

In most developed countries there are rich databases describing urban building densities and various public and semi-public investment in essential economic infrastructure. In the case of natural catastrophes, hazard intensities can be stipulated on the basis of historical data on events, *e.g.,* storms, floods, earthquakes, etc. The same historical event data pool is not available in the case of catastrophes caused by terrorism. In lieu of this, the analysis must be based on assumed events and worst-case scenario analyses.

Figure 7.8. **A Typical Catastrophe Risk Calculation Model**

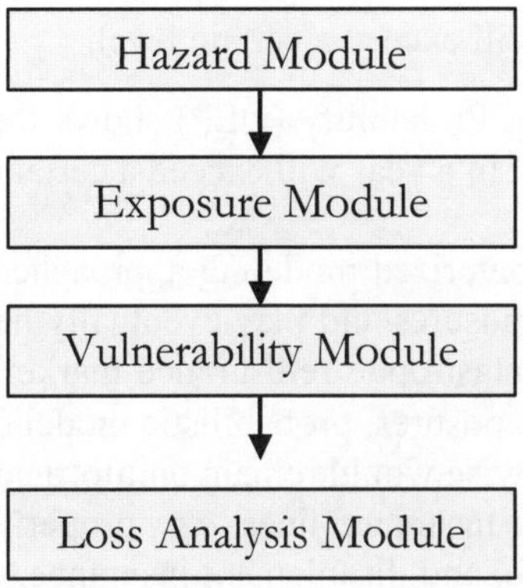

The direct economic risk exposure, the expected loss (EL), is then calculated as:

$$EL = p \cdot v \cdot h \cdot CL$$

where; p $= probability\ of\ the\ hazard\ event$
             v $= vulnerability\ factor\ of\ capital\ asset$
             h $= hazard\ intensity\ factor$
             d $= v \cdot h$ $= damage\ ratio$
             $VAR\ (ICL)$ $= value\ at\ risk\ (insured\ capital\ loss)$

The probability of terrorist events (p) and their intensity (h) are influenced by the level of security in society and specific precautions taken at exposed sites. The expected losses can be categorized by type of economic assets, where we can make a broad distinction between public and private assets. Public and semi-public assets include the central administration, educational facilities, research institutions, hospitals, health centers, etc., and infrastructure such as road systems, airports, harbors, bridges, tunnels, power plants, electric grids, telecommunication networks, etc. Private economic assets may include industrial compounds, small business facilities, residential dwellings, etc. The vulnerability (v) of these economic facilities is a function of asset concentration, internal security, construction resistance, etc. A key objective in the risk assessment is to quantify regional economic exposures and underlying insurance lines based on these considerations. The exposures are often expressed in a number of key measures:

- The average annual loss (AAL) is the expected loss per year measured over an extended period of time. The annual loss figure can be calculated as the sum of the products between all the event losses and the associated event probabilities.

- The probable maximum loss (PML) measures the loss severity expressed in pecuniary terms or as a percentage of the value at risk. Event losses can be much higher than PML, but the measure constitutes a useful comparative statistic. PML is not universally defined, but has been indicated as the largest likely loss corresponding to a 150-year return period[8].

- The loss cost is the part of the insurance premium that pays for the expected repairs or rebuilding of damaged assets. It corresponds to the pure premium charged by an insurance company excluding considerations for administration, adjusting, and underwriting expenses and return on capital.

- Other outputs from the model calculations include two types of loss exceeding probability curves stipulating the probability that catastrophe losses will exceed certain threshold levels.

- The Aggregate Exceeding Probability (AEP) shows the probability that aggregate losses from all events in a year will exceed a certain level.

- The Occurrence Exceeding Probability (OEP) shows the probability that losses from the single largest hazard event in a year will exceed a certain level.

The use of probabilistic computerized modeling approaches is becoming an accepted way to analyze major catastrophe risk exposures and may eventually help reduce some of the underlying uncertainties that challenge the catastrophe reinsurance market[9]. Particularly in connection with the assessment of terrorism risk exposures, probabilistic modeling may help quantify the potential size of economic losses that otherwise would remain uninformed. This approach may also point to interacting effects across different insurance lines, *e.g.,* property insurance, business interruption, workers compensation, health, life, and disablement insurance, etc., that became transparent after the WTC incident. However, terrorism events can take many different forms, *e.g.,* multiple attacks on major economic assets using explosives, spread of biotechnological agents, smaller missile based attacks, suicide bombs, etc. The terrorist events are also likely to change form over time as attention intensifies around specific types of incidents and security is tightened in certain areas. Hence, terrorism activities may converge toward less protected geographical regions and take new forms aimed at breaking down business confidence and public morale, which may have adverse effects on economic activity. In reality, it remains very difficult to outline the likely contours of terrorism exposures, which adds to the uncertainty associated with these types of risk. Nonetheless, the simulation techniques can be useful tools to perform stress testing of worst-case scenarios in country settings and evaluate effects on predefined economic assets and specific insurance portfolios.

Figure 7.9. **Model Estimates – Probabilities of Catastrophe Losses (Layered Reinsurance Program – Example)**

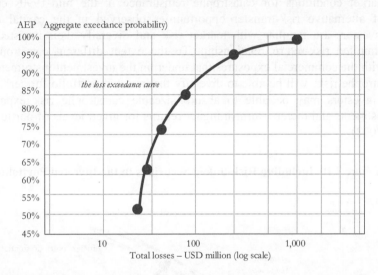

The cyclical nature of capacity and pricing conditions in the catastrophe reinsurance market may be partially ascribed to myophic behaviors in the reinsurance industry as a response to depleted reserves and increased uncertainties after extreme events where regulatory constraints may enforce such outcomes (Jaffee and Russell, 1997). Accounting rules often prohibit the accumulation of surpluses into irreversible reserves dedicated to cover specific future catastrophe losses. Hence, current accounting practices may prevent insurance companies from the ability to effectively smooth the cash flows of premiums and claims over longer periods of time. Furthermore, the retained earnings are considered taxable in many tax jurisdictions, including the United States, also when the retained earnings are earmarked as a capital reserve for future catastrophe losses. Such restrictions may enforce the cyclical nature of reinsurance capacity.

Most commercial property and casualty insurance contracts in the United States excluded or provided very limited cover for terrorism exposures during 2002 while some reinsurance contracts for personal insurance lines provided terrorism cover excluding events using nuclear, biological, and chemical (NBC) agents (Guy Carpenter, 2002). Hence, to accommodate a higher level of coverage the Terrorism Insurance Act was passed in the United States in late November 2002, which gave temporary federal support for insured losses from terrorist events. The act defines a terrorist event as a total loss exceeding US$ 5 million caused by individuals acting on behalf of a foreign interest. The insurance program is mandatory for all insurance companies and imposes a total loss retention on the industry of US$ 10 billion in the first year, US$ 12.5 billion in the second year, and US$ 15 billion the third year. The act is aimed to provide temporary availability of affordable terrorism insurance cover during a transition period where private insurers are assumed to resume commercial coverage, *i.e.,* the current program will expire in late 2005.

The UK has experienced the adverse effects of terrorist events for some time and represents another example of a government supported insurance scheme. Here the UK government has provided unlimited retrocession cover for property insurance with certain payback provisions to a mutual reinsurance company (Pool Re), which in turn is owned by the industry members. The provisions define terrorism as acts by any persons to overthrow or influence the UK government, or any other government, by force or violence. Cover is only provided for damages caused by fire and explosion. The arrangement requires retention per event and annual claims. The retention limits are scheduled to triple over the next four years in the hope that the insurance industry by then is able to provide increased cover on commercial terms.

2.2 Capital Market Instruments

Tighter market conditions for catastrophe reinsurance in the mid-1990s encouraged the exploitation of alternative risk-transfer opportunities observed in the capital market. Large institutional investors are familiar with market risk and diversify their invested portfolios to optimize the implied risk-return relationship. To the extent different catastrophe events are uncorrelated with the commercial exposures that underpin the investment instruments then returns linked to catastrophe risks will be able to diversify the invested portfolio further[10] (Figure 7.10). Hence, large investors may be able to absorb sizeable catastrophe risk exposures in their aggregate investments and thereby furnish higher returns for given levels of portfolio risk (Heike and Kiernan, 2002).

Figure 7.10. **Including Risk-linked Securities in the Invested Portfolio**

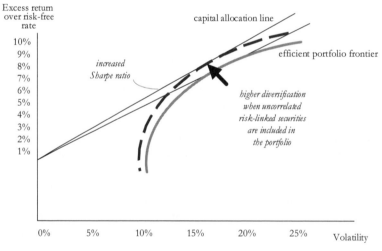

[Sharpe ratio = Excess return over risk-free rate / Volatility]

The industry contemplated alternative risk-transfer opportunities as conditions for reinsurance of catastrophe risk exposures tightened during the 1990s. With a rather finite capacity in the global reinsurance market, insurance companies and financial engineers looked toward the large capital market for takers of catastrophe risk exposures[11]. Based on historical price developments day-to-day changes in the market value of traded stocks and bonds in the US market could reach a size of around US$ 100 billion[12], which is comparable to the estimated size of the property catastrophe reinsurance market. Since investors in the capital market are familiar with these sizeable shifts in fortune, they should be able to absorb the large potential losses associated with disaster risks.

The first capital market instrument linked to catastrophe risk was placed in 1994 when a captive of Hannover Re issued a catastrophe bond linked to worldwide property catastrophe losses[13]. There have been more than 50 risk-linked securities issues since the mid-1990s funding aggregate risk exposures well in excess of US$ 6 billion (Figure 7.11). The issues have covered a variety of catastrophe risks, *e.g.,* hurricane, typhoon, windstorm, earthquake, etc., but not exposures like flood that constitute a significant part of the global catastrophe losses (Sigma 3/2002).

Figure 7.11. **Issuance of Risk-Linked Securities 1997 – 2003 (catastrophe bonds only)**

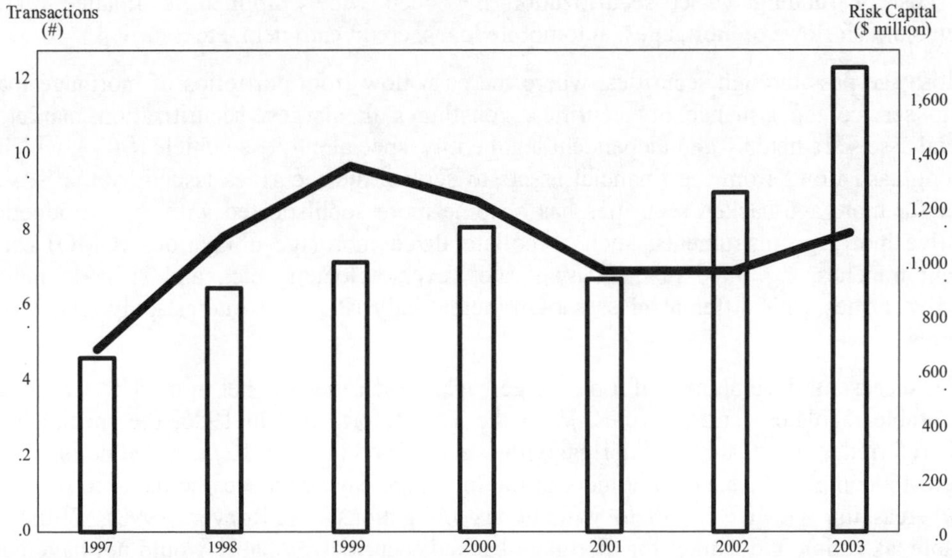

Source: MMC Securities.

The cat-bonds have used different triggers, including actual loss indemnity, catastrophe loss indexes, and parametric formulas based on standardized hazard indicators. The transactions are unique and require the involvement of investment bankers, securities dealers, lawyers, catastrophe analysts, rating agencies, etc. Hence, the transaction costs associated with these issues can be high, but cost savings have been achieved from increased standardization and transparency of documentation, etc. Risk-linked securities are now a well-established element of the capital market with issuance volume reaching an all time high of US$ 1.73 billion in 2003. More recent issues have been targeted to risk-transfer at layers with loss probabilities ranging between 0.4-1.0% corresponding to 250- to 100-year events, but the market is gradually moving towards lower risk layers. Earthquake and storm, both rapid onset hazards, are the two dominant catastrophe risks covered in the risk-linked securities market, whereas emergent events like flood and drought have received little notice. No issues have so far considered mega-terrorism risk directly, but a recent US$ 260 million special transaction covering revenue loss from cancellation of the FIFA World Cup in Germany in 2006 considers threats of natural disasters as well as terrorist events[14]. Another US$ 250 million issue covering excess mortality risk related to life insurance exposures did not explicitly exclude adverse effects caused by terrorist events[15], the terrorism exposure in this transaction, however, is deemed highly remote (Lane, 2004).

The price of risk-transfer in the cat-bond market has been somewhat higher than for conventional reinsurance contracts although prices have been more favorable in the recent market environment. Risk-linked securities have typically provided a premium of 1-5% above the return offered by corporate bonds with the same credit rating[16]. Investors that are unfamiliar with the instruments may require a slight premium to assume this new risk class, whereas issuers may be willing to accept the higher cost to establish an alternative risk transfer mechanism.

In many ways the market for risk-linked securities can be compared to the mortgage backed securities market, which took off in the US during the 1980s partially induced by a favorable tax regime and adherence to a market standard. Asset securitization has grown in importance as an attractive funding alternative for banks and finance companies. The securitization technique uses cash flows from an indigenous financial portfolio to support the issuance of securities that often have higher credit quality than the originator of the financial assets (Blum and DiAngelo, 1998; Fabozzi, 1998). The improved credit rating provides the securitized financing alternative with lower cost of funding. Asset securitization has been widely applied to finance relatively predictable cash flows of mortgages, automobile loans, credit card debt, etc.

Mortgage pass-through securities, where the cash flow from portfolios of mortgage loans is used to service the issuance of securities, constitutes the largest securitization market. The financial assets are held by an independent legal entity, special purpose vehicle (SPV), which uses incoming cash flows from the financial assets to service the securities issued by the SPV. The market for mortgage backed securities has become more sophisticated with the introduction of derivative mortgage instruments, such as collateralized mortgage obligations (CMO) carrying different tranches, *e.g.* fixed rate, floating rate, reverse floaters, etc., and stripped mortgage backed securities with different classes of principal-only (PO) and interest-only (IO) payment structures.

The successful development of a mortgage backed securities market in the US was enhanced by favorable regulatory and tax rules. With the Tax Reform Act in 1986, the special purpose vehicle referred to as a real estate mortgage investment conduit (REMIC) avoided double taxation of interest income as the residual holders of the mortgage payments became liable to pay income tax, whereas the REMIC was held without tax obligations (*e.g.* Roever, 1998). Without this favorable tax ruling, the market for mortgage-backed securities probably would not have been as successful as has actually been the case.

The asset securitization technique was applied to the reinsurance market (Litzenberger et al., 1996; Froot et al., 1998). Through issuance of catastrophe risk-linked bonds, cat-bonds for short, the issuer, typically an insurance or reinsurance company can obtain cover for specified exposures in case of predefined catastrophe events, *e.g.,* storm, hurricane, or earthquake. The catastrophe risk-transfer opportunities have primarily been exploited by insurance and reinsurance companies to obtain complementary coverage in the capital market. Risk securitization has been an attractive alternative for insurers under restrictive market conditions but has also been adopted by a few corporate entities, *e.g.,* Oriental Land Co. (Tokyo DisneySea, Disney hotels and Disney Resort Line).

A cat-bond is typically structured around a special purpose vehicle established in a tax favorable jurisdiction[17] (*e.g.* ISO, 1999; Standard & Poor's, 2000; Goldman Sachs, 2000). The SPV issues the cat-bonds and receives up-front payments from the investors buying the securities. The SPV engages in an insurance contract with the ceding entity, that in turn pays an insurance premium for the entire insurance period or on a pro-rata basis. The insurance contract typically provides the cedant with insurance coverage on an excess-of-loss basis (EOL) corresponding to practice in the catastrophe reinsurance market. Hence, the ceded risk exposure may cover losses associated with particular insurance layers between specified attachment and exhaustion points.

The SPV uses the up-front proceeds from the bond issue less the expenses accrued in connection with the placement to buy a liquid securities portfolio with high credit quality and low interest rate sensitivity. The securities portfolio is placed in a trust account as collateral for the debt service payments due on the cat-bonds (Cook and Della Sala, 1998). The SPV is rated by one of the leading a credit agencies. The SPV often engages into a fixed-floating interest rate swap agreement that converts the interest returns from the invested securities portfolio into monthly

Libor based floating rate payments. The investors receive a relatively high spread above the Libor rate to compensate for the catastrophe risk exposure. The investors only receive the full principal back at maturity if no catastrophe losses materialize in the interim. Hence, the major risk consideration for cat-bond investors is the inherent catastrophe risk exposure (Figure 7.12).

The cat-bonds can use different bases to trigger compensation under the reinsurance contract. Compensation can be triggered as indemnity of actual insurance losses incurred by the ceding party. The trigger could also be based on a defined loss index, *e.g.* the Guy Carpenter Catastrophe Index, the PCS Index, etc., or build on indicators measuring the event magnitude in different ways, *e.g.,* wind speed, wave height, intensity of rainfall, etc. A final approach entails the adoption of parametric formulas, a hybrid methodology, where triggers can be closely associated with the cedants exposure, but at the same time are well defined, objectively measurable, and analyzable.

There is a good potential to transfer parts of the catastrophe risk exposures to the institutional investors in the capital market, and thereby provide an opportunity to diversify the invested portfolios. The risk-linked securities appear to be placed across a fairly diverse investor base without strong dominance by investors in the conventional insurance industry. Whereas issuance of risk-linked securities can be somewhat cumbersome initially until transaction flows have become standardized, this risk transfer market may extend the capacity for certain types of catastrophe risk.

Figure 7.12. **Securitization of Catastrophe Risk – Cat-Bond Structure**

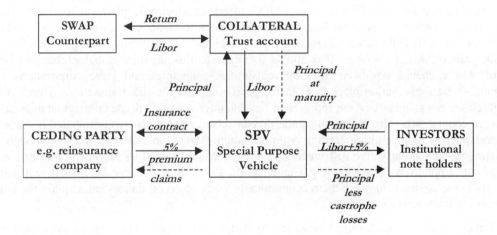

2.3 Financial Derivatives

A number of exchange-traded derivatives linked to catastrophe risk were introduced during the 1990s. The Bermuda Commodity Exchange traded catastrophe options based on the Guy Carpenter Catastrophe Index[18] (GCCI) for catastrophe property losses and the Chicago Board of Trade (CBOT) introduced catastrophe futures contracts based on quarterly property losses reported by the Insurance Services Office[19] (ISO). The exchange also offered trading in a specified catastrophe call spread option contract, which combined the purchase of a call option at a lower strike price and a sale of a call option at a higher strike price[20] (Figure 7.13).

Figure 7.13 **Catastrophe Call Spreads – Long and Short Positions**

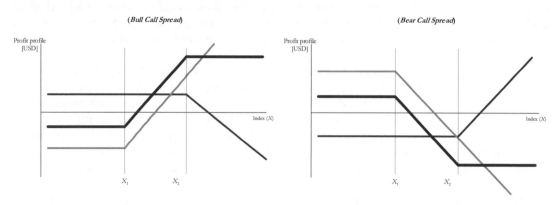

Adapted from T. J. Andersen, *Currency and Interest Rate Hedging*, Simon & Schuster, 1993

In addition the CBOT introduced futures and options contracts based on the catastrophe index established by Property Claims Service (PCS)[21]. All these contract types were standardized futures and options contracts. However, the Bermuda Commodities Exchange suspended trading of its catastrophe futures and options contracts in 1999 due to sluggish trading volume over the preceding two years. The Chicago Board of Trade, the other futures exchange to offer catastrophe derivatives, experienced a declining interest in their contracts and subsequently closed trading of its catastrophe futures.

The Catastrophe Risk Exchange (CATEX) offers an electronic platform to trade tailored reinsurance contracts. This is an Internet-based business-to-business exchange for all types of insurance contracts and related risk management products. The electronic trading system is based on integrative XML technology that allows members to link up to a global exchange posting board. The exchange has been used by reinsurance companies and large corporations as a business-to-business market place to execute specific catastrophe risk transactions. Hence, these contracts are not standardized but represent a flexible interface to facilitate contractual adaptations between counterparts. The trading in standardized exchange contracts was terminated because the general interest and resulting trading volumes simply were unsatisfactory. Even though the catastrophe- linked derivative instruments have been widely touted as promising alternatives to hedge catastrophe risk exposures (*e.g.* Canter et al., 1996), there has not been sufficient market activity in the contracts to make them economically viable. Several factors can explain the fading interest in catastrophe derivatives.

First, the use of standardized contracts to hedge catastrophe exposures is associated with substantial basis risk, which has constituted a significant practical barrier to their use. The effectiveness of the hedges depends on the extent to which the underlying catastrophe loss indexes co-varies with the catastrophe exposures that are hedged. This might not be the case if, for example, the loss index covers property damages in a particular region and the property portfolio to be hedged is scattered across different geographical areas. This discrepancy between the price of the asset underlying the futures contract and the asset portfolio to be hedged is referred to as the basis risk (Figure 7.14). Some studies indicate that standardized futures contracts may cover somewhere around two-thirds of the underlying risk exposures (Major, 1999), which often is considered unsatisfactory.

Secondly, the futures market provides hedgers with opportunities to lock-in at loss levels that correspond to the general loss expectations of the market. As a consequence market participants would have to beat general market expectations in order to earn excess returns compared to the reinsurance market. Since probabilistic expectations supposedly already are reflected in the reinsurance prices, the market for catastrophe futures and options contracts does not represent a true benefit unless insurance companies want to take advantage of arbitrage opportunities between the futures and the underlying reinsurance market, or establish temporary market positions in catastrophe risks. To most insurance companies these types of speculative activities are of marginal interest.

Figure 7.14. **The Basis Risk of Standardized Contract Indexes**

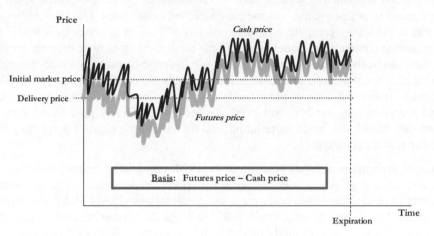

Adapted from T. J. Andersen, *Currency and Interest Rate Hedging*, Simon & Schuster, 1993

Insurance companies are the natural hedgers in the derivatives market whereas there are few natural investors to counter this interest. For example, construction companies could arguably be considered natural investors in catastrophe derivatives because they experience a boom in demand subsequent to severe property damages. However, there are no good arguments for why they should counter this potential windfall by investing in a market that requires highly specialized trading and risk management skills. Acting as an investor in catastrophe risk derivatives requires deep insights into the reinsurance market and specific catastrophe risk exposures that few outside investors possess, and without active investors there will be no successful markets in traded derivatives. Whereas this obstacle is visible in the market for natural catastrophe risk exposures, it is even more apparent in the market for terrorism risk. Therefore, standardized derivatives on terrorism risk exposures do not emerge as a viable risk-transfer market.

In contrast, trading in the weather derivatives offered by the Chicago Mercantile Exchange (CME) has continued to show high market interest. Here we are dealing with contracts that involve a large number of natural counterparts, such as different types of energy producers and energy consumers. Whereas weather derivatives have some correlation to different catastrophe indexes that are influenced by changing weather conditions, these derivatives do not represent an immediate refuge for hedgers that are looking for alternative ways to cover their exposures. The exchange traded weather contracts are used by energy companies and financial institutions to hedge their over-the-counter weather derivatives, which tends to spur further trading activity.

In recent years, financial institutions, energy traders, and energy companies have developed an active dealer-market in a number of over-the-counter weather derivatives based on Heating Degree Days (HDD) and Cooling Degree Days (CDD) temperature indexes[22]. The derivatives are typically construed as call options, put options, and swap agreements. Hence, the holder of a call option is compensated when the index value exceeds the agreed strike price and the writer of the option has to honor the payout. The holder of a put option will receive compensation when the index value falls below the agreed strike price and the writer of the option must honor the payout. The buyer of a swap will receive compensation when the index is above the strike price and will make a payout when the index is below the strike price. The seller of a swap will receive compensation when the index is below the strike price and will make a payout when the index is above the strike price. Hence, the swap buyers and sellers are counterparts that effectively lock-in their energy prices throughout the length of the swap agreement.

In response to the surge in the over-the-counter market for weather derivatives, the Chicago Mercantile Exchange (CME) introduced traded futures and options contracts based on the Heating Degree Days (HDD) and Cooling Degree Days (CDD) indexes[23]. These contracts allow energy producers and users to hedge against volumetric risk effects associated with changes in weather conditions, and as such they compete with the contracts offered in the over-the-counter market. The exchange-traded contracts are widely used by the book runners of over-the-counter products to manage their derivatives risk. The parameters of over-the-counter products are relatively flexible compared to the standardized exchange traded contracts, as size, maturity, and strike price can be tailored to individual counter-party needs. Exchange-traded derivatives are standardized contracts and therefore less flexible. However, standardized contracts post transparent market prices, are actively traded and hence more liquid, and do not impose counter-party risks as in the case of over-the-counter contracts.

A plethora of derivatives emerged throughout the 1990s comprising futures, options and swap agreements, *e.g.,* on energy prices such as crude oil (Brent crude, crude oil light sweet, etc.), refined products (unleaded gasoline, heating oil, etc.), natural gas (Henry Hub), electricity (Palo Verde, California-Oregon border, etc.), credit risk (credit spread options, default swaps, etc.) and so forth. These derivatives are marginally related to the economic effects of different catastrophe events.

As an example, energy prices are correlated with different exogenous events, such as disruptions in economic activity, changes in business confidence, etc. Similarly, the economic risk indicators such as credit spreads and loan portfolios bear some relationship to catastrophe events that affect the entire capital market. These effects may be accentuated if the credit spreads reflect exposures in particularly industries, *e.g.,* energy companies, equipment manufacturers, defense contractors, etc. Hence, a number of price and index relationships might possibly be used to manage particular catastrophe risk exposures. However, many of these relationships remain unexplored and are likely to be wrought with basis risk issues and therefore these venues do not seem to provide an immediate potential to hedge terrorism risk exposures.

Catastrophe risk swaps

The risk transfer characteristics of a conventional reinsurance treaty that also constitute part of a cat-bond structure can be replicated in catastrophe risk swap. The catastrophe risk swap makes it possible to use standardized swap agreements to formalize the contractual obligations of a reinsurance arrangement, which can be advantageous in terms of flexibility and speed. Catastrophe risk swap agreements have emerged as relatively simple over-the-counter instruments to transfer catastrophe risk exposures. But, despite the potential advantages they require specialized legal expertise on swap documentation and swap agreements are generally difficult to unwind once they have been established. Therefore, risk swaps can be an alternative to conventional reinsurance treaties and issuance of risk-linked securities. A swap agreement also entails a counter-party credit just like a reinsurance contract risk as the hedger depends on the other party to honor the obligations, and the risk swap most likely entails an insurance company as counter-party[24].

In a catastrophe risk swap, the cedant makes fixed payments that correspond to the premiums paid in a reinsurance contract, *e.g.,* in a cat-bond structure, against claims compensation in case losses occur. The counter-part to the risk swap receives the fixed premium payments and provides variable payments corresponding to the claims experienced by the cedant (Figure 7.15). Risk swap agreements provide an alternative instrumentation route when engaging in reinsurance arrangements with conventional counterparts, *i.e.,* catastrophe risk swaps are primarily used by insurance companies to manage and diversify their catastrophe risk exposures (Takeda, 2002). Consequently, the "market' for catastrophe risk swaps does not by itself represent an incremental reservoir for risk-transfer that can enhance the capacity to place mega-terrorism risk exposures.

Figure 7.15. **Catastrophe Risk Swap Agreement**

2.4 Catastrophe Risk Financing

Whereas the risk-transfer instruments require that an insurance premium is paid up front to cede a certain risk exposure in the market, the catastrophe financing instruments require the payment of a commitment fee or an option premium to retain access to future financing opportunities (availability of funding) on predetermined conditions (price of funding). Such instruments include committed credit facilities typically available through the banking industry and contingent capital instruments offered by intermediaries in the capital markets.

Risk financing arrangements provide capital replenishment rather than risk transfer solutions and may establish contingencies in the financial markets that make funding available in case there is a need to recuperate after economic losses have been inflicted. The catastrophe risk financing instruments guarantee availability of credit in the future, *e.g.,* to support restoration of productive economic assets. Once the risk financing instruments are drawn down and exercised, the proceeds must be repaid in accordance with underlying loan agreements and bond indentures and therefore adds to the debt burden of the borrower. The risk-transfer arrangements charge larger up front insurance premiums to compensate for the cover of potential catastrophe losses. However any proceeds from subsequent claims recoveries constitute one-way transfers and entail no debt obligations. Hence, there is a trade-off between the payment of higher up-front insurance premiums that reflect the probability of future catastrophe losses, and lower commitment fees for future credit commitments where any loan proceeds will add to a future debt load.

Committed credit facilities

Committed credit facilities ensure that funds can be drawn down at any time on predetermined conditions in case a need arises, *e.g.,* after a major disaster has occurred or any other adverse situation that gives rise to an incremental liquidity need. Different financial institutions, including deposit taking institutions and finance companies may offer committed revolving term facilities that provide funding by rolling over short-term credits at a fixed spread over a variable rate indicator like Libor. Term committed facilities typically require payment of an up-front commitment fee to compensate for the implied liquidity, interest rate, and credit risks.

More advanced forms of committed funding arrangements may constitute syndicated credit facilities shared among banks in larger consortia. The committed credit facilities might also take hybrid forms somewhere between pure bank lines and capital market instruments. The funding arrangement could, for example, be construed as short-term commercial paper or medium-term note issuance facilities where debt instruments are placed directly in the market or are offered to a prearranged panel of financial institutions. These credit facilities would typically be supported by committed back-stop facilities provided by commercial banks to ensure future funding availability in case the capital market dries up or offers funding at uncompetitive rates.

Committed revolving term facilities are usually not conditioned around specific funding needs, but constitute general buffers that serve as reservoirs for unexpected financing requirements[25]. As such, committed credit facilities can be used to make short-medium term financing available to cover immediate liquidity needs that arise in the aftermath of catastrophes including terrorist events.

Contingent capital instruments

Contingent capital instruments are typically offered by insurance affiliates, investment banks, and securities firms that guarantee the issuance of medium term securities or quasi-equity instruments. These instruments constitute put option contracts that give the holder the right to place funding instruments in the market on predetermined conditions. The issuer requires payment of an up-front option premium as compensation for the downside risk assumed by the option writer.

Contingent capital arrangements provide the holders with opportunities to place different capital market instruments on agreed terms and thereby acquire funding in the future on predetermined terms and conditions. Contingent surplus notes guarantee issuance of medium term securities or quasi-equity instruments on fixed terms once the level of an underlying risk indicator has been surpassed (Colarossi, 1999). These option structures are sometimes referred to as knock-in options, because they are activated by an independent trigger.

The issuer of contingent surplus notes provides the holder, *e.g.* an insurance company, with a guarantee that securities can be issued and placed with investors if certain adverse events occur. For regulatory purposes, an insurance company may treat the notes as statutory surplus as it enables the insurance company to finance future losses, but once the underlying credit notes have been issued they must be repaid in accordance with an agreed redemption schedule. Contingent surplus notes with an aggregate market value around US$ 8 billion have been issued in the US primarily to cover the commercial risk of private insurance companies. However, no contingent capital instruments have been issued so far that use natural catastrophes or terrorist events as triggers.

2.5 Assessing Risk Financing Instruments

The choice between alternative risk financing instruments is partially a function of the availability across markets for different risk-transfer and financing instruments and the general pricing and affordability of available covers. However, it is also influenced by the characteristics of the instruments and the implications they have for moral hazard, adverse selection, basis risk, and credit risk exposures.

Moral hazard can arise when a hedger has obtained cover for a particular risk based on realized losses, because the insured party no longer has an incentive to mitigate future losses and hence the insurance provider can be adversely affected in case of a catastrophe event *(e.g.,* Grossman and Hart, 1983; Doherty, 1985). For example, once a terrorism exposure has been insured, the insured party might become negligent on security because they feel covered. Hedging instruments based on an objectively determined index or a parametric formula will generally be less exposed to moral hazards.

Adverse selection can arise when information held by the insured party and by the insurance provider is asymmetric, *e.g.,* the party acquiring insurance coverage often knows more about the risk exposure than the insurance company covering the risk (Hillier, 1997). Hence, the insurance buyer might try to gain an advantage at the expense of the insurance provider. The inverse situation can also arise, whereby the insurer knows more than the insurance buyer. This can lead to "cherry picking", where the insurance company only insure low risk entities while charging a price that reflects the full actuarial risk. In either case, the consequence is an inefficient transfer of risk exposures. Using objectively determined triggers can normally circumvent the problem of adverse selection.

Basis risk can arise from discrepancies between the risk indicators used in the hedging instruments and the underlying risk exposures. For example, if the value of the index that underpins the hedging instrument or insurance contract differs significantly from the value of the risk exposure it is intended to cover, the hedge will be exposed to a high basis risk. Instruments that use standardized indexes will often have high basis risk, because it is difficult to apply a general index to an individualized risk exposure. Instruments based on indemnity of realized losses have no basis risk and parametric formulas can be construed so there is a very low basis risk.

Counter-party risk can arise when the insured party depends on the future solvency of a single counterpart that is responsible for fulfillment under the contract. For example, catastrophe risk coverage from insurance companies with a low credit standing jeopardizes future coverage, because a catastrophe puts added pressure on the solvency of the weakest insurance companies. Exchange traded derivatives and risk-linked securities circumvent the issue of counter-party credit risk (Figure 7.16).

Figure 7.16 **The Trade-Off Between Moral Hazard, Credit and Basis Risks**

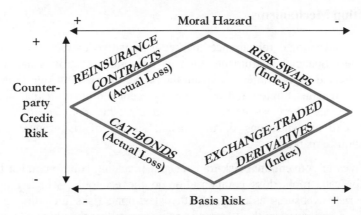

Adapted from N. A. Doherty, *Integrated Risk Management*, McGraw-Hill, 2000

Conventional reinsurance contracts, where the risk cover is based on indemnity claims and actual losses have little basis risk, but are exposed to moral hazard issues and counter-party credit risk. Exchange-traded derivatives such as standardized futures and options contracts potentially expose the hedger to a high level of basis risk, whereas moral hazard and counter-party credit risk exposures are low. Risk-linked securities carry little credit risk because they are collateralized and the securities are placed among a diverse group of investors. Catastrophe risk swaps are exposed to counter-party risk, whereas the level of moral hazard and basis risk depends on the trigger applied in the swap agreement. Subscribing to contingent capital is not exposed to moral hazard and adverse selection, because the arrangements entail no claims coverage, but provide funding that must be repaid according to an indenture agreement. But, committed credit facilities and contingent capital instruments are exposed to counter-party risk and may be prone to basis risk if the loan agreement has limiting covenants or the trigger in the contingent instrument only is loosely associated with the underlying loss exposure.

From a counter-party risk perspective, the issuance of risk-linked securities is favorable. However, the trade-off between instruments is influenced by other factors as well, such as speed, flexibility, complexity, and fee structures. Furthermore, when applying different triggers in the financial instruments, the relationship between moral hazard and basis risk is no longer linear. By using a parametric formula, where the trigger is determined by objective indicators it is possible, at least theoretically, to achieve lower moral hazard and lower basis risk at the same time. The concurrent reduction of these risk elements is possible because the trigger is objectively determined and cannot be manipulated by the hedger, and the basis risk is low because the parametric formula can be construed to closely emulate the value development of the risk exposure. Since risk-linked securities already entail low credit risk, issuance of cat-bonds with parametric triggers seems a good alternative to conventional reinsurance contracts for some types of catastrophe risk.

Hence, the choice of catastrophe-financing instruments should include an evaluation of the inherent elements of moral hazard, adverse selection, basis risk, and credit risk. Insurance treaties, risk-linked securities, catastrophe risk swaps, and contingent capital instruments can have very different attributes. The structure of the financial instruments will influence both the cost and the effectiveness of the insurance covers. Moral hazard and adverse selection issues tend to increase the uncertainty of the catastrophe exposures and may therefore make insurance premiums prohibitively high, while excessive basis risks and doubtful counter-parties can jeopardize the entire risk management exercise and make the instrument irrelevant for hedging purposes. One challenge then relates to the ability to develop triggers that are amenable to key characteristics of potential terrorism events and apply them effectively in the relevant financial markets.

3. Other Compensation Mechanisms

Whereas the conventional reinsurance market is sensitive to recent loss experiences, the introduction of new financial instruments such as risk-linked securities and traded derivative securities have provided opportunities to expand the market for risk-transfer. However, the size of these new markets remains limited and does not represent a dramatic expansion of the current market capacity. Hence, there seems to be a need for other compensation schemes to deal effectively with extreme situations of diminished supply of risk-transfer solutions in the conventional insurance markets.

The alternatives to conventional risk-transfer and financing solutions must be geared to the general needs for catastrophe loss compensation in the economy, which requires systematic analyses of the risk exposures associated with catastrophe risks including potential terrorist events. One of the major issues with catastrophe exposures is that the aggregate loss potentials are so large that they may jeopardize the capital base of major insurance companies and thereby constitute so-called uninsurable risk because no prudent insurance company is willing to offer the insurance cover. In this context there may often a need for some sort of government intervention to make additional market capacity available to insure catastrophe exposures at reasonable prices[26]. Such intervention includes the government-induced creation of specialized risk-transfer vehicles.

3.1 The Risk Management Process

Risk relates to adverse effects on economic activity caused by unexpected catastrophe events and associated uncertainties about future business prospects. A society that ignores potential risk factors will be hit harder when disasters happen because the events were unexpected and insufficient precautions were taken in advance. To the extent potentially adverse catastrophe events are recognized before they happen and potential causes behind such events are analyzed, the element of uncertainty can be vastly reduced. With some ingenuity it might even be possible to reduce the downside risks associated with the uncertainty. In other words, the more effort that is devoted to identify, understand, measure, and mitigate the causes of possible catastrophe events, the more it can reduce the element of surprise and the better the inherent risk exposure can be managed.

A formal risk management process starts with the identification of significant risk factors that might expose economic assets and cause business disruption. Once the important risk factors are identified the vulnerability to the various types of risk, including terrorist acts, should be analyzed and the implied direct economic effects determined. Measures of direct loss effects provide a basis for the analysis of potential benefits from intervention to make insurance cover available and assess the effectiveness of risk mitigation efforts. The risk measures also provide a basis for ongoing monitoring of the economic exposures associated with the key risks in the context of a dynamic and changing environmental context that may require responsive actions. The risk monitoring process can help determine excess exposures that might warrant coverage through various risk-transfer arrangements. Consequently, the efforts to identify, measure, and monitor essential risk exposures also provide a better decision framework to evaluate the need for risk-transfer and financing arrangements and the potential benefits associated with market intervention (Figure 7.17).

Figure 7.17 **The Formal Risk Management Process**

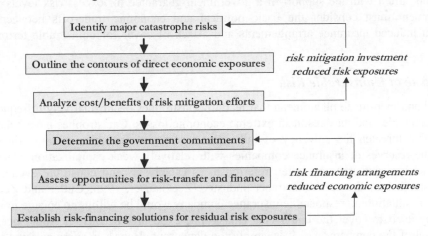

Once the nature of possible terrorism related catastrophe events have been identified and characterized, it is important to consider changing trends in terrorist events and assess the underlying event frequencies and intensities. The patterns evolving in terrorist hazards are dynamic and changing. The potential terrorist events that could occur are driven by human ingenuity and are therefore difficult to predict with any level of certainty, although they might be possible to counterweigh through foresight. Based on assumptions about possible terrorist hazards and predictions on their frequencies and intensities in the future, various vulnerability models can be used to transpose these assumptions into simulated loss estimates of the direct economic losses associated with terrorist events. The introduction of new construction and building techniques, expanded law enforcement and security measures, adherence to global intelligence sharing, diversifying business assets and communication infrastructure, protecting essential human resources, etc., are all activities that have the ability to reduce, and thereby mitigate the economic vulnerability of potential terrorist events. This type of risk mitigation should be pursued as long as the resulting benefits can be justified by reasonable political and economic criteria.

Once there is a good understanding of the potential devastation of economic assets there is a need to determine essential public and private assets that might be in need of financial cover to ensure reconstruction after potential disaster events. These economic assets could comprise private dwellings and commercial facilities as well as major public infrastructure investments including, *e.g.,* health care, educational, research, and administrative buildings. Since there is a limit to how far risk mitigation efforts can eliminate the terrorism risk exposure, there may be a search for ways to ensure that transfer and financing solutions are available for parts of the remaining risk exposure. Advance vulnerability analyses, assessments of the true economic exposures, and monitoring of risk-transfer and financing opportunities are essential elements of the considerations for viable risk management arrangements. It might also include the assessment of discrete risk-transfer vehicles that can offer insurance cover for specific catastrophe risks.

In situations where insurance companies are deemed unable to ensure major catastrophe risks on commercial terms, and if circumvention of expected adverse economic effects justifies it, a government might consider intervening to ensure that risk-transfer solutions are available to the public. These considerations may also take potential secondary economic effects related to social uncertainty and loss of business confidence into account. With a view on the potential economic effects from status quo, the government is in a better position to evaluate the likely benefit associated with intervention, which could involve a cover for excess risk levels as "insurer of last resort". The analyses also provide a foundation from which to determine the potential value associated with the establishment of risk-transfer vehicles. These vehicles may provide a minimum needed risk coverage to public entities on commercial terms, as mandatory or voluntary arrangements, often with the support of a government guarantee for excess risk levels. In short, the government must consider the basic political and economic trade-offs between durable government induced insurance arrangements and a lack of cover for uninsurable terrorism risk exposures.

3.2 The Issue of Uninsurable Risk

Natural and man-made phenomena that lead to catastrophes occur relatively infrequently, are quite unpredictable, and may result in extreme economic losses. Catastrophes have been defined as events that threaten the solvency of individual insurance companies as large direct losses eliminate the reserves of insurance companies with relatively weak capitalization. Catastrophes with extreme loss outcomes are often referred to as cataclysms and constitute events that can strain the stability of the entire insurance industry (Zeckhauser, 1996; Cutler and Zeckhauser, 1999). In this situation no responsible insurance company would be willing to engage in insurance contracts by itself to cover the underlying catastrophe exposures because it would question the very survival of the company, *i.e.,* it is simply too dangerous. Hence, in some extreme situations the catastrophe risks cannot be insured on normal commercial terms, *i.e.,* we talk about uninsurable risk.

Since, individual catastrophe claims within a region are dependent on the same underlying hazard they cannot be diversified within a regional insurance portfolio, so regional insurance companies will have an aversion against insuring these types of events. This is because the size of the potential aggregate losses is so large it may deplete the reserves of the individual insurance companies and jeopardize their viability. These risks might to some extent be diversifiable by ceding excess exposures to the global reinsurance industry. However, the potential aggregate loss exposures might still be so large that appetite is restrained in the reinsurance market as well or the underlying events can be so pervasive and unpredictable that any commercial inducements to insure these risks will vanish *(e.g.,* Jaffee and Russell, 1997; Kleindorfer and Kunreuther, 1999). This has obviously been the case with the extreme economic exposures to terrorist attacks that surfaced in the aftermath of the WTC incident and which at least temporarily constituted an uninsurable risk phenomenon.

In such situations national governments may want to intervene by instituting legal and regulatory requirements to ensure that insurance coverage is available to the public. To many politicians it may be considered unreasonable that citizens and commercial enterprises are unable to obtain insurance coverage for prevalent exposures to common elements of risk including terrorist attacks. Hence, lawmakers can impose mandatory insurance schemes on national insurance carriers or insurance companies operating in the country to enforce the insurance availability. Governments may also encourage the establishment of pooled catastrophe risk funds where lower level risk exposures could be covered by involved local insurance companies on a mutual basis while higher level exposures might be covered partially through reinsurance contracts, issuance of risk-linked securities, and various risk financing arrangements. These, arrangements do not necessarily involve any government funding or guarantees. However, in the absence of government intervention the extreme catastrophe exposures often remain uninsured.

This underscores that governments should engage in formal risk management processes that analyze the socio-economic effects from existing exposures, alternative risk-mitigation efforts, and the imposition of different risk-transfer vehicles to assess the need for intervention. There is general consensus that governments must play some role to ensure that risk-transfer opportunities are available to the public for otherwise uninsurable catastrophe risks, but there is no agreement as to what the precise role of government should be. Hence, it is argued that some types of government imposed catastrophe insurance schemes are necessary, because the uninsurable catastrophe risk exposures constitute excessive loss potentials that cannot be covered through normal commercial insurance arrangements *(e.g.,* Lewis and Murdock, 1996). However, government intervention should not constitute a carte blanche cover for the risk exposures because that will jeopardize actuarial practices and reduce the incentive for risk mitigation *(e.g.,* Epstein, 1996).

The exposure to different types of public sector assets is clearly a central government obligation and does not need the same degree of market intervention as the insurance cover for private economic assets. But it underlines a need to engage in formal risk management processes at the central government level to determine the contours of the exposures on public sector assets. To the extent a government does decide to act as insurer-of-last-resort to the insurance industry, or to entities that manage specific insurance pools, the overall risk obligations should be managed within an integrated risk management system with the aim of taking all catastrophe exposures into account.

It is argued that central governments should be willing to cover otherwise uninsurable risk exposures because public debt has low default risk within the country *(e.g.,* Bohn and Hall, 1999; Cummins, Lewis and Phillips, 1999). Hence, governments can, at least theoretically, issue risk-free debt instruments denominated in local currency and thereby obtain funding for excessive catastrophe losses on an *ex post* basis at the lowest possible costs[27]. However, there are potential downsides associated with excessive government guarantees for catastrophe exposures as they may encourage aggressive behaviors among commercial insurers to the detriment of the solvency among insurance companies (Bohn and Hall, 1999). It is also likely to have an adverse effect on private risk mitigation efforts if the government is willing to carry the brunt of the expected losses.

Others advocate government intervention to cover only the highest layers of the catastrophe exposures that otherwise would remain uninsured in the market. For example, it has been suggested that the government could issue catastrophe call options to the insurance industry in cover of excess losses (Cummins et al., 1999). In this case, the government would charge a premium from the insurance companies as compensation for potential future payouts under the option contracts. Such an arrangement would expand capacity in the catastrophe reinsurance market and at the same time shield the government from any direct involvement in business operations, such as, insurance sales, claims adjustment, and disbursements after major disasters.

This is important because the experience with programs that impose a direct government involvement has mixed results. For example, the US federal government provides catastrophe insurance coverage through disaster relief programs like FEMA, small business loans, and various congressional appropriations. However, these programs have had several unintended side effects and have generally been less effective risk management approaches *(e.g.,* CRS, 1998; Dowton and Pielke, 2001; Larson and Plasencia, 2001). Nonetheless, the private insurance market is often unable to provide cover for pure catastrophe risks and therefore there might be a need for other methods to make insurance protection available to the public. These types of government intervention could take the form of public insurance pools supported by different types of public-private partnerships that engage the insurance industry in the management of the insurance structure. But, these initiatives should carry an appropriate balance between government support and commercial insurance practices. It is also important to consider the trade-off between insurance availability and price, *i.e.,* the purpose should not be to offer subsidized insurance, because it can eliminate risk mitigation incentives and interfere with longer-term capacity revival in the insurance market.

Public non-actuarially determined allocation processes usually turn out to be highly ineffective ways to manage claims disbursements and reconstruction efforts in post disaster periods. Cover for catastrophe exposures could be furnished through insurance vehicles that operate on the basis of commercial and actuarial principles. On the other hand, the set-ups may require some sort of government commitment to act as insurer-of-last-resort, *e.g.,* if losses exceed the capacity of a pool. The reality is, that governments for economic and political reasons may be inclined to provide cover against the direct loss effects from major disasters such as terrorist attacks because it is unlikely to emerge from the commercial insurance industry all by itself. Hence, the challenge is to develop effective vehicles to handle such engagements without institutionalizing government subsidization and political interference in commercial insurance practices.

3.3 Government Induced Insurance Pools

Faced with the inability to insure certain disaster risk exposures in the aftermath of major catastrophes, governments have regularly intervened to ensure availability of coverage. In several industrial countries the governments have intervened to establish mandatory insurance pools providing insurance covers for extreme catastrophe risks. The funds in turn have covered the risk exposures through financing arrangements and reinsurance contracts for different risk layers typically on a stop-loss basis. In some cases, the risk exposures have been covered by a group of regionally based insurance companies[28], which may retain part of the exposure on a mutual basis while a large share of the higher exposure layers are ceded in the reinsurance market.

There are three examples in the US of national insurance pools created to provide effective insurance cover for mega-catastrophes. The Florida Hurricane Catastrophe Fund (FHCF) was established as a consequence of Hurricane Andrew. In this mandatory program the Florida legislature required all insurers operating in the state to participate in a tax-exempt insurance fund. The fund obtained cover for higher risk layers in the reinsurance market a portion of which was provided by the insurance pool itself on a mutual basis. Another example is the California Earthquake Authority (CEA), which was established in the wake of the Northridge earthquake. This voluntary state-run program was funded in part by insurers and obtained a participation of around 70% of all the homeowner insurers operating in the state. The upper layers of CEA's exposure have been reinsured in the market. The Hawaii Hurricane Relief Fund (HHRF) was activated after Hurricane Iniki, but has since stopped writing new policies because the market reestablished sufficient insurance capacity. Thirty-one US states operate so-called FAIR plans (fair access to insurance requirements) to cover uninsurable property risks that otherwise would be unable to obtain coverage from private insurance companies[29].

In France, flooding and earthquake damages have been covered through a special program (Catastrophe Naturelle – Cat Nat for short), which has reinsured all exposures with the government owned reinsurance company (Caisse Centrale de Réassurance – CCR). The insurance companies can establish tax-deductible reserves for major catastrophe events to smooth cash flows over longer time-periods. The CCR has been allowed by law to reinsure terrorism policies since 1982 and terrorism cover was made mandatory on property policies in 1986. However, with the advent of the WTC incident a new insurance pool, Gareat, was established in January 2002 to cover large industrial terrorism risk exposures. Gareat reinsures terrorism risk exposures of commercial insurance companies who provide a substantial cover for the pooled risk on a mutual basis. The entity enjoys government support through its ability to reinsure excess exposures with the CCR.

In Germany a state supported insurance company, Extremus, was established in the fall of 2002 by 16 national insurance and reinsurance companies to provide insurance cover for German terrorism risk exposures in excess of Euro 25 millions. The lower levels of the pooled exposure were backed by insurance companies and international re-insurers while the German government guaranteed a higher layer during an initial three-year period for aggregate losses between Euro 3-10 billions.

The Spanish Consorcio was created in 1941 to cover indemnities from the civil war and was used from 1986 onwards to cover other catastrophe events and as such has provided cover for terrorism risk exposures all along. The Consorcio is a public business institution that, in a subsidiary way, offers insurance coverage for extraordinary risks including natural catastrophes and terrorism events based on policies signed with insurance companies operating in the market that do not want to cover such risks. For this activity, the Consorcio has its own assets (premiums and surcharges provided by the insureds) and it has never used resources from the State. Terrorism is defined as any violent action with the aim to destabilize the established political system or generate fear and insecurity in the social environment in which they are perpetrated. This is, therefore, close to the definition used by Pool Re in the UK. The exposures of the Consorcio are covered by an unlimited government guarantee.

Hence, the governments can ensure the availability of insurance policies to the public with cover for major catastrophe risks through national insurance vehicles that pool together exposures of risk holders throughout the country. This may, for example, allow catastrophe property insurance to be extended widely to households, small businesses, and large industrials and make protection available throughout a region for otherwise uninsurable risks. By pooling the insurance obligations together within an insurance vehicle that operates as an independent economic entity, it becomes possible for the government to induce catastrophe risk management on an arms-length basis and avoid potentially damaging interference in claims distribution, etc. The insurance scheme could offer mandatory insurance policies required by law in order to obtain a sufficient pooling capacity. Alternatively, the pool could operate on a voluntary basis in which case public promotion campaigns might be needed to generate sufficient volume.

Once an insurance pool is established it should analyze its overall catastrophe risk exposure to determine how to manage the pooled exposure. In this analysis the managers of the insurance pool would consider the full scale of available risk-transfer and financing instruments and tools to structure the most optimal cover for the insurance portfolio. These considerations could for example comprise an insurance cover for the lower risk layers provided on a mutual basis by local insurance companies involved in the pool. It is likely to involve cedance of higher risk layers in the global reinsurance market, possibly issuance of risk-linked securities, and relatively low-cost committed credit facilities. The very highest risk layers most likely need some types of government guarantees as insurer-of-last-resort. The insurance vehicle would probably want to retain certain parts of the lower risk layers and cover these through premiums from outstanding policies. The cash reserve should accumulate over time unless major events occur in the interim, and will be paid into a secure fund as a future provision (Figure 7.18). Higher risk layers may often be covered more economically through committed credit facilities, but could possibly be covered through issuance of risk-linked securities for some of the major catastrophe events including specific terrorism risk exposures. Contingent surplus notes might possibly be issued for a wider range of catastrophe risks, including terrorist acts, because these instruments constitute credit obligations that have to be repaid and hence should be less sensitive to uncertainties associated with the underlying loss profiles.

Issuance of cat-bonds may be appropriate as cover for higher risk layers, because a higher risk probability can justify the payment of an interest rate premium paid on these securities. Risk-linked securities have typically been issued to cover higher layer risks with loss probabilities between 0.4 – 1.0% corresponding to 250- and 100-year events (McGee and Eng, 2002). Contingent capital may be appropriate to cover upper-end higher risk layers to reduce the up-front option premium payable on the implied put contracts. However, decisions on the type of cover, *i.e.,* risk transfer versus risk financing, reinsurance versus risk-linked securities, contingent capital versus committed credit facilities, etc., should be based on comparative analyses of relative pricing conditions and simulation analyses that profile the most effective layer structure under different loss scenarios.

Figure 7.18. **Insurance Pool with Layered Risk-Transfer Structure (Example)**

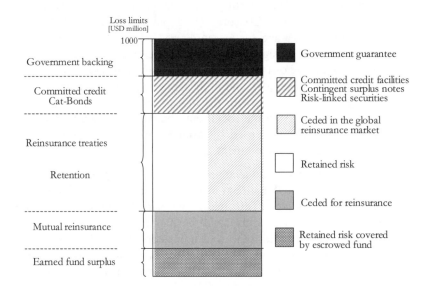

It can be a complex process to evaluate alternative transactional opportunities in different risk-transfer and financing markets and requires specialized expertise, but it is a task that must be pursued on an ongoing basis to make sure that the insurance vehicle continues to operate in an optimal manner. Participants in the local insurance markets will usually not have sufficient capacity to cover all residual catastrophe risks, so there is a need to analyze alternative risk-transfer and financing opportunities available in the financial markets. These alternatives would include reinsurance treaties, issuance of risk-linked securities and cat-bonds, issuance of surplus notes and other contingent capital solutions, as well as different types of committed credit facilities.

It might also be possible technically to establish catastrophe insurance pools over wider geographical areas, *e.g.,* providing cover on a transnational scale. For example, it might be possible for the legislatures in US states with the largest urban concentrations to establish a common terrorism risk pool to cover for certain types of terrorist events. Likewise, it is not inconceivable that exposed countries in Europe could find ways to establish insurance pools in cover of common terrorism risk exposures. Such pools might have the added advantages of higher risk diversification and scale economies. Whereas the political challenges may be substantial, the technical requirements for transnational pools do not seem insurmountable.

4. Alternative Risk Management Solutions

The previous sections analyzed markets for alternative risk transfer and financing solutions and demonstrated the existence of an incremental market reservoir for certain types of financial instruments. The following section tries to specify instrument characteristics that may be conducive to future risk financing transactions and attempts to assess the market capacity for alternative risk management solutions.

4.1 Comparative Analysis of Alternative Instruments

A central feature of catastrophe risk exposure is that the "pure" insurance premium[30] is very sensitive to the uncertainty surrounding the expected loss calculations of the hazard exposure. Hence, it is noted that the relative price of insurance[31] increases exponentially for higher risk layers *(e.g.,* Pollner, 2001). The reason is that it is comparatively easier to predict higher frequency events in the lower risk layers than infrequent events in the higher risk layers where the level of uncertainty can be extreme[32]. Whereas these observations apply to all types of catastrophe risks, the uncertainty element is more pronounced in the case of terrorism risk. Since terrorist events are caused by willful human actions, the catastrophe events do not necessarily follow common routines or patterns but may change character on a continuous basis as terrorists try to adapt to changing conditions in the environment. This human phenomenon of adaptive learning is peculiar to terrorism risk and makes it difficult to use historical event data as a basis for actuarial loss estimates.

Hence, reinsurance prices are a function of the level of uncertainty that permeates the expected loss calculations of terrorism related catastrophe events, which most likely is in excess of the uncertainty level pertaining to natural catastrophe exposures.

Premium (P_{cat}) $= p \cdot (\sigma_{terrorrisk}/\sigma_{catnat}) \cdot (\sigma_{catnat}/\sigma_{non\text{-}cat}) \cdot$ *Cover limit*

where; p *= probability of catastrophe event*

        $\sigma_{terrorism}$ *= standard deviation of expected terrorism catastrophe losses*

        σ_{catnat} *= standard deviation of natural catastrophe losses*

        $\sigma_{non\text{-}cat}$ *= standard deviation of non-catastrophe losses*

Whereas the attack on the World Trade Center has been the most notable terrorist act due to its unprecedented nature and unexpected intensity, terrorist events can take many other forms and are likely to change character over time. As security and various preventive measures are tightened, the possibilities for successful large-scale terrorist acts will diminish. In this situation, active and committed terrorists are likely to adapt their modes of action towards areas that are more difficult to protect and where there is a higher potential success rate.

Hence, the focus of terrorism exposures may converge toward more remote and less protected geographical regions where terrorists may target economic or symbolic facilities. This would predict a future pattern of smaller and more frequent events across many geographical regions[33]. The means of terrorizing might also diverge from more conventional uses of explosives towards suicide bombings, smaller missile based attacks, etc., all of which have happened in different parts of the world. Whereas these forms of terrorist events entail smaller direct economic exposures they have potential secondary economic effects to the extent they are able to break business confidence and public morale. Other possible means of terrorism might be aimed towards events based on extreme uses of nuclear, biotechnological, and chemical (NBC) agents. The use of such agents requires a higher level of technical skill, which may make their occurrence less likely, at least in the short term. However, the uncertainty associated with the potential economic effects of these types of events is high and possibly incomprehensible. Hence, these types of risks, together with war and civil unrest are commonly excluded from insurance covers.

The consequence of the stipulated trends point toward scenarios where mega-terrorist acts are less likely to occur, whereas smaller events will happen more frequently throughout different geographical regions. This will have consequences for the type of insurance exposure we must deal with. Mega-catastrophes by definition constitute uninsurable risk and therefore no market solutions are likely to emerge by themselves that will be able to deal with these exposures, *i.e.,* some type of government intervention will be needed (see the previous section for a discussion). It remains difficult to predict the precise outline of future terrorist events and there continues to be significant uncertainty associated with these risk exposures. However, to the extent we will be dealing with relatively well-defined small to medium sized terrorism exposures, there is a reasonable chance that, *e.g.,* reinsurance contracts and risk-linked securities can be tailored to deal with these risks.

The only examples so far of alternative risk-transfer of terrorism risk exposures to the capital market are FIFA's economic cover for cancellation of the 2006 World Cup in Germany and the Swiss Re sponsored Vita Capital cover for excess mortality risk. FIFA obtained cover through the issuance of risk-linked securities by Golden Goal Finance Ltd (a special purpose vehicle, SPV, created to securitize FIFA's expected revenues from the World Cup arrangement). The US$ 262.5 million transaction was structured by the investment bank CSFB and closed in late 2003 on behalf of FIFA (Fédération Internationale de Football Association) to cover lost revenues to FIFA in the event of incompletion of the World Cup. The need for the cover was prompted by FIFA's marketing partners to secure repayment of prepaid amounts in case of cancellation, abandonment, or curtailment of the scheduled World Cup arrangement. The structure of the transaction follows a conventional risk-linked security (see Figure 7.12). In this transaction, the note holders are scheduled to receive 25% of their initial principal at the interest payment date on December 2005 and, consequently, only 75% the principal amount is exposed to the World Cup cancellation risk. Another new feature of this transaction is that cancellation of the World Cup can be triggered by natural hazards, *e.g.,* windstorm, earthquake, and flood, as well as different types of terrorist events[34].

Golden Goal Finance issued securities in four tranches structured as A1, A2, A3, and B classes. The class A note holders assume the financial risk of cancellation of the World Cup "if no official result has been determined or declared in respect of the final match of the 2006 FIFA World Cup … and no final match will be held on or before 31st August 2007" (Moody's, 2003). The class B note holders assume the financial risk if no official result has been announced by FIFA by August 2007 for scheduled matches other than the final match. The class A notes have all received an A3 rating from Moody's Investors Services whereas the class B notes are unrated[35]. In the rating comments Moody's (2003) list a number of attractive features of the A class securities. They note that FIFA has a strong financial incentive to ensure that the event takes place, *i.e.,* the element of moral hazard is low. There are several alternative sites (stadiums) where the arrangement can be diverted to in case of local incidents, *i.e.,* there are great flexibilities to circumvent adverse economic effects. Only 75% of the note holders' principal is exposed to the risk of cancellation, *i.e.,* there is limited exposure. Whereas Moody's consider man-made catastrophe risks "impossible to predict", they assert that there are a sufficient number of contingencies in place to deal with the consequences of catastrophe events to maintain an A3 rating. Swiss Re acted as sponsor on Vita Capital's issuance of US$ 400 million at-risk variable rate notes. This capital market transaction provides cover in case the combined mortality index for France, Germany, Italy, and Switzerland falls between 130% and 150% of the 2002 level in a single calendar year before final maturity in January 2007. The transaction does not exclude events triggered by terrorist events and, therefore, constitutes a recent example of the securitization of terrorism risk exposures.

The FIFA and Vita transactions are interesting, although the size of these transactions far from qualifies as mega-catastrophe covers, because it shows that some terrorism risk exposures can be covered in the alternative risk-transfer market. The important features that made the FIFA transaction viable relate to the relatively well-defined economic exposure, commitment from the German government to support security around the event (risk mitigation), the existence of risk contingencies, and the absence of moral hazards. There does not appear to be any technical reasons why these features could not be adopted in other financial markets, *e.g.,* reinsurance, contingent capital, and committed credit facilities. However, in this particular situation the alternative markets would be irrelevant to FIFA. A reinsurance contract would expose FIFA to counter-party risk, while contingent capital and committed credit facilities would be uninteresting, because FIFA would need cash compensation in case of cancellation. Similarly, the Vita Capital transaction had a calculated probability of attachment of 0.077%, *i.e.,* the likelihood for this to happen seemed rather remote (Lane and Beckwith, 2004).

Hence, there clearly appears to be a potential to cover terrorism exposures in various risk-transfer and financing markets so long as we are dealing with a relatively well-defined and limited exposure, the government is committed to mitigate the risk, there are viable contingencies in place, and there are no apparent moral hazards. The triggers associated with these transactions would have to be objectively defined, *e.g.,* in the form of unbiased indicators. In the FIFA transaction, the cancellation of the final match is clearly specified as the failure to complete a make-up game within the coming year and in the Vita transaction the combined mortality index is based on general mortality measures. These triggers are different from indemnity of actual terrorism related losses, which would entail potential moral hazard and adverse selection issues, and is closer to indicators or parametric trigger approaches.

4.2 The Potential for New Risk-Transfer Instruments

The relevant financial markets to consider in relation to new risk-transfer and financing instruments include reinsurance contracts, risk-linked securities, contingent capital instruments, and committed credit facilities. The reinsurance market for catastrophe risk is well developed, but market capacity and price developments are highly influenced by recent loss experiences. Furthermore, the insurance premiums for higher risk layers can become excessively expensive if the uncertainties associated with mega-catastrophe events are high. This condition is highly relevant for terrorism risk exposures. The global market capacity for property catastrophe reinsurance continues to be limited[36]. Therefore, major loss events like the WTC incidence can drain capacity from the reinsurance market. Mutual reinsurance arrangements among primary insurers may provide further coverage but is not likely to expand capacity significantly. Hence, the size of this market does not appear high compared to the potential risk exposures that can arise from mega-catastrophes[37], *i.e.,* there seems to be a general lack of coverage for higher risk layers.

The good news is that risk-linked securities have evolved into a relatively independent market segment for catastrophe risk-transfer where the dependency on the traditional reinsurance market is reduced. This might help dampen price volatilities in the global reinsurance market and could gradually help expand reinsurance capacity. As a potential sign of this development, the price reaction to the WTC incidence appeared more measured than the reaction observed after Hurricane Andrews in 1992. FIFA's Golden Goal Finance transaction to cover potential loss of revenues and the Swiss Re sponsored Vita Capital transaction in cover of excess mortality risk also show that it is possible to securitize terrorism risk exposures and that the cat-bond market can provide incremental capacity for terrorism risk insurance.

The ability to diversify catastrophe risks in invested portfolios that are exposed to general commercial risks makes risk-linked securities interesting for a wider audience of institutional investors. If the catastrophe events are unrelated to the returns on conventional financial assets, investors can diversify and improve the portfolios' risk-return characteristics by incorporating different types of risk-linked securities. In the case of mega-terrorism exposures, however, the diversification potential could be challenged because these incidents may have a higher correlation to general commercial risks than is the case with natural catastrophes and consequently may provide less of a risk-return advantage to institutional investors. Also, to the extent that government entities consider issuance of terrorism risk related cat-bonds, it could be associated with moral hazard issues since the government is an important driver of terrorism risk mitigation.

Nonetheless, the market for risk-linked securities has matured in recent years by instituting fairly standardized documentation and catastrophe risk assessment methodologies. Hence, the institutional investors are increasingly familiar with the analysis of catastrophe risk exposures and a secondary market for cat-bonds has emerged to provide continuous trading prices on different cat-bonds. This development has made risk-linked securities a steady element of the capital market and has produced a rather stable annual deal flow that has surpassed an annual deal flow of US$ 1 billion in recent years. Given the more restrictive conditions in the reinsurance market in the aftermath of the WTC incident, transaction volume has increased somewhat, which illustrates that risk-linked securities constitute a realistic alternative catastrophe risk-transfer market albeit of limited size.

5. Summary and Conclusions

Capacity and pricing conditions in the conventional reinsurance market are very dependent on recent loss experiences and display high cyclicality as major catastrophe events occur and drain the loss reserves of the insurance industry. In view of periodically tight conditions in the reinsurance market, new alternative market segments have evolved such as exchange traded catastrophe derivatives, risk-linked securities, contingent capital instruments, and other committed credit facilities. The catastrophe derivatives have not evolved into a viable risk-transfer market for catastrophe exposures. The market for risk-linked securities has been a consistent provider of risk-transfer for rapid onset natural hazards such as hurricanes and earthquake. The market volume has increased slightly but does not appear destined for explosive growth. A recent FIFA transaction indicates that risk-linked securities can be tailored to cover terrorism risk exposures as well. The market for contingent capital has a regular flow of new issues but is not a significant provider of catastrophe risk financing. However, alternative forms of committed credit facilities are available from international banks. In short, there are incremental risk-transfer and financing opportunities available in the international financial markets and together they can expand the risk management capacity to deal with potential terrorism risk exposures. However, they do not by themselves constitute "snap shot' solutions to interim problems of under-capacity in the reinsurance market or uninsurable risk phenomena. Faced with extreme loss potentials of mega-catastrophes, many of these risks are uninsurable and therefore cover for these risks will not be offered on commercial terms in the insurance market.

Hence, some form of government intervention might be needed to cope with the problem of uninsurable risk. Establishing insurance vehicles that pool the risk exposures constitutes one possible approach but before such initiatives are put to sea there is a need to engage in a formal risk management process to guide potential government support. This approach gives insights on expected economic exposures associated with different catastrophe events and provides the means to effectively manage risk mitigation and supportive risk-transfer arrangements. Risk mitigation can have a significant impact on the cost of risk-transfer by markedly reducing the potential losses associated with disaster events such as terrorist acts. Once viable insurance vehicles have been construed to provide cover for uninsurable terrorism risk, they in turn will be able to access alternative solutions available in the international financial markets. Government support for catastrophe damages can have adverse effects because it eliminates incentives to buy insurance and mitigate the underlying exposures. Hence, government initiatives to promote insurance pools should be carried out on an arms-length basis without direct involvement in business operations.

Specific terrorism risk exposures can be securitized and more transactions are likely to emerge in the future. However, as in the case of natural catastrophes, this market segment represents incremental capacity of a limited size. Since there is high uncertainty associated with the assessment of terrorism risk exposures, it might be relatively expensive to place instruments linked to certain types of terrorism events. The dynamic change in the pattern of terrorist events, *e.g.,* toward micro-events that could affect business confidence, etc., might also change the uncertainties associated with these types of risk.

Notes

1   Estimates by the Insurance Information Institute ascribe the largest losses to property, liability, business interruption, life insurance, and workman's compensation (added together property and business interruption losses make up approximately 50% of the total insured losses). Other sources, including the New York City Comptroller, have estimated total direct losses of $85-95 billion and secondary losses in national economic activity several times higher.

2   The insurance penetration in developing countries is significantly lower than the situation in developed countries. Where almost half of the direct losses are covered by insurance in developed countries less than 5 percent of the losses in developing countries receive any type of market coverage.

3   In relatively terms, however, the death toll associated with the WTC incident is considerably lower than the 6,425 victims registered in the Great Hansin earthquake in Kobe, Japan in 1995. The human devastation from the incident is also dwarfed in comparison to some of the largest catastrophes in developing countries over the past decades, the worst of which have counted hundreds of thousands of dead and missing.

4   For example, insurance companies that operate in areas with high potential exposures to specific catastrophes, such as hurricane, flood, etc., might exclude such events from the comprehensive coverage. Losses caused by war and civil unrest are commonly excluded. This is what happened right after the WTC incident, where cover for exposures caused by terrorist events were excluded from insurance policies and reinsurance treaties in the immediate aftermath.

5   For example, if a large meteorite hits earth it may ultimately change life as we know it and thereby eliminate all current economic activity. However, the likelihood that this will occur within our lifetime is very remote.

6   If the insurance premium increases so does the ROL and the relative price (ROL/LOL).

7   This is an estimate of the property catastrophe reinsurance cover offered by global reinsurance companies (Guy Carpenter, 2000). The number may underestimate the aggregate reinsurance capacity somewhat, because a portion of ceded insurance contracts are distributed among primary insurance companies that were excluded from the estimate. There could also be additional coverage for catastrophe risk exposures embedded in proportional and facultative property insurance treaties.

8   A 150-year return period event refers to a hazard impact that occurs with an annual likelihood of $1/150 = 0.67$ per cent. The definition may vary across different types of catastrophes. For example, some professionals argue that hurricane PML is a 100-year and earthquake PML a 250-year return period.

9   Nonetheless, the insurance industry continues to use the probable maximum loss (PML) as a key indicator in simulated model outputs to assess commonly expected loss levels for particular catastrophe risk factors.

10   This is derived from modern portfolio theory, which indicates that a portfolio of financial assets with less than perfectly correlated return characteristics will display a lower variance in the return of the total portfolio, and hence provide investors with the opportunity to construe efficient portfolios that display higher returns for given levels of risk expressed by the standard deviation in return.

11   The global capital market has been roughly estimated around US$ 30 trillion where a substantial part of the market value relates to corporate equity that is exposed to sizeable swings in market prices and bankruptcy risks. Hence, the capital market constitutes a potentially large reservoir for catastrophe risk exposures.

12   The historical volatility of the stock market corresponds to a daily change in market value of approximately 1%, whereas the daily fluctuation in bond returns is closer to .7%. Hence, the expected daily change in the market value of all liquid U.S. securities has had a magnitude of around USD 125 billion.

13   The transaction excluded cover in the US and Japan and claims payments were triggered by actual loss indemnity.

14   US$, Euro, and Swiss Franc denominated fixed and floating rate notes issued by Golden Goal Finance Ltd. in October 2003 with Credit Suisse First Boston as lead manager and Swiss Re Capital Markets as co-lead.

15   US$ denominated floating rate notes were issued by Vita Capital Ltd. sponsored by Swiss Re in December 2003 with an option to extend the transaction to US$ 400 million.

16   Triple-B rated cat bonds have typically offered a premium of 100 basis points (bp) over triple-B rated corporate bonds with the same duration. Double-B rated cat bonds have offered a return of between 100 to 300 bp above similarly rated corporate bonds. Single-B rated cat bonds have offered between 300 to 800 bp above comparable corporate bonds.

17   There currently are a number of tax issues related to the establishment of SPVs to furnish catastrophe risk transfer in the US. Most SPVs have been established in Bermuda, the Cayman Islands or Ireland that allow reinsurance companies to establish the SPVs as separate cells with zero or favorable tax status. Without this tax treatment, the securitzation technique would not be economical.

18   The index reflects insured property losses in US regions (Midwest, Northeast, Southeast, Florida, Gulf) caused by hurricanes, winter storms, thunderstorms, tornadoes and other "atmospheric perils". The GCCI reported on semiannual periods and provided current and aggregate event losses for two sub-periods. The index indicated the ratio of losses over insured values.

19   This reported paid losses of 22 insurers caused by windstorm, hail, flood, earthquake, and riots as registered by the Insurance Service Office.

20   The combined long and short call option positions at a lower and higher strike price respectively is referred to as a "bull call spread". It provides the holder with the opportunity to hedge against catastrophe losses occurring at a range within the two loss ratios (strike prices). The spread position is usually cheaper than buying a single call option, because it entails a simultaneous sale of a call option. Call spread options can be used by hedgers with strong market views to obtain cheaper risk coverage.

21   The PCS Index contracts comprised regional indexes for catastrophe losses in the Northeast, Southeast, East Coast, Midwest, West, California, Florida, and Texas.

22   A heating degree day (HDD) is derived from the average daily temperature corresponding to the level of energy consumption used to heat buildings. The HDD index increases by one point for every degree by which the daily temperature is below 650 F. A cooling degree day (CDD) is derived from the average daily temperature corresponding the level of energy consumption used to cool buildings. The CDD index increases by one point for every degree by which the daily temperature is above 650 F.

23   The contracts are standardized so the HDD and the CDD indexes reflect the accumulated daily HDDs and CDDs over each calendar month.

24   There are formal regulatory restrictions imposed on the wider use of catastrophe risk swaps with the exception of certain off shore markets because the swap agreements often are deemed to constitute insurance contracts that only can be executed by chartered insurance companies.

25   It is, however, important to ensure that no covenants in the underlying loan documentation use specific catastrophe events as default triggers.

26   The determination of what constitutes a reasonable price is obviously political and has to be carefully considered, e.g., intervention that provides coverage at too low prices over extended periods of time introduces moral hazard issues and reduces the incentives to mitigate the underlying risk exposures.

27   In practice, most governments do not have unlimited access to domestic credit sources but are subject to financial constraints, i.e., there are limitations and trade-offs to extreme public borrowing schemes.

28   The insurance pools can consist of large groups of private insurance companies that share large un-diversifiable risk exposures. The insurance pools may be instituted at the request of government authorities to provide coverage for otherwise uninsurable risk exposures.

29   It should be noted that none of these schemes have received direct government subsidies. However, the IRS has allowed capital accumulation in these funds on a tax-free basis, a tax relief the IRS could grant directly to private insurers as well to make the insurance sector more resilient to large catastrophe losses.

30   The 'pure' insurance premium is determined as the expected loss-on-line (LOL) multiplied by the cover limit and hence only takes the actuarial probability of loss into account whereas the total premium charged in the insurance industry also includes provisions for administrative expenses and requirements for return on capital invested in the insurance business.

31   Relative price on insurance = (rate-on-line)/(actuarial probability of loss) – 1.

32   Here the term uncertainty is used to reflect 'Knightean' risk where there are many 'unknowable' elements that make it difficult to make precise actuarial loss estimates.

33   A trend seems to have emerged in recent years towards more loosely linked associations of mind-like terrorist organizations, which increases the likelihood of geographically dispersed terrorist acts in exposed regions of the world (Stern, 2003).

34   The transaction defines an act of terrorism as "any act or acts of one or more persons, whether or not agents of a sovereign power, for political, religious, ideological or similar purposes including the intention to influence any government and/or the public, or any section of the public and whether the loss or damage resulting therefrom is accidental or intentional".

35   Assumed* allocation of securities within tranches in the closed transaction:

Class	Rating	Amount*	Rate basis	Exp. maturity	Legal maturity
A1	A3	US$ 210 mill.	floating	Sept. 2006	Dec. 2009
A2	A3	CHF 30 mill.	fixed	Sept. 2006	Dec. 2009
A3	A3	Euro 20 mill.	floating	Sept. 2006	Dec. 2009
B	NR	CHF 30 mill.	fixed	Sept. 2006	Dec. 2009

36   The total excess-of-loss cover on property insurance was estimated around US$ 75 billion in 2000 indicated as the aggregate loss coverage from the ground up (Guy Carpenter, 2000).

37   The total direct economic losses, insured and uninsured associated with the WTC incidence across all insurance lines was close to the estimate of the aggregate market capacity for property catastrophe insurance.

References

Andersen, T. J. (1993). Currency and Interest Rate Hedging: A User's Guide to Options, Futures, Swaps, & Forward Contracts. Second Edition. Simon & Schuster, New York, NY.

Andersen, T. J. (2001). " Managing Economic Exposures of Natural Disasters: Exploring Alternative Financial Risk Management Opportunities and Instruments". Special Report, Inter-American Development Bank, Washington, D.C.

Andersen, T. J. (2002). "Innovative Financial Instruments for Natural Disaster Risk Management", Inter-American Development Bank, Washington, D.C.

Andersen, T. J. (2003). "Globalization and Natural Disasters: An Integrative Risk Management Approach' in Kreimer, A., Arnold, M. and A. Carlin (eds.), Building Safer Cities : The Future of Disaster Risk. Disaster Risk Management Series No. 3, The World Bank, Washington, D.C.

Alexander, D. (2000). Confronting Catastrophe: New Perspectives on Natural Disasters. Oxford University Press, New York, NY.

Arrow, K. J. (1996). "The Theory of Risk Bearing: Small and Great Risks", Journal of Risk and Uncertainty, 12.

Belonsky, G., D. Durbin and D. Laster (1999). "Insurance-linked Securities", in P. A. Shimpi (Ed.), Integrating Corporate Risk Management. Swiss Re New Markets, New York, NY.

Blum, L. and C. DiAngelo (1998). "Structuring efficient asset-backed transactions' in Issuer Perspectives on Securitization by F. J. Fabozzi (Editor). FJF, New Hope, PA.

Bock, K. J. and M. W. Seitz (2002). "Reinsurance vs Other Risk-transfer Instruments – The Reinsurer's Perspective", in Lane, M. (Ed.) Alternative Risk Strategies. Risk Books, London, UK.

Bohn, J. G. and B. J. Hall (1999). " The Moral Hazard of Insuring the Insurers", in Froot, K. A. (Ed.) The Financing of Catastrophe Risk. The University of Chicago Press, Chicago.

Briys, E. (1999). "Pricing Mother Nature' in Insurance and Weather Derivatives: From Exotic Options to Exotic Underlyings. Risk Books, London, UK.

Canabarro, E., M. Finkemeier, R. Anderson and F. Bendimerad (2000). "Analyzing insurance-linked securities". The Journal of Risk Finance, Winter, pp. 49-75.

Canter, M. S., J. B. Cole and R. L. Sandor (1996). "Insurance derivatives: A new asset class for the capital markets and a new hedging tool for the insurance industry". The Journal of Derivatives, Winter, pp. 89-104.

Chicago Mercantile Exchange (2000). "Weather Futures & Options". Weather Futures and Options Resource Center.

Colarossi, D. (2000). "Capitalizing on innovation in the use of contingent capital". Swiss Re New Markets, New York, NY.

Colarossi, D. (1999). "Contingent Capital' in Integrating Corporate Risk Management by P. A. Shimpi (Editor). Swiss Re New Markets, New York, NY.

CRS Report for Congress (1998). "FEMA and Disaster Relief", Congressional Research Services, The Library of Congress.

Croson, D. C. (2000). "Customizing Indemnity Contracts and Indexed Cat Bonds for Natural Hazard Risks", The Journal of Risk Finance, Spring.

Culp, C. L. (2002). The ART of Risk Management: Alternative Risk Transfer, Capital Structure, and the Convergence between Insurance and Capital Markets. Wiley, New York, NY.

Cummins, J. D. and H. Geman (1995). "Pricing catastrophe insurance futures and call spreads: An arbitrage approach". The Journal of Fixed Income, March, pp. 46-57.

Cummins, J. D., C. M. Lewis and R. D. Phillips (1999). "Pricing excess-of-loss reinsurance contracts against catastrophic loss' in The Financing of Catastrophe Risk by K. A. Froot (Editor). The University of Chicago Press, Chicago.

Cummings, J. D., Lalonde, D. and R. D. Phillips (2002). "Managing Risk Using Risk-linked Catastrophic Loss Securities", in Lane, M. (Ed.) Alternative Risk Strategies. Risk Books, London, UK.

Cutler, D. M. and R. J. Zeckhauser (1999). 'Reinsurance for catastrophes and cataclysms' in The Financing of Catastrophe Risk by K. A. Froot (Editor). The University of Chicago Press, Chicago.

Doherty, N. A. (2000). Integrated Risk Management: Techniques and Strategies for Managing Corporate Risk. McGraw-Hill, New York, NY.

Dong, W., H. Shah and F. Wong (1996). "A Rational Approach to Pricing of Catastrophe Insurance", Journal of Risk and Uncertainty, 12.

Downton, M. W. and R. A. Pielke (2001). "Discretion Without Accountability: Politics, Flood Damage, and Climate", Natural Hazards Review, 2.

Epstein, R. A. (1996). "Catastrophic Responses to Catastrophic Risks", Journal of Risk and Uncertainty, 12.

Fabozzi, F. J. (1998). Valuation of Fixed Income Securities and Derivatives. Third Edition. FJF, New Hope, PA.

Froot, K. A. (1999). The Market for Catastrophe Risk: A Clinical Examination". The National Bureau of Economic Research.

Froot, K. A. and P. G. J. O'Connell (1999). "The Pricing of U.S. Catastrophe Reinsurance", in K. A. Froot (Ed.), The Financing of Catastrophe Risk. The University of Chicago Press, Chicago.

Froot, K.A. and S. Posner (2000). "Issues in Pricing Catastrophe Risk: A Comprehensive Look at the Pricing of Catastrophe Risk", Special Report. Guy Carpenter & Company, New York, NY.

Guy Carpenter (1999). "The emerging asset class: Insurance risk". Guy Carpenter's Review of Catastrophe Exposures and the Capital Markets. Guy Carpenter & Company, New York, NY.

Guy Carpenter (2000). "The world catastrophe reinsurance market". Guy Carpenter & Company, New York, NY.

Guy Carpenter (2002). "The World Catastrophe Reinsurance Market: 2002". Guy Carpenter & Company, New York, NY.

Heike, D. and V. Samari (2001). "Catastrophe-linked Securities: Will 2001 be the Year of the Cat-bond?", Fixed Income Research. Lehman Brothers:,New York, NY.

Heike, D. and J. Kiernan (2002). "Improving Portfolio Performance with Catastrophe Bonds", in Lane, M. (Ed.) Alternative Risk Strategies. Risk Books, London, UK.

Hillier, B. (1997). The Economics of Asymmetric Information. St. Martin's Press, New York, NY.

Insurance Services Office – ISO (1996). "Managing Catastrophe Risk", Insurance Issue Series. New York, NY.

Insurance Services Office – ISO (1999). "Financing Catastrophe Risk: Capital Market Solutions", Insurance Issue Series. New York, NY.

Jaffee, D. M. and T. Russell (1997). "Catastrophe Insurance, Capital Markets, and Uninsurable Risks", Journal of Risk and Insurance, 64.

Khater, M. and D. Kuzak (2002). "Natural Catastrophe Loss Modeling", in Lane, M. (Ed.) Alternative Risk Strategies. Risk Books, London, UK.

Kleindorfer, P. R. and H. C. Kunreuther (1999). "Challenges Facing the Insurance Industry in Managing Catastrophic Risks", in Froot, K. A. (Ed.), The Financing of Catastrophe Risk. The University of Chicago Press, Chicago.

Lane, M. and R. Beckwith (2004). "2004 – Review of Trends in Insurance Securitization", Trade Notes, Lane Financial, Wilmette, IL.

Larson, L. and D. Plasencia (2001). "No Adverse Impact: New Directions in Floodplain Management Policy", Natural Hazard Review, 2.

Lewis, C. M. and K. C. Murdock (1996). "The Role of Government Contracts in Discretionary Reinsurance Markets for Natural Disasters", Journal of Risk and Insurance, 12.

Litzenberger, R., D. Beaglerhole and C. Reynolds (1996). "Assessing Catastrophe-reinsurance-linked Securities as a New Asset Class", The Journal of Portfolio Management, Special Issue.

Major, J. A. (1999). "Index hedge performance: Insurer market penetration and basis risk' in The Financing of Catastrophe Risk by K. A. Froot (Editor). The University of Chicago Press, Chicago.

Major, J. A. and R. E. Kreps (2002). "Catastrophe Risk Pricing in the Traditional Market", in Lane, M. (Ed.), Alternative Risk Strategies. Risk Books, London, UK.

McGhee, C. and Eng, J. (2002). "Market Update: The Catastrophe Bond Market at Year-End 2002". Marsh & McLennan Securities, New York.

Mocklow, D., DeCaro and M. McKenna (2002). "Catastrophe Bonds", in Lane, M. (Ed.), Alternative Risk Strategies. Risk Books, London, UK.

Moody's Investors Service (2003), "Golden Goal Finance Ltd", International Structured Finance, Pre-Sale Report, September 2.

O'Brian, T. (1997). "Hedging Strategies Using Catastrophe Insurance Options", Insurance Mathematics and Economics.

Partner Re (2003). "Terrorism Insurance: Pools & Market Solutions in Europe". Pembroke, Bermuda.

Pollner, J. D. (2001). "Managing Catastrophic Disaster Risks Using Alternative Risk Financing and Pooled Insurance Structures", Technical Paper. The World Bank, Washington, D.C.

Priest, G. L. (1996). "The Government, the Market, and the Problem of Catastrophic Loss", Journal of Risk and Uncertainty, 12.

Risk Management Solutions, RMS (2003). "Managing Terrorism Risk in 2004".

Roever, W. A. (1998). 'The joy of securitization: Understanding securitization and its appeal' in Issuer Perspectives on Securitization by F. J. Fabozzi (Editor). FJF, New Hope, PA.

Rothschild, M. and J. E. Stiglitz (1976). "Equilibrium in competitive insurance markets: An essay on the economics of imperfect information". Quarterly Journal of Economics, pp. 629-650.

Standard & Poor's (2000). "Insurance Securitization: Weathering the Storm", Sector Report. New York, NY.

Stern, J. (2003). Terror in the name of God. Harper Collins, New York, NY.

Swiss Re (2000). "Facultative non-proportional reinsurance and obligatory treaties". Swiss Re Publishing, Zurich.

Swiss Re (2003). "Insurance-Linked Securities", Swiss Re Capital Markets, New York, NY.

Takeda, Y. (2002). "Risk Swaps", in Lane, M. (Ed.), Alternative Risk Strategies. Risk Books, London, UK.

United States General Accounting Office (2003). "Catastrophe Insurance Risk: Status of Efforts to Securitize Natural Catastrophe and Terrorism Risk". Report to Congressional Requesters.

Wang, S. (2002). "Pricing of Catastrophe Bonds", in Lane, M. (Ed.) Alternative Risk Strategies. Risk Books, London, UK.

Zeckhauser, R. (1996). "The Economics of Catastrophes", Journal of Risk and Uncertainty, 12.

Chapter 8

THE ROLE OF GOVERNMENT IN THE COVERAGE OF TERRORISM RISKS[*]

The primary goal of this report is to describe and evaluate alternative forms of government intervention in the market for terrorism insurance. Having highlighted the key features of catastrophe risk insurance, as well as the specificities of terrorism risk, the report begins with an analysis of why private markets systematically fail to provide insurance against catastrophes and, thus, create a need for government intervention.

The initial decision to intervene will generally be made in the aftermath of a major terrorism attack, with private insurers and reinsurers withdrawing from the market, and with rising concerns for major macroeconomic losses if the government does not intervene. In this context, initial government intervention is likely to be both necessary and warranted. The question whether or not the government should intervene is nevertheless discussed in details through the analysis of the arguments developed in two recent papers that make a strong case against government intervention.

The author then turns to the possible modalities of government intervention, from incentives to revive the private markets to explicit government intervention.

After a review of how governments intervene in terrorism insurance markets, the author considers the possible limits and drawbacks to government intervention before presenting a set of policy proposals on the optimal formats for government intervention in terrorism insurance markets.

The report concludes that, ultimately, full success of any government intervention will be measured by the timely return of a well functioning private market for terrorism insurance.

[*]   This report was written by Pr. Dwight M. Jaffee, Willis Booth Professor of Banking and Finance, Haas School of Business, University of California, USA. The author would like to thank Thomas Russell for extremely useful comments on an earlier draft of this paper. Errors, of course, are the responsibility of the author.
The data in this report is current as of end-November 2004.

1. Introduction and Agenda; Executive Summary

Insurance–the transfer and sharing of risk–is by its nature an intrinsically social economic activity. Most other economic activities can be carried out individually (if not efficiently), but insurance requires partners (self-insurance being considered no insurance). Thus, when insurance markets fail to operate effectively, citizens reasonably look to their government for a remedy. And the greater the risks, the greater will be the demand for a government solution.

Terrorism risks, which themselves are intrinsically social, create an immediate and urgent demand for government intervention when private terrorism insurance markets malfunction[1]. As Tom Russell has pointed out (Russell [2002, page 12]):

"Paradoxical as it may be, when the basic notion of the free market itself is threatened, state intervention may be a necessary response."

In a similar vein, Howard Kunreuther and Erwann Michel-Kerjan have written (Kunreuther and Michel-Kerjan [2004], p. 3):

"...we argue that large-scale international terrorism today presents a set of very specific characteristics that make it even more important for the public sector to play a role than they do for other extreme events,"

This is also consistent with what in France is called the "national solidarity principle" which motivates government intervention in the markets for natural disaster and terrorism insurance (Michel-Kerjan and Pedell [2004, p.18]).

The primary goal of this paper is to describe and evaluate alternative forms of government intervention in the market for terrorism insurance. The question whether or not the government should intervene is discussed in Section 1.C, where we review the arguments of Priest [1996] and Smetters [2003] that government intervention in terrorism insurance markets may not be warranted.

The evaluation of alternative forms of government intervention for terrorism insurance requires an analysis of the specific market malfunctions that motivate the intervention. Economic theory provides the framework for evaluating the factors that motivate the government intervention (including a possible private market failure), for considering whether government intervention can redress the failure, and finally for judging the alternatives forms of government intervention. This analysis, however, requires combining the tools of economic theory with an accurate understanding of the institutional structure within which both the insurance industry and the government operate. It is sometimes suggested, however, that economic theory and institutional structure are not the happiest of companions: economic theory often makes assumptions that appear to conflict with institutional reality; and real-world institutions sometimes appear to arise independently of economic needs. In combining them in this Report, we are encouraged by a recent paper by Robert Merton and Zvi Bodie [2004], "The Design of Financial Systems: Towards A synthesis of Function and Structure". In this paper, the authors point out that the institutional structures we observe have often evolved precisely to eliminate the effects of the very transactions costs and frictions that are commonly assumed away in economic models. In other words, the institutional structures have evolved in exactly such a way as to make economic models highly applicable, even when a simple comparison of model assumptions and actual institutions might suggest otherwise. Furthermore, this approach indicates that although countries may vary significantly in their institutional structure (reflecting different underlying costs and traditions), a single analysis can still be applicable in determining how best to fulfil fundamental economic needs.

Gathering institutional information is, of course an empirical exercise. Empirical knowledge concerning private terrorism insurance markets is very limited because government interventions now dominate these markets in most countries[2]. The question, "how well do private markets for terrorism insurance operate?" is now basically a counterfactual query. It is thus essential to enlarge our "database" of empirical information. One strategy in this Report is to use the markets for natural disasters (*i.e.* floods, earthquakes, and wind damage) as an additional source of information where applicable. Figure 8.1 shows the number of "natural" and "man-made" catastrophes and Figure 8.2 shows the corresponding value of insured losses, in both cases from 1970 to 2003 as tabulated by Swiss Re [2004]. The high consequence character of natural disasters is especially apparent in Figure 8.2 since 1992, a period that includes the US Hurricane Andrew (1992), the US Northridge Earthquake (1994), and the European storms Lothar and Martin (1999). Similarly, the terrorist attack of September 11, 2001 clearly stands out in Figure 8.2. It is this shared low probability, but high consequence, character that makes the experience with natural disaster insurance potentially useful in understanding current developments and policies in the markets for terrorism insurance.

It is also clear from the two Figures that a significant number of both natural disasters and man-made catastrophes occur in most years, and that the vast majority of these events individually have relatively minor insurance consequences[3]. Thus, the distinctive feature of both natural disaster and terrorism risks remains that single events can and do occur with very large insured losses. This feature is the focus of our analysis.

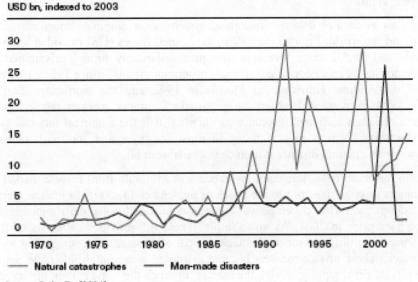

Figure 8.1. **Number of Catastrophic Events**[4]

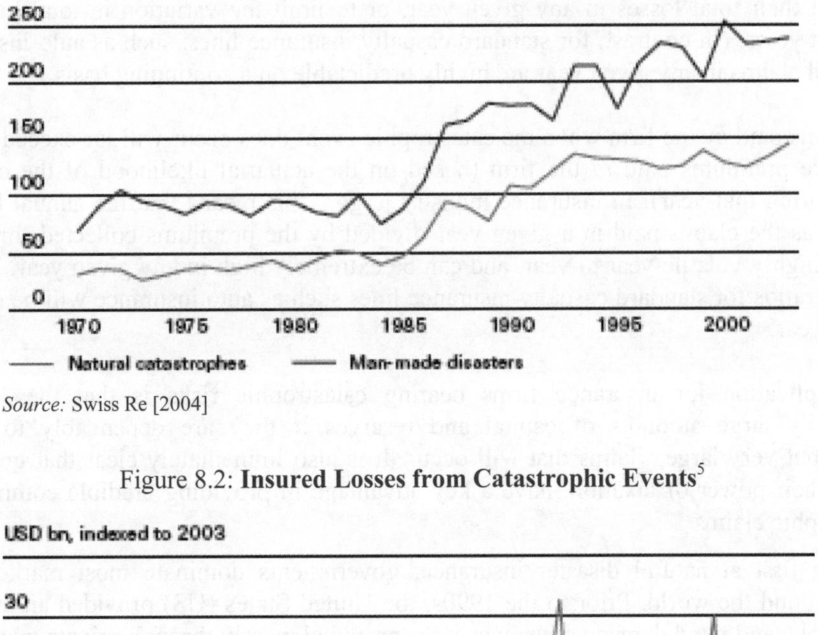

Source: Swiss Re [2004]

Figure 8.2: **Insured Losses from Catastrophic Events**[5]

Source: Swiss Re [2004]

While natural disaster and terrorism risks share the low probability, high consequence, feature, the differences between them must also be carefully considered. These differences, which include the fact that terrorism attacks are intentionally created by human action and that actuarial methods for evaluating terrorism risks are not as well developed, will also be considered in the later discussion. We will also consider the special issues raised by the interdependent nature of terrorism risks, for example that inadequate airport security may allow a building to be attacked by hijacked aircraft, whatever the security precautions taken at that particular building. We will use the term catastrophe insurance when referring to the insurance markets for terrorism and natural disaster risks on a combined basis.

1.A. Key Features of Catastrophe Insurance Markets

Terrorism and natural disaster insurance share the key property that the underlying risks are often created by low probability, but high consequence, events.

This has two important implications for private insurance firms operating in catastrophe lines:

1. Firms holding catastrophic risks cannot rely on *cross-policy diversification* to limit the likely range of their total losses in any given year, or to limit the variation in total losses across different years. (In contrast, for standard casualty insurance lines, such as auto insurance, the expected claims in any given year are highly predictable on a continuing basis.)

2. The claims paid *by* the firm when the catastrophic event does occur will far exceed the *annual* insurance premiums paid *to* the firm (based on the actuarial likelihood of the catastrophic event during that year). In insurance industry jargon, this means that the annual loss ratios– defined as the claims paid in a given year divided by the premiums collected for that year– will be highly volatile year to year, and can be extremely high in any given year. In contrast, the loss ratios for standard casualty insurance lines such as auto insurance will be quite stable year to year.

The implication for insurance firms bearing catastrophic risks is that they must hold extraordinarily large amounts of capital and reserves if they are dependably to cover the infrequent, but very large, claims that will occur. It is also immediately clear that governments, relying on their power of taxation, have a key advantage in providing credible commitments to pay catastrophic claims.

Looking first at natural disaster insurance, governments dominate most markets for this insurance around the world. Prior to the 1990s, the United States (US) provided an exception in that earthquake and wind damage coverages were provided mainly through private markets (flood damage insurance has been a Federal government program in the US since 1968). However, in the aftermath of the Andrew Hurricane in Florida in 1992 and the Northridge Earthquake in California in 1994, even wind damage and earthquake insurance markets required government intervention to maintain sufficient insurance availability. It is the empirical fact that government intervention in some form is present today in most countries and for most natural disaster insurance lines where natural disaster insurance is available at all.

Turning to terrorism risks, terrorism insurance was available from private market insurance firms in a number of countries prior to the attack of September 11, 2001. In France, Germany, and the US, for example, terrorism coverage was commonly included in standard commercial property insurance policies prior to 2001. As an example, Table 8.1 provides estimates of the insured losses that arose from the September 11 attack, based, of course, on coverage that was in place before the attack. These private markets became disrupted immediately after the September 11 attack, with private firms rapidly leaving the market, in much the same pattern observed earlier in the US markets for natural disaster insurance. That is, once the insurance industry recognized the catastrophic nature of the possible losses from terrorist attacks, most firms immediately became unwilling to provide such insurance in the absence of government support. The governments generally obliged, with the new plans introduced in France, Germany, and the US illustrating the range of possible modalities for government intervention. Today, in most countries where terrorism insurance for commercial properties is available at all, the coverage is based at least in part on government participation.

Table 8.1. **September 11, 2001 Attack, Insured Losses by Line** **Source: Hartwig [2002]**	
Insurance Line	Insured Losses ($ Billion)
Business Interruption and event cancellation	12.0
Other Liability	10.0
Property, Other	6.0
Property, World Trade Center	3.5
Aviation Liability and other	4.0
Life	2.7
Workers' Compensation	2.0
Total	40.2

1.B. Why Private Catastrophe Insurance Markets Fail to Operate Effectively

The core of this report begins with an analysis of why private markets systematically fail to provide insurance against catastrophes, thus creating a need for government intervention. It is essential to understand the precise bases for these market failures, since only then can intelligent decisions be made concerning the most effective form of government intervention. We shall see that the low probability, high consequence, nature of catastrophic risks requires that firms offering such coverage have access to large amounts of capital (to cover the payments to policyholders when the catastrophic event occurs). There is strong evidence, however, that access to risk capital is highly limited, for both primary insurers and reinsurers. If catastrophe insurance is offered without access to the necessary amount of capital, then the insurance firm faces a *bankruptcy risk* (called *risk of ruin* in the insurance literature), to the detriment of all its stakeholders. Private insurance firms can, of course, avoid this risk simply by withdrawing from the sale of catastrophe insurance, and the general experience is that insurance firms do exactly this in the absence of government intervention. This discussion is provided in Section 2.A below.

While terrorism risks share with natural disaster risks their low probability, high consequence, character, terrorism risks also have the unique feature that they are *man-made*. It is thus critical to understand the impact that the man-made feature of terrorism risks has on the provision of terrorism insurance, whether provided by private markets or the government. For example, the government will likely have better information than the private markets concerning the probability and location of a future terrorist attack, which provides one reason why private firms may be unwilling to provide coverage against such risks. It is also possible that terrorism events have greater spillover effects on the overall economy, creating another basis for the failure of private insurance markets. On the other hand, it is also possible that terrorists may choose not to attack insured targets, which would increase the willingness of private firms to offer terrorism insurance. The discussion of this and related topics (including the complexity of underwriting terrorism risks) is provided in Section 2.B below.

1.C. The Initial Decision to Intervene

The initial decision to intervene will generally arise following a major terrorism attack, with private insurers and reinsurers withdrawing from the market, and with rising concerns for major macroeconomic losses if the government does not intervene[5]. In this setting, the government will have no choice but to intervene, for the following three reasons:

1. The government will possess the best information concerning the likelihood of future attacks. It must demonstrate to its own citizens, the insurance industry, and perhaps also to the terrorists, that it can control the problem. Its willingness to commit government resources to provide indemnification against future losses provides a very credible tool for this purpose.

2. Major macroeconomic losses could follow from the failure of the private markets for terrorism insurance. Government intervention will offset, if not eliminate, these losses. Indeed, government action is likely to go forward in all but the most extreme case, even if calculations suggest that the plan costs actually exceed the likely macroeconomic benefits (Russell [2002]).

3. Whatever the immediate macroeconomic effects, *were a further attack to occur soon thereafter*, there would be serious regret not to have intervened initially.

This is the setting in which the government must determine the most advisable form for its intervention. Before developing our main conclusions in this regard, however, it is useful to review two recent papers that argue firmly against government intervention. The papers are Priest [1996], "Government Insurance Versus Market Insurance," which argues against government intervention in any insurance market, and Smetters [2003], "Insuring Against Terrorism: The Policy Challenge," which argues against the US government's intervention in terrorism insurance following the September 11 attack.

The starting point for the Priest [1996] paper is the position of Kenneth Arrow, who had made the case for government intervention in insurance markets in a series of famous papers. Priest quotes the core of Arrow's position as (Arrow [1963], p. 961):

"The welfare case for insurance policies of all sorts is overwhelming. It follows that the government should undertake insurance in all those cases where this market, for whatever reason, has failed to emerge".

Priest does not directly take exception to the affirmative aspects of Arrow's position. Instead, the focus of his critique is a series of issues that Arrow did not consider, or at least did not emphasize:

1. Priest points out that insurance purchased from private markets is always *voluntary*, ensuring that such purchases always make the individuals or firms better off. In contrast, Priest argues that government insurance is frequently *compulsory*, raising the possibility that individuals could be made worse off. In particular, he suggests that government insurance systems typically use some degree of risk pooling–in which high-risk and low-risk individuals are charged the same insurance premium. In this case, the low-risk individuals are overcharged, and thus might prefer not to participate in the government plan at all, if that were an option.

2. Priest argues that government insurance facilities are intrinsically *less efficient* than their private market counterparts. He focuses on the presumed failures of government insurers to diversify risks by selecting the clientele, to control adverse selection through the use of risk rating, and to control moral hazard through deductibles and coinsurance. The inefficiencies that arise with government insurance not only raise the costs of the

insurance, but they may also distort the allocation of resources, for example by providing homeowners incentive to build on river banks.

3. Priest argues that government insurance plans often derive from a desire to *redistribute resources*, in particular toward high-risk individuals. Priest's argument here is not with redistributional policies in general, but with regard to redistributional policies that masquerade as government insurance plans, and as a result may not be properly evaluated.

Our purpose is to evaluate Priest's argument only in the very narrow focus of our topic, namely government intervention in terrorism insurance markets. In this regard, a key factor is that the observed government interventions in terrorism insurance markets arose because private sector firms were no longer willing to provide such coverage. Therefore, points (1) and (2) above appear largely irrelevant, since there is no private market with which to make the comparison. It is also noteworthy that the plans reviewed here are basically voluntary, with the partial exception that terrorism insurance is required on a class of policies providing property damage insurance in France. Point (3) is more complex, since it is true that the government interventions in terrorism insurance may well be redistributing resources toward high-risk individuals and firms. However this redistribution appears not to be hidden, since it is the explicit goal of the policy to help those facing terrorism risks. Thus, we conclude that Priest's arguments, whatever their more general applicability, do not provide strong grounds for avoiding government intervention in terrorism insurance markets. Nevertheless, the concerns raised in his paper are exactly the reason that (i) government plans should be designed to minimize the crowding out of private market activity and (ii) the plans should be organized to provide an orderly sunset as soon as possible

The analysis of Smetters [2003] provides a critique of the US government's intervention in the terrorism insurance market following the September 11 attack. His analysis covers three key areas:

a) Smetters provides evidence suggesting that the private markets for terrorism insurance in the US actually failed much less badly following the September 11 than is the conventional wisdom. For one thing, he points out that by the Fall of 2002, the time at which the US intervention was actively considered in Washington D.C. (and more than one year after the attack), the private markets for terrorism insurance in the US were already showing substantial improvement relative to the initial shock. For another, he points out that the low take-up rates for terrorism insurance during 2002 could as well reflect low demand as low supply (based on arguments similar to those we made above in Section 3.B.2).

b) Smetters questions the validity of factors often used to motivate government intervention in terrorism insurance markets. First, he questions whether the difficulty of evaluating terrorism risks can explain the private market failure (based on arguments similar to those made above in Section 2.3.B). Second, he argues that private market firms could have limited their exposure by using devices such as retroactive premiums or the equivalent.

c) Smetters notes that many of the likely explanations for the failure of private markets for terrorism insurance reflect government action, including tax and accounting policies; see also our discussion below in Section 2.A).

In conclusion he writes (Smetters [2003], p. 30):

"Private commercial property and casualty insurance markets are likely able to insure against terrorism and even war losses if government tax, accounting, and regulatory policies were changed in order to reduce the insurer cost of holding capital as well as to support the securitization of large risks. Modifying these fiscal policies would have likely been much more efficient than the approach taken in TRIA, which has created several

potential problems: Crowding out the development of private insurance; excess demand for subsidized insurance by diversified shareholders; ex-ante and ex-post moral hazard, and, unfunded liabilities on future generations".

Smetters' analysis is by and large consistent with the positions taken in this Report. In particular, we share the conclusion that the "first best" solution for terrorism insurance is to create conditions that allow the revival of the private insurance market, and that changes in the government's tax, accounting, and regulatory rules are a critical first step in this direction. On the other hand, we disagree with Smetters' position that it would have represented better public policy to allow the private markets for terrorism insurance to stand on their own in the Fall of 2002. This difference of opinion arises primarily from our alternative evaluations of the evidence concerning how badly the terrorism insurance markets had failed and of the likely costs this would have imposed on the economy. Looking forward to the forthcoming termination dates of the existing country plans, we certainly join with Smetters in the hope that we will have reached the point at which private firms are again prepared to insure against terrorism without direct government support

1.D. Modalities for Intervention in Catastrophe Insurance Markets

We next turn to the possible modalities of government intervention. A particularly simple, and thereby appealing, form of government intervention has the government provide specific and direct incentives to revive the private markets to functionality. In other words, the government would help *to recreate the private markets*, rather than *to create a public substitute for the private markets*.

The provision of tax incentives or other subsidies to lower the cost of capital for private firms that bear catastrophic risks is one example. The idea is that if insurance firms hold sufficient capital, then the risk of ruin from a catastrophic event can be reduced to a manageable level, thus allowing the reemergence of a private market for catastrophe insurance. Government action to expedite the development of financial instruments that allow insurance firms to transfer risk to capital market investors is another example. Catastrophe bonds, which insurance firms have used on a small scale to transfer catastrophe risks, represent a specific case. These and other examples of government incentives to recreate private markets for catastrophe insurance are described in Section 3.A below. Unfortunately, as we shall see, initiatives to recreate private markets for catastrophe insurance have had limited success to date, although there are now proposals pending for further regulatory and tax-law changes in the US that might significantly expedite the recovery of the private insurance markets for catastrophe risks in the US.

This leads to a review of the alternative modalities for explicit government intervention. The many existing government interventions in the terrorism insurance markets illustrate the wide range of possible formats. To organize an analytic understanding of these various formats, it is useful first to distinguish the *market micro structures,* through which the sale of policies and the settlement of claims occurs, from the *insurance functions* through which risk bearing occurs. Most existing government interventions are mixed private/public enterprises with the private markets handling most, if not all, of the market micro structure functions, while the government is responsible for varying amounts of the insurance functions. Although we will comment on the features of alternative market micro structures in our discussion of individual country plans, our primary focus is on the alternative modalities used for risk bearing and how it is shared between the private and public sectors.

The following list provides examples of the key distinguishing features that are observed in the various existing government formats for insurance activity:

- How is risk shared among the government, capital market investors, and insurance firms?
- Is participation in the government plan mandatory?
- Does the government subsidize the costs for the reinsurance coverage it offers?

- What are the limitations in the type of terrorism risks that are covered?
- Are there maximum limits with regard to the exposure of insurance firms and/or the government?
- Do private firms retain a role in setting underwriting standards and risk-based prices?
- What sunset provisions are adopted to end the government participation by a future date?

These and other components of the existing government interventions in catastrophe insurance markets are discussion in Section 3.B.

1.E. Limits and Drawback to Government Intervention in Terrorism Insurance Markets

Having reviewed how governments intervene in terrorism insurance markets, it is critical to consider the possible limits and drawbacks to government intervention. A particularly important question, from both economic and political perspectives, is whether the government intervention *crowds out* or otherwise displaces private markets. The government intervention will, of course, be viewed much more favourably if it does not displace functional private markets.

Unfortunately, it is very difficult empirically to determine if crowding out of private terrorism insurance is occurring, since it requires counterfactual knowledge as to the behavior of private terrorism insurance markets in the absence of government intervention. The US markets for wind damage and earthquake insurance, however, do provide an interesting perspective since the private markets have become partly reestablished as time has passed since the date of the major disaster that triggered the primary market failure. The discussion in Section 4.A below takes up the general question of crowding out by government insurance plans and evaluates specific cases.

The possibility that government interventions may displace private actions to mitigate the damage that may be created by terrorist actions is another possible drawback to government activity in terrorist or natural disaster insurance markets. This reduction in mitigation can be understood as an application of the principle of *moral hazard,* in which the provision of insurance provides individuals and firms incentive to take on *greater risk.* On the other hand, insurance providers normally use *risk-based pricing* to create price incentives for the insured parties to take their own actions to mitigate the risks. The interplay of these two forces are considered when we discuss the impact that government intervention has on terrorism risk mitigation in Section 4.B below. Also, given the public nature of terrorism risks, some mitigation efforts will be influenced by factors other than the narrowly definite economic incentives, and some of the effects of terrorism will exceed the reach of mitigation by private sector firms and individuals. These topics, as well as how mitigation activity is influenced by the interdependent nature of terrorism risks, are discussed in Section 4.B.

Individuals will generally anticipate that governments will provide emergency aid and relief following a catastrophic event (either natural disaster or terrorist attack), independent of any formal government insurance program. In the US, for example, this aid is provided on a continuing basis by the Federal Emergency Management Agency (FEMA). The primary activity of this agency is emergency disaster relief – providing victims with immediate medical care and shelter on a short term basis – with little or no intention to provide compensation for lost assets. Individuals, however, may think the relief agency also provides financial compensation for losses incurred, in which case issues of moral hazard may arise. The Victim Compensation Fund, created to provide compensation for the victims of the 9/11 attack, provides another example, where the government has decided to provide *ex post* compensation, even though there was no *ex ante* commitment. These issues are discussed in Section 4.C below.

1.F. Optimal Formats for Government Intervention in Terrorism Insurance Markets

When intervention does occur for terrorism insurance, it is important to ascertain the optimal format for that intervention. Key questions will include:

- What should be the overall extent of the government's participation?

- What should be the duration of the intervention-transitional to rebuild private capacity, or long-term reflecting a fundamental market failure?

- What should be the financial modality of the government intervention? For example, the government could act as the primary insurer, as reinsurer of last resort, or as ex-post lender of last resort. What determines the most appropriate modality?

These and other policy proposals are covered in Section 5.

2. The Failure of Private Insurance Markets for Catastrophic Risks

Private insurance markets for catastrophic risks – covering natural disasters and terrorism – generally fail to operate effectively on a world-wide basis. Instead, active markets almost always involve a strong element of government intervention. In this section, we explore the features of catastrophe insurance that make it so susceptible to a private market failure. We first consider the markets for natural disaster insurance, then we turn to the additional issues raised by terrorism insurance.

2.A. The Failure of Private Markets for Natural Disaster Insurance

Natural disasters – such as floods, earthquakes, and wind damage–have always occurred and inflicted large losses on individuals and firms. We would therefore expect well functioning private markets to exist to provide insurance against these risks. In reality, natural disaster insurance is government-based in most countries of the world. The virtual absence of private catastrophe insurance markets makes it very difficult to ascertain what factors led to the market failure, or to determine whether or not the government interventions are crowding out what would otherwise be well-functioning private markets[6].

Fortunately, the United States (US) provides a partial exception to the general absence of private natural disaster insurance markets. First, prior to the 1990s, earthquake and wind damage insurance were provided primarily by private firms in the US. Then, following the Andrew Hurricane of 1992 and the Northridge Earthquake of 1994, most private firms began to withdraw from these markets, forcing the state governments in Florida and California to create quasi governmental entities to ensure coverage[7]. Most recently, private insurance firms have started to re-enter these markets.

Since the private market collapses of the 1990s clearly preceded the government interventions, there is no possibility that the government intervention initially crowded out what would have been well-functioning private markets. This leaves open, however, the question whether the private markets might have reopened more rapidly in the absence of the government intervention[8]. More generally, the observation of insurance firms withdrawing from catastrophe markets, and to some degree returning later, provides a useful laboratory for understanding why the private markets fail, which is exactly the focus in Jaffee and Russell [1997] and [2003]. The following discussion in this section is a summary of the key points of those papers.

The unique problem presented by catastrophe insurance, in comparison to standard lines of property and casualty insurance such as auto insurance, is that the benefits of *cross-policy diversification* are not generally available to catastrophe insurance firms. The problem is best illustrated by the following simple example[9]. First, consider an auto insurer with a total insured coverage of $100 million. If the expected annual loss rate were 1%, the firm would anticipate $1 million of claims annually. If it charged an actuarially fair premium–that is, a premium commensurate with those losses–the income would also be $1 million annually, providing exactly the funds needed to cover the expected losses[10]. Of course, the actual losses for the year might vary from the expected amount, but, assuming a well diversified insurance portfolio with a large number of relatively small individual risks, these deviations should be relatively small and thus covered by a relatively small amount of additional capital.

Now consider a catastrophe insurer, also with a total insured coverage of $100 million, facing an expected annual loss rate of 1%, and charging an annual premium of $1 million. But now assume–consistent with the character of catastrophe risks–that the firm faces claims of either $0 (99% of the time) or $100 million (1% of the time); this is the proverbial once in a hundred years event. This firm will need $100 million in resources to guarantee to pay its claims when the catastrophic event occurs. Since annual premiums are $1 million, this leaves $99 million to be raised as capital or from other sources. Thus, in contrast to standard casualty lines such as auto insurance, catastrophe lines require a large amount of capital, or its equivalent, if the insurance firm is to pay the catastrophic losses when they occur. Otherwise, the firm will face a major bankruptcy risk, which would likely be unacceptable to potential policyholders and its own shareholders alike[11].

Adequate capital is thus the nub of the issue for any firm providing catastrophe coverage[12]. And, unfortunately, the following list indicates insurance companies face fundamental impediments when attempting to raise large amounts of capital to underwrite catastrophe risks[13].

- Accounting Requirements. Generally accepted accounting principles (GAAP) preclude an insurance firm from earmarking capital or retained earnings for use only to pay for future (not yet incurred) catastrophe losses.

- Tax Provisions. Casualty insurance firms in the US are not allowed to take tax deductions against premium income even if they use retained cash flows to create reserve allocations against future expected losses; thus retained earnings are a highly taxed means for accumulating capital[14]. Furthermore, even if insurance firms do set aside capital or retained earnings to cover expected future catastrophe losses, the earnings on these funds will be fully taxable, further increasing the cost of capital. Harrington and Niehaus [2002] estimate that the disadvantageous tax treatment of catastrophe insurance firms creates an implicit expense that may equal in size the expected loss itself, thus effectively doubling the premium that must be charged insurance customers.

- The US insurance industry has evolved methods to moderate the disadvantageous tax treatment it faces. For one thing, while a primary insurance firm must be chartered in the US state in which it sells policies, it can purchase reinsurance from firms that operate in off-shore tax-haven areas such as Bermuda. The goal is that the reinsurer's offshore tax benefits be reflected in lower reinsurance costs for the primary insurer. The use of offshore reinsurance entities, however, raises questions of performance risk. For another solution, the firms can issue subordinated debt (including catastrophe bonds), instead of retaining earnings or issuing equity shares. The benefit here is that bond financing creates it own tax-shield., but catastrophe bonds represent a newly developed market that has found only limited use so far. Reinsurance and catastrophe bonds are discussed further just below.

- Takeover Risk. The two factors above not withstanding, if a firm still accumulated a large base of capital and reserves, it would then face a significant takeover risk. The acquiring entity would just have to wait one year until the existing policies all expired, following which it would have complete access to the capital trove for any purpose it wished[15].

Reinsurance provides primary insurance firms with an alternative to capital accumulation as a means to lay off catastrophe risks. Reinsurers and primary insurers, however, face the same capital issues, so reinsurance really only pushes the capital problem back one stage. Indeed, in the US following the Andrew Hurricane of 1992, the Northridge Earthquake of 1994, and the terrorist attack of September 11, 2001, primary insurers and reinsurers withdraw their coverage for catastrophe line simultaneously, in parallel attempts to protect their capital positions against possible large future losses[16].

Exchange-traded catastrophe futures and options provided insurance firms with a mechanism to transfer catastrophe risks to capital market investors, thus bypassing the reinsurers. Such instruments were introduced in the US financial markets in 1992, but they failed to become actively traded and they no longer exist. Part of the problem was the unwillingness of investors to place capital at risk, given that there was (i) no standard methodology for pricing the instruments, (ii) no mechanism for hedging the risks, and perhaps most importantly (iii) a fear of asymmetric information. There was also a lack of demand by the insurance companies, due in part to counterparty risk–the fear that counterparties would not have sufficient resources to make the required payments if and when a major catastrophe actually did occur.

Catastrophe bonds provide insurance firms with another mechanism to transfer catastrophe risks to capital market investors, while avoiding the counterparty risk of exchanged-traded options[17]. An insurance company issues a catastrophe bond in the same way as a corporate bond. The purchase price paid by investors, however, is deposited in a special collateral account and used to purchase government bonds. Investors receive interest payments funded by the government bonds plus a premium from the insurance company to compensate for the annual expected loss from the catastrophe. If no catastrophe occurs, the investors receive their principal back at maturity through the liquidation of the government bond account. On the other hand, if the catastrophe occurs, then the *insurance firm* receives a payment based on the liquidating value of the government bonds, and the investors receive no principal repayment and no further interest payments[18].

Following the Andrew Hurricane and Northridge Earthquake disasters of the early 1990s, the first catastrophe bonds were issued by insurance firms. The premiums required by investors in these bonds, however, far exceeded any reasonable valuation of the expected loss. For example, for a catastrophe bond on which the expected annual loss was 1% (and thus the expected bond coupon could have represented little more than a 1 percentage point spread over the risk-free government bond rate), the actual spread was often 7 percentage points or more, representing a huge risk premium[19]. This high spread appears to be the result of a variety of factors[20]. Perhaps the main one is the difficulty of evaluating catastrophe risks, with the effect that only investors with specialized knowledge have been attracted as investors in these bonds. Other more traditional factors may also be at work including asymmetric information (the possibility that the bond issuer has special information) and agency problems (employees within an investment firm may avoid securities with potentially large losses). Finally, there are a number of more technical tax and accounting issues that are obstacles to the widespread use of catastrophe bonds; these issues are discussed in detail in Section 3.A.2.

Insurance firms have continued to experiment to find formats for catastrophe bonds that are more appealing to investors, and the risk premiums on recent issues are lower. One change has been to replace indemnity bonds (in which catastrophe losses are measured by the issuing firm's book of business) with "parametric" bonds (in which the loss is determined by a specified event– such as an earthquake size 7.0 or higher in a given region), which reduces the problem of asymmetric information. Another change has been to include a variety of catastrophic losses within the same bond, which means that investor returns have a more traditional pattern, instead of the "all or nothing" character created by traditional catastrophe bond structures. Nevertheless, catastrophe bonds do not yet provide insurance firms with a sufficiently dependable vehicle to motivate these firms to provide catastrophe insurance on a wider scale[21].

Opportunistic insurance firms might be expected to enter catastrophe insurance markets *following* major events, given that premium levels will be high as other firms exit the market. In practice, it appears that new entry is not sufficient to forestall government intervention. One explanation is that the capital market conditions immediately following a major event make it difficult for a firm to raise new capital because investors in new equity issues are wary that (i) the funds will be used to pay off past losses, not to support new activities; and (ii) the issuing firm may have asymmetric information regarding the underlying risks. An additional explanation is that principal-agent issues make it unlikely that employees within an insurance firm will recommend entry into a market where the existing firms have just suffered major and unexpected losses. To be sure, opportunistic entry does occur, but it seems to be highly isolated[22].

Behavioral impediments in the evaluation of catastrophe risks represent a further factor that may help explain why both insurance firms and capital market investors avoid catastrophe insurance markets following major events, even when their participation would be well compensated. *Ambiguity aversion* is a particularly good example. Ambiguity aversion is said to occur when the premium required to bear risk is based on the most pessimistic model of the event (given that alternative models do exist). For example, ambiguity aversion might be responsible if, following a catastrophic event, insurers or investors raise their estimated probability of another event to a level above what would be suggested by normal Bayesian updating[23]. This would occur, for example, if the insurers or investors became unsure of their knowledge concerning the process that determines the catastrophic events, and thus require an additional premium for *model uncertainty*, over and above their best estimates of the expected loss.

The Andrew Hurricane and Northridge Earthquake events occurred more than ten years ago, and no further natural disasters of equivalent impact have occurred in the US. And we now see the re-entry of private firms to these natural disaster insurance markets. Private market coverage is currently available, however, only for specific risks, typically low-risk locations and structure types, where the government plan is charging comparatively high prices. But the activity is expanding, which is consistent with an ambiguity aversion effect that dies away as new events do not occur, and insurers become more confident in the estimates of risks provided by the existing models. On the other, it is expected that were another major event to occur, insurers would once again leave the market for natural disaster insurance. We return to the topic of natural disaster insurance in Section 3, where we discuss some features of government interventions in these markets.

2.B. The Failure of Markets for Terrorism Insurance

Prior to the terrorist attack of September 11, 2001, terrorism coverage was routinely included in standard commercial property insurance policies in many countries, including, for example, France, Germany, and the United States. But these markets were disrupted following that attack, in a pattern similar to the withdrawal of insurance firms from the markets for natural disaster insurance in the US during the early 1990s, as just discussed[24]. Today, terrorism insurance, like natural disaster insurance, involves at least some government participation in most countries. It appears that the same issues of capital adequacy and bankruptcy risk that motivate private firms not to provide natural disaster insurance also motivate these firms not to provide terrorism insurance. There is no need to repeat the discussion written just above, but Congressional testimony given a few months after the 9/11 attack by a Director of the US Government Accounting Office on the existing conditions in the private market for terrorism insurance provides a useful summary (Government Accounting Office [2001], p.15):

"It seems clear, given insurers increased recognition of their exposures in the aftermath of the unprecedented events on September 11, 2001, that coverage for terrorist acts is not now amenable to normal insurance underwriting, risk management, and actuarial techniques. As a result, insurers and reinsurers are concerned about their ability to set an

appropriate price for insurance coverage for terrorist acts. Given this uncertainty if this kind of insurance were to be offered at all, it is likely that either the prices insurers set would be prohibitively high or so low as to invite insolvency. However, even if we conclude that insurers cannot price and, therefore, cannot sell this kind of insurance, defining the nature of the problem facing both the economy and the insurance industry is a critical first step."

We now complete our discussion of the market failure for terrorism insurance by discussing several features that distinguish terrorism insurance from natural disaster insurance; see also Kunreuther, Michel-Kerjan, and Porter [2003] and Kunreuther and Michel-Kerjan [2004]. These features include (i) the man-made nature of terrorism risks, (ii) the possibility of very large spillovers on the macroeconomy, and (iii) the greater complexity in modelling terrorist risks. We discuss these in turn.

2.B.1. The Man-Made Nature of Terrorism Risks

Terrorism risks are *man-made*, in contrast to the relatively benign (*i.e.* non-strategic) behavior of "mother nature" as the source of natural disaster risks. In many respects, the human involvement in terrorism makes these risks even more difficult for private markets to insure, although there are some offsetting aspects. The following summarizes the main effects of the man-made nature of terrorism risks:

- The government will likely have better information than the private markets concerning the probability and location of a future terrorist attack. This should allow the government to assess risks more accurately than can private insurance firms, and could allow the government to set more accurate prices for terrorism insurance. It is unlikely, however, that the government would allow its detailed information to be used for setting insurance premiums. For one thing, terrorists could then deduce what the government knew, or thought it knew, by analyzing the pattern of posted insurance premiums. For another, owners and residents in locations that received high risk ratings would want to know the basis for these valuations, creating pressure for the government to release confidential information[25].

- The upshot is that if insurance premiums reflect detailed risk ratings at all, then they are likely to be based only on information directly available to the private insurance firms. These firms will recognize, of course, that more accurate evaluations could be made using the government's information, and this would likely lead to higher premiums, in compensation for the ambiguity created by the firm's limited access to information.

- The willingness of the government to serve as the insurer of last resort, thus committing the resources to make payments if and when a terrorist attack occurs, will lend credibility to its programs that have the goal to stop terrorism attacks from occurring in the first place.

- Terrorists will choose their targets strategically, and the strategy may include picking targets based on their insurance status. For example, if the terrorists choose to target insured structures, then private market insurance would be especially costly, if available at all[26]. More generally, any element of moral hazard–in which the likelihood of a loss rises when insurance is provided–will create higher insurance premiums; also see Kunreuther and Michel-Kerjan [2004].

- The actions that individuals and firms take to mitigate the likely damage from a terrorist attack will depend on the strategy the terrorists are expected to employ in choosing targets. For example, if terrorists are expected to focus on unprotected targets, then private mitigation activity is more likely to occur. In this case, however the social benefit of mitigation will be limited, to the extent that it only serves to change the location at which an attack will occur.

2.B.2. Spillovers on the Macroeconomy

The spillover effects on the overall economy are likely to be greater for terrorism than for natural disaster events, since (i) the direct losses could well be greater (as witnessed by the 9/11 attack), (ii) the failure to stop the attack will be seen as a failure of the government, and (iii) terrorists may well aim their attacks to maximize the overall impact on the economy.

Insurers (including private investors holding securitized insurance risks) will be less willing to bear terrorism risks when they fear that the realized losses will coincide with negative macroeconomic periods. The mechanism for this relationship starts with the notion that suffering a loss, whether due to a terrorist attack or just a macroeconomic slump, causes investors to place a higher value on an additional unit of wealth or income. Thus, if a terrorist attack creates both direct property losses and a more general macroeconomic slump, then the "cost" of the property damage may be greatly magnified. Investors and insurance firms cannot easily avoid the macroeconomic slump, but they can avoid the magnified effect of the direct property loss simply by avoiding the terrorism insurance risks.

In financial market terms, terrorism risks that also create bad macroeconomic conditions and falling stock market prices have a positive Beta statistic, meaning that the terrorism insurance losses have a high (*i.e.* positive) correlation with depressed share prices in the stock market. To induce investors to take on high-Beta risks, or to purchase high-Beta securities, the market must offer a higher expected return on the capital tied to those investments–this is the compensation for holding the high-Beta risks. The implication is that the insurance premiums that compensate those holding terrorism risks will be higher to the extent that the direct losses from a terrorist attack are expected to spillover to the general economy and the stock market.

2.B.3. Modelling Terrorism Risks

It is often suggested that terrorism risks are more difficult to evaluate in an actuarial sense than are natural disaster risks, and that terrorism risks are certainly more difficult to evaluate than most other lines of casualty insurance. This is attributed in part to the more limited record of historical terrorism experience, and in part to the man-made and strategic aspects of terrorism risks. Based on this premise, it is possible to argue that (i) private insurance firms may be reluctant to participate at all in terrorism insurance markets, or that (ii) they will charge higher than expected premiums to compensate for the ambiguity. It is also possible that the difficulty in modelling terrorism risks complicates the efforts of individuals and firms to act to mitigate their possible future losses from a terrorist attack.

To evaluate these propositions, it is important to note that there are many examples where insurance firms have offered, and continue to offer, coverage even when there is highly limited information concerning the risk to be insured. Marine insurance was available starting in the earliest Roman times, using a combined loan and insurance contract called *bottomry*, which is also an early form of a catastrophe bond[27]. Surely this insurance was offered on the basis of very limited information–including the possibility that boats might sail off the flat edge of the world! In a later era, in 1688, Lloyds of London created its reputation by providing marine insurance even in the highest risk situations. A more recent example is that private firms insured the first commercial earth satellites, even in the absence of a significant historical record. And most currently, the Towers Perrin [2004] report discusses how loss estimates provided by a modelling firm were used to set premiums for a proposed, industry-wide, terrorism reinsurance facility; also see the discussion below in Section 3.A.3.

The implication is that high uncertainty and a limited historical record are not sufficient to deter insurance firms from offering coverage. The more likely impact of modelling uncertainty is that the insurance firms will charge relatively high premiums, as compensation for accepting the inherent uncertainty and ambiguity concerning the correct probabilities and expected losses. In fact, a willingness to supply, but at a suitably high price, does appear to characterize the current status of insurance coverage across a wide range of high-risk casualty lines.

These facts change when we consider the catastrophe lines–both natural disasters and terrorism. Here we find a very limited willingness of the private market to supply coverage (in the absence of government support). To be sure, the catastrophe coverages do have greater modelling uncertainty, and the terrorism risks have the greatest uncertainty, but the distinction with risky casualty lines such as marine, satellites, and product defect appears more a matter of degree than of kind. The key feature of the catastrophe lines is that when losses do occur, they are likely to be large, indeed catastrophic, quite possibly enough to threaten firm insolvency. It is our opinion, therefore, that it is the *joint occurrence of catastrophe-sized losses and modelling uncertainty* that creates the possibility of supply disruptions in the natural disaster and terrorism insurance lines[28].

3. Modalities for Government Intervention In Terrorism Insurance Markets

The discussion in the preceding section has made the case that, around the world, insurance is generally available for protection against catastrophe risks–both natural disasters and terrorism– only when we observe significant government intervention in the market. In this section, we review the primary modalities for the observed government interventions in the markets for terrorism insurance. The discussion here focuses on the economic aspects of the plans. More detailed descriptions of the country plans are provided in separate Reports of this Project.

3.A. Government Interventions to Recreate Private Markets for Terrorism Risks

The most desirable form of government intervention is to create the conditions that will allow private markets for terrorism insurance to operate again. This form of intervention responds directly to the factors that created the private market failure in the first place, in essence a "first-best" solution. Several specific policy actions can be considered in this category.

3.A.1. Direct Remedies to Improve Access of Insurance Firms to Capital Sources

The direct approach is to create conditions under which insurance firms can readily raise capital dedicated to support terrorism insurance lines of business. As described earlier, the primary impediments, at least in the US, are accounting rules and tax regulations, which in turn raise the cost of capital and create firm takeover risks. It does not seem a Herculean task to change the accounting rules to allow capital to be earmarked for use only to pay terrorism claims, or to change the tax rules to allow expected losses from future terrorism events to be deducted against current unearned premiums. Nevertheless, it is now three years since the September 11, 2001 event, and no significant action has occurred in either dimension. There is also the empirical question whether such actions would be sufficient to reactivate private terrorism insurance markets. In this regard, there are two pieces of evidence, one from the United States (positive), the other from Europe (negative).

The positive US evidence is provided by two features of the quasi-public agencies created to provide insurance coverage for wind damage (Florida) and earthquakes (California). First, the capital raised by each agency is available only for paying claims on its natural disaster coverage, since the quasi-public agencies are fully protected against any take over attempts by private market firms[29]. Thus, the plan structures effectively circumvent the accounting rules that otherwise preclude the earmarking of capital to specific expected future losses. Second, both agencies acquired special tax exemptions from the Internal Revenue Service (IRS, the US tax authority). Indeed, there was a stage at which the IRS had denied the tax exemption for the California Earthquake Authority, and the state's response was that this would be a "deal breaker". Ultimately, the IRS agreed, no doubt motivated by the quasi-public nature of the Authority and the political support it was able to muster. Thus, the state-based agencies did achieve structures that solved both the accounting and taxation issues, and this was essential to their success in reviving activity in their respective natural disaster markets. It is intriguing, of course, that the quasi-public agencies were able to circumvent the accounting and tax impediments, while the US accounting and tax authorities appear unwilling to provide similar opportunities to private sector entities.

Evidence from the Economic Union (EU) suggests, however, that while solving the accounting and taxation issues may be a necessary condition to raise capital for catastrophe insurance, this is not a sufficient condition. Insurance firms in the EU face accounting and taxation rules that are more flexible with regard to capital to support catastrophe insurance, but these EU insurance firms still do not offer catastrophe insurance. While it is beyond the scope of this Report to analyze the possible reasons that private EU insurance firms do not offer catastrophe coverage, the main point is that flexible accounting and tax regulations provide necessary but not sufficient, conditions to recreate active catastrophe insurance markets.

3.A.2. Improved Access for Catastrophe Bonds

The market for catastrophe bonds has been steadily, but slowly, evolving since the first such bond was introduced in 1997. A total of 51 catastrophe bonds have been issue as of mid-year 2004, accounting for a risk transfer of about $8 billion. In 2003, 8 new transactions were completed, for a total issuance amount of $1.73 billion (see Bowers [2004]). The market thus continues to grow, but it has not yet become a comprehensive solution for the funding of catastrophe insurance capital needs.

There are currently three regulatory issues relating to the use of catastrophe bonds by US insurance firms (see US Government Accounting Office [2002], [2003]). The first issue concerns accounting standards that do *not* allow insurance firms to reflect the risk transfer achieved by *non-indemnity* catastrophe bonds on their financial reports filed with state insurance regulators. Non-indemnity catastrophe bonds, which release capital to the issuing insurer based on a triggering event, such as an earthquake of level 7.0 or higher in a specified geographic region, have become increasingly popular with investors because the payout is not based on the issuing firm's book of policies (as it would be with an indemnity-based catastrophe bond). The National Association of Insurance Commissions (NAIC, the association of all US state insurance regulators) is currently considering a proposal to make this change.

The second issue refers to a new Financial Accounting Standards Board (FASB, which establishes GAAP accounting rules) proposal that clarifies accounting rules for *special purpose vehicles* (SPVs), including those that hold the government bond collateral for catastrophe bonds. The proposal enlarges the conditions under which the assets and liabilities within the SPV must be consolidated on the books of the issuing firm; it was initiated in response to the incomplete consolidation of SPVs by Enron. The change will be detrimental to the use of catastrophe bonds by insurance companies if it is determined to apply in these cases. The interpretation and implementation of FASB Interpretation No. 46 is currently in process.

The third issue is an attempt to obtain more favourable tax treatment for the SPV in a catastrophe bond, creating benefits that are currently available only to multiple class loan securitizations such as mortgages. Without this favourable tax treatment, the SPVs for catastrophe insurance structured instruments are typically located in offshore tax-havens, similar to those used for reinsurance firms. Unfortunately, these offshore entities also introduce new transaction costs that significantly offset the tax benefits they provide. A legislated tax-free conduit status was critical to the development of the US mortgage-backed and asset-backed security markets, and it could be equally significant in the development of the catastrophe bond market.

While action on any of the three issues would improve the usefulness of catastrophe bonds for raising capital to back catastrophe insurance, it is unlikely that this will be sufficient to activate private markets in natural disaster or terrorism insurance. The primary issue is that the evaluation of catastrophe bonds continues to require specialized knowledge and skill, and investors without these attributes have been inclined to invest elsewhere[30]. Indeed, other insurance firms are among the largest investors in catastrophe bonds, with little or no participation from "generic" capital market investors. In principle, this problem could be solved by creating catastrophe bond *investment or mutual funds* with the bonds chosen by professionally skilled managers. The failure to create such funds, however, likely reflects the judgment within the fund industry that it would be difficult to market a fund with the unique, that is *catastrophic,* attribute of catastrophe bonds.

3.A.3. The Creation of Mutual Risk Retention Pools

Mutual risk retention pools, organized within the private markets, represent another possible device to help recreate private markets for the provision of terrorism insurance. Such pools can be organized either within a group of insurance users, or by a group of insurance firms. Historically, farmers who were without access to established insurance markets, or who considered the premiums of insurance firms to be too high, joined to together to provide mutual coverage. More recently, and following the September 11 attack, a group of US airlines organized a mutual pool called *Equitime*, but it never become operational, perhaps due to the continued subsidization of the industry by the US government (Kunreuther and Michel-Kerjan [2004]).

Another recent and instructive example is the attempt of 14 US insurance firms to create a mutual reinsurance pool to cover their workers' compensation risks that arise from terrorism events. The issue of terrorism risks for workers' compensation insurance in the US is particularly severe because almost all states require that terrorism risks be covered in every workers' compensation policy. The firms engaged the Tillinghast and Reinsurance businesses of Towers Perrin to study the potential of a mutual pool to support the private market activities of the participating firms (Towers Perrin [2004]). Although the study ultimately determined that such a mutual pool was not practical at this time (for reason described below), the methodology they employed and the information they gathered are useful to review here.

The goal of the workers' compensation reinsurance pool was (Towers Perrin [2004], p.2):

"...to maximize the effective use of industry-wide capacity and minimize the potential for insurer insolvency/ruin resulting from large and unpredictable terrorism events."

The key issues confronted and solutions offered included:

- The pool would provide aggregate excess reinsurance, reimbursing members for 90% of their losses above a specified member retention level. The excess pool design was favoured over first-dollar coverage because the former provided greater flexibility to individual firms and it was more efficient in using the available aggregate capital.

- Participating members would pay annual premiums to the pool as a function of the coverage they required. Risk Management Systems (RMS), a catastrophe risk modelling firm, was hired to provide examples of the premiums that would be charged based on the book of business of alternative firms. It was concluded that it was feasible to determine premiums in this fashion, which appears to belie the contention that terrorism risks are uninsurable due to modelling uncertainty; see also the discussion above in Section 2.B.3.

- It was determined that a tax-free conduit status would likely be required if the mutual pool concept were to be economically feasible. This would parallel the tax-free status provided for the quasi-public pools established in California and Florida for earthquake and wind damage coverage respectively.

- RMS also estimated the aggregate losses that would be expected from various large terrorism events. The most severe case considered was a downtown New York City Anthrax release, which was estimated to create $91 billion in aggregate losses. It was determined that the pool resources would be inadequate to cover major terrorism events, based on the estimated losses over a range of such events. It was thus recommended not to go forward with more detailed planning.

In summary, although a mutual industry pool would help smaller firms survive moderate terrorism events, the pool's resources were inadequate to help any of the firms survive a major terrorism event. Simply put, the premium income of the US workers' compensation industry is about $30 billion annually, and this is insufficient to protect the industry against major terrorism losses that are potentially three times that amount. The report thus concludes that a US government backstop for terrorism reinsurance continues to be required[31].

3.B. The Modalities for Explicit Government Interventions in Terrorism Insurance

We next turn to a review of existing modalities for explicit government interventions in terrorism insurance markets. We develop a framework for analysis by organizing the discussion in terms of the functional features of the alternative plans. More detailed discussions of the individual country plans will be available in other Reports for this project.

It useful first to distinguish the *market micro structures* from the *insurance functions* that are embedded in the alternative plans. Market micro structures refer here to the actual marketing and the sale of policies at the initial date and then the settlement of claims when losses occur. Insurance functions refer to the alternative modalities through which coverage is defined, policy premiums are set, and risk is held. Most existing government interventions are mixed private/public enterprises with the private markets handling most, if not all, of the market micro structure functions, while the government participates in varying degrees in the insurance functions. Although we will comment on the features of alternative market micro structures in passing, our primary focus is on the alternative modalities used for coverage, price setting, and risk bearing.

3.B.1. Full Government Insurance

The most extreme intervention has the government serving as the *primary insurer*, taking on all insurance functions, including defining the coverage, setting the prices, and bearing the risk. This is well illustrated by the complete coverage provided in Israel for injury, life, and property risks arising from terrorism. The coverage is given to all persons within Israel without direct cost. The Israeli government bears the entire risk, which is funded from general tax revenues[32]. Northern Ireland offers a similar restitution program for losses due to terrorism. Full government insurance was also provided by the United States during World War II and the Korean War, for coverage against property damage incurred from attack upon the US. Here too the government defined the coverage, bore the risk, and planned to finance the costs from general tax revenues.

Equity across individuals is a main motivation for a country to provide complete government insurance, which would seem appropriate when the losses incurred are the result of a common national policy such as a war. Free government insurance also has a positive incentive effect, since it motivates people to remain in the country and even in the regions at highest risk. For the same reason, however, complete government insurance reduces the incentive for individuals to mitigate what will be their actual losses in case of an attack. This latter point was emphasized by Hirshleifer [1953], writing about US war damage insurance introduced during the Korean War. He recommended that incentives to mitigate possible damage be created through a schedule of risk-based premiums. Hirshleifer also noted that comparable incentive effects to mitigate could be obtained by offering no government insurance or compensation at all, but he feared this would create a plan for *ex post* restitution for losses, which would then eliminate the desirable incentive effects.

The California Earthquake Authority (CEA), created after the 1994 Northridge Earthquake, provides another type of full government insurance. The CEA is a quasi-public entity, created by action of the California state legislature, with stand-alone status, but operating under constraints imposed by the legislation. We have already noted the fundamental differences that exist between natural disaster and terrorism risks, and we do not mean to suggest that the CEA provides a useful architecture for government intervention in a terrorism insurance market. The CEA program experience, however, provides unique insights into a insurance plan in which coverage is voluntary and explicit premiums are charged. The CEA is empowered to set premiums and to bear the risks, but under three legislated constraints:

1. The legislation determined the classes of real estate losses which are and are not covered. This created a so-called "mini policy", which, had it been in effect at the time of the Northridge Earthquake, would have reduced the insured losses in half. More recent legislation also requires the CEA to take actions to increase earthquake risk mitigation.

2. The legislation requires premiums be set on an "actuarial basis"; the CEA is using estimates from modelling firms to determine risk-based benchmarks for different geographic regions and structure types. In practice, the quoted CEA premiums have been "tempered," moderating the price differences across regions. While this represents premium tempering, as well political "tampering," it should be recognized that the geographic premium differentials provided by the modelling firms are themselves subject to potentially large errors of estimation.

3. The legislation required large initial capital contributions from the private insurance firms, which were thereby relieved of the need to provide direct coverage. The legislation allows the CEA to purchase reinsurance, but denies access to public funds. An immediate effect is that, based on current premium levels, CEA resources are adequate only to provide complete coverage for an event about double the size of the Northridge Earthquake. Beyond that level, policyholders would receive only partial indemnification.

Unlike the Israeli and US war damage plans considered earlier in this section, participation in the CEA plan is voluntary, and significant premiums are charged. As a result, private firms may and do compete with the CEA, although to date, they mainly offer policies for low-risk locations and structures, undercutting what are the relatively high CEA premiums for these risks. It thus appears that the CEA is not crowding out competitors who offer coverage on low-risk location and structures, while the absence of private sector competitors on high-risk properties leaves open the possibility that crowding out is occurring at these higher risk tiers.

It is also intriguing that the percentage of all California properties with earthquake coverage (with either the CEA or private firms), has declined significantly, from about 33% in 1996, when the CEA was created, to about 15% currently (California Department of Insurance [2004]). It seems that many homeowners consider the premiums to be high relative to the coverage provided; for many homes, the earthquake premium equals or even exceeds the premium for standard fire, theft, and liability coverage[33]. The CEA has been trying to raise demand by altering contract features, especially the deductible amounts, but these have not been successful to date[34].

The CEA experience suggests it is a complex matter to determine how best to serve consumer needs for direct catastrophe insurance. The most intriguing fact is that many consumers consider the premiums charged too high to warrant insurance purchase, even though the premiums approximately equal the estimates of expected losses provided by independent modelling firms.

Furthermore, the political tempering of premiums should actually increase demand, since *tempering reduces the premiums on high-risk properties, while private firms compete in providing fairly priced coverage on low-risk properties*.

3.B.2. Government as Reinsurer of Last Resort for Terrorism Insurance

We next consider terrorism insurance plans in which the government serves as the reinsurer of last resort[35]. Under these plans, the government mainly provides reinsurance at the highest risk levels, while private insurers and reinsurers retain some or all of the lower tiers of risk. The sharing of risk with the private industry is achieved through a mandatory deductible limit at the lowest risk level and through coinsurance at intermediate risk levels. The current plans for terrorism insurance in France (GAREAT), Germany (Extremus), the UK (Pool Re), and the US (the Terrorism Risk Insurance Act, TRIA) all have these features, at least in general terms[36]. While these plans all share the concept of the government as the reinsurer of last resort, they differ in other dimensions, which we now analyze.

Mandatory Participation

Mandatory or automatic participation in a government plan has two primary effects, one positive and one negative:

- Mandatory or automatic participation eliminates adverse selection, a benefit for the plan[37].

- Mandatory or automatic participation will likely crowd out private sector reinsurance for the risk layers at which the government plan provides coverage, an economic cost.

In all the country plans reviewed here, participant in the government plans is not mandatory, although in some cases it may be automatic; also in some cases the offer or provision of terrorism insurance to clients by the primary insurers may be mandatory[38]. The US TRIA plan requires insurers to offer coverage to their policyholders; all insurers then automatically participate in the government plan. French law requires that all property insurance contracts provide terrorism insurance. Participation in the GAREAT pool is not compulsory, but membership is currently automatic for insurance company members of the Fédération Française des Sociétés d'Assurances (FFSA) and mutual insurers in the Groupement des Entreprises Mutuelles de l'Assurance (GEMA); see OECD [2004]. In the UK Pool Re plan, participation is voluntary, although customers must opt for terrorism coverage for all of their properties if they wish to have any terrorism coverage at all. In Germany, coverage of terrorism risks and participation in the Extremus plan are both voluntary.

In all these plans, *private sector reinsurance* is generally purchased by the members to control their risks at the lowest (deductible) and intermediate (coinsurance) levels. Thus, the complete crowding out of private reinsurers could occur only at the highest risk tier, where the government serves as the unique insurer of last resort. Given that the government interventions were initiated by the failure of the private markets to offer reinsurance at this highest tier, crowding out at these risk levels was certainly not an issue initially[39]. Nevertheless, it is worth remembering that private market reinsurers are unlikely to have a major market presence in any risk tranche at which the government continues to intervene actively.

Government Plan Reinsurance Premiums

The plans differ in how premiums are set for the government's reinsurance facility. The US plan charges no *ex ante* premiums for the reinsurance facility, but has an option to require *ex post* (*i.e.* retrospective) compensation. Whether or not *ex post* compensation would be carried out will presumably depend on the financial status of the insurance industry at the time the decision is made. The French, German, and UK plans all charge *ex ante* premiums, with no provision for *ex post* restitution (an earlier version of the UK did have restitution). Only the UK plan uses risk-based premium charges, and these are now limited to only two geographic rating zones. For all the other plans, the reinsurance premium depends only on the insured coverage amount.

It is worth noting that government plans providing natural disaster insurance in Japan, Florida, and California all provide for risk-based pricing. The use of risk-based premiums in government-based natural disaster reinsurance plans may occur because better methods exist to determine risk-based premiums for natural disasters. Likewise, the absence of risk-based premiums in government reinsurance for terrorism risk may arise to avoid the implication that the government can judge the locations or building types that are most likely to attract an attack.

Primary Insurance Premiums

Generally speaking, insurance firms in the countries reviewed here have wide discretion to set the premiums they charge their customers for terrorism coverage[40]. In the US TRIA plan, the revised UK Pool RE plan and the German Extremus plan, the primary insurers have complete discretion to determine their premiums for terrorism coverage. In France, the reinsurance premium charged by the government plan is proportional to the total property coverage premium charged the policyholder by the primary insurer; but this still leaves the primary insurer in control of the premiums it charges its clients. In other words, the GAREAT terrorism reinsurance charge is basically a tax on all applicable property damage insurance premiums received from clients.

Primary insurers will generally use risk-based premiums to obtain compensation for the risks in their own portfolio and to pass through the cost of the risk-based premiums they are charged by private market reinsurers and by the government plans. On the other hand, to the degree that the government reinsurer charges flat premiums (which are zero in the US plan), the observed degree of risk-based pricing passed through to the consumer will be moderated. The effect is to limit risked-based pricing at the consumer level, and thus to limit the incentive for mitigation activity at the consumer level[41]. To be clear, the premiums posted by primary insurers for their clients may still include risk-based components, reflecting the need to control their own retained risks and to pass through any risk-based costs on the private market reinsurance they purchase.

Risk Coverage Limitations

The country plans all vary in terms of what defines a "terrorist act", whether chemical, biological, nuclear, and radiological (CBNR) attacks are covered, and for which insurance lines is coverage available. In the US and UK, CBNR attacks are covered as long as the respective Treasury department certifies that an act of terrorism–based on the legal definition–has occurred[42]. In France and Germany the legally set definitions of a "terrorism" event are applied directly, but Germany excludes all CBNR attacks, whereas France excludes nuclear attacks. In all countries, legal disputes may arise whether an event is act of war (in which case it would not be covered) or an act of terrorism (in which case it could be covered). The US TRIA law has the further important limitation that it does not apply to acts of domestic terrorism.

In all these countries, the government plans are directed primarily to commercial property damage. The France, Germany, and the UK plans also cover business interruption risks, whereas the US plan does not. The US plan, on the other hand, covers excess, workers' compensation and surety insurance lines, which may not be covered in the other countries. We return in a moment to the impact these various coverage limitations may have on consumer demand for terrorism insurance coverage.

Pool Structure

The French, German, and UK plans all create an explicit reinsurance pool, into which reinsurance premiums are paid, and from which compensation for losses is received (including the additional support provided by the government as insurer of last resort). This creates an automatic mutualization of the risk, which moderates the risks retained by the insurance firms (Michel-

Kerjan and Pedell [2004]). In contrast, the US TRIA plan creates no *ex ante* pool, thus requiring the primary insurers to generate their own mechanisms for risk sharing. This can be seen as a positive feature if it allows the private markets to develop efficient mechanisms for risk sharing, or as a negative feature if turns out that the private markets are unable to develop such risk-sharing structures for terrorism risks.

Maximum Retained Risks

The success of any government plan will depend critically on its ability to provide dependable limits to the amount of risk that is retained within the private sector. For example, in California following the 1994 Northridge Earthquake, the insurance firms were prepared to transfer significant sums of capital (almost $4 billion in total) to the new California Earthquake Authority in order to shed any and all exposure to earthquake losses[43].

For the terrorism reinsurance plans considered here, in contrast, participation in a plan reduces a firm's exposure, but still leaves varying amounts of the risk to be held in an industry pool or by the firm directly. In Germany, there are limits to the government's retention at the highest risk tier, and amounts above that would revert to the industry pool. In the revised Pool Re plan in UK, in contrast, the risk of individual insurers is now capped per event and per annum, with the cap levels depending on the firm's market share. In France, insurance firms face losses as a function of the total losses to be paid by pool members, but the French government retains all the risk at the highest tier. In the US, there is also an overall cap, beyond which neither the government nor the insurers are responsible for paying claims. Overall, the greater the amount of risk transferred from the private sector by the government plan, the greater that plan's contribution to the revival of the terrorism insurance market, but also the greater the extent to which it might crowd out future private market activity.

Sunset Provisions

Government intervention in the terrorism insurance market runs the risk that it may induce a self-fulfilling need, by crowding out otherwise feasible private market initiatives. The plans in France, Germany, and the US all have fixed termination dates within the next two years, and the UK plan is subject to periodic review. However, it may prove difficult to terminate any of these plans, particular if terminating the government plan means switching from a high level of government support to zero on a single date. In contrast, a plan in which the government's role is gradually but steadily reduced through time may have a greater chance ultimately to be eliminated. The US TRIA plan, for example, explicitly allows the possibility of steadily reducing the government's retention (see Michel-Kerjan and Pedell [2004]). More generally, it may prove useful for countries to adopt *an explicit path to sunset*, as well as a literal and *final sunset date*. At the same time, an understanding of the need and techniques for government intervention in the terrorism insurance markets is likely to be evolving rapidly. Thus, all sunset provisions should allow flexibility in case the evolving nature of terrorism risks requires a modification in the sunset plan.

Why Consumer Demand is So Limited

The plans for terrorism insurance described here (France, Germany, UK, and US) are all functioning, with full, if not necessarily enthusiastic, participation of the private terrorism industry[44]. It is thus a surprise to find that demand, not supply, appears to be the factor limiting the volume for terrorism insurance (excluding France, where coverage is automatically applied to applicable commercial properties). The available reports for the US show limited demand, with 20% to 36% of potential customers accepting coverage (even in New York City); see Michel-Kerjan and Pedell [2004] and US Government Accounting Office [2004a] and [2004b]. A recent survey of 2,400 US businesses by Marsh & McLennan [2004] finds that 27.3% had adopted coverage in the 2nd quarter of 2003, rising to 32.7% by the 4th quarter of 2003. Although these coverage ratios are in line with previous reports, the Marsh & McLennan report is hopeful that a positive trend is developing. On the other hand, Michel-Kerjan and Pedell [2004] report that as few as 2.75% of eligible German firms are using used the Extremus facility. It will also be instructive to see how much demand materializes in the UK, given that Pool Re has now expanded its coverage, but at the same time doubled its premiums.

A variety of factors have been suggested as explanations for the limited demand[45].

- The existing terrorism plans have many exclusions; the exclusions range over acts of war, chemical, biological, nuclear, and radiological (CBNR) attacks, losses on assets held outside the country, and acts by domestic (that is, not foreign) terrorists. Although it may be intuitively appealing that reducing the coverage could significantly reduce demand, the literature on "background uncertainty" suggests a more complicated relationship. To see why, suppose coverage is initially available and purchased for protection against two risks, say Acts of War and Acts of Terrorism. Now, if Acts of War coverage were to become unavailable, then the demand for the remaining insurable category, Acts of Terrorism, will actually rise as individuals and firms attempt to control their total retained risk as much as possible[46]. The implication is that the greater the range of observed terrorism coverage exclusions, the greater the insurance demand we would expect for those terrorism risks where insurance remains available[47].

- Commercial properties owned by large public companies, or properties with landmark or "trophy" status, face a much higher likelihood of terrorist attack than do small commercial or residential properties, based both on their strategic interest to terrorists and on location. Casualty insurance, however, may not be essential for a publicly owned company, to the extent that the incurred losses are reflected in a decline in the firm's share price, which means that the loss is automatically spread across all the shareholders[48]. Indeed, the academic literature has searched to find reasons why public corporations would purchase casualty insurance at all[49]. It is thus plausible that corporate managers may not consider it essential to purchase terrorism insurance (particularly in view of the behavioral and pricing factors we describe in the next two points).

- Behavioral factors may reduce the demand for terrorism insurance, reflecting a tendency for consumers to set very small probabilities to zero, or to assume "it won't happen to me." Kunreuther and Pauly [2004] provide a specific model based on search and transaction costs, as well references to a larger literature.

- Individuals and firms may consider terrorism insurance too costly, either because they cannot afford the premiums, or because they feel the premiums exceed the expected loss by too wide a margin. It is noteworthy that the Marsh & McLennan [2004] report, referred to earlier in the context of the limited demand for terrorism insurance coverage, attributes the recent increase in US demand to the sharply declining premium charges for the coverage. Similarly, as discussed earlier, the perception of high prices also seems to be a primary reason the demand for earthquake insurance is so low in California. Hurricane insurance in Florida, in contrast, is one catastrophe coverage in which the demand remains high even given the perception of high premium costs. The explanation, however, is that mortgage lenders require hurricane insurance for Florida properties, whereas they do not require earthquake insurance for comparable California properties[50].Although mortgage lenders continue to require terrorism insurance on commercial property mortgages, the lenders appear to have become more flexible in how they enforce this requirement.

To summarize, it appears that corporate risk-spreading, behavioral factors, and high prices combine to limit the actual demand for terrorism insurance. It is an intriguing thought that if consumers and firms reveal a limited actual demand for government terrorism insurance, then this should dampen, if not eliminate, the concern for the social costs of a failed market, which created the impetus for the government intervention in the first place.

4. Limits and Drawbacks to Government Intervention in Terrorism Insurance Markets

Having reviewed how governments actually intervene in terrorism insurance markets, it is critical to consider the possible limits and drawbacks to government intervention. In this section, we review three potentially important drawbacks to government intervention in terrorism insurance markets: crowding out, mitigation effects, and emergency relief.

4.A. Crowding Out

By *crowding out*, we mean that the government intervention displaces private market activity that would have otherwise taken place. In countries such as Israel and Northern Ireland, where the government provides complete indemnification against terrorism losses at no cost, it is obvious that private terrorism insurance cannot compete. At the same time, crowding out is not really an issue in these countries since (i) in no case would private firms offer insurance while the extreme terrorist threats persist, and (ii) the government intervention arises from political as much as economic motives.

More relevant cases arise in countries such as France, Germany, UK, and US, where the government serves as the reinsurer of last resort. We now apply a simple framework which demonstrates how the existence of crowding out depends primarily on the prices for terrorism reinsurance set by the government plan and by the private market in the absence of the government intervention. We assume that consumers purchase insurance from the low cost supplier. Several alternative cases and outcomes are illustrated in Table 8.2.

Table 8.2. **Crowding Out Based on Private and Government Insurance Prices**

	Government Plan Price PG	Private Market Price PM	Private Market Insurance Activity (No Government)	Crowding Out
Case 1	PG = EL	PM >> EL	0	No
Case 2	PG = EL	PM > EL	Positive	Yes
Case 3	PG < EL	PM = EL	Positive	Yes
EL = expected loss for provision of terrorism insurance.				

Case 1 in Table 8.2 makes two key assumptions:

1. PG = EL: the government plan price for reinsurance PG equals the expected loss EL.

2. PM >> EL: the private market price for reinsurance PM *far* exceeds the expected loss EL.

The assumption that private insurers charge significantly higher prices than the government could reflect the response of private firms to the risk of ruin and/or the effects of ambiguity aversion (uncertainty over the process generating the likelihood and location of possible future attacks). Whatever the basis, the assumption for Case 1 is that the private market price is so high that there is no demand for private insurance even in the absence of the government intervention (see column 3 in Table 8.2). Since no private market activity arises even in the absence of the government intervention, there is *no crowding out* (see column 4 in Table 8.2). This case becomes more likely, of course, the higher the risk premiums charged by the private market insurers. This result would also hold if private insurers refuse to provide coverage at any price (this being equivalent to charging a price so high that no coverage is demanded).

Case 2 differs from Case 1 because the private market price is no longer so high as to deter all activity in the absence of the government plan. Since the demand for private insurance is positive only when the government insurance is not offered (because PG < PM), there is crowding out. The welfare significance of such crowding out, however, is unclear because the private sector insurance is supplied only at actuarially unfair prices (that is, PM > EL). For example, if the private market's high price simply reflected inaccurately high expected losses, then the government intervention might still be desirable[51].

In Case 3, the government plan sets a subsidized price, while the private market sets it price equal to the expected loss (in the fashion of a fully efficient market). This case also creates crowding out, and now there is a greater presumption that the crowding out indicates the government plan has created a welfare loss. However, even in this case, it could be that the government subsidy reflects an attempt to increase the supply as the result of a positive externality associated with the purchase of terrorism insurance.

These simple cases demonstrate that the welfare implications of crowding out are complex. In Case 2, where the private sector price exceeds the expected loss, crowding out may actually be desirable if the private sector price reflects private market inefficiency in providing terrorism insurance. In Case 3, where the government price is less than the expected loss, crowding out again may be desirable if the government subsidy reflects an externality in the provision of terrorism insurance. The conclusion is that welfare interpretations of crowding out phenomena require a careful analysis of the fundamental factors that create the crowding out phenomena.

The crowding out discussion has so far assumed that insurance prices are set once and for all. More realistically, private firms will reduce their prices over time, perhaps reflecting the gradual elimination of ambiguity aversion, while the government plan prices remain fixed. In this case, we would observe increasing market penetration by the private firms, essentially a beneficial *crowding in of private sector activity*. This result requires, of course, the government to maintain fixed prices at the initial level. As noted earlier, the US markets for hurricanes in Florida and earthquakes in California both appear to be evolving in exactly this way.

4.B. Mitigation Incentive Effects

The possibility that private sector mitigation efforts may fall as the result of a government intervention into terrorism insurance is another possible drawback to such an intervention. The economics literature analyzes the impact of insurance on mitigation based on two key forces:

1) Insurance availability tends to reduce mitigation, since insured individuals will receive indemnification for their losses independent of their mitigation effort. *ex post* indemnification for losses incurred, as in the case of government provided emergency aid, similarly decreases the incentive to mitigate the amount of expected losses.

2) Risk-based premiums, however, provide an incentive to mitigate, which at least offsets the negative incentive created by the availability of insurance.

The failure to apply risk-based premiums in most government reinsurance programs creates an incentive against mitigation[52]. The flat pricing must thus be motivated by some other factor. For example, the government may fear that risk-based pricing, by revealing the government's information with respect to the locations and structures it knows to be at the greatest risk, would be used by the terrorists themselves. Or the government might consider it inequitable to charge higher premiums for the higher risks, given that international terrorism is the source of the risks.

The possible negative effects of the availability of insurance on mitigation requires, of course, that consumers and firms actually purchase the insurance. For example, if the government premiums are set at such high levels that no insurance is purchased, then of course there would be no negative impact on mitigation effort. This can be seen, in fact, as an extreme example of risk-based pricing, illustrating the case in which risk-based prices fully offset the negative mitigation incentives created by the availability of insurance. Similarly, limitations on the coverage, such as high deductible and coinsurance requirements, or ceilings on the maximum coverage, will all have the positive effect of creating greater mitigation effort. On the other hand, mitigation efforts will be reduced when coverage is mandatory as it is in France.

The highly publicized nature of terrorism risks may introduce several additional factors, beyond the narrowly defined economic incentives, which may influence private sector mitigation efforts. First, property owners and firm managers may decide to act to control terrorism risks in the interests of safety and welfare, independently of any direct economic incentives to do so. Second, firm employees are likely to take actions to force greater mitigation efforts by their firms if they feel their safety and welfare is in jeopardy. Finally, some of the losses created by terrorism occur at the macroeconomic and societal levels (such as simple fear), and these are likely beyond the reach of private sector mitigation efforts.

The complex process through which terrorism risks arise, especially the expected strategic intent of the terrorists, may also have a special impact on the willingness of individuals and firms to undertake actions to mitigate their future losses from terrorist risks. One key feature here is that the risk facing an individual or firm may depend in part, and possibly in large part, on the mitigation efforts taken by others, often called *interdependent risks*. The relationship between interdependent risks and mitigation activity has been studied recently by Kunreuther and Heal [2003a] and [2003b]. As one example of this approach, consider what mitigation efforts would be undertaken by an airline to protect against a luggage bomb, given that luggage is presented directly by passengers (which the airline can readily inspect) as well as transferred from other airlines (which may impossible to inspect). In this situation, if one airline suspects that the other airlines are lax in inspecting luggage, then the first airline may decide also to limit its own security measures, creating a vicious circle of lax security. On the other hand, if terrorists are also known to focus on airlines with lax security, then the benefit of creating a reputation for high security may induce all airlines to spend resources on security, a virtuous circle of high security. Not only can there be quite different outcomes depending on the particulars of the situation, but the equilibrium may switch from one to another even if only a small number of firms initially change their behavior. This provides an interesting possibility for public policy, initiated either by an industry trade association or the government, in which a switch to a more positive equilibrium is initiated by inducing even a small number of firms to invest in a greater degree of mitigation.

Keohane and Zeckhauser [2003] discuss another type of interdependent risks, in which the reaction of terrorists to mitigation efforts becomes a key determinant of the mitigation efforts. They consider two alternative regimes. In one regime, terrorists are motivated to attack targets which create a large aggregate damage. Individual actions that mitigate the likely damage will create a positive externality, by reducing the overall likelihood of an attack, thus benefiting all individuals and firms in the target area. In another regime, individual mitigation efforts have the negative externality of directing the terrorist attack to another target. Behavior based on both regimes may occur at the same time.

A particularly interesting aspect of the Keohane and Zeckhauser model is that individual responses to government actions may undermine the purpose of the government action; it is as if the government action crowds out at least some of the individual efforts to mitigate losses. As an example, suppose that the government takes action to reduce the likelihood of an attack against a particular city. Individuals and firms may then respond to the reduced risk in that city by moving new activities there. This would raise the likelihood of an attack on that city, offsetting and possibly even negating the positive benefit created by the initial government action.

4.C. The Impact of Emergency Relief on Insurance

Certainly in the countries for which specific plans are being evaluated here–France, German, UK and US–citizens will generally anticipate that governments will provide emergency aid and relief following a terrorism event. For example, the Victim Compensation Fund (VCF), was created by act of the US Congress to compensate victims of the September 11th terrorist attack. Overall, more than 5,500 awards were issued in an average amount slightly above $2 million each. Although the attack victims clearly would not have anticipated the attack or the creation of the VCF, individuals today who are anticipating future attacks would factor in the possibility that *ex post* aid will provided. As a further example, the US maintains a formal agency–the Federal Emergency Management Agency (FEMA)–with the express role of providing emergency disaster relief. To be clear, the primary task of FEMA is to provide victims with immediate medical care and shelter on a short term basis–with little or no interaction with any primary insurance coverage. Individuals, however, may think the relief agency also provides financial compensation for losses incurred, or that they will receive less compensation if they are insured. It is thus interesting to see the how the September 11 VCF handled this (US Department of Justice [2002], p.1):

> *"While the congressional act requires certain deductions from collateral source monies– life insurance, pensions, etc. it did allow the Special Master discretion in calculating the appropriate deduction. As a result of the extensive review conducted during the comment period by the Department and Special Master, the Final Rule allows the offsets to be minimized and, in turn, increase the awards to claimants. Although the legislation does not permit the creation of a mandatory minimum pay out for all eligible claimants after the deductions, the Special Master believe it will be very rare that a claimant will receive less than $250,000".*

When citizens come to expect that the government will provide *ex post* aid at no cost in the event of a terrorist attach, there are likely to be harmful ramifications in terms of crowding out and mitigation (as discussed in the above sections)[53]. *Ex post* aid is likely to create a harmful form of crowding out, since the aid can be seen as the equivalent of a zero-cost government insurance program. *Ex post* aid is also likely to create disincentives to mitigate, to the extent there is the expectation that the government will indemnify losses, whatever their size.

While these crowding out and mitigation effects of *ex post* aid programs are undesirable, realism suggests that governments will continue to provide such aid in the face of unexpected events, and that citizens will expect their government to do so. The only practical solution, therefore, is to control the details of the *ex post* aid in a way that minimizes the undesirable effects of crowding out and mitigation. For example, it is important to clarify that purchasing insurance will not reduce the payout that otherwise would be expected from *ex post* aid. It is also useful to tie aid payments in a positive way to the amount of *ex ante* mitigation that was carried out. The problem, however, is that *ex post* aid is normally provided on the basis of *emergency need*, and it may not be credible for the government to announce on an *ex ante* basis that it will not reduce award payments based on insurance in force or mitigation actions taken.

5. Policy Proposals

We now provide our conclusions in terms of a set of proposals for government intervention in the terrorism insurance markets.

5.A. The Preferred Format for the Proposed Intervention

The existing government interventions in catastrophe insurance, for both natural disasters and terrorism risks, provide highly useful information. As described earlier in this Report, we observe certain features that are common to many of these plans, and which seem to be effective. On the other hand, certain aspects, particularly with regard to the government's coverage at the highest risk tranche and the government's pricing for this coverage, exhibit substantial variations across countries, at the same time that there has been no practical testing (meaning that, fortunately, no events have occurred requiring payouts from these highest risk tiers). In this section, we first summarize what we take to be the points of similarity and agreement, then we discuss the issues of pricing and coverage at the highest risk tier.

5.A.1. The Uniform Factors of Government Intervention in Terrorism Insurance

The following features are common to most government plans for intervention in catastrophe insurance markets for commercial properties and related coverages, and they appear to work well. They are listed here with only brief comment:

- The market micro structure functions, through which the sale of policies and the settlement of claims occur, should be carried out by private market insurance firms. The private sector firms are experienced with carrying out these activities and are likely to perform them better than a new government entity. In addition, goals such as risk-based pricing and an early termination for the government intervention (discussed further below) will be best served by keeping the private firms engaged in the market.

- Government intervention should give high priority to actions that reactivate the private markets. As discussed in Section 3.A, these actions include steps to improve the access of catastrophe insurance firms to capital market resources, including the further development of the market for catastrophe bonds. While improved capital market access has significant long-run potential, and should remain a key part of government initiatives, it is unlikely to create a rapid recovery of a private insurance market immediately following a major event. Also, as discussed in section 3.A.3, the creation of private industry mutual assistance pools should be encouraged by government action, for example, by providing such pools with tax-free conduit status. Here too, there are important long-term benefits from helping the industry make more efficient use of its capital resources, but such pools do not create the new capital that is required in the short-run following a major event.

- For the foreseeable future, the centrepiece of government interventions should remain a reinsurance facility. As observed in most existing government plans, the coverage should require a significant deductible requirement (at the lower risk tier) and coinsurance component (at the middle risk tiers). This format provides good economic incentives for risk management. Furthermore, plans that allow the voluntary participation of insurers and reinsurers are generally preferred, since they create a cooperative private/public partnership, in which the re-emergence of a private industry is likely to be encouraged. The pricing and delivery mechanism for the government reinsurance coverage is discussed below.

- Premium setting at the retail level should remain fully in control of the private firms. This should entail risk-based pricing, with the prices reflecting each firm's expected losses based on the risks it retains, the cost of private sector reinsurance (or other risk transfer mechanisms), and the cost of the government plan.

- The government plan should provide a clear path, or at least a strategy for a path, to termination. One credible mechanism is to require that the extent of the government reinsurance be steadily reduced, albeit at a pace consistent with the capacity of the private industry to reinsure the evolving levels of risk. It is also important to continue to encourage private firm participation, for example by not reducing the prices charged for the government coverage, even if expected losses decline.

5.A.2. The Variables of Government Intervention in Terrorism Insurance

Pricing is perhaps the most difficult question in designing a government plan for terrorism insurance. This involves both the initial level of the premium relative to the expected loss, and how the premium should be modified over time. It also involves questions whether *ex post* retrospection compensation should be included (which is comparable in most respects to a *lender* of last resort component). We begin with this question.

Ex post (Retrospective) Compensation and a Lender of Last Resort

A premium component that includes *ex post* or *retrospective* payments is a common feature in both primary and reinsurance contracts. A simple example occurs when auto premiums rise on the basis of claims made. This basic structure occurs whenever current and future insurance premiums are determined, at least in part, by the insured losses that have occurred historically. It is commonly used where the proper actuarial basis for premium determination is unclear, which includes cases where moral hazard may be an important component of expected losses. As long as the contract terms are binding, the insurer is basically acting as a lender, providing cash flow payments when the loss occurs, but receiving premium repayment in future years.

All of the government terrorism insurance plans considered here (for France, Germany, UK and US) include a component of *ex post* payments. These are explicit in the US (TRIA) plan, but arise in the other plans as part of the required, pool-based, coinsurance payments. Such a feature is understandable, given the difficulty of determining the proper actuarial premium and the desire of the government to minimize its budgetary obligations, *as long as the arrangement is successful in attracting the needed supply of terrorism insurance by the private market firms*. The latter depends, ultimately, on whether the failure of the private market for terrorism insurance arises from the inability of the insurance firms to access the necessary risk capital on a short-term basis (for which *ex post* premiums are a useful device) or whether the supply failure arises because providing terrorism insurance is basically a *negative present value project*, in which case retrospective premiums will not increase the supply of coverage.

The concept of *lender* of last resort has precise parallels to *ex post* premium payments[54]. It could be applied to terrorism insurance if a government agency, possibly the Central Bank, stood ready to make loans to insurance firms who were in need of liquidity. The notion is that private insurance firms may refuse to offer terrorism coverage, even when premiums exceed the expected loss, due to the costs of financial distress that arise if the firm does not have access to the resources to pay future losses. Thus, a lender of last resort may serve to activate the private market for terrorism insurance at low cost to the government.

The loans might appear similar to catastrophe bonds, but (i) would be issued only after the losses occurred, and (ii) would be collateralized by the insurance firm's assets. The loans would be repaid from the insurance firm's ongoing profits. A difficulty, of course, is that the government would face potential default risk on these loans. Furthermore, it is an open question whether access to such a lender of last resort, without an insurer of last resort, would provide sufficient incentive for major insurance firms to continue to commit their capital and other resources to terrorism insurance. It should be recognized that such a loan facility is indistinguishable in its cash flow attributes from a government insurance plan in which payment for coverage is made only *retrospectively*, given that the same time pattern of cash flows apply to the loan.

Auctions for Excess of Loss Coverage

Auctions provide an alternative and potentially attractive system through which the government may provide reinsurance to the private markets. The key advantage of the auction device is that the private insurance firms play a key role in determining the price they must pay to obtain the government's reinsurance contract, in contrast to the existing programs in which the price is administratively set by the government. The system requires the government to set the total quantity of reinsurance coverage it wishes to make available. The price is then determined at that level at which the private industry demand, as revealed through its bidding, equals the government's supply. The process can be thought as similar to that used by governments when they auction Treasury bonds or mineral rights.

The auction sale would apply to contracts providing excess of loss payouts, with the government providing its reinsurance compensation when industry losses from an event exceed a specified value. The instrument could take a specific form similar to either exchange trade catastrophe options or catastrophe bonds, both of which were described earlier in Section 2.A. A number of authors have discussed such a proposal, including Lewis and Murdoch [1996 and 1999], Cummins, Lewis and Phillip [1999], Cummins and Doherty [2001], Jaffee and Russell [2003] and Smetters [2003].

A key advantage of the auction mechanism is that the private market sets the price at which it is willing to demand coverage. The devil, however, may be in the details, since the government must determine all the auction conditions, including how much aggregate coverage to offer, and the conditions under which new "tranche" will be available, if at all, in the future. Also, since the contracts would most likely include triggers and payouts based on *industry-wide* losses, individual firms would face basis risk[55].

Given the difficulty of creating a completely new auction structure immediately following a terrorist attack, it is not surprising that such a format has not been attempted. However, this format becomes quite an appealing way to continue government backing, while terminating the complete coverage that was instituted immediately following the initial and unexpected attack. This approach would also help to develop the market for insurance linked securities, such as catastrophe bonds.

5.B. Concluding Thoughts

Following a major terrorism act, private insurance firms are likely to suspend their terrorism insurance activities and to request government intervention in the terrorism insurance market. A positive government response will not only improve the supply of terrorism insurance, but it will be viewed as a credible and symbolic representation that the government is alive and well, and prepared to defend the country and its economy. It is in this context that the initial government intervention is likely to be both necessary and warranted. The initial intervention, however, should emphasize that the goal of government policy is not to replace the market, but rather to complement the market until it is again able to operate by itself.

Over time, the private industry should require a decreasing level of government intervention. Among other things, time will allow the industry to develop better capabilities to model terrorism risks, as well as to recover and then expand its capital base. The best plan would have the government intervention decrease as the private industry's potential rises, *pari passu*. Also, during this intermediate time span, the government should carry out the tax, accounting, and regulatory actions that are under its control and which will expedite the recovery of the private markets for terrorism insurance.

Ultimately, full success of the government intervention will be measured by the timely return of a well functioning private market for terrorism insurance.

Notes

1.   Terrorism insurance may provide coverage for a variety of risks, including property damage, liability, business interruption, workers compensation, and life insurance risks. Countries vary as to whether chemical, biological, nuclear, and radiological (CBNR) attacks are included under terrorism coverage; in some cases these forms of terrorism risks are not covered at all.

2.   To be clear, most countries have mixed private/public systems for the delivery of terrorism insurance, but a critical part of the risk is generally held by the government. Existing systems are compared in Section 3.B.

3.   The small amount of insured losses created by most events arises in part because most losses are not insured. Nevertheless, these events do contribute, in the aggregate, to a "background" level of about $5 billion annually in insured losses for each category.

4.   Natural catastrophes include cold waves and frost, droughts and forest fires, earthquakes, floods, storms, and other (such as hail and avalanches). Man-made disasters covers events associated with human activity, such as aviation, mining road, railroad, shipping, space, and terrorism disasters; see Swiss Re [2004], p. 40, for further details.

5.   In principle, the issues of intervention should be addressed before an attack, and the planning should take a long-term outlook, including within it the possibility that attacks will occur. The text describes the more realistic scenario in which government interventions in such situations are usually event driven.

6.   See Jaffee and Russell [1997], US Government Accounting Office [2001], and Nutter [2002] for discussions of how natural disaster insurance is provided around the world.

7.   To be precise, the insurance entities were created by Acts of the respective state legislatures, and government officials sit *ex officio* on their governing boards. The entities, however, are not formally part of the state governments.

8.   Government interventions for natural disaster insurance in the US occur mainly at the state level, not the federal level. Our discussion in the text focuses on the interventions in the state of Florida following the Andrew Hurricane and the state of California following the Northridge Earthquake, but other US states have also intervened in natural disaster insurance markets. As examples, the state of Hawaii became a direct provider of hurricane insurance following the Iniki Hurricane in 1992, and the state of Texas established the Texas Windstorm Insurance Association in 1971 following Hurricane Celia in 1970.

Brown, Cummins, Lewis, and Wei [2003] suggest a less important role for government intervention following the Andrew Hurricane and the Northridge Earthquake. Their comments are directed primarily, however, to the limited role of *federal intervention* in these markets, not the major state interventions that did occur.

9   A similar example is given in Harrington and Niehaus [2001].

10   In practice, of course, premiums exceed actuarial levels, allowing firms to cover operating costs and to earn profits.

11   Insurance markets in which insurance companies face recognizable bankruptcy risks have been analyzed in recent papers, for example Phillips, Cummins and Allen [1998] and Cummins and Mahul [2003]. Shareholders will particularly wish to avoid bankruptcy risks if the insurance firm has significant "going-concern value" based on its franchise in other, non-catastrophic, insurance lines.

12   See Froot [2001] for an empirical description of the limited capital available to the catastrophe insurance industry, and an additional analysis of why this is the case.

13   The list pertains only to US insurance firms, based on US accounting, insurance, and tax regulations. The regulations that apply, for example, to European Union insurance firms are different.

14   US casualty insurance firms can take tax deductions for claims paid, and even for anticipated payments when the loss event has already occurred. However, when very large catastrophic events actually do occur, the firm may well end up with negative net income for tax purposes, and thus the tax deduction will be fully usable only as a tax loss carry forward against future positive income. This feature reduces the present value of the tax deduction.

15   It is a fair question to ask why a firm with a cash trove takes on such exceptional value, that is, a value beyond its net cash position. The likely answer is that capital market imperfections make it easier to obtain such cash when it is within an established firm, as opposed to the task of borrowing the same amount directly from a bank. Whatever the reason, it seems an established fact that a firm with a large amount of unprotected cash may face a high takeover risk.

16   See Froot [2001] for further discussion of the limited role played by reinsurers in supporting the US markets for disaster insurance following the Andrew Hurricane and Northridge Earthquake.

17   See McGhee [2002] for a good description of the historical development of the catastrophe bond market, as well as an accessible, but detailed, discussion of how the bonds work and the current shortcomings that must be resolved.

18   In recent versions of catastrophe bonds, the repayment of principal to investors is deferred for a long period, but is not literally cancelled. The credit ratings provided on catastrophe bonds have improved as a result of this change.

19   Froot [2001] discusses of the development of the catastrophe bond market and the observed pricing patterns.

20   Bantal and Kunreuther [2000], Kunreuther, Michel-Kerjan, and Porter [2003], and Kunreuther and Michel-Kerjan [2004] discuss a variety of factors that have so far precluded the emergence of a fully effective market in catastrophe bonds.

21   The US Government Accounting Office [2003] indicates that at year-end 2002, catastrophe bonds outstanding equaled less than 3% of the total reinsurance in force on a worldwide

basis. The report also draws a pessimistic conclusion regarding the likelihood of using catastrophe bonds to support terrorism insurance in the near future. The only explicit terrorism catastrophe bond issued to date provides very specialized coverage for the World Cup football games to be held in Germany in 2006.

22   Opportunistic entries by insurance firms controlled by Warren Buffett and his holding company Berkshire Hathaway are particularly telling, since his firms have access to ample capital and his leadership precludes normal agency issues; see Buffett [1996] and [2001]. His National Indemnity firm significantly under-priced the competition to provide reinsurance to the California Earthquake Authority, the quasi government entity created in the aftermath of the 1994 Northridge Earthquake. Buffett's firm was also one of the few to offer terrorism insurance, for selected risks and under specified conditions, following the terrorist attack of September 11, 2001, even though its General Reinsurance subsidiary suffered significant losses due to that attack.

23   See Bantal and Kunreuther [2000], Hogarth [2002], and Kunreuther and Michel-Kerjan [2004] for discussions of ambiguity aversion in the context of catastrophic events. Jaffee and Russell [2003] describe a range of behavioral factors that may impact the willingness of insurance companies to provide catastrophe coverage.

24   Cummins and Lewis [2003] provide a discussion of the similarities in market reactions to the Andrew Hurricane, the Northridge Earthquake, and the 9/11 attack. There is general agreement that the market for terrorism insurance became disrupted–including both rising prices and limited availability--following 9/11, but there is disagreement whether this should be characterized as a market failure. The US Government Accounting Office and various real estate and trade groups tended to consider it a market failure (see US Government Accounting Office [2002]), while other observers offer a contrary view (see for example Smetters [2003]).

25   In the case of hurricane and earthquake risks in the US, government agencies are also very knowledgeable (the US National Weather Service for hurricanes, and the US Geological Survey for earthquakes), and both agencies must and do release their information in publicly available reports.

26   For discussion of the strategies that might be employed by terrorists, and the implications for the nature of the risks and the impact on terrorism insurance, see Woo [2002], as well his other papers and other reports on the web site of Risk Management Solutions, at *http://rms.com/* .

27   With a bottomry contract, the lender (and insurer) provided the shipowner with funds to purchase the ship and the inventory of tradable goods. If the ship returned safely, the lender received the loan principal back with interest. But if the ship were lost at sea, then the lender received no repayment at all from the shipowner–this is the insurance component. This pattern of payoffs to the lender is identical to that of a modern catastrophe bond.

28   The willingness of private insurance firms to re-enter the US markets for hurricane and earthquake insurance following extended periods in which no new unexpected losses have occurred is consistent with a moderation of the modelling uncertainty that arose immediately following the initial events.

29   It is possible, however, that another government entity might "takeover" the capital resources of a disaster insurance agency. In fact, this has happened at least twice, in both cases where the government took the capital assets in the context of a budgetary crisis. One

case occurred in New Zealand in 1990, when the earthquake fund was taken, the other in the US state of Hawaii in 2003, when the state wind damage agency was closed (under Hawaii House Bill 1466).

30   See Bantwal and Kunreuther [2000], Kunreuther, Michel-Kerjan, and Porter [2003], and Kunreuther and Michel-Kerjan [2004] for discussions of ambiguity aversion and similar behavioral traits that have plagued the development of an active market in catastrophe bonds.

31   Although the report's analysis appears valid, it is worth noting that it is in the best interests of the industry to conclude that the US government provision of a reinsurance facility be continued (at zero cost to the industry).

32   The coverage is provided under two different programs. The Property Tax and Compensation Fund provides property and casualty insurance, funded by a mandatory national property tax. The Law for the Victims of Enemy Action covers life and medical insurance, and is funded by the government's standard health insurance program.

33   This result is not likely explained by consumer expectations of *ex post* aid, since the same expectations would have been present prior to the Northridge quake. This result is also not likely explained by consumer concern that the CEA will not be able to pay claims in the face of a very large event. Here, the contrary evidence comes from the Hawaii Hurricane Relief Fund (HHRF), which was structured in a manner very similar to the CEA, and faced a similar low level of demand. In an attempt to raise demand, the HHRF offered a new policy backed by higher levels of reinsurance, but also requiring a higher premium. Very little demand appeared for this higher quality coverage.

34   The initial CEA contract required a deductible equal to 15% of the amount covered. More recently, a 10% deductible option was introduced (at a higher premium), but this has created only limited additional demand.

35   Information about the plans has been taken from a variety of sources, including Kunreuther [2002], Russell [2002], US Government Accounting Office [2002], Swiss Re [2003], Kunreuther and Michel-Kerjan [2004], Michel-Kerjan and Pedell [2004], and OECD [2004]. Each country plan also has a useful web page. The French plan for terrorism insurance, GAREAT (Gestion de l'Assurance et de la Réassurance des Risques Attentats et Actes de Terrorisme), is integrated with the French plan for natural disasters CCR (Caisse Centrale de Réassurance).

36   Many of the features that are described here for terrorism insurance are also reflected in the plans for earthquake insurance in Japan and New Zealand, and in the Florida hurricane reinsurance program, see US CBO [2002].

37   Mandatory participation may also appear as a way to force the private sector to provide a specific type of coverage. In California, for example, firms offering home owner's insurance were required to provide an earthquake option. In France, firms offering commercial property insurance are required to include terrorism coverage. Such regulatory "tie-in" arrangements, however, break down if the private firms are prepared to leave the market entirely, in order to avoid the tie-in (which happened in California after the Northridge Earthquake and in France after the 9/11 event). On the other hand, Switzerland has a similar requirement for the provision of natural disaster (but not earthquake) insurance and this appears to be working well, without any further direct government intervention.

38   Spain represents one case where both the provision of terrorism insurance and participation in the government plan are mandatory; see OECD [2004].

39   Crowding out could, however, evolve over time, in the sense that the private market might have recovered were it not for the existing government program. This possibility is discussed below in Section 4.A.

40   In the US, state insurance regulators often have significant power to approve premium levels on consumer policies (such as auto and homeowner insurance). In most cases, however, for commercial lines, which are relevant to the terrorism coverage discussed here, significant premium regulation does not occur.

41   Russell [2002] points out, for example that the reimbursement structure of the US TRIA plan will cause primary insurers to treat small and large terrorism risks very similarly. He leaves it as an open question whether this represents an intentional subsidy to large cities, perhaps based on the expected economic benefits of agglomeration.

42   For the US plan, the government reinsurance facility does cover losses from a CBNR terrorism attack. However, a US Treasury ruling noted that while US insurance firms are required to offer terrorism insurance, they are not required to offer coverage against CBNR terrorism attacks unless separately required by State law.

43   By contributing the capital and joining the California Earthquake Authority (CEA), the firms satisfied the state law requiring any firm offering homeowner's insurance also to offer earthquake insurance. The CEA members maintain limited liability with respect to earthquake losses that exceed the financial resources directly held by the CEA.

44   Brown, Cummins, Lewis and Ran [2003] show that the stock market prices of US insurance firms dealing with terrorism risks generally declined as the passage of the US government intervention (TRIA) became more assured. This suggests that stock market investors, at least, did not consider TRIA to be a net benefit for the insurance industry.

45   For a parallel discussion, see also Smetters [2003].

46   See Guiso and Appelli [1998] for a formal analysis of the impact of uninsurable risks on the demand for insurable risks.

47   To be clear, in our example, while consumers will substitute the available Terrorism insurance for the unavailable War insurance, the total demand (War and Terrorism insurance combined) should decline when War insurance becomes unavailable.

48   This changes if the loss can be sufficiently large to force the company into bankruptcy. In this case, it would be appropriate to buy insurance in order to avoid bankruptcy, or more specifically to avoid the extra costs that are created by a bankruptcy.

49   In addition to avoiding bankruptcy costs, as described in the previous footnote, the academic literature notes that it may become rational for public companies to purchase casualty insurance if stock market investors interpret the stock price declines created by a casualty losses as reflecting negatively on the firm or on the firm's management in a more fundamental sense.

50   This raises the question, of course, why mortgage lenders require hurricane insurance in Florida, but not earthquake insurance in California. The answer seems to be that earthquake damage on a wood-frame house rarely exceeds the 20% equity stake required of homebuyers by mortgage lenders, whereas hurricanes readily create a complete loss. In this context, it also becomes more understandable why California consumers balk at the high deductibles required on earthquake insurance.

51   See Barker [2003] for a more general analysis of the welfare aspects of terrorism insurance, with a particular focus on whether the government prices involve an element of subsidy.

52   The programs in France, Germany, and the US provide no risk-based pricing. The UK program now creates 2 pricing zones across the entire UK, with uniform pricing across structure types.

53   This is sometimes described as the *Samaritan's Dilemma*, see Buchanan [1975]. This and related drawbacks to such government intervention are discussed in Brown, Kroszner, and Jenn [2002].

54   The discussion in this section is based in part on Jaffee and Russell [2003].

55   See Cummins, Lalonde and Phillips [2003] for a discussion that suggests the basis risk created by aggregate triggers on reinsurance instruments may be manageable for insurance firms.

References

Arrow, Kenneth, "Uncertainty and the Welfare Economics of Medical Care," *American Economic Review*, 53, pp. 941-973, 1963.

Bantwal, Vivek and Howard Kunreuther, "A Cat Bond Premium Puzzle," *Journal of Psychology and Financial Markets*, Vol. 1, No.1 76-91, 2000.

Barker, David, "Terrorism Insurance Subsidies and Social Welfare," *Journal of Urban Economics*," 54, 328-338, 2003.

Bowers, Barbara, "Creative New Uses for Catastrophe Bonds Help General More Capital, Deals, and Investors," *Best's Review*, June 2004.

Brown, Jeffrey, David Cummins, Christopher Lewis and Wei Ran, "An Empirical Analysis of the Economic Impact of Federal Terrorism Reinsurance, Working Paper, Department of Insurance and Risk Management, The Wharton School, 2003.

Brown, Jeffrey, Randall Kroszner, and Brian Jenn, "Federal Terrorism Risk Insurance, NBER Working Paper No 9271, 2002.

Buchanan, James M. "The Samaritan's Dilemma." In *Altruism, Morality and Economic Theory*, edited by E.S. Phelps,71-85. New York: Russell Sage Foundation, 1975.

Buffett, Warren E. Chairman of the Board, Berkshire Hathaway, to the Shareholders of Berkshire Hathaway, 2001, available at http://www.berkshirehathaway.com/2001ar/impnote01.html.

Buffett, Warren E., Chairman of the Board, Berkshire Hathaway, Annual Report to Shareholders, Management Discussion, 1996 , available at:
http://www.berkshirehathaway.com/1996ar/mda.html.

Collins Center for Public Policy, *Final Report of the Academic Task Force on Hurricane Catastrophe Insurance* (Tallahassee, Fla.: Collins Center for Public Policy, 1995).

Cummins, David and Neil Doherty, "Federal Terrorism Reinsurance: An Analysis of Issues and program Design Alternatives, paper presented at NBER Insurance Conference, 2002.

Cummins, J. David, Neil Doherty, and Anita Lo, "Can Insurers Pay for the "Big One'? Measuring the Capacity of the Insurance Industry to Respond to Catastrophic Losses", *Journal of Banking and Finance*, 26, 557-583, 2002.

Cummins, David, David Lalonde, and Richard Phillips, "The Basic Risk of Catastrophic-loss Index Securities," Financial Institutions Center, Working Paper 00-22-B-B, 2000.

Cummins, David and Christopher Lewis, "Catastrophic Events, Parameter Uncertainty and the Breakdown of Implicit Long-Term Contracting: The Case of Terrorism Insurance," *The Journal of Risk and Uncertainty*, 26:2/3: 153-179, 2003.

Cummins, David, Christopher Lewis, and Richard Phillips, "Pricing Excess of Loss Reinsurance Contracts Against Catastrophic Loss," in Kenneth A. Froot, ed., *The Financing of Catastrophe Risk*, Chicago: University of Chicago Press, 1999.

Cummins, David and Oliver Mahul, "Optimal Insurance with Divergent Beliefs About Insurer total Default Risk," *The Journal of Risk and Uncertainty*, 27:2: 121-138, 2003.

Froot, Kenneth A., "The Market for Catastrophe Risk: A Clinical Examination," *Journal of Financial Economics*, 60, 529-571, 2001.

Gollier, Christian "Insurability" (paper presented at the National Bureau of Economic Research Conference on Insurance, Cambridge, Mass., February 1, 2002).

Guiso, Luigi and Tullio Jappeli, "Background Uncertainty and the Demand for Insurance Against Insurable Risks, *The Geneva Papers on Risk and Insurance Theory*, 23: 7-27 1998.

Gron, Anne and Andrew Winton, "Risk Overhang and Market Behavior," *Journal of Business*, vol. 74, No. 4 (October 2001), pp. 591-612.

Gron, Anne and Deborah Lucas, "External Financing and Insurance Cycles," in David F. Bradford, ed., The Economics of *Property-Casualty Insurance* (Chicago: University of Chicago Press, 1998), pp. 5-27.

Harrington, Scott E. "Rethinking Disaster Policy,"*Regulation,* vol. 23, No. 1 (2000), pp. 40-46.

Harrington, Scott E. and Greg Niehaus, "Government Insurance, Tax Policy, and the Affordability and Availability of Catastrophe Insurance), Journal of Insurance Regulation, 19, pp. 591-612, Summer, 2001.

Harrington, Scott E. and Greg Niehaus, "Capital, Corporate Income Taxes, and Catastrophe Insurance, *Journal of Financial Intermediation*, 12, pp. 365-389, 2003.

Hartwig, Robert, "September 11, 2001: The First Year," Insurance Information Institute, 2002.

Hirshleifer, Jack, "War Damage Insurance," *The Review of Economics and Statistics,* Volume 35, Issue, 144-153, May 1953.

Hogarth, Robin, "Insurance and Safety After September 11: Has the World become a "Riskier' Place?" Social Science Research Council, On Line Essays at http://www.ssrc.org/sept11/essays/hogarth.htm.

Jaffee, Dwight and Thomas Russell. "Catastrophe Insurance, Capital Markets, and Uninsurable Risks." *Journal of Risk and Insurance* 64 No.2 (June, 1997): 205-230.

Jaffee, Dwight and Thomas Russell, "Markets Under Stress: The Case of Extreme Event Insurance," in Richard Arnott, Bruce Greenwald, Ravi Kanbur, and Barry Nalebuff editors, *Economics for an Imperfect World: Essays in Honor of Joseph E. Stiglitz*, MIT Press [2003].

Keohane, Nathaniel and Richard Zeckhauser, "The Ecology of Terror Defense," *The Journal of Risk and Uncertainty*, 26:2/3; 201-229, 2003.

Kunreuther, Howard, "The Role of Insurance in Managing Extreme Events: Implications for Terrorism Coverage," *Business Economics,* National Association for Business Economics, April 2002.

Kunreuther, Howard and Geoffrey Heal, "Interdependent Security," *The Journal of Risk and Uncertainty*, 26:2/3; 231-249, 2003a.

Kunreuther, Howard and Geoffrey Heal, "You Only Die Once: Managing Discrete Interdependent Risks," NBER Working Paper No. w9885, August 2003b.

Kunreuther, Howard, and Erwann Michel-Kerjan, "Dealing with Extreme Events: New Challenges for Terrorism Risk Coverage in the US," Working Paper 04-09, Risk Management and Decision Process Center, University of Pennsylvania, April 2004.

Kunreuther, Howard, Erwann Michel-Kerjan, and Beverly Porter, "Assessing, Managing and Financing Extreme Events: Dealing with Terrorism, "National Bureau of Economic Research Working Paper No. 10179, December 2003.

Kunreuther, Howard and Mark Pauly, "Neglecting Disaster: Why Don't People Insurance Against Large Losses", *The Journal of Risk and Uncertainty,* 28-1, 5-21, 2004.

Lewis, Christopher and Kevin Murdock, "The Role of Government Contracts in Discretionary Reinsurance Markets for Natural Disasters," *Journal of Risk and Insurance,* vol. 63, No. 4 (1996), pp. 567-597.

Lewis, Christopher and Kevin Murdock, "Alternative Means of Redistributing Catastrophic Risk in a National Risk-Management System," in Kenneth A. Froot, ed., *The Financing of Catastrophe Risk* (Chicago: University of Chicago Press, 1999), pp. 51-85.

Marsh & McLennan, "As Costs Come Down, Businesses Warm to Terrorism Insurance–One Firm in Three Buys Coverage," *News Release*, May 10, 2004.

McGhee, Christopher, "Risk-Linked Securities: Increasing Catastrophe Coverage for Consumers and Businesses," Viewpoint (a Marsh and McLennan Company Journal), Volume XXXI, Number 2, 2002.

Merton, Robert, and Zvi Bodie, "The Design of Financial Systems: Towards a Synthesis of Function and Structure, National Bureau of Economic Research Working Paper No 10620, June 2004.

Michel-Kerjan, Erwann, and Burkhard Pedell, "Terrorism Risk Coverage After 9/11: A Comparison of New Public-Private Partnerships in France, Germany, and the US," Working Paper, Risk Management and Decision Process Center, University of Pennsylvania, 2004.

Moss, David A. , "Courting Disaster? The Transformation of Federal Disaster Policy Since 1803," in Kenneth A. Froot, ed., *The Financing of Catastrophe Risk* (Chicago: University of Chicago Press, 1999), pp. 307-355.

Nutter, Frank., "The Role of Government in Financing Catastrophes, *The Geneva Papers on Risk and* Insurance, vol. 27, No. 2, 283-289, April 2002.

OECD [2004], "Terrorism Risk Insurance Schemes in OECD Countries – Comparative Table."

Phillips, Richard, David Cummins, and Franklin Allen (1998), "The Financial Pricing of Insurance the Multiple-Line Insurance Company," *Journal of Risk and Insurance*, Vol 65, pp. 597-636.

Priest, George "The Government, the Market, and the Problem of Catastrophic Loss," *Journal of Risk and Uncertainty*, vol. 12, No. 2/3 (1996), pp. 219-237.

Russell, Thomas, "The Costs and Benefits of the Terrorism Risk Insurance Act: A First Look," NBER Insurance Conference paper 2003, available at http://www.nber.org/~confer/2003/insurance03/russell.pdf.

Smetters, Kent, "Insuring Against Terrorism: The Policy Challenge, presented at the 2004 Conference of the Brookings-Wharton Papers on Financial Services.

Swiss Re, "Natural Catastrophe and Man-Made Disasters in 2003," *Sigma*, No. 1/2004.

Swiss Re, "Terrorism Risks In Property Insurance and their Insurability after 11 September, 2001," available at http://www.swissre.com/ under Publications/Risk Perception/Terrorism Risks.

Towers Perrin, "Workers' Compensation Terrorism Reinsurance Pool Feasibility Study," March 2004, on line at http://www.towersperrin.com/tillinghast/publications/reports/WC_Terr_Pool/WC_Terr_Pool_Study.pdf.

US Congressional Budget Office, *Federal Reinsurance for Terrorism Risks,* CBO Paper, October 2001.

US Congressional Budget Office, *Federal Reinsurance for Disasters,* CBO Study, September, 2002.

US Department of Justice, Press Release, "Final Regulations of September 11th Compensation Announced," March 7, 2002.

US General Accounting Office, "Terrorism Insurance: Rising Uninsured Exposure to Attacks Heightens Potential Economic Vulnerabilities, Statement of Richard J. Hillman." GAO-02-472T, 2002.

US General Accounting Office, "Catastrophe Insurance Risks, The Role of Risk-Linked Securities and Factors Affecting Their Use, GAO-02-941, September, 2002.

US General Accounting Office, "Catastrophe Insurance Risks, Status of Efforts to Securitize Natural Catastrophe and Terrorism Risk, GAO-03, 1033, 2003.

US General Accounting Office, "Terrorism Insurance, Effects of the Terrorism Risk Insurance Act of 2002, Statement of Richard Hillman, GAO-04-720T, April 2004a.

US General Accounting Office, "Terrorism Insurance, Effects of the Terrorism Risk Insurance Act of 2002, Statement of Richard Hillman, GAO-04-806T, May 2004b.

Woo, Gordon "Quantifying Insurance Terrorism Risk" (paper presented at the National Bureau of Economic Research Conference on Insurance, Cambridge, Mass., February 1, 2002), available at: http://rms.com/NewsPress/Quantifying_Insurance_Terrorism_Risk.pdf.

Chapter 9

THE COVERAGE OF TERRORISM RISKS AT NATIONAL LEVEL[*]

This Report deals with certain general features of terrorism insurance in OECD member countries and, in greater detail, with the creation and development of specific terrorism insurance schemes in the eight OECD countries in which they now operate (Australia, Austria, France, Germany, the Netherlands, Spain, the United Kingdom and the United States).

After an introduction covering various general issues, the Report deals with developments over OECD countries as a whole and then with the main features of terrorism acts covered by the different schemes, before going on to focus on the specific features of the schemes for terrorism insurance in the eight countries mentioned above. The Report then analyses each of the schemes in terms of its history and purpose; definitions; operation, extent, lines covered and perils covered; exclusions; state involvement and layers of cover; non-state reinsurance/retrocession; extent of compulsory insurance; and period of operation.

In its final sections, the report draws some conclusions on the common problems faced and how these have been resolved, including a final section pointing to areas of good practice that other countries, within and beyond OECD, may regard as worthy of attention.

---

[*] This report was written by Mr. John Cooke, International Economic Relations Consultant, London (UK). The data in this report is current as of mid-May 2005.

1. Introduction

1.1. Background

The period since the destruction of the World Trade Center has demonstrated its steadily widening effects in terms of reactions and responses in individual insurance markets. Within the first weeks afterwards it became clear that the scale of the losses represented the biggest ever insurance claim and exceeded any comparable recent catastrophe. In addition, September 11 occurred at a time of significant volatility, both in world stock markets and in property/casualty premium rates. All these factors together contributed to a widening ripple of economic effects in national insurance markets, bearing down on the operations of non-life insurers and life assurers alike.

It was only gradually, and at varying speeds, that governments and insurance industries in different markets both within and outside OECD appreciated the full extent of changes flowing from September 11. But, in terms of the prospects for terrorism coverage at national level, a number of factors became identifiable relatively soon:

- a sudden alteration in the perception of "risk". True, "risk" may always have been viewed as possibly including suicidal perpetrators of destruction: but a change of scale became evident, taking account of the potential for thousands of civilian casualties, and of the possible use of biological, chemical or nuclear weapons;

- the emergence of a new debate as to whether there might be a fresh and different class of risks arising from actions akin to acts of war, and whether such "risks tantamount to war risks", ought to be regarded as different in kind, as well as in degree, from conventionally insurable risks. In the event, an approach of this kind, focusing on identifying a new definition of "risks tantamount to war risks", proved not to be helpful; and in most markets it was not pursued. But the debate was necessary and instructive. It is likely to re-emerge, in some form or other, if or when there were another major terrorist occurrence, because the question of whether certain risks are, by their nature, different in kind, remains in contention;

- a shift in conceptions of the cumulative magnitude of possible losses. The losses on 11 September were greater than previously envisaged in disaster scenarios, involving cumulative consequences going further beyond a specific risk than previously imaginable;

- an increased focus on the role and responsibility of commercial enterprises involved in higher risks (such as tall premises), and the need for them to cater for novel hazards through disaster recovery plans. For their part, insurers in virtually all national markets, towards market pricing that took greater and move explicit account of their commercial clients' approach to disaster contingency planning;

- a shift by insurers towards more rigorous and detailed disaggregation and pricing of the types of risk and liabilities defined and underwritten in insurance policies, with a more cautious approach towards covering certain hazards previously regarded as routine;

- a consequent sharp reduction in the availability and/or affordability of certain types of insurance, including compulsory classes of cover, as reinsurers and direct insurers alike took measures to reduce or shed completely their terrorism risks;

- a realisation that there was a new phenomenon of uninsurability, and a perception that, "as any potential terrorist event moves farther into the future and primary insurers are successful at shedding more, even if not all, of their terrorism risks, any losses will be increasingly left to affected businesses, their employees, lenders, suppliers and customers. These entities lack the ability to spread such risks among themselves as insurers can"[1].

All of these factors played their part in the development, post September 11, of new approaches to the coverage of terrorism risks at national level. They led to wide acceptance by governments and insurers alike that, even in peacetime and in markets with strong domestic insurance industries, there were limits to the extent to which conventional insurance could be relied upon to cover huge and cumulative hazards that were not amenable to traditional modelling or assessment. Hence governments faced a choice of whether to "stand behind" their insurance industries, as insurer or financier of last resort, if such hazards were to continue to be insurable, or whether to accept that the risks in question might be transferred to individuals and entities in civil society, on an uninsured basis.

1.2. Structure of the Report

The present Report on the coverage of terrorism risk at national level is designed to offer a detailed description and analysis of national schemes that have been established to insure or compensate damages entailed by terrorism. This Report accordingly covers the following elements:

- main features of terrorism acts covered;

- terrorism insurance in OECD countries;

- specific schemes for terrorism insurance in OECD countries, including:

   - insurance lines covered;

   - whether terrorism insurance has been made compulsory (obligation for individuals/corporations to be insured and/or obligation for insurance companies to cover insurance risks);

   - the various "layers" of cover (policyholder deductible, insurer retention, reinsurance, governmental backing (when relevant), rationale and functioning of the layer system, choice of intervention thresholds, etc.);

- Good practice – in theory and practice, for the attention of countries that have no specific terrorism insurance scheme or that contemplate the modification of the scheme currently enforced;

- Conclusions.

2. Main Features of Terrorism Acts Covered

2.1. Definitions: General Questions

Given the separate OECD Recommendation on a check-list of criteria to define terrorism for the purpose of compensation, this Report need not offer a detailed study of the problems arising in defining terrorism in terms of acts by individuals or groups with or without political intent. Suffice it to say that defining terrorism has proved to be a difficult exercise. As the OECD conclusions make clear, past work on a general definition of terrorism has often been controversial, and no consensual definition has emerged at the international level. Decision makers in the insurance sector seeking a workable definition have therefore sometimes had recourse to definitions used at national level, in criminal law for instance. More often however they have elaborated definitions tailored to the specific constraints of insurance and/or compensation operations. In the meantime, the question of definition, as guidance for private entities, remains open in many countries where no definition has been agreed at national level through, for instance, insurance associations.

2.2 Definitions: Elements of Commonality and Divergence in OECD Countries

Nor need this Report offer a detailed study of how definitions may vary from one OECD member to another, as these are also covered by a separate document. Definitions vary, reflecting each member's legal system, history, and approach to distinguishing between statutory definitions of terrorism as a crime and insurance definitions of terrorism as a risk. In the majority of members there is a statutory definition (whether located in criminal law or in legal measures providing for terrorism insurance and reinsurance), although in a significant minority of members the task of definition has been left with the insurance industry. Most members' definitions have common elements in terms of aim (an ideologically motivated act) and actors (individual or group). There is somewhat greater divergence as to means used (commonly physical violence or threat of physical violence; sometimes intimidation or terror; sometimes not specified). There is also divergence as to targets (sometimes people and goods; sometimes unspecified). The newer the definition, the wider its likely scope: older definitions tend to focus on targeting human life and property by means of weaponry or explosions, while newer definitions often go wider, covering biological, chemical and nuclear contamination and psychological terror.

2.3. Definitions: Checklist of Key Elements

Whatever the difficulty of these and other considerations, it is clear that an acceptable definition of terrorism lies at the heart of establishing any terrorism insurance regime. The OECD has developed a checklist of elements of a definition for the purpose of compensation, arranged under a number of criteria (means and effects; intention; technical insurability; economic insurability; legal/regulatory insurability; compensability by the state; and/or compensability through non-governmental mechanisms). Among these criteria, the criterion of technical insurability merits particular comment, having regard to the terrorism insurance schemes that have developed in certain OECD member states. True, assessability of risks (in terms of quantifiable probability, frequency and severity of losses) must always be one of the key yardsticks of technical insurability. But its importance is not equal or identical for private sector entities and government entities that may be involved in covering terrorism risks:

- For private sector insurers, prospective assessability is a prerequisite: private sector insurers cannot cover risks where the probability, frequency and severity of losses cannot be satisfactorily assessed in advance, and the correct premium charged.

- For government insurers (as financiers/insurers of last resort) assessability may be retrospective: if a government entity is providing the ultimate layer of cover in the form of, effectively, a loan from potentially unlimited contingent capital, it has the option of charging an initial premium which may or may not be finely calculated, relying on its ability to recoup the balance of retrospectively-assessed losses over an extended repayment period.

Although government practice in relation to prospective and retrospective assessability varies widely, the distinction between prospective and retrospective assessability will emerge repeatedly as one of the factors inherent in the varying structure of different state-backed terrorism insurance schemes under study.

3. Terrorism Insurance in OECD Countries

3.1. General Features

It is not easy to give a detailed view of developments in terrorism insurance across all OECD countries, particularly those countries where no specific terrorism insurance scheme has been introduced. The general picture is of course well known, and reflects the position stated in the introduction to this Report: a shift by insurers and reinsurers towards more rigorous and detailed disaggregation and pricing of the types of risk and liabilities defined and underwritten in insurance and reinsurance policies, with a more cautious approach towards covering certain hazards previously regarded as routine, accompanied by a consequent sharp reduction in the availability and/or affordability of certain types of insurance, including compulsory classes of cover, as reinsurers and direct insurers alike took measures to reduce or shed completely their terrorism risks.

The precise effect of these developments in different OECD markets – and in particular the price of cover, when available – is however difficult to research and quantify. The reasons for this are unsurprising. Although the period since September 2001 now runs to more than three years, reliable historic data (which always lags by a considerable period) is only beginning to be available for insurance markets over the start of the period (mainly for 2001-03) and is not yet available on a reliable comparable basis.

3.2. Extent of Cover for Terrorism Acts in OECD Members

Certain features emerge as tending to be prevalent over OECD markets as a whole. A key driver in most markets has been the changed attitude of reinsurers towards reinsurance cover for terrorism risks. This manifested itself at different times in different markets, depending on renewal dates for insurance contracts. In many OECD markets the change came on 1 January 2002; but in certain others the change was less immediate (*e.g.* Japan, where renewal dates tended to coincide with the end of the fiscal year on 31 March 2002).

The overall effect of this change was to reduce the availability and affordability of reinsurance cover for terrorism risks, with consequently higher retentions by direct insurers. Again, the extent of the change manifested itself in different ways in different markets, depending on the demand for terrorism cover and the willingness of direct insurers to compete to supply it: in the Greek insurance market, for instance, where no terrorism exclusion applied before September 11, and where direct insurers have continued to offer terrorism cover (as a competitive matter) despite the withdrawal of reinsurance, there has been a dramatic shift of ultimate financial responsibility for terrorism claims from reinsurers to insurers. It is estimated that while reinsurers provided 69% of Greek terrorism insurance capacity up to 31 December 2001, their involvement was reduced to less than one percent from 1 January 2002.

Nonetheless, the overall effect of these developments appears to be that there is a certain balance between supply and demand for terrorism insurance at the time being (mid-2004) in those OECD countries without a specific terrorism insurance scheme. A number of factors appear to have contributed to the general absence of a supply crisis that might otherwise be expected. First, despite the known risks of terrorism, may businesses, particularly small and medium-sized enterprises, do not appear to be regarded as significant risks and are not therefore excluded from cover: the Scandinavian markets (Denmark, Finland, Norway and Sweden), to take one example, appear generally to conform to this. Secondly, cover appears to be available, at a price, where it is required. It has to be said, however, that these market circumstances probably owe a good deal to the fact that no really significant terrorist incident has occurred since September 11 in an OECD market without a specific terrorism insurance scheme. If such a market were to suffer a significant incident, the balance of future supply and demand would probably be very severely tested.

Against that background, it is worth examining two major OECD insurance markets that have no specific terrorism insurance scheme, Italy and Japan:

Italy

The majority of insurance policies covering property damage in Italy exclude terrorism risks where the total sum insured is in excess of €50 million. As risks in the personal lines sector and small to medium-sized risks in the commercial lines market generally fall within this limit, the options open to insurance companies are fairly restricted. Insurers usually apply a terrorism exclusion clause to policies covering property risks with a total sum insured in excess of €50 million and/or for top locations with values in excess of €50 million. Throughout 2002 insureds with large industrial risks have had to seek terrorism cover through facultative reinsurance. If available at all, terrorism cover in excess of €50 million was very costly.

In 2003, however, the Associazone Nazionale fra le Imprese Assicuratrici (ANIA, the Italian association of insurers) submitted a proposal to the government to create a tax-exempt joint-liability insurance/reinsurance Pool, on the analogy of the Italian Environmental Damage Liability Insurance Pool. Insurers joining the Pool (which would be open to all Italian and foreign insurance undertakings operating in Italy with policies operational on Italian national territory) would insert in their policies identical terrorism definition wordings[2] approved by the Pool. The Pool would cover direct and indirect claims (provided that the latter were contingent on risks directly covered) from private natural and legal persons for property risks including fire and technological hazards (subject to certain exclusions)[3], provided that the base policies do not explicitly exclude the coverage of indirect damage. ANIA envisaged a Pool of indefinite duration, subject to review of its capacity, rules and *modus operandi*, probably after an initial period of two years.

The administration of the Pool would be in the hands of the pool administrator (managing financial, administrative, accounting and IT matters) while the Pool itself would be responsible for technical matters including conditions, rates (calibrated by risk the premium), exclusions, and reinsurance decisions. Ceding insurers would remain responsible for claims (except where a Cooperation Clause required the active involvement of the Pool in the event of serious claims exceeding a certain threshold). Premiums paid by primary insurers to the Pool would be kept in a temporary fund for 7-10 years. In the event of a surplus, the capital would be used to either return premium paid by the primary insurers or to reimburse the government, if the latter had had to intervene in the payment of losses.

It is understood that the Italian legislative process has so far proved an obstacle to bringing the proposed Italian Pool to fruition.

Japan

In the case of Japan, the adverse effect of September 11 needs to be seen against the background of the prolonged stagnation of the Japanese economy. Reviews by the Marine and Fire Insurance Association of Japan (currently the General Insurance Association of Japan) concluded, after successive revisions, that estimates of losses arising from September 11 totalled approximately 143 billion yen at the end of March 2002. The business results for fiscal 2001 (April 2001-March 2002) of non-life insurers accounting for 95% of the total Japanese market showed an increase in net premiums of 0.4 % (6,811.8 billion yen) and a 0.4% improvement in the average loss ratio, thanks to decreased losses from natural catastrophes. However, both ordinary profits and net profits went into the red for the first time since fiscal 1947. Ordinary profits fell by 137.5%, and net profits by 249.4%, as a result of the overlap of two specific factors: first, the increase in claims payments and the provision of outstanding loss reserves caused by the impact of overseas reinsurance losses including those related to the terrorist attacks on September 11; and, secondly, the large losses caused by the devaluation of the book value of securities due to a fall in stock prices. (All these losses were treated by Japanese insurers as expenses in fiscal 2001 account, and so did not have an impact on business in fiscal 2002).

"War risks" such as war and civil war are commonly excluded in the general policy conditions for ordinary Japanese non-life insurance products. However, acts of terrorism are generally treated differently, and many Japanese non-life insurance companies cover acts of terrorism under general policy conditions. There were no exclusion clauses for acts of terrorism in

Japanese insurance policies before 31 March 2002 (the usual insurance and reinsurance renewal date, linked to the year-end financial closing). Since then, many non-life insurance companies have set limits on terrorism losses to be covered under renewed contracts for commercial risks, matching the trend in world-wide reinsurance markets, as follows:

- Threshold Terrorism Exclusions: these vary in their operation. For property insurances where the sum insured exceeds 1 billion yen, a special exclusion clause operates, and terrorism risks will not be covered even from the first loss. Property insurances for factory risk with an insured amount exceeding 1.5 billion yen carry the same exclusion. In other cases (*e.g.* miscellaneous pecuniary loss comprehensive insurance for corporations, business interruption insurance and business continuing expenses insurance), many contracts with an insured amount exceeding 1.5 billion yen exclude terrorism risks.

- General Exclusions: Many insurers exclude terrorism cover in other contracts (*e.g.* movable comprehensive insurance, contractors' all risks insurance, machinery and erection insurance), irrespective of the amount insured.

In other insurance contracts however (*e.g.* commercial fire insurance for sums insured within the limits mentioned above, automobile insurance, personal accident insurance and insurance for personal risks) there appear to be no exclusions for terrorism risks.

Together with these changes, the Japanese non-life insurance industry also recognised the importance of strengthening insurers' overall operational management through scrutiny of business operations (including the proper retention of risks appropriate to insurers' capacity, the proper operation of risk management and the provision of adequate disclosure in a timely manner to respond to the rapid changes in business conditions) and more specific attention to reinsurance (including selection of reinsurers, matters to be considered in underwriting reinsurance contracts, and figures for reinsurance underwritten by line).

The Japanese insurance market has also pressed for the creation of an industry-wide terrorism risk pool. Under the Insurance Business Law, concerted actions are limited to a joint reinsurance pool for ordinary insurance, and such joint actions are restricted to common decisions on conditions of reinsurance contracts, amount of reinsurance transactions, reinsurance premium rates, reinsurance commissions (slightly more relaxed rules apply to earthquake insurance for dwellings, compulsory motor insurance, aviation insurance and some nuclear energy insurance, because of their specific nature and social importance). In view of extraordinary aspects of and social problems inherent in acts of terrorism, Japanese insurers regard it is crucial to be able to deal on a common basis with terrorism risks and to obtain the government's financial support as a last resort.

The Japanese non-life insurance industry would therefore like to see the creation of a joint pooling system with the government's financial support, together with clearance for concerted insurance industry action in not only reinsurance business but also in direct business. Public opinion is seen as a crucial factor in persuading the Japanese government to give financial support for terrorism risks; and the Japanese industry has been engaged in efforts to create a terrorism risk scheme. However, there is still only limited support for the proposal from large corporate customers, and there has been no strong public demand. One probable reason for this is that employers' liability insurance in Japan is the subject of a government insurance scheme and is therefore not the subject of private insurance and the difficulties attending it in other markets (*e.g.* the United Kingdom and the United States) in connection with terrorism risks. As a result, commercial demand for terrorism insurance is not particularly strong, and can generally be met by insurers when required. Discussions on the idea of a terrorism risk pool with government financial support are therefore in abeyance in Japan.

The examples of Italy and Japan suggest that, while in both markets a pool might be the preferable solution, ways have been found towards a fairly satisfactory supply/demand balance, as in other OECD markets without a specific terrorism insurance scheme.

4. Specific Schemes for Terrorism Insurance in OECD Countries

As is recognised in the Task Force's Check-List for a Definition of Terrorism, terrorism risk insurability is a complex and evolving concept. While the criteria for insurability are outside the scope of this Report, it is relevant to ask whether governments were influenced by questions of social and economic welfare ("externalities") in devising specific schemes for terrorism insurance cover, and how far these questions were reflected in the shape of specific schemes.

4.1. "Externalities"

Insurance, like any other good or service, is subject to costs of production (from which the supply curve is derived); and its price can be expected to reflect the costs to insurers of supplying the service. But in certain cases a good or service imposes external costs or provides external benefits ("externalities") to society that are not captured in the supply curve. Terrorism insurance, it can be argued, may well confer two categories of external benefits ("positive externalities") to society:

- Pre-Loss Benefits: businesses with adequate terrorism insurance may be less prone to forego otherwise beneficial activities (*e.g.* construction projects) than businesses lacking such insurance;

- Post-Loss Benefits: insured businesses suffering losses from terrorism events may be less likely to be subject to financial distress or failure, thereby preserving jobs and minimising destabilising economic effects.

The potential benefits of these positive externalities can be illustrated as follows:

4.2. Market Failure

In certain circumstances (*e.g.* when a class of risks becomes more expensive to insure, or uninsurable, through conventionally available or affordable insurance cover) the insurance market, left to itself, will not deliver these positive externalities. Faced with such non-delivery ("market failure"), governments have a hierarchy of potential responses. They may:

- Provide incentives for business and civil society to take their own measures towards risk mitigation;

- Change levels of post-disaster assistance;

- Encourage the development of alternative risk transfer (ART) vehicles (catastrophe bonds, catastrophe options, swaps, etc.);

- Alter the tax treatment of catastrophe reserves.

Ultimately, however, such "market failure", it can be argued, lies at the core of economic justification for more direct government involvement in terrorism insurance[4]. This Report therefore aims to bring out the extent to which governments and the insurance sector have been influenced by such policy considerations, as well as by history and past practice in their own country and their own insurance market. It will also examine how far both governments and insurers have been influenced by whether they could call on pre-existing institutions when framing national solutions, or whether they had to develop entirely fresh institutions and mechanisms.

4.3. Specific Schemes[5]

A number of OECD countries have developed specific schemes of a mixed private/public nature to cover terrorism insurance. Some already existed before 11 September 2001, while others were created in direct response to it. All are worthy of description and analysis, as representing the most advanced insurance markets' responses to the problem of providing cover for terrorism risks. The factual and quantitative characteristics specific to each scheme are set out in the tables in Part II Chapter 5 of this publication and need not be repeated in full. But the following comparisons and comments are offered, to illustrate qualitative differences in the origins of specific schemes, their ambit in terms of protection offered, and the extent to which they have been developed or modified in direct response to 11 September:

4.3.1. Australia

History and Purpose

The Australian Reinsurance Pool Corporation (ARPC; a statutory corporation under the Terrorism Insurance Act 2003) was established by the Australian Government in direct response to the withdrawal of terrorism cover by Australian insurance companies following terrorist attacks in various countries and in particular the attack on the WTC. The primary function of the ARPC is to provide insurance cover for eligible terrorism losses (other functions can be prescribed by regulations, and could relate, for example, to wider compensation for losses arising from terrorist incidents). Apart from a retention specified by government regulation, the ARPC provides 100 per cent reinsurance of the terrorism risk for insurers. Premiums paid for this reinsurance cover contribute to the pool of funds available to pay claims for eligible terrorism losses and to meet the ARPC's administrative costs.

In setting up the ARPC the Australian Government's declared policy[6] was to establish an interim intervention measure to address a market failure arising from the inadequate supply of terrorism risk cover, on the basis of a mixture of a pool and post-funded model. The intervention would need to be consistent with:

- the need to maintain, to the greatest extent possible, private sector involvement;

- ensuring that risk transferred to the state was appropriately priced and that the state was compensated by those benefiting from the assistance;

- allowing for the re-emergence of commercial markets for terrorism risk cover; and

- the development of global solutions.

After industry consultations, the Australian government adopted a hybrid pool/post-funded model broadly consistent with these parameters and principles. The Scheme involved the accumulation of a cash pool of $300 million funded by premiums, backed by a commercial line of credit of $1 billion and a government indemnity of $9 billion, together expected to provide sufficient certainty and public confidence of cover against terrorist risk, at premiums lower than the then current market prices.

The Australian government also made clear that it did not wish to be involved in the insurance market in the long term. Its involvement was accordingly directed at alleviating problems faced by commercial property owners unable to obtain terrorist risk insurance. For this reason, other classes of insurance were not included (such as domestic property, marine and aviation insurance). Similarly, coverage did not extend to damage resulting from nuclear causes (such damage having long been excluded from insurance, and being unlikely ever to be commercially available). It is a feature of the ARPC scheme that it will be regularly reviewed (every three years) with a view to testing the extent to which the commercial market may be re-emerging for terrorist risk insurance. The Australian government was therefore aware that the extent to which the scheme covered such risks could limit the state's ability to withdraw. Components of the Scheme, including pricing, classes of insurance required to provide terrorism risk cover and level of underwriting available, are deliberately flexible, not being set in legislation, in order to encourage the reemergence of the commercial market.

It is noteworthy that financial services interests were one of the driving forces behind the establishment of the Australian scheme. These included banks, who wanted to be sure that they would be repaid if properties over which they held mortgages were destroyed as a result of an act of terrorism, and the Property Council, representing the large commercial property owners. Both feared the economic consequences of any insurance market failure resulting from the inability or unwillingness of the relatively small Australian commercial insurance sector to continue to offer property cover. It is a particular feature of the Australian savings and investment market that many large properties in Australia are owned by Listed Property Trusts; and the units in these trusts are held by superannuation/pension funds and institutional investors, together with a substantial number of ordinary private investors. It was a major concern of the Australian authorities that if a property that was not covered for an act of terrorism were destroyed, the effects, particularly on private savers, could be far-reaching.

Definitions

The definition of "terrorist act" for the purpose of the scheme, together with the process to determine when an event is a "terrorist act", is set out in Section 6 of the Act. An Australian government declaration (from the Treasurer, following consultation with the Attorney General) is required for an act to be recognised as a "terrorist act" for the purpose of the scheme.

Operation, Extent, Lines Covered & Perils Covered

The ARPC scheme supplies replacement terrorism insurance coverage for commercial property or business interruption. It renders terrorism exclusion clauses in eligible insurance contracts ineffective in relation to loss or liabilities arising from a declared terrorist incident affecting eligible property located in Australia, and provides that compensation payable to holders of eligible contracts will depend on the underlying coverage of the contract.

The scheme covers insurance for loss of or damage to commercial property owned by the insured, insurance for business interruption arising from loss of or damage to or inability to use eligible property, and insurance for liability of the insured arising from ownership or occupation of eligible property. Private residential property is not included. Risk cover is for any declared terrorist incident, except events involving damage from nuclear causes. Cover is available for Commonwealth and State business enterprises as well as Commonwealth-owned airports leased commercially. Farms benefit from cover for terrorism risk if they hold insurance against business interruption.

Exclusions

The Scheme regulations exclude certain other types of insurance cover, including: marine insurance, aviation insurance, motor vehicle insurance, life insurance, health insurance, private mortgage insurance, medical indemnity insurance, and professional indemnity insurance.

State Involvement & Layers of Cover

Insurance companies can reinsure the risk of claims for eligible terrorism losses through the ARPC[7]. Reinsurance premiums paid by insurers to the ARPC will build up the first layer of funds (an expected pool of $300 million) available to cover claims from declared terrorist incidents. The pool will be supplemented by a back-up bank line of credit of $1 billion, underwritten by the state, as well as an Australian government indemnity of $9 billion, giving aggregate cover of up to $10.3 billion when the pool is fully funded.

The following rating structure for reinsurance premiums was mandated for the Scheme at its inception:

Premium Structure for Reinsurance			
Class of insurance		Initial rate (from 1 October 2003)	Maximum rate (after an event)
Commercial Property	- Tier A	12%	36%
	- Tier B	4%	12%
	- Tier C	2%	6%
Business Interruption	- Tier A	12%	36%
	- Tier B	4%	12%
	- Tier C	2%	6%
Public Liability		–	2%

In essence, there is a two tier reinsurance premium structure: an initial "standard rate' scale targeted to building the premium pool at a rate of about $100 million per annum; and a maximum post-terrorist event rate scale, targeted to rebuilding the resources of the Scheme in the event of a major incident.

For commercial property and associated business interruption, an initial premium of 2 per cent of underlying base premium generally applies (Tier C), with surcharges of 10 per cent and 2 per cent applying to properties located in most capital city commercial business districts (CBDs) (Tier A) and other urban areas (Tier B), respectively (with Tier A and Tier B to be designated by postcodes). No initial premiums for public liability have been charged.

Non-State Reinsurance/Retrocession

It is not compulsory for insurers to reinsure the risk of eligible terrorism losses through the ARPC. Insurers might choose to accept the risk themselves, or to seek reinsurance from a commercial reinsurer.

Extent of Compulsion and Choice

Compulsory Insurance: Terrorism insurance cover is compulsory for all insurance classes covered by the ARPC scheme (commercial property, infrastructure facilities business interruption and public liability).

Compulsory Recourse to ARPC: As noted above, it is not compulsory for insurers to reinsure the risk of eligible terrorism losses through the ARPC.

Period of Operation

The scheme has operated from 1 July 2003. There was a transition period for eligible insurance contracts entered into before 1 October 2003, as terrorism risk cover was deemed into existing contracts without any charges for such cover being levied until the date of renewal. During this transition period, reinsurance was provided by the ARPC free of charge. There is no terminal date for the operation of the ARPC scheme, which remains under periodic review.

4.3.2. Austria

History and Purpose

Following September 11, Austrian insurers in the Verband der Versicherungsunternehmen Österreichs (VVO, the Austrian insurance association) set up a mixed co- and reinsurance pool (Österreichischer Versicherungspool zur Deckung von Terrorrisiken) on 1 October 2002. The VVO's primary goal in setting up the new pool was to grant affordable property cover against terrorism exposure, *i.e.* covering risks arising from an insured peril triggered by terrorism. The pool is open to insurers and reinsurers writing business in Austria; and some 99% of primary insurance companies that are members of the participate in it, their share of the pool being pro-rated to their market share in property insurance.

The Austrian Pool represents the response of a relatively small advanced insurance market (regarded before September 11 as facing a relatively low and infrequent terrorist threat) which, even with optional terrorism insurance, would otherwise face a degree of market failure. The Austrian government has decided not to offer a third layer of cover, in the form of a state guarantee, at the time being. The Austrian Ministry of Finance has made clear that it welcomes the action taken by the insurance insurance but wishes to avoid any steps that could deter the private sector from taking measures itself to accommodate terroism risks as far as possible. In the period since its creation the Austrian Pool has not had to face a serious test.

Definitions

No Austrian government declaration is required for an act to be recognised as a "terrorist act" for the purpose of the scheme. Instead, the VVO has drawn on the German definition developed by the GDV: "Terrorist acts are all acts of persons or groups of persons with a view to achieving political, religious, ethnic, ideological or similar goals, and which are apt to put the public or sections of the public in fear, thereby influencing a government or public bodies".

Operation, Extent, Lines Covered & Perils Covered

Under the terms of the Pool scheme cover for terrorism risks (limited to the territory of Austria) extends to all lines of property insurance business other than transport insurance, with a cover limit of €5 million per single event per year, and covers property insurance in respect of industrial, commercial and private lines. A further €20 million cover is available for an additional premium.

Exclusions

The Austrian Pool is subject to the following main exclusions:

- business interruption (except in respect of direct consequential damage);
- liability;
- marine, aviation and transport;
- damage resulting from failure to supply;
- damage due to biological or chemnical contamination resulting from terrorist attack;
- art insurance.

State Involvement & Layers of Cover

The Austrian Pool currently operates without a state guarantee and offers cover totalling up to €200 million without deductibles, in two layers:

1. the first layer, up to an annual aggregate of €50 million, to be co-insured by direct insurers, in proportion to their market share;

2. the second layer of €150 million, up to a total annual aggregate of €200 million, to be underwritten by the international reinsurance market.

The following rating structure for reinsurance premiums has been mandated for the scheme:

– for participants in the Pool: from 0.75% to 4.0% of the sum insured;

– for non-participants in the Pool: from 2.25% to 12.0% of the sum insured.

Non-State Reinsurance/Retrocession

Given that the Austrian state is not involved, all reinsurance and retrocession is on a non-state basis.

Extent of Compulsion & Choice

Compulsory Terrorism Insurance: Terrorism cover remains optional in Austria for most lines, being provided on a private, facultative and conditional basis. Exceptions are commercial passenger and third party liability for aviation, railways and other "no fault" liability classes, where terroism cover is mandatory.

Compulsory Pool Membership: Pool membership is optional, but 99% of VVO members belong to the Pool.

Period of Operation

The Austrian Pool has been in operation since 1 October 2002. There is currently no terminal date for its operation.

4.3.3. France

History and Purpose

Following September 11, the French authorities were the first to respond, with the creation of the GAREAT (Gestion de l'Assurance et de la Réassurance des Risques Attentats et Actes de Terrorisme) Pool to insure major industrial risks against terrorism.

The rapid creation of the scheme owed much to the pre-existence of the Caisse Centrale de Réassurance (CCR), the French state-backed entity created in 1983 to guarantee terrorism reinsurance cover. France has had a long history of acts of terrorism since the Second World War. A wave of attacks took place at the beginning of the fifties with the end of the colonial period for ex French territories in North Africa. This was followed by other regional and international waves. Terrorism covers have subsequently been part of Property insurance policies, either as specific or as additional covers, since they were first offered in the fifties. Following the increase of political risks in the seventies, they developed into extended covers also covering riot, civil commotion, malicious acts and sabotage.

Those extended covers, although optional and considered as low frequency risks, nevertheless were developed for industrial risks. As the frequency of attacks increased in the late seventies, new schemes to protect individuals or properties were set up by the State. Following the establishment of the CCR to reinsure terrorism policies, cover for direct property losses and business interruption has been a compulsory element of French insurance policies covering property damage, including motor policies, since 1986.

In the years after 1986 French direct insurers generally opted to reinsure with the CCR, until in the 1990s increasing competition led to falls in premium income for direct cover, leading insurers to prefer traditional lower-cost reinsurance treaties to the higher-cost CCR alternative. In the mid-1990s the CCR withdrew from its few existing treaties, but remained in place as a potentially available state-backed reinsurance institution.

The CCR reinsurance scheme of the 1980s had been based on the concept of individual reinsurance covers for each direct insurer in the French market, based on all terrorism property risks. Under this concept, France prohibited property insurers from excluding terrorism or even establishing separate limits or deductibles to address it. Property policies had to pay losses for violent acts of others, and the government guaranteed reinsurance payments for claims arising from acts it determined to have been acts of terrorism. This policy changed in the wake of September 11, however, with a new decree allowing for separate treatment of terrorism for risks with insured values above certain levels. It followed that GAREAT, as created in 2001 and operative from 1 January 2002, did not represent a simple return to this: under the GAREAT scheme only major risks are covered, insurers' retentions are much higher, and maximum use is made of the reinsurance market even though the overall level of state intervention is much higher.

The GAREAT structure reflects circumstances in the French insurance market after September 11, when direct insurers had difficulty in offering renewal terms on many commercial lines policies, following announcements by most reinsurers that terrorism exclusion clauses would apply within reinsurance treaties incepting on or after 1 January 2002. The GAREAT scheme was a twofold response to this:

- GAREAT was set up as a reinsurance pool covering commercial and industrial risks from the start of 2002 for direct property losses and business interruption arising from acts of terrorism where the sum insured is in excess of €6 million. GAREAT provides reinsurance protection to direct insurers provided that they cede the terrorism risk forming part of all qualifying policies within their portfolio;

- the French state agreed to act as reinsurer of last resort, through the CCR, for damages caused by acts of terrorism resulting in aggregate annual losses in excess of €1.5 billion (€2.00 billion from 1 January 2004).

GAREAT membership is open to insurance companies operating in France and also to other insurers covering French risks, provided that these risks are located in Metropolitan France, French Overseas Departments (DOM) and Territories (TOM) and Mayotte.

GAREAT can be seen as incorporating five fundamental principles:

- separation of small risks from medium/major risks: the pool protects medium/major risks on the basis of a firm commitment by reinsurers to provide sufficient market capacity for all Property risks (including homeowners' risks, other commercial risks and motor);

- maximum mutualisation for medium/major risks: a key feature of the scheme is cover for virtually all medium/major risks of all types, linked to compulsory terrorism cover in Property policies, thereby obviating adverse selection and providing an adequate premium base;

- maximum cover (perils, amount and frequency): the scheme covers virtually all risks (with very few exclusions, to avoid any mismatch with original policies) with an annual excess of loss market retention, a reinsurance line and, ultimately, unlimited reinsurance through the CCR with its State guarantee;

- pricing on a progressive scale: net reinsurance premiums are pro-rated to the Property premium (as best indicator for the basic risk) on a scale of 1-3 the minimum rate (according to size). Overall, original rates are adjusted on a real scale of 1.0 to 1.5, and the weighted average reinsurance rate is around 12% of the Property premium (*i.e.* around 0.012% of the sum insured, based on the average actual quotation for the segment in question);

- unlimited Motor cover: the scheme includes a waiver of subrogation rights against motor insurers in the event of a terrorist attack involving a vehicle, reflecting the principle that no private company can take on unlimited losses arising from intentional damage. This frees motor insurers and their reinsurers from major potential commitments in the event of legal action against such a vehicle's insurers (around half of significant terrorist attacks worldwide have involved use of a vehicle).

The breadth of the GAREAT scheme means that virtually any adverse economic consequences of possible insurance market failure are prevented.

Definitions

No French government declaration is required for an act to be recognised as a "terrorist act" for the purpose of the scheme, but provided an event meets the definition in the French Criminal Code all types of terrorism (regional, national and international) in any form (including nuclear, chemical and biological risks) are covered for all French property risks.

Operation, Extent, Lines Covered & Perils Covered

The GAREAT scheme offers very wide coverage, including all types of terrorism (regional, national and international) in any form (including nuclear, chemical and biological risks) for all French property risks, on the same terms as the original policy, with no restrictions in terms of time or sums insured. Specifically, the scheme protects the following lines of business:

- For nuclear risks (excluding liability), local and public authorities, buildings, public law administration facilities and institutions, exhibitions and special risks, parking for fleets of vehicles or goods: property damage cover (*i.e.* fire, all risks & multi-peril packages, and business interruption if the business interruption is linked to property damage);

- For construction, engineering and financial institutions: cover for machinery breakdown, erection all risks, construction all risks, computer all risks, bankers' blanket bonds.

GAREAT's reinsurance coverage is restricted to commercial, professional and industrial risks where the sum insured for direct property damage and business interruption is in excess of €6 million, subject to the following:

- where there is a contractual indemnity limit in the policy, the contractual indemnity limit will be taken as the insured value;

- where insured values cannot be identified with certainty, risks ceded to the pool will be those where the insured premises cover more than 20,000 square metres, or those for which the premium for natural catastrophe cover is in excess of €6,000;

- cession of a policy covering several buildings is optional where the buildings are more than one kilometer apart and the aggregate insured value of all buildings is greater than €6 million but each individual building has a value below €6 million. However, cession to the pool becomes compulsory if any single building has an insured value of €6 million or more.

There is the following rating structure. Direct insurers set the rates to be applied on original business. Pool members then cede the following rates (expressed as percentages of property insurance premiums) to GAREAT:

- Insured value between €6 million and below €20 million   6%

- Insured value between €20 million and €50 million   12%

- Insured value above €50 million   18%

Exclusions

There are the following principal exclusions under the GAREAT scheme:

- Life, accident and health insurance (for which there is a separate French Compensation Guarantee Fund for Victims of Terrorist Acts);

- Liability;

- Financial losses;

- Risks covered by marine, aviation and transport policies;

- Nuclear weapons;

- War, strikes, riot and civil commotion;

- Other malicious acts, vandalism;

- Theft, looting or fraud following acts of terrorism.

State Involvement & Layers of Cover

The GAREAT pool scheme operates on a four-layer basis, the layers in the twelve months from 1 January 2005 being shown in the table below:

Layer	Limit/Excess
1st	€400 million in annual aggregate Co-reinsurance provided by pool members (*i.e.* direct insurers, in proportion to their market share)
2nd	€1.60 billion in annual aggregate Coverage provided by international reinsurance market
3rd	€2.00 billion in annual aggregate Coverage provided by international reinsurance market
4th/Overspill	CCR offers unlimited protection backed by state guarantee

Non-State Reinsurance/Retrocession

It is not compulsory for French insurers (see below) to reinsure terrorism losses through GAREAT. Foreign or captive insurers might choose to accept the risk themselves, or to seek reinsurance from a commercial reinsurer.

Extent of Compulsion & Choice

Compulsory Terrorism Insurance: terrorism cover for direct property losses and business interruption has been a compulsory element of French insurance policies covering property damage, including motor policies, since 1986.

Compulsory Pool Membership: GAREAT membership is not compulsory. But it is currently automatic for insurance company members of the Fédération Française des Sociétés d'Assurances (FFSA) and mutual insurers in the Groupement des Entreprises Mutuelles de l'Assurance (GEMA) to be members of the pool. The pool therefore benefits from very widespread support, which, by being "automatic" for FFSA and GEMA members, is tantamount to compulsory.

Period of Operation

GAREAT has been in operation since 1 January 2002. The current GAREAT agreement with the French state runs until 2007 but can be renegotiated.

4.3.4. Germany

History and Purpose

Historically, terrorism cover has been included in many German insurance policies. But terrorism cover was not compulsory before September 11 and remains optional. Nonetheless, the widespread inclusion of terrorism cover highlighted the vulnerability of German insurers to terrorist risks. In the wake of September 11 the Gesamtverband der Deutschen Versicherungswirtschaft (GDV) therefore embarked on negotiations with the Federal German government, leading to the creation of EXTREMUS Versicherungs-AG in September 2002.

EXTREMUS is a specialist insurance company writing only terrorism business. It has a share capital of €50 million, and the founding shareholders are sixteen insurance and reinsurance groups active in the German market.

There are some distinctive features to the development of EXTREMUS-AG, which will probably remain critical to its future fortunes. One is the German government's insistence on a liability cap, before it would consider providing backup cover for terrorism claims: this has acted as a disincentive to insurers to offer terrorism cover for large risks that are difficult to assess. Another is the fact that terrorism cover remains optional in Germany: this naturally reduces the pool of risks covered, compared with those countries where compulsory terrorism cover, or requirements for an insurer to reinsure all terrorism risks with the pool, results in a broad base of terrorism risks covered. A third is EXTREMUS's policy of only insuring companies within Germany, which means major German multinationals have to purchase additional policies for their buildings in foreign countries.

The result is that, despite the existence of EXTREMUS, take-up of terrorism insurance remains limited, and terrorism insurance premiums remain high. Early on in the life of the EXTREMUS initiative there were uncertainties as to whether the EXTREMUS concept would prove a sufficient response to the German insurance industry's real requirements, and whether the take-up of terrorism insurance would be adequate to generate sufficient funds to the €1.5 billion primary limit required for EXTREMUS-AG to function. These uncertainties remain: EXTREMUS announced (March 2004) that demand had continued over 2003 to be much lower than anticipated. After initially predicting in 2002 earnings of €300 million that could increase to €500 million in later years, EXTREMUS subsequently forecast premium income for 2004 as likely to be 20% lower than in 2003: nonetheless a renegotiation of its reinsurance terms allowed EXTREMUS to report a technical profit for 2004.

Definitions

No German government declaration is required for an act to be recognised as a "terrorist act" for the purpose of the scheme. But it is necessary for a the consequences of a terrorist act to satisfy the GDV's definition, *i.e.* "Acts of terrorism shall be acts by persons or groups of persons committed for political, religious, ethnic or ideological purposes suitable to create fear in the population and thus to influence a government or public body".

Operation, Extent, Lines Covered & Perils Covered

EXTREMUS only offers terrorism cover for risks located in Germany under policies with a total sum insured (for property damage plus business interruption) in excess of €25 million. Cover can be limited to buildings only, or to the contents of buildings, or to losses arising from business interruption, provided that there is a relevant original property insurance policy for a sum insured above €25 million. The maximum (first loss) aggregate limit of indemnity is €1.5 billion per policyholder per year. In the event of a loss, the policyholder retains 1% of the annual limit of indemnity. All risks below €25 million continue to be covered under the usual property policies.

EXTREMUS protects the following lines of business: commercial and industrial property damage and business interruption (provided that the business interruption is linked to an insured property damage loss) arising from fire, explosion, collision or falling objects from aeroplanes or flying objects as well as vehicles of all types, parts thereof or their cargo, or other malicious damage.

Ratings are between 0.25‰ and 0.60‰ of the sum insured. Pricing is simple and does not vary with the location of the risk. The premium rate depends only on the original sum insured for the conventional cover and the yearly aggregate limit purchased by the insured. If the later is lower than the original sum insured a discount may be given and the ratings may even remain at 0.25‰.

Exclusions

The main exclusions are:

- War, war-like events, civil war, revolution, rebellion or insurrection;

- Atomic and nuclear energy risks;

- Contamination arising from terrorist acts;

- Marine and aviation losses;

- Losses to works of art;

- Losses to data processing plants and data carriers other than those originating from property damage (*e.g.* hacker attacks, virus attacks and other cyber risks);

- Business interruption interdependency losses.

State Involvement & Layers of Cover

At its inception EXTREMUS offered cover up to an amount of €13 billion per year. It ceded 100% of its business to reinsurers. About 50 domestic and foreign insurers and reinsurers provided reinsurance cover up to €3 billion, while the German government was liable for up to €10 billion where annual aggregate losses were in excess of €3 billion. The layered reinsurance structure was in three layers, as follows:

Layer	Limit/Excess
1st	€1.5 billion in the aggregate (Primary) Provided by primary insurers and reinsurers domiciled in Germany
2nd	€3.0 billion in the aggregate Excess of €1.5 billion Coverage provided by international insurance market
3rd	€13 billion in the aggregate Excess of €10 billion State guarantee

In 2004 and 2005, however, the layer structure was altered, with a reduction in overall capacity. For 2005 it is as follows:

Layer	Limit/Excess
1st	€2.0 billion in the annual aggregate (Primary) Provided by domestic primary insurers and domestic and foreign reinsurers
2nd	€10.0 billion in the annual aggregate Excess of €8 billion State guarantee

This change in capacity is due to a decrease in EXTREMUS's premium income in 2004 and reflects decisions to reduce the second layer and merge it with the first layer in order, it is reported, to allow EXTREMUS AG to cover its operating costs.

Non-State Reinsurance/Retrocession

There is scope for non-state reinsurance and/or retrocession, to the extent that the EXTREMUS scheme itself caters for the first layer of cover to be reinsured in the market, and to the extent that contracting with EXTREMUS-AG is in any case not compulsory.

Extent of Compulsion and Choice

Compulsory Terrorism Insurance: terrorism cover was not compulsory before September 11 and remains optional.

Compulsory Pool Membership: As EXTREMUS AG is a primary insurance company (not a pool) there is no membership.

Period of Operation

EXTREMUS-AG came into operation in November 2002, without limit of time.

4.3.5. Netherlands

History and Purpose

Before the attack on the WTC in September 2001 it was a feature of the Dutch insurance market that unlimited covers were offered in almost all lines of business (general, personal, health and life). Following September 11, insurers in the Netherlands, in line with insurers around the world, sought to review and restrict terrorism coverage. Although exclusions could be brought into non-life policies by endorsement or at subsequent renewals, in the Netherlands (as in many other countries) a life contract, once begun, could not be varied. The Verbond Van Verzekeraars

(VVV: the Dutch insurers' association) accordingly discussed with the Dutch Government the extent to which the financial impact of terrorist activity could be considered a risk that could be carried through commercial insurance, as then existing. The Dutch Ministry of Finance published a report in November 2002 analysing various scenarios, focusing on the scenario of an attack on a full sports stadium resulting in total insured losses spread across all sectors of the market, including a very significant proportion of life claims. In the light of this report the government, the Dutch Insurance Supervisory Authority (Pensioen- & Verzekeringskamer (PVK)) and the VVV considered proposals for a pool covering insurance of terrorist acts against "Dutch" risks.

The VVV then negotiated arrangements with the Dutch Government, under which it was agreed that the VVV would co-operate with the Government in setting up a dedicated reinsurance company (the Nederlandse Herverzekeringsmaatschappij voor Terrorismeschaden (NHT) or Terrorism Risk Reinsurance Company (TRRC)). It was also agreed that emergency legislation (the Noodwet Financieel Verkeer, or Emergency Law on Financial Transactions) would be applicable, if required, to restrict terrorism exposures in in-force life policies where these could not be amended by insurers to conform with the overall TRRC exposure limit of €1 billion (*i.e.* virtually all in-force life policies). The underlying purpose and rationale for these arrangements was to limit total terrorism risk exposures to a level that was reasonable, and could reasonably be expected to be reinsured. Taken together, these steps represented an intervention measure to address a market failure arising from the inadequate supply of terrorism risk cover, embracing the following:

- A unified approach to all insurance lines, linked to definitions of terrorism, malevolent contamination and precautionary measures;

- Voluntary participation in the TRRC by direct insurers authorized to carry on insurance business in the Netherlands (in practice including virtually all members of the VVV);

- Guarantees by participants in the TRRC (pro-rated to a proportion of their gross premium income) to secure its reinsurance liabilities;

- Limited capacity of €1 billion per year, in three layers;

- A "Terrorism Cover Clause", where feasible, in all policies, providing for overall terrorism exposures to be limited, and for terrorism risks to be reinsured by the TRRC, on the basis of the capacity limit of €1 billion per year;

- Application of the Emergency Law on Financial Transactions in cases where the "Terrorism Cover Clause" restriction on cover could not be applied (*e.g.* in the case of in-force life policies);

- Restriction of TRRC reinsurance cover to Dutch risks;

- Certain exclusions.

The TRRC was duly established as a reinsurance company with a relatively small equity, owned by a non-profit-making foundation set up by the VVV. Under the arrangements, the Dutch insurance industry is the first port of call in the event of a major terrorist atrocity; but the Dutch Government is involved as a participant in the pool. The TRRC, overseen and administered by the VVV, began its operations on 1 July 2003, triggering the simultaneous withdrawal of terrorism cover by reinsurers for their cedants in the Netherlands (the risks from that date being covered by the Pool). The likely establishment of the Pool was common knowledge beforehand, and reinsurance treaties for 2003 incorporated clauses to give effect to this.

Definitions

No Dutch government declaration is required for an act to be recognised as a "terrorist act" for the purpose of the scheme, which is based on three definitions:

- Terrorism: any violent act and/or conduct (outside the scope of one of the six acts of war referred to in Article 64(2) of the Insurance Business Supervision Act 1993) in the form of an attack or series of attacks connected in time and in intention, resulting in injury and/or impairment of health (whether or not resulting in death), loss of or damage to property, or any other impairment of economic interests, making it likely that the attack(s) have been planned and carried out (whether or not in an organizational context) with a view to serving certain political and/or religious and/or ideological purposes;

- Malevolent Contamination: any spreading, active or otherwise, (outside the scope of one of the six acts of war referred to in Article 64(2) of the Insurance Business Supervision Act 1993) of germs and/or substances capable, through their (in)direct physical, biological, radioactive or chemical effects, of resulting in injury and/or impairment of health to humans or animals (whether or not resulting in death), loss of or damage to property, or any other impairment of economic interests, making it likely that such spreading, active or otherwise, has been planned and carried out (whether or not in an organizational context) with a view to serving certain political and/or religious and/or ideological purposes;

- Precautionary Measures: any measures taken by the authorities and/or insureds and/or third parties to avert the imminent risk of terrorism and/or malevolent contamination, or (if such a peril has manifested itself) to minimize its consequences.

Operation, Extent, Lines Covered & Perils Covered

The TRRC's operations are confined to Dutch risks in all lines of business underwritten by the original reinsureds. Participating insurers are deemed to cede all their terrorism exposure to the pool. Because a participant's entire portfolio is "pooled", there is no obligation on an insurer to declare individual risks to the pool.

In the case of non-life contracts, the location where the risk is situated is regarded as:

- The state where the property is situated, if the insurance relates to immovable property, or to immovable property and its contents insofar as both are covered by the same insurance contract;

- The state of registration, if the insurance relates to vehicles or vessels, of whatever kind;

- The state where the policyholder has taken out the contract, if the contract is for four months or less and relates to travel or holiday risks, regardless of the insurance lines covered;

- In all other cases, the state of the policyholder's regular residence, or, if the policyholder is a legal entity, the state where the legal entity is established.

Life contracts are only covered if the policyholder's regular residence is in the Netherlands, or, in the case of a legal entity as policyholder, if the legal entity's registered office is in the Netherlands.

Exclusions

The following are excluded from TRRC cover:

- Aviation hull;

- Aircraft liability;

- Any nuclear compensable by the Dutch Nuclear Pool;

- Insurances making express provision for terrorism as a named peril.

For property loss or damage there is an indeminity limit of €75 million per policyholder for any one location per year for all participating insurers irrespective of the number of policies issued.

State Involvement & Layers of Cover

The TRRC has capacity of €1 billion per calendar year, in three principal layers, together with a threshold:

Layer	Limit/Excess
1st	€400 million in the aggregate Pooled cover provided by participating primary insurers
2nd	€800 million in the aggregate Excess of €300 million provided by international reinsurers
3rd	€1 billion in the aggregate Excess of €200 million provided jointly by the international reinsurers and the Dutch state

The scheme is technically reinsurance, with three layers:

1. The first layer operates on a pool basis, with capacity of € 400 million provided by direct insurers.

2. The second layer of € 400 million is provided by the professional reinsurance industry and purchased in the commercial market for a premium.

3. The top layer of € 200 million is provided jointly by the international reinsurers and the Dutch Government acting as reinsurers and charging a premium.

Within the pool layer of €400 million, claims will be allocated to insurers in proportion to their premium income from Dutch business. This will be calculated upon total premium volume for life and non-life business, but will exclude reinsurance. Participant will bear their respective proportion of all losses arising, whether life or non-life.

Should the aggregate limit of €1 billion ever be exceeded, there would be pro-rated reductions in amounts to be paid against claims, to ensure a proper and fair functioning of the insurance system, in accordance with a detailed protocol established by the TRRC. Claims would then be scaled back to prevent the €1bn limit from being breached. In the event of a threat to the life insurance industry from heavy claims under policies falling outside the scope of the TRRC the Dutch government could take action under emergency powers assumed by the Finance Ministry under legislation governing financial emergencies, so as to further reduce life insurers' exposure, where the terms of current life policies would not otherwise allow this.

Non-State Reinsurance/Retrocession

Under the scheme, the second and third layers (€600 million in aggregate) are reinsured in the international reinsurance market.

Extent of Compulsory Insurance

Compulsory Terrorism Insurance: terrorism cover was not compulsory before September 11, but most lines of business covered it.

Compulsory Pool Membership: Although participation in the TRRC is voluntary, Dutch Government statements created pressure to join; and only a relatively small number of specialist/single-line insurers have stayed out.

Period of Operation

The TRRC became operational on 1 July 2003. It has been periodically extended for additional periods, and is expected to be further extended as long as market conditions require.

4.3.6. Spain

History and Purpose

Among OECD countries, Spain was the first to develop an institution providing compensation for terrorism losses, in the form of the state-owned Consorcio de Compensación de Seguros (CCS). The CCS was established in 1941, with the initial aim of funding large insured losses in respect of civil commotion in the Spanish civil war, for which the Spanish insurance market had insufficient reserves. Following a series of major catastrophes in the 1940s, CCS gained permanent legal status in 1954 as a state company attached to the Ministry of Finance. Although a public sector entity, CCS is managed as a private company with a board drawn half from the insurance sector and half from the civil service. CCS has its own status and assets, distinct from the state, and is subject to the same legal obligations as a private company. The Spanish state would intervene in CCS's support only if a loss were to exceed CCS's accumulated resources (which has never occurred in CCS's history). CCS's activities are financed from surcharges paid by policyholders.

Since 1954 cover has been compulsory for "extraordinary risks" including natural catastrophes (earthquake, volcanic eruption, flood, windstorm), and political risks (strike, terrorism, civil commotion). CCS functioned as a state insurance facility guaranteeing such cover. After deregulation in 1990 it became possible to insure these risks privately; and since then CCS provides cover for "extraordinary risks' where this is not available from private sector insurers, subject to a continuing requirement for all policyholders to pay a CCS premium (which their insurers collected on CCS's behalf) to maintain full mutualisation for all terrorism risks. After September 11, with growing scarcity of reinsurance capacity for industrial and commercial risks, CCS was approached by UNESPA (the Spanish insurance association) to broaden its operations in relation to terrorism to include business interruption cover and from 1 January 2002, under a reinsurance agreement with UNESPA, CCS offered reinsurance for terrorism-related business interruption risks located in Spain, provided that the direct insurers seeking such reinsurance were signatories to the agreement. In 2004, however, business interruption was included in the Spanish system as part of every "extraordinary risk" cover (direct cover) and the reinsurance agreement accordingly came to an end.

In terms of loss experience, the proportion of total losses paid by the CCS for extraordinary risks in the period 1987-2003 is shown below. Terrorism and associated risks (civil commotion) represent 11.43% (€186.5 million for insured property).

Percentage of total losses by cause (period 1987-2003)

Causes	% Losses
Floods	84.96
Earthquake	1.03
Volcano	0.00
Wind	2.47
Meteorite	0.00
Riot	0.04
Terrorism	8.88
Civil Commotion	2.55
Acts by Armed Forces	0.07
Total	**100.00**

To date, the highest individual loss (€12.7 million) to the CCS, considering all the extraordinary risks, resulted from a terrorist act committed in 1982 on a building of the Telefonica Company. This act also had political consequences with a substantial threat of social disruption at a difficult moment of political transition.

Definitions

Terrorism is defined as follows: "every violent act committed with the object of destabilizing the established political order or generating fear or insecurity in the social environment in which it is perpetrated".

No Spanish government declaration is required for an act to be recognised as a "terrorist act" for the purpose of the scheme, given that CCS's activities are governed by private law and cover "extraordinary risks" including natural catastrophes (earthquake, volcanic eruption, flood, windstorm), and political risks (strike, terrorism, civil commotion).

Operation, Extent, Lines Covered & Perils Covered

The lines of business protected by CCS are:

- Material Damage:

    - Fire & perils (alone or when in combined policy)

    - Theft (alone or when in combined policy)

    - Glass (alone or when in combined policy)

    - Machinery breakdown (alone or when in combined policy)

    - Motor vehicles (own damage only)

    - Civil works

    - Business interruption

- Personal Accident (PA):

    - Group PA

    - Individual PA

    - Any ancillary PA included in life and pension policies

Exclusions

The main exclusions from CCS cover are:

- Life
- Marine, aviation, space
- Third party liability
- Credit and bonds
- Health
- Legal expenses
- Travel insurance
- Agricultural insurance
- Construction all risks and erection all risks

State Involvement & Layers of Cover

Given the CCS's history and mode of operation as a state company, its establishment does not entail a system of layers backed by a state guarantee.

Non-State Reinsurance/Retrocession

It remains open to insurers and reinsurers to have recourse to non-CCS reinsurance and retrocession. But the CCS now covers all Property policies for the vast majority of catastrophe risks without need of the international reinsurance market.

Extent of Compulsion & Choice

Compulsory Terrorism Insurance: terrorism insurance has been compulsory since 1954, but only if linked to a basic policy that covers the lines protected by the "extraordinary risks" system and is underwritten by a private insurer (not the CCS).

Compulsory Pool Membership: not applicable, as CCS is not a pool.

Period of Operation

CCS has operated in its present form since 1954, with important amendments in 1990, 2002 and 2004. There is no terminal date.

4.3.7. *United Kingdom*

History and Purpose

For a decade before 11 September the United Kingdom had had Pool Re as a government-backed terrorism reinsurer. This meant that the UK was better positioned to deal with terrorism than many other OECD members. The Pool Re scheme was established in 1993, in response to restrictions in the scope of terrorism reinsurance cover available to the UK commercial property insurance market.

The restrictions in cover that led to the establishment of Pool Re in 1993 followed the spate of terrorism incidents in London and elsewhere in England, related to the situation in Northern Ireland at that time. When Pool Re was originally established the reinsurance cover provided by the scheme was only the cover withdrawn by the international reinsurance market, namely cover for an act of terrorism that resulted in fire and/or explosion. Under the scheme the UK government agreed to enter into an agreement with Pool Re to make funds available to pay claims should the assets accumulated by Pool Re become exhausted. In entering these agreements in 1993, the U.K. Government made clear its intention to withdraw from the arrangement when the insurance market is able to provide Terrorism Cover without the requirement for Government support.

Between 1993 and 2002 Pool Re funded losses consequent upon acts of terrorism, by contributing a total of £612M on claims arising under its Members' policies, the most significant incidents being:

Date	Event	Pool Re Paid
April 1993	Bishopsgate, City of London	£262M
February 1996	London Docklands	£107M
June 1996	Manchester City Centre	£234M
August 2001	Ealing, West London	£7M
1993 to 2001	Other Events	£2M
	Total	**£612M**

At the time of September 11 Pool Re's statutory scope was limited to property damage caused by fire and explosion and consequential loss. It provided cover for terrorism as defined by the Reinsurance (Acts of Terrorism) Act 1993; one of the explicit purposes of this Act was to give a definition of terrorism for insurance purposes. Coverage granted to policyholders, through buyback of the terrorism exclusion in commercial property policies, was individually reinsured to Pool Re, at rates prescribed in the Pool Re tariff. The Terrorism Act 2000 widened the definition of terrorism to include for example acts which "create a serious risk to the health or safety of the public" or acts which were "designed seriously to interfere with or seriously to disrupt an electronic system"[8]. At the time of September 11 insurers protected these exposures – to the extent that they covered them in original policies – through their commercial reinsurance arrangements, while Pool Re limited itself to property damage and business interruption losses arising from fire and explosion, but did not provide cover against other forms of terrorist attack.

Following the attacks on the World Trade Centre and other locations in the USA on 11th September 2001, substantial changes took place in the reinsurance market with regard to coverage for terrorism. Before September 11 reinsurance cover available in the UK from the international reinsurance market had been designed to dovetail with the cover provided by Pool Re since 1993; hence insurers did not face a gap between the reinsurance cover available from Pool Re and the cover available from the commercial market. After September 11 reinsurers took the view that they were no longer in a position to continue to provide cover to the same extent: they accordingly applied exclusions in respect of damage caused by perils other than fire and explosion and also applied to their exclusions a wider definition of what constituted an act of terrorism.

Immediately after 11 September it was recognised that steps would need to be considered to extend the scope of Pool Re to cover the full range of property damage and consequential loss perils traditionally provided in the market. It was clear that, given the statutory restriction of its scope to property damage and consequential loss, Pool Re was unlikely to provide a solution if, for example, reinsurance cover for liability classes was withdrawn. Nor did Pool Re cover war, which is generally excluded (by "war exclusion" clauses) for first party policies when war is declared by the Government. However the entry into operation of the war exclusion clauses is not solely dependent on Government definition, because the war exclusion clauses exclude not only war but also an act of foreign enemy, and hostilities (whether war be declared or not). There were questions about the extent to which future events would fall within these definitions; and these questions clearly assumed greater importance after 11 September.

There was also concern, post-September 11, that the range of terrorist weapons was potentially far wider than previously envisaged. An obvious example was chemical or biological attack – most evidently anthrax. The use of terrorist weapons of this kind could result in claims under two extensions to commercial property policies – especially those aimed at the hotel and retail sector – notifiable infectious and contagious diseases, and loss of access due to action by competent authorities. There could also be product recalls by businesses as a result of contamination, or cases where biological or chemical attack required decontamination, resulting in claims under all risks Material Damage or Business Interruption policies.

In addition, there was concern in the UK market to continue to provide terrorism cover in policies covering commercial risks. Household policies in the UK do not explicitly exclude terrorism; and events which result in a claim under a household policy, even if caused by terrorism, would be met. Until September 11 terrorist attacks had been targeted on commercial property, and household losses were expected to be small and incidental. It was argued that, post-11 September, potential exposures to household losses were now greater.

Finally, there were certain unresolved issues relating to terrorism and employer's liability (EL) cover in the UK market. UK law requires employers to insure their liability to employees. It was not difficult to imagine scenarios in which terrorist activity could result in EL claims – for instance, if lax security resulted in terrorists entering business premises and harming employees. However, a key question was the extent of the exposures. In the UK, EL is tort based, and negligence on the part of the employer has to be proved (in this it is different from no-fault workplace compensation scheme such as the US workers' compensation system). In the UK terrorist activity which results in employees being killed or injured will not generally result in successful EL claims unless the employer has negligently contributed to these deaths and injuries. Before September 11, terrorism had not generally been excluded from EL policies; but it was open to insurers to exclude it and so withdraw cover for terrorist-related EL risks. But employers' liabilities would not be extinguished by the withdrawal of insurance cover; and there was therefore a major question of how to provide employers with the necessary cover to meet these continuing legal liabilities.

As a result of discussions towards the end of 2001 the UK Treasury announced its willingness to enter into discussions with the insurance industry, Pool Re and other interested parties to review the operation of the Pool Re scheme. In July 2002 announcements were made on the agreements reached to widen the cover, and amend certain other essential features of a scheme in a way which responded to the changes which had taken place and the needs of the UK insurance market. While there is still a potential gap between the terrorism cover offered by the scheme and the broad exclusions which sometimes appear in Members' reinsurance arrangements, the gap is tending to close, with many reinsurance programmes again providing back-to-back cover.

Definitions

The issue of a certificate by the UK Treasury (or, if refused, then by a decision of a Tribunal) is required for an act to be recognised as an "act of terrorism" for the purpose of the Pool Re scheme, under the Reinsurance (Acts of Terrorism) Act 1993. The Act defines "acts of terrorism" as "acts of persons acting on behalf of, or in connection with, any organisation which carries out activities directed towards the overthrowing or influencing, by force or violence, of Her Majesty's government in the United Kingdom or any other government *de jure* or de facto", and specifies that "organisation" in this definition "includes any association or combination of persons."

Operation, Extent, Lines Covered & Perils Covered

Pool Re is a mutual reinsurance company. Membership is not obligatory, but any insurance company or Lloyd's syndicate that is authorised either by the UK or an overseas regulatory authority to transact property insurance in the UK is eligible to be a member. Direct insurers that are members are obliged to provide terrorism cover, in the terms of the scheme, to those policyholders that request such cover. Reinsurance is provided to Members for material damage and business interruption cover, at rates stipulated in an Underwriting Manual supplied to each Member. The material damage rates are related to geographic zones by postcode within the United Kingdom; in broad terms these are grouped in Central and Inner London, other city centres, and the rest of England together with Scotland and Wales. There is a single rate for business interruption, which is not allocated to particular zones. Rates are applied to the full value at risk.

Members are free to set their own terrorism premiums for their underlying policies, according to normal commercial arrangements. Premiums are paid to members by policyholders, and members must remit the corresponding reinsurance premium to Pool Re within one month of the close of the quarter in which those terrorism risks had attached. No reinsurance commission is paid to Members by Pool Re. However Members decide to pay whatever intermediary commission they may determine.

Under the current arrangements it is important for Pool Re to have detailed information on the exposure carried by Members, and by the scheme overall, to allow rates to be set which will achieve an appropriate level of fairness in their application between Members. Each year Members are requested to submit up-to-date details of portfolio exposure data, incorporating location information by postcode and size of exposure for the risks included.

The Underwriting Manual is an extension of the Reinsurance Agreement and it is a condition that Members comply with it in every respect. Original Insureds are not permitted to select which properties are insured for terrorism cover. Their choice is to select to have terrorism cover either for all of their properties or none at all. It is permissible for an insured purchasing terrorism cover for material damage to elect not to do so for business interruption.

Due to the unique nature of the scheme great importance is placed on the detail of its Members' compliance. It is obviously critical that funds flowing into the pool reflect the outcome of the application of the rating structure to risk exposure at any point in time. Accordingly, Pool Re reviews Members' underwriting and accounting practices in relation to the scheme. Similarly, a pro-active approach is taken regarding claims management, with a review process which considers Members' claims and contingency procedures. These include both technical response and administrative control, in anticipation of major terrorist incidents, should these occur at any time in future.

The territorial scope of the reinsurance cover is limited to England, Wales and Scotland excluding the territorial seas. The scheme does not extend to the Channel Islands or the Isle of Man. Should a Member offer wider territorial cover, the cover for other territories would not be protected under the Reinsurance Agreement.

The aim of the arrangement is to ensure that original insureds have cover available under policies issued by Members for Acts of Terrorism to the full extent of their policy limits. The categories of cover ("Heads of Cover") under original contracts of direct insurance that are eligible for reinsurance under the scheme are:

1. Buildings and completed structures
2. Other property (including contents, engineering, contractors and computers)
3. Business interruption
4. Book debts

Cover provided by Pool Re to its Members is no longer restricted to Acts of Terrorism resulting in fire and/or explosion only, and is offered on an "all risks" basis, including chemical, biological, radiological or nuclear attack. Hence there is the facility for individual policyholders to attach terrorism cover to their general policy, which may be wider than the general cover.

Exclusions

The only losses now excluded under the Pool Re scheme are those in respect of war and related perils and computer hacking, virus and denial of service, although certain losses resulting from terrorism (*e.g.* contamination) are often excluded from household policies by Pool Re members.

State Involvement & Layers of Cover

Pool Re functions as a mutual reinsurance company authorized to transact reinsurance business for Property and Business Interruption and related classes, including residential property in commercial ownership (but not household property in the ownership of individuals). The scheme covers Property and associated Business Interruption losses resulting from an Act of Terrorism, as defined in the enabling Act of Parliament, the Reinsurance (Acts of Terrorism) Act 1993.

Pool Re's Retrocession Agreement with HM Treasury provides funding for Pool Re in the event that it exhausts all its financial resources following claim payments. Pool Re is required to pay a premium for this protection to the Treasury. Any amounts claimed by Pool Re under the Retrocession Agreement have to be subsequently repaid to the Treasury. Up to now such repayments have been funded by requiring members to pay an additional premium of up to 10% of the reinsurance premium paid to Pool Re in an underwriting year which resulted in a loss to Pool Re (matched by arrangements for each member to receive a return premium of up to 10% for any year in which Pool Re made an underwriting profit); but Pool Re now has sufficient amounts of premium funds for this arrangement to be discontinued.

Under the arrangements, the government (HM Treasury) undertakes to issue a certificate whenever a particular event is deemed to be an Act of Terrorism. Pool Re responds to claims only where such a certificate has been issued, although there is a facility to refer to an independent tribunal in cases of dispute over the certification of a particular event as an Act of Terrorism.

The relationship with the government is reinforced through HM Treasury's entitlement to appoint a director to the board of directors of Pool Re. This director reports formally to HM Treasury on how Pool Re has performed against a set of objectives, at least annually. He may raise other issues with HM Treasury that have a bearing on the objectives or other aspects of the public interest.

Under the Pool Re scheme, the reinsurance cover provided to Members is subject to a maximum loss retention per event per member (or members forming part of a Group) combined with an annual aggregate limit. The amounts of the retentions are based on the extent of Members' participation in the Pool Re scheme. The retention for each insurer is set annually, as a proportion of an industry-wide figure and advised to Members before the start of the relevant underwriting year. It has been agreed that the industry-wide retentions will be increased as follows:

Applying in	Per Event	Per Annum
2003	£30 million	£60 million
2004	£50 million	£100 million
2005	£75 million	£150 million
2006	£100 million	£200 million

Non-State Reinsurance/Retrocession

To the extent that membership of Pool Re is not compulsory, it is open to direct insurers to reinsure, and for reinsurers to retrocede, terrorism exposures to other reinsurers and retrocessionaires.

Extent of Compulsory Insurance

Compulsory Terrorism Insurance: terrorism cover was not compulsory before September 11 and remains optional. But under the Pool Re scheme original insureds are not permitted to select which properties are insured for Terrorism Cover. Their choice is to select to have Terrorism Cover either for all of their properties or none at all (except where an insured wishes to exclude properties whose value falls completely within a large deductible). An insured purchasing terrorism cover for material damage may elect not to do so for Business Interruption.

Compulsory Pool Membership: membership of Pool Re is not compulsory.

Period of Operation

Originally in operation in its present form since 1993, Pool Re's current scope of terrorism cover has been offered since July 2002. There is no terminal date, but the steady increases in industry-wide retentions in 2003-06 can be viewed as gradually reducing the state's potential exposure and increasing that of the market.

4.3.8. United States

History and Purpose

The Terrorism Risk Insurance Act of 2002 (TRIA) was passed on 19 November 2002, as legislation specifically designed to offer, for the first time, a financial backstop, to enable commercial insurers operating in the United States to underwrite terrorism risks by safeguarding them from potential insolvency from those risks.

In the year between September 11 and TRIA there was considerable debate within the US in 2001-2002 as to the appropriate form of support and the extent of governmental involvement. The debate focused on two alternative concepts:

- Government Loans: this was based on the concept of interest-free governmental loans to insurers (with a cap on total government liability) combined with restrictions on certain classes of lawsuit in the aftermath of a terrorist act.

- Coinsurance: this was based on the concept of a free co-insurance plan, under which the government would repay a prescribed percentage of losses above a designated figure in the first plan year and a further designated figure in the second plan year, with total government disbursements being subject to an annual cap. Insurers' shares of losses qualifying for prescribed percentage repayment would be pro-rated to their market shares; and, once any insurer's qualifying losses had been repaid at the prescribed percentage, further losses would be repaid at a reduced percentage until the ceiling imposed by the annual cap on government disbursements had been reached.

In the event, TRIA drew on some of these elements, but not others. Intended as a short-term solution to the economic and social impact from the unavailability of terrorism coverage for U.S. risks, TRIA creates a shared compensation mechanism under the Department of the Treasury through which the costs of terrorism claims in property/casualty policies over the three years 2003-2005 are allocated between the insurance industry and the Federal Government.

The immediate effect of the Act, from its inception as law (26 November 2002), was that all terms and/or special conditions in policies previously in place that restricted terrorism cover (as defined in the Act) in whole or in part, were be deemed null and void. TRIA concurrently reinsured any terrorism coverage already in place that was consistent with the Act's definition of "insured losses". Commercial insureds automatically had this cover during the period of the time it took for insurers to issue notices of premium increases for the cover to the insureds (90 day limit) and for the insureds then to consider those increases and respond (within 30 days of receipt of those notices). The terrorism exclusion can only be reinstated if the insured fails to pay the premium increase identified for this coverage or if the insured signs a statement asking that the terrorism exclusion be reinstated. Policies for which unrestricted terrorism coverage was already in place were not directly affected by the passage of the Act.

Finally – and reflecting debate preceding its enactment – TRIA includes built-in mechanisms that may allow the provisions of the Act to extend into other areas of insurance. For this purpose the Act requires:

- An "expedited study" of the affordability and availability of catastrophe terrorism reinsurance for group life policies to determine whether such coverage should be included in the Federal program;

- A study by experts in the field of the effects of terrorism on life insurance and other insurance lines, to be completed within nine months of the Act's enactment, and to be used to determine whether the program should be further expanded to include these other lines. In the event, the study led to a determination that TRIA would not be extended to group life insurance lines;

- A similar expert study of the effectiveness of the Federal program and of the likely capacity of commercial property/casualty insurers to offer terrorism cover in the future, to be completed no later than 30 June 2005.

Definitions

An "act of terrorism" means any act that is certified by the Secretary of Treasury, in concurrence with the Secretary of State and the Attorney General:

1. to be an act of terrorism;

2. to be a violent act or an act that is dangerous to (a) human life, (b) property, or (c) infrastructure;

3. to have resulted in damage in the US (or outside the US in case of an air carrier or vessel or the premises of a US mission); and

4. to have been committed by an individual or individuals acting on behalf of any foreign person or foreign interest, as part of an effort to coerce the civilian population of the US to or influence the policy or affect the conduct of the US Government by coercion.

However acts committed by domestic terrorists or in the course of war as declared by Congress (except as covered for purposes of workers' compensation), are not covered under the Act; and the aggregate losses resulting from the terrorist act must exceed $5 million to be subject to the program.

Operation, Extent, Lines Covered & Perils Covered

Under the terms of the Act, all insurers – direct, surplus lines, and alien – that write primary and/or excess property/casualty insurance for U.S. risks are required to participate in the program. These include those licensed to provide primary insurance in at least one state, excess insurers, certain surplus lines insurers (*i.e.* those appearing on the National Association of Insurance Commissioners (NAIC) Quarterly Listing of Alien Insurers), and insurers who are approved by a Federal agency in connection with maritime, energy or aviation activity. The Secretary of the Treasury, in consultation with the NAIC, may determine to apply provisions of the Act to municipal and other self-insurance programmes, captives, or other insurance classes if that determination is made before a trigger event. And, as previously noted, TRIA also called for an expedited study on the extension of the program to group life insurers (leading, in the event, to a determination that TRIA would not be extended to group life insurance lines), as well as for later studies concerning other insurance lines.

For at least two years (and subsequently extended by Treasury to a third year), property/casualty insurers are required to make available terrorism cover on all policies covering U.S. risks, identify the portion of the policy premium attributable to terrorism cover, and offer cover in a manner that does not differ materially regarding terms, amounts or other limitations of cover offered for acts other than terrorism. Key lines covered are:

- Commercial property and casualty lines including:

    - Excess insurance;

    - Workers' compensation;

    - Surety.

Losses covered are those insured under primary and/or excess property/casualty insurance, workers' compensation, and surety contracts.

The recoveries provided by the Act flow to property and casualty insurance companies as reinsurance. Policy provisions that exclude terrorism risks that are defined in TRIA and are in force in property/casualty policies (except for those pertaining to non-payment of premium) are voided as from the date of Presidential signature to the Act. For policies that were either in force or issued within 90 days after enactment of TRIA, insurers must provide notice to insureds of the additional premium charge associated with the mandated cover within 90 days. For policies issued more than 90 days after enactment, insurers are required to disclose the charge as a separate line item within the policy. In all instances, the applicable exclusion can be reinstated if the insured requests so in writing or fails to pay the identified premium for the TRIA cover within 30 days of receiving notice from the insurer.

Guidelines concerning the insurers' pricing of terrorism cover are not defined, other than by inference from the requirement that terrorism cover must not differ materially from terms, amounts or other limitations for other property/casualty cover. Since the Act left unchanged the role of state regulators in rate approvals it has not resulted, so far, in either exorbitant rates from underwriters or deeply discounted rates that recognize the support from the federal reinsurance plan.

Exclusions

The following are excluded from the program:

- losses under federal crop covers, including privately issued or reinsured crop or livestock insurance;

- private mortgage insurance;

- title insurance;

- financial guaranty cover issued by monoline entities;

- medical malpractice insurance;

- health or life insurance;

- flood insurance;

- reinsurance;

- retrocessional reinsurance.

State Involvement & Layers of Cover

In essence, the Act establishes a Terrorism Reinsurance Program, administered by the Department of the Treasury, under which insurers are required to offer terrorism cover, with the Program acting as reinsurer for the bulk of any resulting losses. Any terrorism exclusions in existing insurance policies inconsistent with TRIA cease to have effect. Each participating insurer is required to pay losses up to a retention amount based on the insurer's direct earned premium written in the previous year. During a "Transition Period" up to 31 December 2002, the deductible was equal to 1% of prior year's premiums, rising to 7% (for 2003), 10% (2004) and 15% (2005).

For losses in excess of these deductibles cover will be subject to 10% quota share participation by each insurer, with the Federal Government covering the remaining 90% of those losses up to a combined aggregate program limit of $100 billion annually (*i.e.* government covers 90% of the insurer's losses above the insurer's retention amount, with the insurer paying the remaining 10%). Insurers are permitted to reinsure their deductible and quota-share exposures in the program if they so choose. Federal payments will not be offset by any such reinsurance. Under the provisions of the Act, insurers are not liable for losses in excess of the program's $100 billion annual cap. If losses exceed the cap, Congress will determine the sources and procedures for the excess payments.

The Act contains "recoupment provisions" under which the Secretary of the Treasury is required to recoup portions (varying year by year) of the payments made by the federal government under this program. These "Recoupment of Federal Share" and "Insurance Marketplace Aggregate Retention Amount" provisions stipulate that if the federal government pays for insured losses during the course of a year, the Treasury Secretary will be required to recoup the difference between total industry costs (the aggregate of insurers' losses up to their deductibles, plus the 10 percent cost share above the deductibles) together with the following fixed Dollar amounts per year: $10 billion for Year 1, plus the interim period at the close of 2002; $12.5 billion for Year 2; and $15 billion for Year 3. The recoupments will be made via policyholder surcharges collected by insurers on property/casualty policies subject to TRIA that are in force after the date of the Secretary's determination. The surcharges may not exceed 3% of a policy's annual property/casualty premiums and will be remitted to the Federal Government by the insurers. The Secretary can make discretionary and other adjustments to recoupments on the basis of their economic impact in certain instances.

Non-State Reinsurance/Retrocession

There is scope for non-state reinsurance and/or retrocession, to the extent that insurers' deductibles can be reinsured within or outside the program, as preferred.

Extent of Compulsory Insurance

Compulsory Terrorism Insurance: Insureds are free to reject the offer of TRIA terrorism cover and negotiate different (non-TRIA) cover, or to opt to be uninsured for an act of terrorism.

Compulsory Program Membership: Under the Act, all insurers – direct, surplus lines, and alien – that write primary and/or excess property/casualty insurance for U.S. risks are required to participate in the program.

Period of Operation

The overall program under the Terrorism Risk Insurance Act 2002 remains in operation until the end of 2005. TRIA required the Secretary of the Treasury to determine, no later than 1 September 2004, whether to extend beyond the end of 2004, and up to the end of 2005, the requirement that property/casualty insurers make available terrorism cover on all policies covering U.S. risks, identify the portion of the policy premium attributable to terrorism cover, and make cover available in a manner that does not differ materially regarding terms, amounts or other limitations of cover offered for acts other than terrorism. On 18 June 2004 the Secretary of the Treasury announced that the "make available" requirement would be extended until the end of 2005. In early 2005 two Bills were introduced in Congress (H.R. 1153 and S. 467) to extend TRIA through 2007, but no action is likely on any extension measure until after June 30, 2005, at which time Treasury's required Report on TRIA will be submitted to Congress.

5. Good Practice – in Theory and Practice

With few exceptions, most existing terrorism insurance schemes (or, in their absence, current national market practice) have been brought into existence, or significantly adapted, in the wake of 11 September 2001. It is therefore too early in their life-cycle to draw firm conclusions regarding successful good practice in their establishment and operation. But this Report can usefully try to analyse potentially important areas of good practice, not least for the attention of countries that have no specific terrorism insurance scheme or that contemplate the modification of the scheme currently enforced. It could also prove helpful for governments and insurance industries in OECD countries to have some kind of commonly endorsed checklist of good practice when devising national solutions.

5.1. Likely Areas of Good Practice

Terrorism insurance schemes can be viewed as ranging across a spectrum, from relatively simple market arrangements, at one extreme, through mutual risk-pooling arrangements, to state-supported schemes, and finally, at the other extreme, state-run insurance. Given that all such schemes involve a degree of intervention in the marketplace, usually to remedy market failure and to capture, on a continuing basis, the "positive externalities" that terrorism cover brings with it, the following have been generally recognised as likely areas of good practice in setting up and operating schemes:

Timescale: it is very important for any approach to take account of the long term (so far as possible in so unpredictable a field as international terrorism), rather than a "quick fix";

Flexibility: any approach is likely to need to allow for flexibility and provide scope for modification to match both the actual level of threat and market conditions, present and future;

Balance: a balanced and proportionate approach needs to be taken, assigning an appropriate role to the insurance industry, financial markets and (where relevant) the government as insurer/financier of last resort, and taking account of the fact that the balance between these may ebb and flow depending, for instance, on the availability of capital in the insurance market and financial markets;

"Crowding Out": it is important for approaches involving the public sector to follow a principle of avoiding institutionalising a role for government that "crowds out" competition from the private sector and discourages adaptation in insurance markets and/or limits the attractiveness of insurance markets for new investment;

Externalities: it is important for any approach to look further than the immediate cost and availability of insurance cover, so as to take account of the wider economic costs of insufficient cover, and hazards such as business interruption, economic instability and discouragement of investment and wealth-creation that may result from such wider economic costs[9].

The above list of likely areas of good practice for schemes with state involvement is not exclusive: there are other features with implications for good practice, particularly as regards distortion of competition within an insurance market or between different countries' insurance markets. What is more, perceptions of good practice need to take account of market circumstances, market history and market strengths and weaknesses in particular countries, and of the different forms that state involvement may take: in certain countries a degree of state involvement in the coverage of extraordinary risks may be viewed by the market itself as appropriate and necessary, may be regarded as market-strengthening rather than in opposition to market forces, or may be seen as a permanent, if subsidiary and specialist, feature of the wider market. Views of good practice accordingly need to calibrated against local circumstances.

Assuming however that the above elements of good practice are generally desirable in theory, how far have they proved achievable in practice? Are they in fact achievable? Or are some or all of them inconsistent with the mix of requirements necessary for the establishment of a terrorism insurance scheme that is stable and viable? The question can be approached by analysing some of the common questions faced by the eight OECD members (Australia, Austria, France, Germany, the Netherlands, Spain, the United Kingdom and the United States) that have set up specific terrorism insurance schemes. There are no fixed boundaries between these questions, but they can perhaps be broadly categorised in terms of two broad questions:

- How do different schemes approach market failure, and how do they structure the role (if any) of the state?

- Are scheme dynamics compatible with theoretically desirable good practice?

together with two further, rather more specific, questions:

- How far can terrorism be regarded as a separate peril, and is it viable to offer "stand-alone" insurance cover for it?

- The significance to be accorded to elements of compulsion in any system?

As will be readily seen, these questions shade into one another, but will be taken in turn.

5.2. *Approaches to Market Failure*

In the "History and Purpose" paragraphs of each country section, this Report has sought to bring out the extent to which governments and their insurance sectors have been influenced by an analysis of market failure. As has been said, market failure is not simply a matter of supply failing to meet demand: if a conventional insurance market fails to provide sufficient available and affordable terrorism insurance cover, certain additional positive externalities will also be lost. There is a question whether, taking any particular scheme, the precise pattern of insurance lines covered in that scheme bears a relationship to the relevant state's motivation for deciding on the extent of its involvement in the scheme.

It would be logical to expect such a relationship. For instance, in the case of the United Kingdom, the UK Treasury took the view that the UK government should take on the role of financier of last resort only if *two* criteria were met: *first*, there needed to be evidence of *market failure* (*i.e.* evidence that the insurance market, left to itself, would fail to provide cover for certain risks); and, *secondly*, that market failure needed to have *economic consequences* going beyond mere transfer of risk (*i.e.* consequences such as decisions by international businesses, faced with carrying the risks associated with the destruction of their premises, to migrate to other countries). In the case of risks to commercial premises, where these two criteria were met, the UK government agreed to participate in the public/private Pool Re scheme. In the case of other risks, such as risks to domestic property or sports facilities, the UK government judged that market failure, if it led to transfer of the risk, would not result in economic consequences such as cessation or migration of business, and the Pool Re scheme accordingly does not extend to such risks.

It seems clear that all governments that have considered state-backed terrorism insurance schemes have been influenced by a similar set of broad perceptions. But not all have been influenced in the same way; nor have all reached identical conclusions, whether in terms of justification for intervening or in terms of coverage (where approaches are notably variable). The reasons for differences of approach may reflect the politics, geography or economic culture of different states. They may also reflect the availability, in some cases, of existing institutions on which to build. These features are taken in turn:

- Politics: politically, the likelihood of terrorism is simply perceived as much greater in some countries than in others, reflecting the international political profile of the country concerned, the extent of internal political differences, the way these are traditionally expressed, and other factors. In turn, these differences in perception are reflected in variations in consumer demand for cover;

- Geography: geographically, the potential of terrorism as an instrument of economic disruption will be related to whether a country is perceived as having a single economic, political and cultural capital, or whether economic, political and cultural activity is divided between a political and commercial capital or, even more widely, spread among various conurbations or sub-federal hub-and-spoke centres. Again, there will be consequent variations in consumer demand for cover;

- Economic Culture: the economic culture and tradition of different states and markets is a significant factor. Some states are markedly less willing than others to countenance a long-term role for the state in insurance. This has implications for structuring the role of the state in any scheme, in terms of the point at which the state begins to have a role (e.g. the level at which an insurance risk is transferred to the state), the point at which the state's role ends (depending on whether the state assumes a liability that is limited or, in effect, unlimited), and whether the state's role is limited in time (*e.g.* by a "sunset clause");

- Availability of Existing Institutions: can existing institutions be built upon, or does a scheme require the creation of institutions de novo?

These differences were reflected in variations of approach to market failure, and institutional choices, by different OECD governments:

- Variations of Approach: on market failure, the Australian government provided an explicit statement of motivation in the Explanatory Memorandum to the Terrorism Insurance Act 2003, focusing on market failure and the government's intention of temporary and proportionate intervention limited to commercial property, business interruption and public liability. The Austrian government stood aside from state backing for the Austrian pool, implicitly viewing any market failure as insufficient to require state involvement. The French GAREAT and Spanish Consorcio schemes, to the extent that they were built on existing institutions, may not have needed to reassess market failure issues in the same way. On the other hand the UK adaptations to Pool Re, despite building on an existing institution, were taken as the opportunity for a fairly fundamental review of how (and indeed whether) market failure issues needed to be addressed in the way that Pool Re had addressed them in the period 1993-2002. The same is true of the US crafting of TRIA, which perhaps goes furthest as a very large-scale structured intervention to address market-failure, on the one hand, coupled with provisions strongly militating in favour of its being temporary, on the other. Finally, the German and Dutch approaches both address market failure, but in a context where terrorism insurance is in any case not compulsory;

- Economic Culture and Structuring the Role of the State: differences of economic culture have made for a range of approaches to the degree of state involvement in schemes. In the French and Spanish schemes, the state acts through a specific state insurance entity. In most – but not all – other schemes, the scheme gives rise to a mutual or co-operative private insurance entity, behind which the state stands as guarantor or financier of last resort. In most schemes, there is a point at which the State's role begins (usually at above a certain layer of retentions, or when a layer of commercially-purchased reinsurance is exhausted): this is exemplified in the French and German schemes, and also in the UK (in retentions by Pool Re members). Similarly, state involvement ends at a finite point in certain schemes (*e.g.* EXTREMUS, which has a limit on state liability, and TRIA, which is time-limited) while being unlimited in most others (France, Spain, the UK);

- De Novo vs. Existing Institutions: of the three OECD members that had the option of building on existing institutions, Spain probably went furthest in leaving the underlying Consorcio structure unaltered, while adding to its range of cover. In the case of France and the UK, existing institutions played a major role: in France the CCR proved the foundation for the GAREAT structure, while in the UK Pool Re provided an existing state-backed mutual reinsurer. All three, as long-standing entities, provided sample models for consideration as the new Australian, Austrian, German, Dutch and US schemes were developed; but none provided a complete blueprint for any of these new schemes, each of which drew on different elements as regards structure, cover and mechanics.

The above elements may all be seen as variable predisposing factors influencing the approach of any state or market to setting up and operating a terrorism insurance scheme and in determining its coverage.

5.3. Scheme Dynamics

Whatever the external predisposing factors, any scheme has also to meet a number of compelling internal requirements in order to be successful. These too are variable, but centre on the proposition that it is almost axiomatic that there are no truly "willing" participants in any terrorism insurance scheme. The insurers are naturally wary of underwriting risks that cannot be easily modelled and predicted, while governments are guarded about the extent to which taxpayers' money should be applied, at present or in the future, to financing (whether directly, or as financier/reinsurer of last resort) schemes which, once established, may be difficult to bring to an end. Insurance consumers (businesses or individuals) likewise may be unwilling to pay increased premiums for terrorism insurance. Distributors will have interests in the way the scheme is marketed. To be successful, any scheme must strike a reasonable balance, in local market circumstances, to cater for these different interests.

Comparisons between schemes suggest that a number of features need to be present if a scheme is to work successfully. "Success" is, of course, related to objectives; and not all schemes will have identical objectives. However, it can be assumed that one objective of most schemes will be to ensure that the economy of the country in question benefits from the increased resilience that that cover for terrorism should bring. This objective may be pursued "actively" (through a scheme under which terrorism cover may be compulsory) or "passively" (through a scheme under which terrorism cover is at least available to those seeking it). Under either scenario, certain features can be identified as relevant to success:

- Diversity and Volume of Risk Portfolio: to be successful, any scheme offering terrorism cover (whether "actively" or "passively") must avoid focusing only on the worst risks.

Schemes need to be designed so as to cover a wide diversity of risks, on an aggregated basis where possible (thus minimising the scope for adverse selection by the insured) and so as to attract an adequate volume of premium (thus building reserves both to cover costs and meet terrorism insurance claims);

- Distribution: to be successful, a scheme needs to go beyond ensuring simply that cover is available. It is as true of terrorism cover as of other forms of insurance that "insurance is sold, not bought" (if only because few businesses or individuals will regard themselves as terrorism targets); and any successful scheme needs to have a distribution system that works with the grain of market practice (*e.g.* as regards taking advantage of customer propensity to insure – where such a propensity exists – or making commission arrangements attractive to brokers) so as to encourage customer take-up via established market networks;

- Continuing Price Stability: to be successful, a terrorism insurance scheme needs to offer cover at reasonable and predictable prices, little subject to change. In a good number of schemes, this is achieved by transferring the insurance risk to the government, with the scheme provider paying a premium to government in return for the transfer of the risk. But there are exceptions to this pattern: in the case of CCS, CCS maintains its own funds, with no payments to the Spanish state, which would intervene only if a loss were to exceed CCS's accumulated resources; in the case of TRIA, no payment is made to the US Treasury, which however may exercise a right of "recoupment"; in the case of Pool Re, while a payment is made to government, Pool Re retain the risk, with a right to draw on funds from the UK government (as financier of last resort) if necessary, the government in its turn having the right to seek repayment, over an extended period, of funds advanced. Whatever the precise arrangement, price stability, continuity and predictability are essentially achieved via a mechanism under which government ensures availability and affordability of insurance by offering a form of price-smoothing. In turn, these features militate against insureds abandoning the scheme at times when terrorism risk is perceived as low, thereby favouring the maintenance of reliable premium flows to finance the scheme;

- Approach to Limited State Liability and/or Terminal Date ("Sunset") for the Scheme: whatever the desirability, in terms of good practice, of prescribing a limited role for the state, or a terminal date for a scheme, there are practical factors (in terms of scheme volume, long-term distribution arrangements, and price-stability) that may militate against this (together with historical, political and economic factors influencing a particular market). True, limited state liability, and/or a "sunset clause", offers the clearest possible signal encouraging the re-entry of conventional insurance into the market. But signals, however strong, cannot ensure that conventional insurance, to the extent that it is present in the market, or returns to it, will offer sufficient capacity to meet economic need – the key test of whether the market can satisfy demand. And an accelerated end to a scheme, with a consequently compressed repayment timetable, may be structurally inconsistent with the objective of offering a smoothing mechanism under which government recoupment, spread over an extended period, effectively reschedules the timetable for meeting the costs (to the economy as a whole) of terrorism insurance. To that extent, state involvement that is limited in quantum or time, although appropriate to an explicitly temporary scheme, may be intrinsically defective in the case of a scheme that is designed to meet longer-term macroeconomic goals and incorporates the mechanisms necessary for achieving those goals.

All eight schemes in OECD countries have taken different approaches to catering for the different interests and for the inducements to be offered to potentially unwilling partners in schemes. At one extreme, the French GAREAT and Spanish Consorcio offer fairly comprehensive approaches, offering very wide risk coverage and attracting wide participation from direct insurers. Perhaps at the other, the UK Pool Re scheme (as extended) could only attract participation from the UK government, on a more extensive basis than before, by maintaining a role for the market (albeit with a very high level of participation in Pool Re) and by providing for a progressive increase in industry-wide retentions. The US TRIA leans in the same direction, as regards insurers' retentions. Other schemes fall at different points along this spectrum.

It is noteworthy that TRIA alone provides for "sunset clause" under which it ceases to operate at the end of 2005, although the Australian scheme provides for periodic reviews. It is not clear, at this relatively early stage of the life-cycle of different schemes, and the relative unpredictability of any recrudescence of major terrorist events, whether such mechanisms can or will have their expected effect. There must be a particular question over the likelihood of conventional insurance cover ever being available for nuclear, chemical and biological risks in major economic centres regarded as high-risk targets.

5.4. Terrorism: a Separate Peril with Stand-Alone Cover?

It is noteworthy that, with the exception of the Spanish Consorcio scheme (and to some extent the French GAREAT scheme), all schemes in OECD countries treat terrorism as a distinctive peril, to be differentiated from other forms of disaster, natural or man-made. This is matched by a provision in many countries' terrorism insurance schemes (*e.g.* those of France, the United Kingdom and the United States) that the government, rather than insurance underwriters, determines when an act of terrorism has occurred.

This view of terrorism risks as distinctive needs to be recognised, however, as a relatively new perception. Before September 11 brought forth the present range of terrorism insurance schemes, only one scheme (the United Kingdom Pool Re) stood out (in Europe, at any rate) as attempting to isolate terrorism as a distinctive peril and treat it separately from other violent perils. In contrast, Spain had adopted a different approach, enabling the Consorcio to cover losses from a wide range of "extraordinary events," including natural catastrophes such as flood and earthquakes as well as manmade events such as riots, terrorism, and "popular unrest" and requiring "Extraordinary Event Cover" to be included with a wide range of commercial property policies. Such an approach, while distinguishing between acts of terrorism and other violent acts according to their legal definitions, brings them all under the same system of cover, thus resembling reinsurance pools in South Africa and Venezuela, which insure a range of violent acts in countries where political violence is endemic. By effectively prohibiting insurers from making any distinction for terrorism, this avoids the question of distinguishing terrorism from other violence, and deflects consideration of terrorism as a factor against doing business in the country concerned; it also caters for an understandable desire not to let terrorists set a country's economic agenda.

The current view, however, tends towards the perception that acts of terrorism in their latest form represent a new and different class of risk, arising from actions akin to acts of war, and that such risks, with their cumulative levels of aggregation, should be regarded, for underwriting purposes, as different in kind (*i.e.* not just different in degree) from conventionally insurable risks. Yet there is a paradox here, with fundamental implications for the operation of terrorism insurance schemes. It is this: while terrorism risks are, and should be, recognised as perils with separate, distinctive characteristics for underwriting purposes, the success of any broadly-backed terrorism insurance scheme depends on finding effective ways of aggregating them with other risks and ensuring that insureds are under a degree of pressure to insure the aggregated risks together. There are good, market-driven reasons for this: it is more efficient to offer cover for terrorism risks with other covers; terrorism cover will be governed by similar clauses to those governing other general insurance risks; as a result, terrorism cover can be readily distributed with other covers. But, above all, as has been said, the viability of a terrorism insurance scheme depends on building a broad-based portfolio of risks, offering a degree of protection from adverse selection.

This is not to say that terrorism risks cannot be catered for on a stand-alone basis: the market has developed increased capacity for covering terrorism on a stand-alone basis, but only to a limited extent (between $100 million and $300 million for any one risk). There are instances (certainly in the UK and Germany) of businesses preferring to insure a terrorism risk on a stand-alone basis, outside the pool, for reasons of cost. But these instances (which show selective competition from private underwriters offering limited stand-alone cover on a carefully defined basis) only underline the problems faced by schemes when offering less selective stand-alone cover for terrorism risks. These can be clearly seen in the case of EXTREMUS, which offers stand-alone terrorism cover, on a voluntary basis, in the German market, not combined with wider general insurance cover: there has been a significant shortfall in German take-up of terrorism insurance from EXTREMUS, resulting in unmanageable costs for EXTREMUS (which has had to restrict its operations) and (presumably) in EXTREMUS not meeting its policy objective of ensuring that the German economy benefits from the added resilience which widespread take-up of terrorism cover is intended to bring.

5.5. Inclusion of Elements of Compulsion in Schemes

As has been seen, there are two principal elements of possible compulsion in schemes: compulsory terrorism insurance and compulsory pool membership. All eight schemes display differences of approach. In Austria, Germany, the Netherlands and the United Kingdom neither is compulsory. In Australia, France, and Spain terrorism insurance is compulsory, but scheme membership is not. In the United States, the elements of compulsion take a different form: participation in the TRIA program is compulsory for all insurers writing property and casualty insurance as defined in TRIA; and it is compulsory for all such insurers to offer terrorism insurance; but an insured may specifically opt out of cover for terrorism risks.

Yet a classification of this kind risks over-simplification, unless it is accompanied by an analysis of the market situation in each country (in terms, for instance, of insurance penetration) and the degree to which compulsory terrorism insurance, where it exists, is confined to particular lines on a stand-alone basis. In the same way, distinctions between optional and compulsory membership of a pool need to be treated with care: in some cases (Austria and the Netherlands, for instance) pool membership may be officially optional, but it is virtually universal (and indeed expected) that insurers will be members. In the UK, membership of Pool Re is optional, but any property insurer joining Pool Re is compelled, under the terms of membership, to reinsure a policyholder's entire portfolio of property risks with Pool Re, thereby militating against adverse selection.

It follows that a form-based approach to compulsion, as such, is not necessarily a useful yardstick against which to analyse or classify schemes. The more important aspect is the totality of the way in which a terrorism insurance scheme, as an effects-based system operating within the circumstances of its own market, secures all the pre-conditions necessary for its viability.

6. Conclusion

It is not easy to draw any overall conclusions from this Report. As has been said, it is too early in the life-cycle of most terrorism insurance schemes in OECD countries to make firm assessments regarding successful good practice in their establishment and operation. Equally, the outlook for future international terrorism acts and events remains uncertain, as does the potential response of insurance markets to them. In addition, it is hard to rank terrorism's future position among other priorities (e.g. environmental risks) competing for fresh injections of insurance capital. Finally, it remains unclear how far terrorism risks are, ultimately, amenable to insurance, whether or not supported by specific insurance schemes: after all, insurance is a vehicle for compensating losses, and terrorism acts with consequences going beyond compensable losses (*e.g.* the need to permanently relocate people or economic activity away from a contaminated area) would give rise to requirements, in terms of public policy and private investment, that insurance could not meet.

Despite these caveats, however, some tentative conclusions can be attempted, as regards the elements of good practice identified in the previous section (timescale, flexibility, balance, "crowding out" and externalities), as follows:

Timescale: all approaches can be characterised as taking account of the reasonably long term, rather than a "quick fix". There is a question-mark, in this respect, over TRIA: it is certainly not a "quick fix"; but it remains the only scheme with a sunset clause. It is not clear whether, whatever the market signal sent by the sunset clause, the market will spring back to the extent necessary to provide terrorism cover conferring the necessary long-term economic benefits;

Flexibility: all approaches appear to allow for flexibility and provide scope for modification to match both the actual level of threat and market conditions, present and future. Even the most comprehensive state schemes (those of France and Spain) have been adapted to meet post-September 11 requirements, and could be adapted again;

Balance: it is less easy to say whether all schemes will prove to have adopted a balanced and proportionate approach, assigning an appropriate role to the insurance industry, financial markets and (where relevant) the government as insurer/financier of last resort, and taking account of the fact that the balance between these may ebb and flow depending on the availability of capital in the insurance market and financial markets. At the time being, most appear to have done so; but some schemes are under strain (EXTREMUS being a notable example, on account of the limited role of the state, combined with offering stand-alone terrorism cover on a basis that is arguably too narrow to secure a broad portfolio of risks);

"Crowding Out": although more than three years have passed since September 11, it remains too soon to tell whether schemes – particularly relatively new schemes involving a role for government – will prove to have successfully followed the principle of avoiding an institutionalised role for government that "crowds out" competition from the private sector and discourages adaptation in insurance markets and/or limits the attractiveness of insurance markets for new investment. In certain markets, an actual or potential role for government has been present over an extended period, for reasons relating to public policy and local circumstances. Nonetheless, the recent hardening of markets has attracted new capital into the general insurance sector; and this, combined with a limited return of private sector terrorism insurance, suggests that the private sector has not necessarily been crowded out. What is less clear, in present circumstances, is whether conventional terrorism insurance, if and when it fully reappears, will be truly available or affordable on a basis of sufficient capacity to meet market demand. And, at this relatively early stage of the life-cycle of schemes, and given the unpredictability of any recrudescence of major terrorist events, there must be a particular question over the likelihood of conventional insurance ever being available for nuclear, chemical and biological risks in major economic centres regarded as high-risk targets;

Externalities: most schemes, it can be said, have sought to look further than the immediate cost and availability of insurance cover, so as to take account of the wider economic costs of insufficient cover, and hazards such as business interruption, economic instability and discouragement of investment and wealth-creation that may result from such wider economic costs. That said, no scheme, with the exception of the Spanish Consorcio, has experienced a major terrorism-related loss since September 11.

However this assessment of good practice, while generally positive, must remain tentative. It needs to be underlined that, as stated above, there are important dynamics determining the viability and durability of terrorism insurance schemes; and these dynamics (driven by the need for diversity and volume in a scheme's risk portfolio, distribution requirements, and pressure for continuing price stability) may well be in tension with the good practice desiderata (timescale, flexibility, balance, avoidance of "crowding out") that have been identified as favoured policy objectives. Indeed, there may be plain inconsistency between them: this is particularly likely if the good practice prescriptions require a degree of tentativeness in any scheme's approach to its role in the marketplace, while the scheme's internal dynamics require the development of strong and durable relationships and marketplace practices.

These opposing forces (if that is what they are) need not be taken as a counsel of despair. They need not entail an entrenched place for terrorism insurance schemes, at their current level, in the insurance markets of the future, should circumstances change. Rather, they illustrate that terrorism insurance schemes, even if successfully designed to be as non-price-distorting and competitively neutral as possible, probably represent a degree of intervention that will inevitably result in certain marketplace changes. In turn, such changes may require a creative effort if the time comes for them to be reversed, rather than a naïve expectation that the role of specific terrorism insurance schemes will smoothly ebb away in the face of any new surge of private sector capacity that may come to the terrorism insurance market. That is however in the nature of interventions in the marketplace, and does not obviate their validity, when made for good and sufficient reasons. The macroeconomic benefits to be captured, after the shock of September 11, were clearly such reasons.

Notes

1   Cluff and Jonkman (2002) p. 217.

2   "Terrorist offences are all those intentional acts or menaces perpetrated by one or more persons being part of structured groups, with the aim of intimidating, conditioning or destabilizing a State, a population or a part of a population." A specific institutional body specified by law (as in Germany, Spain and United Kingdom) would have to declare officially whether an act is an act of terrorism, triggering action by the pool.

3   Excluded risks:
        1. Damage due to acts of war, civil war, insurrection, military occupation, invasion and similar;
        2. State authority interventions: forfeiture, nationalization, requisitioning, destruction or damage to property caused by a Government or local public authority intervention;
        3. Sabotage and vandalism;
        4. Damage, loss, costs and expenses directly or indirectly caused by nuclear, biological or chemical contamination and explosion;
        5. Indirect damage when not linked to direct damage;
        6. Any type of indirect damage deriving from the inclusion of supplier and purchaser clauses or from access limitations;
        7. Damage, loss, costs or expenses directly or indirectly caused by supply lines failure (gas, electrical energy, water, telephone lines, etc.);
        8. Fraud or willful deception;
        9. Aviation risks;
        10. Cyber risks;

11. Insurances coming from other pools;
12. Military bases and risks pertaining to the Police, Financial Police and Carabinieri.

4   For a general discussion of these issues see G.L.Priest: *Government Insurance versus Market Insurance* (26th Annual Lecture of the Geneva Association, 12 September 2002).

5   The following section of this Report draws on various sources, including (for European schemes) Partner Re's description and commentary *Terrorism Insurance - Pools and Market Solutions in Europe* (2003, revised 2004). The author gladly acknowledges his debt to the Partner Re report, and in particular to three contributors, François Vilnet of Partner Re (whose text on the history and purpose of GAREAT is largely followed in this Report), Ignacio Machetti of Consorcio de Compensacion de Seguros (whose updated text on the loss experience of CCS 1987-2003 is followed in this Report) and Steve Atkins of Pool Re (whose published note on the Pool Re scheme forms the basis for the sections on Pool Re in both the Partner Re report (to which Mr Atkins contributed) and in this Report.

6   Explanatory Memorandum to the Terrorism Insurance Act 2003.

7   The premium paid by policyholders will not necessarily equal the reinsurance charge paid by insurers, since insurance companies will need to recoup administrative expenses and separately price the risk (up to $1 million per annum) that they must retain when reinsuring with the ARPC.

8   The Pool Re scheme however continues to be based on the definitions in the Reinsurance (Acts of Terrorism) Act 1993.

9   An example is the UK Office of Fair Trading's recent (15 April 2004) exemption of Pool Re from antitrust sanctions on the grounds that the benefits provided by Pool Re, such as "helping businesses survive a terrorist act, minimizing the adverse economic impact, and ensuring that all commercial properties are covered" mitigate conflicts with antitrust rules.

References

Aon Re Worldwide: "Terrorism Insurance and Reinsurance Solutions: A Revolution in Europe", 2003.

Associazione Nazionale fra le Imprese Assicuratrici (ANIA): "ANIA Project: Terrorism Pool" (ANIA Working Draft), 27 May 2004.

Atkins, Geoff and Tim Pitt: "Terrorism Insurance" (Australia and New Zealand Institute of Insurance and Finance Journal, Vol. 26, No. 3), June-July 2003.

Brown, Jeffrey R., J. David Cummins, Christopher M. Lewis, Ran Wei: "An Empirical Analysis of the Economic Impact of Federal Terrorism Reinsurance" (NBER Working Paper No. w10388), March 2004.

Cluff, Lawrence D. and Stefanie Jonkman: "Terrorism Insurance Post 9/11: Principles for Designing Private/Public Programs" in "Insurance and September 11: One Year After: Impact, Lessons and Unresolved Issues", Geneva Association, August 2002.

Dutch Terrorism Risk Reinsurance Company (TRRC Note), May 2003.

Dutch Terrorism Risk Reinsurance Company: Clauses Sheet Terrorism Cover (TRRC Note), January 2005.

EXTREMUS Versicherungs AG Überblick: "Ausführung zu Terrordeckungen im Ausland".

International Underwriting Association of London : "World @ Risk 2004", 2004.

Kunreuther, Howard C., Erwann Michel-Kerjan and Beverley Porter: "Assessing, Managing and Financing Extreme Events: Dealing with Terrorism" (Wharton School), October 2003.

Kunreuther, Howard C.: "The Future of Terrorism Insurance", Risk Management Review (Wharton Risk Management and Decision Processes Center), Fall 2002.

Marine and Fire Insurance Association of Japan, Inc: "Current condition of Japanese insurance market after terrorist attacks on September 11" (by Katsuo Matsushita) in "Insurance and September 11 – One Year After: Impact, Lessons and Unresolved Issues" (Geneva Association), 2002.

Partner Re: "Terrorism Insurance: Pools & Market Solutions in Europe" Pembroke, Bermuda.

Pool Re note: "Changes to the Pool Re Scheme", 2003.

Priest, George L.: "Government Insurance versus Market Insurance" (26th Annual Lecture of the Geneva Association), 12 September 2002.

Schweizerischer Versicherungsverband (SSV): "Angebot für einen koordinierten Einkauf von Rückversicherung für Terrorrisiken in der Sachversicherung" (circular to SSV general business members), 12 September 2003.

Skipper, H. D. (Ed): "International Risk and Insurance: An Environmental-Managerial Approach", Irwin McGraw-Hill 1998.

Swiss Re: "Nuclear risks in Property Insurance and Limitations of Insurability" (Focus Report), November 2003.

Swiss Re: "Terrorism – Dealing with the New Spectre", Focus Report 2002.

Swiss Re: "Terrorism Risks in Property Insurance and their Insurability after 11 September 2001" (Sigma), 2003.

"Terrorism in the Turkish Insurance Sector" (Note by the Turkish Insurance Association) 2004.

"Terrorism Insurance" in Deloitte Touche & Tohmatsu's "Indicator" Vol. 3/2004.

Thomas A. Player and Anthony C. Roehl: "Insuring Global Terrorism Risks" Morris, Manning & Martin LLP 2003 (2003, revised 2004).

"To Pay or Not to Pay: Business Weighs the Cost of Terrorism Coverage" (Knowledge@Wharton), 7 May 2003.

"War and Terrorism – Legal Considerations" (Holman Fenwick & Willan), 2003.

and numerous other government announcements, press releases, newspaper reports, articles, brokers' circulars, websites, statistics and other data describing individual terrorism insurance schemes and changes to them.

Annex

Terrorism coverage in non-member countries: Israel, the Republic of India and South Africa[*]

Introduction

This chapter is aimed at presenting and discussing the main features of terrorism risk coverage schemes implemented in selected Non-Member Countries, in the broader context of the current debate on the respective potential roles of insurance companies, financial markets and governments in the coverage of terror-related losses. The focus of the analysis, in particular, will be placed on the current situation in South Africa, in Israel and in the Republic of India[1]. These countries, in fact, with their peculiarities and specificities, offer a good sample of different types of institutional arrangements[2].

1. The South African Experience: SASRIA

Before 1979, private insurance companies in South Africa offered insurance cover for riot, strike and malicious damage. The standard policies available on the market, however, systematically excluded:

- civil commotion amounting to a popular rising;

- any act of any person, acting on behalf or in connection with any organisation with activities directed towards the overthrow by force of the Government *de jure* or de facto, or to the influencing of it by terrorism or violence; and

- loss or damage caused by war, invasion, act of foreign enemy, hostilities or warlike operation, whether war be declared or not, civil war, mutiny, political riot, military or popular rising, insurrection, rebellion, revolution, military or usurped power, martial law, or state of siege.

During the seventies, moreover, due to a considerable escalation of violence and unrest in South Africa, the number of politically-motivated malicious damage, such as bomb blasts, sabotage, etc. greatly increased. In this context, it became evident that there were certain gaps in the cover offered by the conventional insurance market. The problem was exacerbated by the fact that many politically-motivated acts would be excluded from the coverage offered by standard insurance policies.

As soon as the Soweto 1976 riots started, moreover, many insurance companies, anticipating heavy losses, declared that it was never their intention to cover claims for riots and malicious damage which were politically-motivated. In addition, as regards riot, there were several grey

---

[*]   This report was written by Pr. Alberto Monti, Bocconi University (Milan, Italy).

areas on causation, which made it very difficult to determine whether the riot was politically-motivated or not.

As a consequence of the progressive withdrawal of conventional coverage the South African Insurance Association (S.A.I.A.) was approached by the Government, who recognized the crucial need for political riot and strike cover. The Government made clear that they were prepared to take a role in public-private partnership, but they also emphasised that they did not want to crowd out the private sector.

Under the auspices of the S.A.I.A., the industry had a number of meetings, and arising from these meetings, it was decided that an organisation would have to be formed as a separate corporate or statutory entity, the intention of which would be to provide facilities for full politically motivated malicious damage and political riot cover, including acts of terrorism.

As a result, SASRIA was formally established on 25 January 1979, when it was registered under Section 21 of the Companies Act as an Association Incorporated Not For Gain. By specific exclusion under Section 10 of the Income Tax Act, SASRIA was not liable to pay tax[3].

As a Section 21 Company, SASRIA does not have shareholders. Instead, it has participating members who are all of the insurance companies writing fire coverage. Participation in SASRIA embodied reinsurance obligations of each Member company and the Government, in turn, agreed to act as a reinsurer of last resort[4].

SASRIA is a registered insurance company, whose objectives were set out in the Articles of Association as the provision of insurance cover to protect assets against certain defined events, being primarily politically motivated acts, and acts of terrorism and political riot. The objectives of SASRIA also included the promotion of community interests, pursuant to Section 21 of the Companies Act.

Financing of SASRIA was by way of premia for policies or coupons, issued to protect motor vehicles and private and commercial property, including loss of rent. After payment of modest administration and acquisition costs, plus claims, the balance generated to the build-up of a Fund. In addition, the SASRIA members, per agreement, agreed to take a total net line of R5 million (approx. USD 785,000.00) for their own account, and SASRIA produced a formula for calculating what each individual member's proportion of this R5 million (approx. USD 785,000.00) line would be[5].

The method of dealing with claims then, in any one insurance year, was to consume in the first instance, all the current year's earned premia and accumulated general reserves. Member companies would then be called upon to pay the next R5 million (approx. USD 785,000.00); if claims still exceeded this limit, the Government would then be responsible for the excess as a stop loss reinsurer. The reinsurance layer afforded by member companies was however dispensed within 1989 as it had become meaningless and insignificant. From 1989 SASRIA arranged international reinsurance coverage on a "per-risk' excess of loss basis coupled, in latter years, with a quota share treaty[6].

At inception, there was only a very limited statistical background. These limited statistics did reveal that certain areas would have to be designated as higher rated areas. It was nevertheless felt desirable to adhere to a simplified rating structure, based on an objective underwriting philosophy, which differs from conventional insurers. A conventional insurance company will assess each risk, and allocate a premium to it, in accordance with the risk. SASRIA, on the other hand, applies its rates across the board within specified classes of business.

It is one of the basic preconditions for SASRIA cover to exist, that there must be in existence an underlying fire policy, covering the conventional insurance risks (non-motor). The theory behind this is that the insured should be covered for every insurable eventuality, so that in the event of a claim, either the SASRIA policy or the underlying policy should respond, thereby limiting the existence of gaps in coverage. Every conventional insurance policy excludes war and associated risks, as well as any peril covered by SASRIA. War and associated risks are also excluded from the SASRIA policy, these being considered uninsurable risks and the responsibility of the South African Government.

During the early years of SASRIA's existence, several discrepancies arose between SASRIA and the conventional insurers and it became clear that there were certain issues, which still needed to be addressed. Certain losses took place where there was disagreement as to whether the event was an ordinary riot or whether there was a political motivation, in which case SASRIA and not the conventional insurer would respond.

During the mid-eighties, overseas reinsurers to the South African market gave final notice of their intention to exclude all riot and strike cover from their treaties, whether such riot and strike was the result of politically motivated acts or not. This meant that insurers would be unprotected above their normal net retention. They therefore threatened to stop riot and strike cover in total. In January 1987, the Finance Act was amended to extend the cover originally granted by SASRIA by the inclusion of cover in respect of loss or damage caused by non-political riot, strike and public disorder. Acts of malicious damage would, however, remain to be covered by conventional insurers. It was at the time specifically agreed by the conventional insurance markets that they would include the so-called malicious damage extension to their policies, which provides cover for ordinary malicious damage[7].

One of the basis precepts of the SASRIA cover is that it is non-cancellable and non-refusable. Provided that the application for SASRIA complies with the SASRIA regulations, no risks may be refused by SASRIA and no policy may be cancelled by SASRIA. In addition, no insured person may cancel his SASRIA cover mid-term. This is in conformity with SASRIA's objective underwriting philosophy.

Bearing in mind SASRIA's vast exposure, it was deemed prudent by SASRIA to cap losses and impose a loss limit in the interests of maintaining an adequate fund for the benefit of all policyholders. In consequence, and at present, a holding company and all of its subsidiaries will be entitled to a loss limit of R300 million (approx. USD 47 million) per calendar year. Companies with insured values in excess of R300 million (approx. USD 47 million) are entitled to a loss limit discount which is calculated on a sliding scale. The higher the total asset value, the higher the discount. Such companies are referred to by the SASRIA policy wording as "One Insured" entities.

In order that an adequate fund could be built up to cater for losses within South Africa, it was deemed necessary by the insurance market and by SASRIA, to create an exclusive underwriter. In the past, the only competition came from Lloyd's of London, who had been writing political riot cover for three or four years prior to SASRIA's formation. This was considered undesirable as Lloyd's were in a position to pick and choose the better risks and to come in at lower premia than SASRIA could offer, thus taking premium outside of the Republic. Thus in 1984 the Finance Act was again amended to provide that SASRIA was the only insurance company in the Republic of South Africa entitled to insure against the specific SASRIA risks, effectively affording a legislated monopoly. The Conversion of SASRIA Act to date, still allows for this exclusivity but does provide that the shareholder may terminate it at a future, undetermined date.

After growing pressure from member companies, organised industry and commerce, SASRIA approached Government in order to extend the SASRIA cover to consequential loss covering the standing charges of commercial enterprises, *i.e.* those costs which would still have to be paid despite damage to the premises of the insured – *i.e.,* salaries and wages, water, electricity and rates, advertising costs and all of those non-variable charges which carry on when no machinery is turning. This was agreed to by Government, and as from the 1st March 1985 SASRIA cover was extended to cover such risks.

The claims experience of SASRIA is by and large dictated by the political and labour climate. Due to the nature of the risks involved, SASRIA has paid large claims[8]. Despite the claims experience, nothing stopped the SASRIA Fund from escalating at a very rapid rate, considerably helped by the enormous income generated by investment of the Fund. This was however reduced with the implementation of the Conversion of Sasria Act.

During 1989, SASRIA was approached by the Urban Foundation and was requested to participate as an insurer for SASRIA perils on a mortgage loan scheme, which they had initiated. The underlying policy took the form of a loan guarantee policy issued to certain lending institutions. Having been issued with such loan guarantee policies, the relevant lending institutions became more willing to grant loans to low income groups, where these housing loans constituted a high financial risk. The over-riding intention of course, being to alleviate the housing shortage to an extent. SASRIA readily announced acceptance of its participation in the mortgage loan scheme and this type of cover was added to the current SASRIA perils with the consent of the Government.

Up until 1999, SASRIA was a not for gain legal entity. As such, SASRIA was not able to distribute profits and at the end of 1999, had accumulated a fund in excess of R11 billion. (approx. USD 1.7 billion) Since this was in excess of the insuring needs of SASRIA, after negotiation with the Government and the insurance industry it was decided that the optimal use of the excess funds of SASRIA would lie with an effort to reduce State debt. The Conversion of Sasria Act was thus enacted.

The Act effectively converted SASRIA to a limited company with effect from September 1999. At this date, the South African Government became sole shareholder of SASRIA. During October 1999, an independent actuarial analysis was completed which determined assets surplus the company's needs. This surplus was declared as a dividend to the shareholder and duly used by the Government to off-set the interest on State debt. In terms of the Conversion of SASRIA Act, the Government also ceased to be the ultimate reinsurer to SASRIA. Sufficient reinsurance was however purchased in both the local and international markets. Full privatisation of SASRIA is expected to be complete by end-of 2005.

The SASRIA administrative function is undertaken, per agreement with SASRIA, by SASRIA's member companies comprising most of the registered fire underwriters. Any person or company that wishes to acquire the SASRIA cover will approach the conventional insurer who will then issue a SASRIA coupon in conjunction with their own fire cover or a stand alone SASRIA policy, in the case of vehicle insurance. Premium is collected by the agent companies and submitted to SASRIA after deduction of administration fees. By the same token, claims are reported, *ab initio* to member companies. Where the member company is of the view that the claim is excluded in terms of the S.A.I.A exclusions, the claim is then submitted to SASRIA.

2. The Isreali Compensation System

It is well known that terrorism characterizes the political history of Israel since its inception. As a consequence, the Israeli legal system has taken a comprehensive and permanent approach to the issue of compensation for harm caused by terrorism[9]. On the one hand, the Victims of Hostile Action (Pensions) Law, 1970 ("VHAP"), provides compensation for bodily injuries suffered in terrorist attacks, as well as compensation to family members of deceased victims; on the other, the Property Tax and Compensation Fund Law ("PTCF"), 1961, provides compensation for property damage caused by terrorism. Yet, not all types of harm caused by terrorism are covered by these permanent legislative schemes[10].

Compensation for Bodily Injuries and Death

In 1970, the Israeli government passed the Victims of Hostile Actions (Pensions) Law. The political decision was to equate the benefits given to injured civilians and to the families of victims of war or terrorism with the benefits provided to injured soldiers and to the families of soldiers killed in action, respectively. In light of the peculiar situation in Israel, the rationale of providing compensation to civilians randomly hit by terrorist actions may be viewed as an extension of customary compensation of members of the armed forces injured during war operations[11].

As a result, the VHAP makes no distinction between civilians injured by war and civilians injured by terrorism. Both cases are defined under the law as "enemy-inflicted injury" which consists in any of the following:

- An injury caused through hostile action by military or semi-military or irregular forces of a state hostile to Israel, through hostile action by an organisation hostile to Israel or through hostile action carried out in aid of one of these or upon its instructions, on its behalf or to further its aims (All hereinafter referred to as "Enemy Forces");

- An injury inflicted by a person unintentionally in consequence of hostile action by Enemy Forces or an injury inflicted unintentionally under circumstances in which there were reasonable grounds for apprehending that hostile action as aforesaid would be carried out;

- An injury caused through arms which were intended for hostile action by Enemy Forces, or an injury caused through arms which were intended to counter such action (excluding an injury inflicted upon a person age 18 or older while committing a crime, or a felony involving willfulness or culpable negligence).

The above definition encompasses not only harm inflicted by a terrorist act, but also harm caused by defensive measures aimed against terrorist aggression (so-called "friendly fire"). A special "approving authority" appointed by the Minister of Defense is in charge of the determination as to whether an event constitutes a "hostile act". It shall be note, however, that the VHAP law provides a rebuttable presumption:

"Where a person has been injured under circumstances affording reasonable grounds for believing that he has sustained an enemy-inflicted injury, the injury shall be regarded as enemy-inflicted unless the contrary is proved."

Victims who are injured by a hostile act are entitled to medical care and to a stipend while receiving medical care. Those who remain permanently disabled are entitled to disability benefits. All benefits under VHAP are administered by the National Insurance Institute ("N.I.I.")[12]. VHAP also provides benefits for families of victims killed as a result of "hostile acts". The structure of benefits is based on the benefits paid to the families of soldiers who die during and as a result of active duty.

A victim who has a claim under the VHAP and who may have a separate personal injury claim for compensation under another law may choose between compensation and rights according to the VHAP and compensation and rights according to the other law. In other words, the law provides for a choice of remedy, rather than an exclusivity of remedy[13].

Compensation for Property Damage

As with damage for personal injury, the compensation of victims of terror for property damage is an extension of the compensation to civilians for war damage. To this purpose, in 1961, Israel adopted the Property Tax and Compensation Fund Law (PTCF). The PTCF Law (n.5721-1961) is a consolidation of pre-existing pieces of legislation, but it also added new important features to the state compensation mechanism. The law and its implementing regulations are the basis of the current compensation system for property damage caused by war and terrorism. The Fund established under the law was originally financed by tax on property[14]. Over the years, and especially since 1981, only a small percentage of the property tax collected was actually used for the compensation fund, and finally the link between the assets subject to the property tax and the assets covered by the compensation provisions was completely detached. The compensation scheme, however, is still administered by the income tax authorities[15].

Under the law and regulations, compensation for damage to household items is set at full replacement value rather than at the depreciated value of the assets affected. Since the regulations set certain limitations of coverage as to quantity and total value, Israeli residents may purchase additional insurance on the voluntary market to cover what exceeds the PTCF coverage. In light of the above, at present the PTCF scheme works as a social support system, complementing the private insurance market, financed by the general taxpaying public.

The PTCF covers both direct "war damage" and "indirect damage".

Pursuant to the terms of the law, war damage means:

"A damage caused to the substance of a property as a result of warlike operations by the regular armies of the enemy or as a result of other hostile actions against Israel or as a result of warlike operations by the Israel Defense Forces"

In turn, "indirect damage" is defined as follows:

"A loss or the preclusion of profit as a result of war damage within the area of a border settlement, or by reason of the impossibility of utilising properties situated within the area of a border settlement as a result of warlike operations by the regular armies of the enemy or as a result of other hostile acts against Israel, or as a result of warlike operations by the Israel Defense Forces"

Both direct and indirect damages, consequently, are defined as to include terrorist acts as part of the expression "*other hostile actions against Israel*". It shall be noted, however, that the PTCF law does not provide a presumption similar to that of the VHAP that borderline events would be considered as hostile acts.

Direct damage to property is covered in accordance with the Property Tax and Compensation Fund Regulations (Payment of Compensation) (War Damage and Indirect Damage), 1973, promulgated under the law. Under the regulations, the compensation is limited to the "Actual Damage," defined as the lower amount of:

- the difference between the value of the asset before the damage occurred and the market value of the asset immediately after the damage occurred; or

- the cost of restoring the asset to its prior condition. In addition, compensation will be paid for reasonable expenses incurred during the occurrence of the damage and aimed at mitigating the damage.

The system is aimed at restoring life to normalcy as soon as possible after a terrorist act.

Indirect damage, including business interruption and loss of earnings, nevertheless, was usually remained uncompensated, except for those damages suffered by businesses in border settlements. In 2001 the PTCF Law was amended to allow the government to compensate for indirect damages caused by hostile acts[16]. Compensation is now available provided that:

- the damage was caused by actions which the Minister of Defense declared as hostile actions; and

- the damage occurred in a location which the Minister of Finance, with the approval of the Knesset's Finance Committee, declared as an area damaged by hostile actions.

When both conditions are met, the law authorizes the payment of compensation for damage to assets, loss of earnings, or the inability to use assets located in the affected area.

The Regulations provide that in the event an owner of property is entitled to receive compensation for the damage from the Tax Authority as well as another source, such as a private insurance company, the compensation paid under the PTCF will only cover the difference between the amount received from the other source and the amount of recoverable damage.

Even if terror-caused pure economic losses are not compensated under the scheme, Israel has certainly one of the most generous compensation mechanisms for damages caused by war and terrorism. This permanent and comprehensive legislative system aimed at compensating terror victims must be viewed in the context of the high and constant exposure of this country to war and terrorism risks, as well as of the general welfare policy of the Israeli State.

**Table A.1. South Africa and Israel Terrorism Risk Insurance Schemes
Comparative Table (30 Dec. 2004)**

	South Africa	Israel
Name of scheme	SASRIA LIMITED	Property Tax and Compensation Fund
Date of establishment	1 August 1979	The current law was passed on 6 April 1961
Basic structure	Sasria is a short term insurer offering cover for Riot, Strike, Public Disorder, Terrorism and Acts of politically motivated malicious damage. Policies are coupon policies attaching to conventional covers and are sold to the public by conventional insurers. Sasria cannot refuse or cancel cover once issued. Government acts as a stop loss reinsurer offering cover of R1 bn ($150m approx)	The government compensates through the Fund for any loss of property as result of a hostile act, at market value. In certain (limited) areas, indirect damage is also covered. The fund's financial source is tax money. Any Israeli resident is entitled to compensation.
Layers of coverage	Cover from ground up to R300m ($45m approx) per one insured entity in South Africa. Catastrophe excess of loss reinsurance of R3bn excess R200m. 50% Quota share treaty – limit R5bn gross. Government stop loss reinsurance of R1bn excess of reserves and reinsurances.	Direct damage to property, other than household contents: unlimited (actual damage + costs of mitigating the damage). Direct damage to household contents: up to about €20,000 (the sums vary according to family structure). Additional coverage can be purchased at 0.3% of the property value, up to a limit of about €140,000. It is also possible to purchase coverage for property outside of Israel at a rate of 0.5%-4.5% of its value.
Limitation of exposure of private sector	No limit of exposure but policy limits apply (R300m per one insured per calendar year)	Not relevant. The private sector sells insurance only for damages not covered by the Fund (indirect damage etc.).
Temporary/permanent government participation	Temporary. Currently to end 2005 but renewable thereafter.	Permanent
Gratuity of government coverage	Yes. Government receives no premium for stop loss cover.	The Fund is financed through a tax on property.
Voluntary/mandatory	Voluntary.	The basic coverage is given free of charge to any Israeli resident.
Minimum sum insured	None	-
Type of events covered (definition)	Riot (political and non political), strike, public disorder, terrorism and acts of politically motivated malicious damage. No Government declaration is required, the operative wording of the policy applies.	Damage caused to property as a result of warlike operations by the regular armies of the enemy or as a result of other hostile acts against Israel or as a result of warlike operations by the Israel Defense Forces.
Coverage of CBRN terrorist attacks	All policies contain the CBRN exclusion clause.	Covered
Lines covered	Commercial, industrial and personal lines. Risks for direct property loss and standing charges. No full business interruption.	Property. When indirect damage is covered: loss of profits.
Pricing mechanism	Rating is done on an objective basis where one rate applies per risk class	There is no link between payment and eligibility for compensation.

	irrespective of value, location or nature of risk. Rates are as follows: Commercial – 0.012% Personal lines – 0.003% (Others include money, marine, standing charges, motor and contractors).	An exception is the additional coverage for household contents, priced at 0.3% of the additional property covered.
Other public sector victims compensation schemes	Government disaster relief funding mechanisms.	The Property Tax and Compensation Fund also compensates for drought damages. The Victims of Hostile Acts Law – any citizen or resident of Israel affected by acts of terror or hostile acts in Israel and abroad, as well as anyone who entered Israel in a lawful manner, is eligible for compensation.

3. The Indian Terrorism Risk Insurance Pool

Following the withdrawal of the cover for the risks of terrorism and sabotage by the international reinsurers after the September 11, 2001 events in the US, private non-life insurance companies licensed to operate in India have pooled their resources to establish a Terrorism Risk Insurance Pool starting from April 1, 2002[17].

The Terrorism Risk Insurance Pool fully reinsures all terrorism risks underwritten by the primary companies participating in the venture. Excess of loss retrocessional coverage is then purchased on the international market. The General Insurance Corporation of India (GIC), on behalf of all the non-life insurance companies manages this pool including maintenance of accounts, investment of funds, etc. For this purpose a handling fee of 1% of the premium on the cessions is recovered from the participants. The cover is available only in respect of fire, engineering and fire/engineering sections of miscellaneous policies. The rates charged for this cover are administered by Tariff Advisory Committee (TAC). The entire premium charged for this cover is ceded to the pool after deducting 2% as service charges for the cedant company.

At the beginning, Indian corporations – especially power utilities – were reluctant to take terrorism cover. The few corporations that had decided to purchase terrorism risk coverage included petroleum refiners and some ports[18]. Power utilities' reluctance to take terrorism cover was partly driven by the potential adverse impact on their bottom lines. Insurance costs of power utilities are restricted to 2.5 per cent of the operation and maintenance costs. Consequently, taking terrorism risk implied that the costs of the high premia would have to be treated as additional expenditure, with the concomitant impact on the rates of return. Few power utilities, especially independent power producers, were prepared to accept this rate of return reduction.

Moreover, domestic insurers were also not very enthusiastic on selling such terrorism risk covers. This was partly because of the steep reinsurance premia and tight caps on maximum reinsurance liabilities. Reinsurers had capped their liabilities to a maximum of Rs 200 crore (USD 40 million). Besides, reinsurers starting from 2002 were not willing to accept terrorism as part of the treaty arrangements any more. As a result, most of the domestic non-life insurers had to pool their risks or take reinsurance on a facultative basis, which were prohibitively expensive.

According to the available information, terrorism risk premia have been recently reduced in a significant manner[19]. In a circular issued to all the non-life insurers in the country, the Tariff Advisory Committee (TAC) of the Insurance Regulatory and Development Authority (IRDA) reduced the premium from 0.05 per cent per mille (50 paise per Rs 1000 of sum assured) to 0.03 (30 paise per Rs 1000). Industry sources said that reduction in the premia was partly driven by the low claims ratios in terrorism insurance. In fact, very few corporations in the country have made claims on terrorism-related losses. The reduction might also be driven by the reduced risk perception and/or reduce cost of international retrocessional coverage.

After an initial period in which the maximum coverage per risk was set at Rs. 200 crores (USD 40 million), from January 2004 the Pool had the financial capacity to offer terrorism cover up to Rs. 300 crores (USD 60 million) per location. Along with the above mentioned premium reductions, the coverage limits have been recently raised to Rs 500 crore (USD 100 million) per event per location. The changes took effect on February 1, 2005[20].

As a result, effective from February 1, 2005 the premium/coverage factor for Terrorism Risks has been set by the Authority[21] as follows:

Table A.2.

Sl. No.	Total Sum Insured per location (MD+LOP) Rs. Crores	Premium on Total sum Insured	Rate (Per Mille)	Overall (MD+LOP) liability cap per location / ompound
1	Up to 500	Full rate of a) Industrial risks b) Non-Industrial risks a) Residential risks	0.30 0.20 0.10	TSI
2	Up to 500 and Up to 2000	First 500, as per (1) above **Plus** on the balance Sum Insured Full rate of a) Industrial risks b) Non-industrial risks	0.25 0.15	Rs.500 Cr.
3	Over 2000	First 2000, as per (2) above **Plus** on the balance Sum Insured Full rate of a) Industrial risks b) Non-industrial risks	0.20 0.12	Rs.500 Cr.

Source: Circular TAC/4/04 of December 16, 2004 – Cover for Terrorism Risks under Fire, Engineering & IAR tariffs

Conclusions

The analysis conducted above shows that the compensation schemes implemented in South Africa, Israel and the Republic of India considerably vary from one another. Both in South Africa and in Israel the State has taken a prominent role in a longstanding institutional arrangement. In India, on the other hand, only recently private insurance companies pooled their resources to create a Terrorism Risk Insurance Pool. In this country, therefore, the government is not directly involved in an *ex ante* insurance scheme aimed at compensating losses resulting from terrorism[22].

The Israeli system of compensation is certainly the most stable and comprehensive. It shall be noted, however, that it is not an insurance system, but rather a direct State compensation scheme financed by the general taxpaying public. In this perspective, it must be viewed in the context of the high and constant exposure of this country to war and terrorism risks, as well as of the general welfare policy of the Israeli State.

The South African and Indian solutions, to the contrary, are insurance-based pooling schemes that rely heavily on the private insurance sector. The State initially acted as reinsurer of last resort in South Africa, while now it is the sole shareholder of SASRIA. Terrorism coverage is priced and sold separately both in India and in South Africa[23], in light of the peculiar insurability problems posed by terrorism risk.

This brief overview of terrorism risk compensation schemes in selected Non-Member Countries reinforces the view that there is no ready-made solution that governments should adopt to solve the problem of terrorism risk coverage, and each arrangement will have to be tailored to the specific needs of each market. Institutional responses in OECD and Non-Member Countries may widely vary, to adapt to the different levels of country exposure to terrorism risk and of insurance penetration, among other factors.

Notes

1   The author wishes to thank Michael Strydom (Managing Director, SASRIA), Yoav Ben Or (Israeli Ministry of Finance, Non-life Insurance Dept.) and Isaac Shavit (Israeli PTCF Administration) for their valuable contributions to this paper.

2   It shall be noted that terrorism risk compensation arrangements have been also implemented in other Non-Member Countries. In the Russian Federation, for instance, a terrorism risk pool was set up by private insurance companies in December 2001 following the events of September 11 2001. Reportedly, it has 25 members and at present has a financial capacity exceeding 943 million rubbles per contract of terrorism risk insurance (or of USD 32.5 million). The insurance rates vary between 0.0125% to 0.2% of insured value depending on the economic activity of the policyholder. In the first half of 2004 the volume of premia collected by the Russian terrorism risk pool exceeded USD 400.000 and 220 new contracts were underwritten. Since the Pool was founded in 2001, 480 contracts were concluded; potential liability on insured risk is estimated at 60 billion of rubble (USD 2.1 billion) while total premia amounted to 36 million rubbles (USD 1.3 million). The current financial insurance and reinsurance capacity of the Pool is therefore very limited as compared to the losses that could arise from terrorists' attacks in aviation, energy and other industries. Moreover, the Pool encounters difficulties to reinsure on international markets since Russia is highly exposed to the terrorist risks; reinsurance premia therefore remain extremely high. The Russian Federation is currently considering a draft law that would introduce a requirement for organizers of mass events to purchase civil liability insurance against terrorism risk.

3   This exclusion was however withdrawn and SASRIA became a tax paying entity with effect from 1 January 1997.

4   It is important to note that despite participation of Members and Government neither had proprietary rights in SASRIA or its assets.

5   This was calculated as a percentage of the net fire premium of each member.

6   See Strydom (2004), *Political, Terrorism and Labour Insurance: the South African Experience*, unpublished manuscript on file with the author.

7   See Strydom (2004).

8   The 1991 Ciskei Coup d'etat: R70 million; the 1993 Mining Claims: R120million; the 1994 Bophuthatswana Riots: R250 million; the pre-election 1994 Johannesburg bomb blast: R15 million; the 2000 Pretoria station claim: R30 million.

9   See Sommer (2003), *Providing Compensation for Harm Caused by Terrorism: Lessons Learned in the Israeli Experience*, 36 Ind. L. Rev. 335.

10   The loss of income suffered by businesses, for example, is generally not compensated.

11   See the discussion in: Sommer (2003), cit., p. 338 et seq.

12   See Ben Or, *Insuring Terror & War Risk in Israel* (2004), unpublished presentation on file with the author.

13   See Sommer (2003), cit., p. 351 et seq.

14   See Shavit (2004), *Israel's Property Tax and Compensation Fund Law*, unpublished presentation on file with the author.

15   See Sommer (2003), cit., p. 357 et seq.

16   See Sommer (2003), cit., p. 354 et seq.

17   See IRDA Journal, Volume III, Number 3 (February 2005), p. 23.

18   See Shivkumar (March 28, 2005), *General insurers pitching to provide risk cover to port trusts*, The Hindu Business Line.

19   See Shivkumar (December 24, 2004), *Terror risk premia sharply down*, The Hindu Business Line.

20   See: IRDA Journal (February 2005), p. 23.

21   On January 28, 2005 (Circular TAC/1/05), moreover, the Tariff Advisory Committee has approved the following clarifications effective from February 1, 2005: *1)* It is not permissible for the Terrorism risk endorsement to be cancelled and re-written effective from February 1, 2005 or any later date in order to take advantage of the reduction in rates for insurances effected on or after February 1, 2005. If an insured chooses to cancel a policy and have a fresh policy issued, on such a policy, the old rates continue to apply until the next renewal date. *2)* The endorsement extending insurance for Terrorism risk shall carry the following cancellation clause: "*Notwithstanding the cancellation provisions relating to the basic insurance policy on which this endorsement is issued, there shall be no refund of premium allowed for cancellation of the Terrorism risk insurance during the period of insurance except where such cancellation is done along with the cancellation of the basic*

insurance. Where a policy is cancelled and rewritten mid-term purely for the purpose of coinciding with the accounting year of the insured, pro-rate refund of the cancelled policy premium will be allowed. If the cancellation is for any other purpose, refund of premium will only be allowed after charging short term scale rates as per Tariff." 3) In order to correspond with the increased cover on insurances of Terrorism risk attaching on or after February 1, 2005, the limit of insurance on existing insurance of Terrorism risk shall stand automatically increased to Rs.500 crores per event per location.

22　　The Indian Tariff Advisory Committee (TAC), however, plays a role in the determination of the premium/coverage factor.

23　　In South Africa, it is one of the basic preconditions for SASRIA cover to exist, that there must be in existence an underlying fire policy, covering the conventional insurance risks (non-motor).

OECD PUBLICATIONS, 2, rue André-Pascal, 75775 PARIS CEDEX 16
PRINTED IN FRANCE
(21 2005 02 1 P) ISBN 92-64-00872-1 – No. 54079 2005